S0-AUM-315

THE CHRISTIAN FAITH

THE
CHRISTIAN FAITH

PERSONALLY GIVEN IN
A SYSTEM OF DOCTRINE

BY

OLIN ALFRED CURTIS

οὐχ ὅτι κυριεύομεν ὑμῶν τῆς πίστεως,
ἀλλὰ συνεργοί ἐσμεν τῆς χαρᾶς ὑμῶν

KREGEL PUBLICATIONS
Grand Rapids, Michigan 49501

Library of Congress Catalog Card Number 56-9279
ISBN 0-8254-2310-4

First Edition, September, 1905.
Reprinted in 1906, 1908,
1956, 1971 and 1978.

LITHOPRINTED IN THE UNITED STATES OF AMERICA

O
145c

LIFE Pacific College
Alumni Library
1100 West Covina Blvd.
San Dimas, CA 91773

L.I.F.E. College Library
1100 Glendale Blvd.
Los Angeles, Calif. 90026

TABLE OF CONTENTS

INTRODUCTION TO THE SYSTEM OF DOCTRINE

PART FIRST—MAN

PART SECOND—THE CHRISTIAN RELIGION

THE SYSTEM OF DOCTRINE

The First Doctrinal Division
Man's Need of Redemption

The Second Doctrinal Division
Jesus Christ, Our Lord and Redeemer

024657

The Third Doctrinal Division
Our Lord's Redemptive Work

The Fourth Doctrinal Division
Redemption Realized in the New Man

The Fifth Doctrinal Division
Redemption Realized in the New Race

The Sixth Doctrinal Division
The Triune God Revealed in Redemption

PREFACE

NEITHER in claim nor in spirit is this book dogmatic. As indicated in several ways by the book itself, there is no attempt to speak the final word, no aim to be, or to become, "the recognized authority" of any church, or of any school, or of any man. After years of preparatory waiting, I have, I believe, caught an important vision of the Christian Faith as an organic whole of doctrine, and I am eager to help other men to catch the same vision.

In reading the book, many peculiarities of view and method will be discovered; but the main clue to all can be found in one thing, namely, in the junction of the two ideas, personal responsibility and racial solidarity. Every man is a responsible moral person; but no man is complete in himself—he is made to be a fragment of an entire race. Instead of being content with one of these ideas, I use them both in junction, and with equally serious emphasis. In this peculiar junction there may be, I sometimes hope, a fair mediation between Arminianism and Calvinism.

From many teachers and authors I have received suggestions; but there are four names that should be amply noted in this preface; for without the influence of these four men the book, in all probability, would never have been conceived. First, Dr. Daniel Whedon. He it was, and he alone, who convinced me beyond possible doubt that the necessitarian has no case in Ethics, and almost no case in Psychology. Second, Thomas Carlyle. For as much as ten years, in my early ministry, my mind was dominated by Carlyle. And at last he compelled me to appreciate the ethical appeal of the prophets of the Old Testament; and from this appreciation the entire moral fiber of my message has surely come. Third, Professor Borden P. Bowne. As Whedon and Carlyle, together, led me to see the moral significance of personality, Bowne led me to see its cosmic significance. And this cosmic significance of personality is now basal in all my thinking. This statement, though, is not to be taken to mean that I pretend to represent Professor Bowne in definite opinion or tendency. I wish simply to pay an unstinted tribute to his influence without allying him to my theology. Fourth, Bishop Martensen. Not only did he create my *confidence* in Systematic Theology, also he *started* my present conception of the organism of Christian doctrine. Yet more ought to be said—the courage to wait for a vision of the total faith was kept alive in me by reading Martensen's Christian Dogmatics.

As to my discussions, there are, I am aware, places where the items are not fully in harmony. Sometimes this want of harmony results from my determination to preserve every mood in which the book was written. I would not cut out a passage to secure consistency, for I cared more for a full testimony than I did for a flawless argument. At other times the inconsistency is more deeply rooted, and means that I have not yet worked out all the implications of my Psychology. In a few most subtle situations I am not quite sure as to the real data, and so I waver in my estimate.

Another matter—the scheme of quotation—requires a word of explanation. The primary purpose of this scheme is to provide *an atmosphere* for my discussion. But under this primary purpose a quotation is, at times, used to illustrate or confirm or enlarge a conclusion; or in

justice to state an important view which is different from
my own. In every instance where a quotation from a
foreign language makes such a contribution as may be
of large value to the reader, it has been carefully translated. In other instances, I have yielded to my own
taste.

OLIN A. CURTIS.

The Drew Theological Seminary,
    Madison, New Jersey

INTRODUCTION TO THE SYSTEM OF DOCTRINE

FRAGMENT OF A CONVERSATION BETWEEN A PROFESSOR OF MORAL SCIENCE IN AN AMERICAN COLLEGE AND A STUDENT JUST ABOUT TO GRADUATE FROM A CERTAIN THEOLOGICAL SEMINARY:

Professor. "Are you entirely satisfied with your course in theology?"

Student. "No; the course has been of value to me, but it has one lack."

Professor. "What? I am interested."

Student. "In studying the Bible and Christian doctrine no connection was anywhere made with moral science."

Professor. "I am not surprised. The theologian is quite wont to forget that a sinner is a man."

THE INTRODUCTION

———

PART FIRST
MAN

FINDING A MAN

To have a note of reality in our theology, we must see what actually takes place in the life of a man. In the last century much was written about man; new search was made in psychology, in ethics, in anthropology, and especially in sociology; and some of this search resulted in positive contribution to our knowledge; but from nearly all of this scientific work we turn away in disappointment. It is not merely that the view is partial, that the selection of data is often arbitrary, that the intrinsic human elements are never all vitally combined—the root of the failure lies deeper. These writers themselves care for science and not for living men. They have not the eye of love, and so they do not and cannot find a real man at all. It seems like "a spacious phrase," but it is the truth, that in the poetry of Robert Browning one can come closer to the whole reality of human life than he can in any scientific treatise published in the last hundred years. . . .

I too may fail, for the task is oftentimes baffling in the extreme; but I am eager to find a man. I want to see, and then to help you to see, a real man's real life—not to be caught and held fast in the accidental overlay, not to be misled by the conventional estimate, not to be swept away by the scientific tendency, but to see for myself a real man's real life. . . . And to be true, patiently, comprehensively true, to our own fellow, the common man, *(God help us there!)* to be open to the meanings of all things in his experience, low things as well as high things, high things as well as low things; to enter into his most flashing and evasive moods; to commune with him as friend communes with friend—yes, to love him with an everlasting love; and out of all this, to tell the entire wonder of his story. . . .

And I would discover, not only what a man is by nature, but also what he may become by the grace of God. To borrow a line from John Bunyan's quaint Apology, I want to show you how a man

"runs and runs
Till he unto the gate of glory comes."
—*From the notes for a course of Seminary Lectures.*

THE MAN AND THE ANIMAL

Lower than God who knows all and can all,
Higher than beasts which know and can so far
As each beast's limit, perfect to an end,
Nor conscious that they know, nor craving more;
While man knows partly but conceives beside,
Creeps ever on from fancies to the fact,
And in this striving, this converting air
Into a solid he may grasp and use,
Finds progress, man's distinctive mark alone,
Not God's, and not the beasts': God is, they are,
Man partly is and wholly hopes to be.
            —*Robert Browning*, A Death in the Desert.

When I speak of transition I do not in the least mean to say that one species turned into a second to develop thereafter into a third. What I mean is that the characters of the second are intermediate between those of the two others. It is as if I were to say that such and such a cathedral, Canterbury, for example, is a transition between York Minster and Westminster Abbey. No one would imagine, on hearing the word transition, that a transmutation of these buildings actually took place from one into another.—*Thomas Henry Huxley*, Life and Letters, ii, 428.

In the scientific sense evolution is neither a controlling law nor a producing cause, but simply a description of a phenomenal order, a statement of what, granting the theory, an observer might have seen, if he had been able to inspect the cosmic movement from its simplest stages until now. It is a statement of method and is silent about causation. . . . The causality of the series lies beyond it; and the relations of the members are logical and teleological, not dynamic. In that case much evolution argument vanishes of itself. Survivals, reversions, atavisms, and that sort of thing become only figures of speech, which are never to be literally taken. In a phenomenal system these things can literally exist as little as they can in a piece of music, for in such a system only laws and ideas abide. —*Borden P. Bowne*, Theism, Deems Lectures for 1902, pp. 104, 108.

THE CHRISTIAN FAITH

I. THE MAN AND THE ANIMAL

NECESSARILY here we touch the dominant theory of evolution. There are, as Professor Bowne has pointed out, two different ways of regarding the process of evolution in nature, namely, as a causal process and as a phenomenal process. For illustration take the series A B C. Our questions are: Did A by dynamic efficiency produce B, and then B in the same causal manner produce C? Or did A simply first appear in a progressive plan which next required B, and then culminated in C? Readily we perceive that these questions pertain to two distinct provinces, the first question to that of metaphysics, the second to that of natural science. Evolution as a theory of natural science, aiming to furnish an account of phenomenal relations in nature, I can receive and receive with enthusiastic gratitude toward such naturalists as Charles Darwin and Alfred Russel Wallace; but evolution as metaphysics, aiming to furnish a philosophy of causation, I must reject as utterly superficial and unconvincing.

Perhaps we can handle the subject with more clearness and interest by making reference to that popular exposition by Charles Morris, called Man and His Ancestor. In a brilliant chapter, "How the Chasm was Bridged," Mr. Morris teaches that the ape may have "emerged into man" by means of his first use of tools.

To "some wise-headed old man-ape" there came, perhaps, the idea of binding a stone to the end of a club. Thus was made not only the earliest form of the battle-ax, but, as "our progressive ancestor" soon perceived, a veritable tool with which objects could be shaped. In this fortuitous manner, it is imagined, began the long and splendid line of human invention and manufacture!

This is exceedingly interesting; but even more interesting than this event is the "wise-headed old man-ape" himself. What is meant by saying that he "emerged into man"? Is it that he passed from mechanical volition into self-conscious volition? If so, then Mr. Morris has missed the true point of emphasis. The method of this passage into the experience of self-consciousness is not the remarkable thing. It is no more remarkable that a creature, if capable of self-consciousness at all, should become self-conscious by binding a stone to the end of a club than that Jean Paul should become self-conscious by sawing wood. The true point of emphasis is the *possibility* of the fact and not the way in which the possibility is at last actualized. And is it not plain enough that the possibility of self-consciousness, wherever found, implies an initial, an inherent, capacity for self-consciousness? Could you begin with any haphazard thing and bring it on to self-consciousness by mere procedure and environment? Dropping details, my contention will amount to just this: If ever an "ape" became a self-conscious man it was because he was, in initial capacity, in fundamental plan of being, not an ape, but *an undeveloped man*. If Mr. Morris, or any naturalist, prefers to name this undeveloped man a "man-ape," wise-headed or otherwise, that is nothing but a convenience in classification, and in no degree does it impair or change the fact, the stupendous fact, that now for the first time in the onward sweep of life we have

an individual creature with inherent capacity for manhood. This capacity, this basal plan, "this possibility
timidly looking toward a zenith"—this, I insist, is the
one significant thing precisely as it is the one significant
thing in any child born in any human home to-day.

Having in mind now this undeveloped man, the question comes up, Was he an evolution from a lower
animal? More sharply, Was the first creature with
capacity for self-consciousness evolved out of a creature
having no such capacity? As already indicated, the
term evolution is ambiguous and so the question can be
taken in either of two ways. It might mean, Did the
lower animal, by inherent dynamic, *cause* the undeveloped
man? Or it might mean, Did the lower animal merely
grant the *occasion*, the phenomenal point of demand?
Was the lower animal simply man's immediate antece-
dent in a progressive teleological plan? If the causal
meaning be intended, we are estopped, and must instantly answer, *No!* And we are estopped not by any
presupposition of a special creation, but by the one fact
that the lower animal, however similar to man in structure, appearance, and habit, evinces no adequacy for such
causation. The very feature of our natural constitution
which seeks a cause at all also requires an adequate
cause; and that an ape, or any lower animal, was an
adequate cause for the primeval man is, as far as I
can see, not only altogether without proof, but totally
inconceivable.

Nor are we aided by any formula such as the "bio-
genetic process" provided by Professor Ernst Haeckel.
These *evolutionistic formulæ* are for the most part sheer
generalities, arbitrary and empty. They are more
vacuous, if that be possible, than those amazing scholastic definitions which gave motive to the acid line in
Faust, "Mit Worten ein System bereiten." Even when

a scientific formula is of value, it is but a description of a natural method as observed, and can have no dynamic efficiency whatever. Indeed, it is beyond understanding how any serious thinker can ever believe that laws, processes, collocations, and concatenations in nature ever do anything!

To many, though, the crucial question is this: Did that undeveloped man have a simian parentage? This is a clear-cut question; but the answer given will depend not so much upon the array of argument as upon one's personal valuation of the kind of evidence afforded. As the significance of this personal estimate of the worth of evidence is seldom appreciated, and as it must be appreciated before the present theological situation can be fully understood, I will single out and dwell upon an item used in proof by both Mr. Morris and Mr. Darwin. This item I have selected not because it is more finical than many other items given, but because it is strikingly and interestingly characteristic and quickly serves to show the point which I have in mind. The hairs on a man's upper arm grow in direction opposite to that of those on his lower arm; and they all, above and below, point toward the elbow. This peculiarity is not found, it is said, in the lower mammals; but it is found in some of the gibbons and in the larger anthropoid apes. Mr. Darwin's ingenious explanation is this: These apes, when in the rain, originally made a water-shield by covering the head with the hands, "the hairs turning so that the rain could run downward in both directions toward the bent elbow." A man, of course, now makes no such water-shield, but all the hairs on his arm still point toward the elbow; and in this insistent peculiarity we have a "survival" in proof of simian parentage.

To some men this kind of evidence is forcible, and for full conviction they need only a quantity, larger or smaller; but to other men such an argument, however enlarged, is but a pronounced material fallacy. Nature is too vast, too complex, too secretive, and man's origin is too remote in time, for us sanely to draw so positive a conclusion from any number of similarities, whether superficial or structural. Biology now seems to an on-looker to be unusually hesitant; theories confidently held only a few years ago have been given up; and no man can tell what theory will fill the horizon ten years hence; but this much is certain—no theory based entirely upon the kind of evidence now used by evolutionists will ever satisfy all truth-seekers.

But this question itself of man's parentage, while important in certain lines of discussion, is not so crucial as is usually, and on both sides, taken for granted. Establish, say, a *tarsiid* parentage for the primeval man, and what would it amount to as bearing upon any profound defense of the Christian faith? Nothing one way or the other. The connection between parents and offspring would be superficial—phenomenal—and the demand for an adequate cause would be precisely as urgent as it was before. Neither would this phenomenal connection require us to modify the fundamental Christian conception of man's nature, condition, and destiny.

My own general position as to the theory of evolution can be summarily gathered up in this way: In nature there are two kinds of progress, one kind of the plan, and the other of the individual. The progress of the plan is by means of a series of concrete individuals, the first making the start, then each one gathering up the meaning of the past and fixing a new point of departure toward the final goal. The progress of the individual is by growth, or development, until its inherent capacity, or its primal scheme of being, is realized. No individual can become another. No individual can efficiently cause another. But whenever an individual is a certain thing, or has by development reached a certain condition, then another sort of an individual may be required to carry out the whole plan in its further reach. As phenomena, transient or abiding, two individuals may be closely connected under the plan; and this connection, as in the case of a human mother and child, may be of large and possibly everlasting significance; but fundamentally, in causation, every individual is as isolated, and as utterly provided for by the plan, as though there were no other individual in existence. The law of heredity itself is nothing but the plan's method by which an individual is made a deposit for the meaning of the past. And the total plan is a bare method, too. It never takes care of itself. It never does any dynamic task. It has no secret, potent, resident forces which produce things and push things. No natural law or power makes either the corn grow or the winds whistle. On the one hand, the system of nature is not a deistic machine, wound up once for all to perform its own set task. And, on the other hand, it is not a pantheistic organism, forever self-sufficient for its own necessary process. It needs God, the immanent and yet transcendent God. In every point and in every movement nature needs the Absolute Will. Outside of one very limited realm, which requires no emphasis here, there is no causation other than that of this Divine Will. Forces, laws, processes, evolutions— they all but express the personal power and manners of the Lord God Almighty. The poetry of the psalmist was in direct trace of the ultimate truth when he said, "The God of glory thundereth."

Most tersely said, evolution is but a series of individual items planned for culmination; each item, after the start, getting from adjacent items an occasion for being, and also all phenomenal relations; and the entire series making one coherent, ever-moving scheme to manifest in time the purpose of the Creator.

Once I saw the sketches used by William Morris Hunt in painting the Flight of Night. With these sketches before me, I could grasp the underlying plan of the picture, and see how and why one figure was related to another. A certain figure grew under treatment until it was filled out in form, color, and expression, and then its completion made another related figure necessary to the further development of the whole plan. Looking at a consequent figure from an artistic standpoint, one could properly say, "That figure was evolved out of those before it." But the remark would mean only that the consequent figure was *occasioned*—that is, it received from the preceding figures a fitness of position and a peculiar accentuation in form, color, and expression. And even more might be said. Not only does the consequent figure have characteristics which surely it would not have as an unrelated item, but also some of these characteristics are borrowed (inherited) because the underlying plan requires a thematic emphasis by repetition. But whatever was done, it was done with items under a plan by the artist. The Flight of Night did not paint itself. No item of the picture did anything. William Morris Hunt did the whole thing. He alone was the efficient cause.

A man is an animal. But this is because in certain features he is like an animal. In other words, it is mere classification. And man is like an animal not because he was evolved out of an animal, or dynamically caused by an animal, but because the underlying plan of the living God, at this point in its progress, calls for a being that gathers up the meaning of all animal life before rising into the dignity of personality.

PERSONALITY

Man is but a reed, the weakest thing in nature, but he is a thinking reed. It is not necessary that the entire universe arm itself to crush him. A breath of air, a drop of water, suffices to kill him. But were the universe to crush him, man would still be more noble than that which kills him, because he knows that he dies, and the universe knows nothing of the advantage it has over him.—*Pascal*, Thoughts, xviii, xi.

We here found that consciousness, when deeply scrutinized, is an act of opposition put forth against our sensations; that our sensations are invaded and impaired by an act of resistance which breaks up their monopolizing dominion, and in the room of the sensation thus partially displaced realizes man's personality, a new center of activity known to each individual by the name I; a word which, when rightly construed, stands as the exponent of our violation of the causal nexus of nature, and of our consequent emancipation therefrom. —*James Frederick Ferrier*, Philosophical Works, iii, 207.

Among all the errors of the human mind, it has always seemed to me the strangest that it could come to doubt its own existence, of which alone it has direct experience; or to take it at second hand as the product of an external nature which is known only indirectly, only by means of the very mind to which we would fain deny existence. —*Hermann Lotze*, Microcosmus, Clark, i, 263.

II. PERSONALITY

In his fragmentary book, Facts and Comments, Herbert Spencer notes a psychological problem. It is suggested to him by those "invading melodies"—"often those vulgar ones originating in music halls and repeated by street pianos"—which lodge in the consciousness and are not easily expelled. Probably we all recognize his fact—we have had our own attention to higher things impaired by the insistence of some prowling tune! This humiliating invasion, Mr. Spencer thinks, throws an important side-light on the dispute concerning the *Ego*, and renders dubious the contention that there is an innate knowledge of personality. For, he asks, if there is a distinct person, a central self, how will you explain this invasion? You cannot relate it to the unit of the *Ego;* and if the rebellious thing cannot be unified with the *Ego,* what is it? In a word, how can there be any unitary person when there is no harmony in consciousness?

This skeptical puzzle would be amusing were it not so extremely pathetic. It is something as if a man in crossing Brooklyn Bridge should begin to doubt the existence of the bridge, the one thing which enabled him to be up there at all! Mr. Spencer's annoyance, his effort to expel the "invading melodies," his quick discernment of the psychological problem—yes, his very doubt itself—would be impossible were he himself nothing but an incoherent series of conscious momenta, "a loose bundle of mental states." There could be no realization of the flying and conflicting elements of consciousness were there not over against all these an abiding point of personal unity. Paradoxical as it is,

personality is never more largely evident than it is when
we begin to doubt its existence.

Herbert Spencer's primary failure, a failure vitiating
his entire system of philosophy, lies in this one thing: He
is never true to man's total experience. Every man has
a dual life. There is a coherent side and an incoherent
side. In this very instance, the invasion cited, there is
plain duality. The man, when invaded, is just as conscious of himself trying to expel the prowling tune as he
is of the invasion itself. Then, why not say so? A
philosopher ought to be true to both sides of man's experience; he has no right to cover up one side, or to neg-
lect one side; he has no right to explain one side at the
expense of the other. Real philosophy is at the root an
ethical matter. It demands that we cherish all reality;
that we treat every fact as if it had come, like a shining
spark, from the Moral Law.

This primary failure leads to another failure. Mr.
Spencer is unable to appreciate the significance of the
difference between the being conscious of things and the
being conscious of self. When merely conscious of
things, a man is, like an animal, a bare individual in
automatic response to all the influences which reach him.
As Dr. James E. Latimer once said, "Nature passes
through him unhindered as water passes through a
spout." This individual response is, I repeat, automatic,
as much so as when a locomotive instantly "shivers" at
the first move of the lever. Not only sensations, emotions, individualistic tempers are automatic; but even
thoughts and volitions may be automatic also. Man is
a highly sensitive machine, that is all, save in those upper
moods when he is conscious of himself. And even then
he is only "an inhabited machine." This self-consciousness, admittedly, gets its psychological inception
in ordinary consciousness; but there is no unitary worth,

no personality, until self is held in consciousness with such clarity as to provide a new, personal purchase for the leverage of the will. And even now, with self clearly seized, there is only a beginning in personal life. In self-consciousness there is a point of unity; but it is, at first, a bare point, not only subject to such invasions as disturbed Mr. Spencer, but now and again violently and completely overwhelmed. And the surprising torment of the matter is that a man must be both the individual and the person, and so on both sides of his own battle. In the striking words of Hegel, a man is "both the fighter and the fight itself." And it is this very peculiarity which makes human life so profoundly sad, often so profoundly tragic, and yet so martially glorious. If we tried in one swift sentence to sum up the first inner meaning of man's life, we could hardly say a better thing than this: *To personalize the entire individual.* This personal mastery of the individual cannot be completed in this world; but we can begin, and then with God's help do more and more. It is like a man who "preëmpts a claim" on one of our Western prairies. At first the settler is there with only one point of civilization—a stake fixed in the ground. Then he clears out the tangle for a dooryard; then he builds a cabin large enough for a home; then he enters into a long, weary, unyielding struggle, until the man is master of the wilderness!

Analysis of Personality

In psychology it is often taught that personality is grounded in the power to become self-conscious. This is true, but self-consciousness itself requires the most searching analysis. In such a close analysis, we find two features. The first I will name *self-grasp*; the second, *self-estimate*.

Consideration of Self-grasp. Looking at man's attainment of personality as a process, the preparatory thing
in the personal process is the start in emancipation from
the dominion of nature. In how low a phase of animal
consciousness this self-severance from nature begins, we
do not know. One modern philosopher says, "The
crushed worm writhing in pain undoubtedly distinguishes
its own suffering from the rest of the world." "Undoubtedly" is a rather strong word here; but, however
it may be with the worm, the higher animals do, undoubtedly, make a distinction between subject and object. When, for example, the ponies in the Fife mines
steal and open the miners' piece-boxes, eat the bread and
jam, and then carefully return the boxes, each box to its
proper place, these ponies can hardly be considered as
mixing up the miners, the boxes, the food, and themselves in one opaque clutter. But this ability to distinguish between subject and object does not amount to
personality—is really no element of personality. Certainly it is the beginning of a movement toward personality; but it is only the end of the personal process
which has the quality of personality. A man just starting
up the Mount Washington road, eight miles long, is
surely on that particular road; but he has no more of the
summit-experience than has a man fast mired in a distant
swamp. And it remains to be seen whether our man on
the mountain road shall prove himself to be enough of a
climber to achieve the vision at the top of the mountain.
So this Fife pony can be scientifically regarded as in the
personal process, but he is not thereby a person; indeed,
for all practical discussion of reality, he is no nearer personality than is a juniper tree. All this needs to be firmly
said because the tendency now is to cheapen personality
in the name of a more scientific study of the animal
world.

By this term "self-grasp," then, I mean much more than self-severance from nature—I mean such a complete self-severance that the man can fully seize himself, can hold himself distinctly and steadily at the central blaze of his vision, can think his way clear around himself. "I lifted myself up out of the underbrush and said, 'There, there you are.'" In simple formula, the state of consciousness in self-grasp may be expressed thus: "I am not this—nor this—nor all these—I am simply I myself."

In a passage of In Memoriam (XLIV) Tennyson has remarkably sung the truth, exactly what I mean by personal self-grasp:

> "The baby new to earth and sky,
>   What time his tender palm is prest
>   Against the circle of the breast,
> Has never thought that 'This is I.'

> "But as he grows he gathers much
>   And learns the use of 'I' and 'me,'
>   And finds, 'I am not what I see
> And other than the things I touch.'

> "So rounds he to a separate mind
>   From whence clear memory may begin,
>   And through the frame that binds him in
> His isolation grows defined."

Consideration of Self-estimate. In grasping self, though, however strong the grasp, there is no finished import. The personal worth of the seizure lies in the fact that it renders inevitable some estimate of self. When I realize that I am "other than the things I touch," I also, in the very act, discern a certain peculiarity in myself. This discernment of self-peculiarity is the basis of all self-judgment. Right here allow me to hold our discussion for a moment of emphasis. Do you not see a long out-sweep from this point where a person discovers a peculiarity in himself? It is just now that we first hear the breaking surf of the mighty deep of moral concern! Not that this incipient self-valuation is moral at all, but it prepares the way for a personal sense of responsibility under ethical demand. Were a man unable to perceive any peculiarity of self, he could never judge himself over against an ideal, and so could never feel responsibility toward the right, and so could never acquire moral character.

Of course, this estimate of self is a changing, a growing thing—is, in truth, never absolutely perfect. Surprise after surprise awaits every man, especially at any crisis of his life, when the unsounded mystery of his individual being flings to the surface new things or new combinations. Phillips Brooks once said (I condense it): "My future is to me a perpetual curiosity because I know so little about myself." But this imperfection of self-estimate matters not greatly, for all we now need is such an estimate as will provide for the on-going of the personal and moral life. We are not here seeking a perfect individual, or even a perfect person, but simply a real person. In convenient phrase, the state of consciousness in self-estimate may be expressed thus: "I am not like this— nor like this—nor like any of these—this is what I am."

Consideration of Self-consciousness. By self-consciousness some writers mean no more than I mean by self-grasp. The terminology is not of extreme moment, if we only in some way keep self-estimate as an important feature of personality; but, after much testing, I must myself regard normal self-consciousness as having two sides, necessarily interlaced, self-grasp and self-estimate. At one stroke in consciousness you get both an entity and a peculiarity. The instant you think, "I am not this," you also think, "I am not like this." In every full act of self-consciousness, I hold, a person must consider himself *as existing—in peculiarity.*

The Culmination in Self-decision. The final feature in personality is the power of self-decision. So very important is this feature that writers with the tendency of Maine de Biran make it basal in personality. And even Julius Müller held that there could not be self-consciousness without self-determination, the two always "making their appearance together." To me, however, self-consciousness seems to be psychologically the more fundamental; and I would say that sometimes there is self-consciousness without any such volition as amounts to self-decision. And yet self-decision is the most important feature of the entire personal process, and for the simple reason that it is the culmination. What, then, do we mean by this term "self-decision"? Whenever we will anything, supremely conscious of self, that volition is self-decision. It is not, as certain theologians teach, the quality of the end-in-view, but just intense self-consciousness alone, that turns an impersonal volition into a self-decision. Nor is self-decision any decision made by a person. A person can will and does will many things, yes, and many important things, which are not self-decisive. I would dare to say that in the last third of the battle of Waterloo not one order came out of the personality of Napoleon. In truth, the victory was due not so much to the important fact that Wellington and Blücher were there as to the much more important fact that, in full selfhood, Napoleon was not there! We are not now considering personal responsibility, but long before we are ready to consider it we need to see that countless volitions are not true expressions of personality. Again, then, what is self-decision? This: Whenever a man sees himself *out there* as an existing, isolated, peculiar individual, and then, in the flash of that vision of self, wills anything, that volition is self-decision. The person first makes himself the clear, full object of his own thought, and then makes that definite point of his person the original initiative of his choice. And so the significance of self-decision becomes tremendous because the decision is charged with the conception, with the entire valuation, which the man has of himself. The state of consciousness in self-decision may be expressed thus: "I—just this separate and peculiar myself—will do this."

FORMAL SCHEME OF THE PERSONAL PROCESS

I. The Process in Outline

1. The process *begins* in self-separation of the lowest degree; where there is a bare distinction in consciousness between subject and object.
2. The psychological *basis* of personality is in the power—
   (1) Of self-grasp } interlaced in self-consciousness.
   (2) Of self-estimate
3. The process *culminates* in self-decision.

II. Definitions in Approach to Personality

1. *An organism* is a complex of essential parts; all the parts in dependent reciprocity; and every part making constant contribution to a common end.
2. *An individual* is any item that cannot be divided without losing identity.
3. *A man*, fundamentally considered, is an organic individual that is a person. Or, a man is a personal, organic individual.
4. *A person* is any being having capacity for personality.

III. Definitions of Personality

1. *Analytical Definition.*
   Personality is the power of self-grasp, self-estimate, and self-decision.
2. *Concise Definition.*
   Personality is the power of self-conscious decision.
3. *Popular Definition.*
   Personality is the power to think, "Of myself I will do this thing."

IV. Final Definition of a Person

A person is any being capable of self-conscious decision.

THE MORAL PERSON

On n'empêche pas plus la pensée de revenir à
une idée que la mer de revenir à un rivage.
Pour le matelot, cela s'apelle la marée; pour le coupable,
cela s'apelle le remords.   Dieu soulève l'âme comme l'océan.
—*Victor Hugo*, Une Tempête sous un Crane.

Men get embarrassed by the common cases of a misguided conscience; but a compass may be out of order as well as a conscience,
and the needle may point due south if you hold a powerful magnet
in that direction.   Still, the compass, generally speaking, is the true
and sure guide, and so is the conscience; and you can trace the de-
ranging influence on the latter quite as surely as on the former.—
Thomas Arnold, Life and Correspondence, from a letter dated October
21, 1836.

This secret consciousness it is, of variance from the only True, of
distance from the only Real, of alienation from the only Holy, which
wakes up at the touch of human suffering and fear, and turns them
from a bare quivering of the flesh into a fruitful anguish of the spirit.
It is by appealing to this that the true prophet breaks the contented
sleep of instinct—rings the alarm in the chambers of the soul—flings
the animal nature convulsed with shame upon the ground, and by a
purifying sorrow lifts it up into responsible manhood.   In vain
would the preacher light his torch from the fires of hell did he address
only physical susceptibility and abject consternation; it is the moral
history written within, the felt interval between what is and what
might have been, which these things passionately express and which
make them credible at all.—*James Martineau*, The Seat of Authority
in Religion, pp. 452, 453.

With regard to nature, it is experience, no doubt, which supplies
us with rules, and is the foundation of all truth; with regard to moral
laws, on the contrary, experience is, alas! but the source of illusion;
and it is altogether reprehensible to derive or to limit the laws of
what we ought to do according to our experience of what has been
done.—*Immanuel Kant*, The Critique of Pure Reason, the Müller
translation, p. 259.

III. THE MORAL PERSON

WHILE fundamentally a man is a person, actually he is more—he is a moral person. At times he is not only self-conscious, but also conscious of a peculiar background of moral demand. This moral background we call conscience.

In an address, delivered in Tremont Temple, Boston, March 25, 1879, James Freeman Clarke tried to prove that dogs have conscience. In point, he told the audience of a dog that was punished for stealing a piece of meat. A day or two after the punishment the dog stole another piece. Mr. Clarke, unaware of the second theft, came quite suddenly upon the dog and began to pet him; but, strangely enough, he slunk away like a culprit. "This," said Mr. Clarke, "convinced me that the dog was conscience-stricken." But it convinces me of no such thing. It is nothing but an instance of associational fear. The dog was punished for taking the meat; and after that experience he associated the taking of meat with the pain of the punishment; and Mr. Clarke's sudden appearance brought to mind the association as fixed; and the fondling was not sufficient to break the fixture. When the dog slunk away he was in no moral distress at all.

To understand the work of conscience it is first of all necessary to see that moral distress never comes from associational mechanism. In moral distress a man is not afraid of any external tribunal. He is afraid of an inner, spiritual tribunal. At times, indeed, a conscience-stricken person seeks, actually seeks, exposure and public castigation in his endeavor to escape the awful forensic condemnation within. Rather would he suffer any possible external penalty than endlessly to endure this mysterious, searching, unpliable presence that says in his soul, "You did wrong!" Moral distress is a feeling of self-blame under the notion of right and wrong.

THE NOTION OF RIGHT AND WRONG

The notion of right and wrong is a personal intuition that there is the right and the wrong; that the two are absolutely antagonistic; and that a person ought to do the right. There is, therefore, in the intuition an insistence upon three notes—existence, antagonism, and obligation. But this insistence upon the existence of right and wrong is entirely empty of concrete indication. Conscience never tells us *what* is right, or *what* is wrong. We have simply the *unfilled notion* that something is right and we ought to find it and take sides with it; and then we ourselves fill up that empty moral form and get a concrete moral obligation. This content—this "what of moral concern"—is naturally a varying thing; sometimes determined by powerful influences belonging to our environment; at other times determined by long, careful personal search and practical tests; and not infrequently determined, as I believe, by desperate, willful dashes at duty. Once clearly grasp this distinction between the intuitive, unfilled notion of right and wrong and the same notion applied, filled up, rendered concrete, and you can begin, anyway, to appreciate man's pathetic moral history. Men have always agreed that there is a right; but never yet have they agreed as to what is right.

Take the case of our civil war. Beneath the political question which had come down to us from the conflict between Alexander Hamilton and Thomas Jefferson was the moral question of slavery. But slavery as a positive wrong was not the bottom of the ethical situation. That bottom—"the unspeakable sorrow of the war"—lay in the fact that the deadly struggle was between brothers, all believing in the right, and all seeking the right, and yet entirely unable to agree as to what was right. In one of his later books Mr. W. D. Howells has written these words: "In the South there was nothing but a mistaken social ideal, with the moral principles all standing on their heads in defense of slavery." It is as much as twenty-five years too late to write such careless words. They are inadequate and even misleading. We must not for one instant fail to recognize the truth that there was just as much moral purpose in the South as there was in the North. The trouble was not in moral character, but in the moral judgment by which the empty notion of the right gets its concrete application.

The Institution of Taboo

This institution, found in the customs of certain savage tribes, is, I believe, the crudest expression of moral life. A "thing taboo" is considered dangerous, so very dangerous that one must not touch it or even look at it. A corpse, a newborn child, shed blood, a sick person, and hundreds of other things and persons are taboo. Mr. Frazer tells of an Australian who discovered that his wife had been lying on his blanket and "died of terror in a fortnight." In his Magic and Religion, Andrew Lang gives a utilitarian explanation of this institution. He says that these taboos were sanctioned by the tribal counselors as the result of experience, not their own, perhaps, but that of the clairvoyants, and other ministers of mystery. "Other taboos, as to women, are imposed for very good reasons, though not for the reasons alleged; and broken taboos are not (in actual ordinary experience) attended by penalties, which, however, suggestion may produce."

Over against this utilitarian explanation, I wish to quote a passage from Principal Jevons's Introduction to the History of Religion: "How primitive man settled what things were not to be done there is no evidence to show. We will therefore content ourselves with the fact that as far back as we can see in the history—or rather the prehistory—of man taboo was never grossly material. It marked the awe of man in the presence of what he conceived—often mistakenly—to be the supernatural; and if his dread of contact with blood, babes, and corpses appears at first sight irrational, let us remember that in these, the three classes of objects which are inherently taboo, we have man in relation to the mystery of life and death, and in his affinity to that supernatural power which he conceived to be a spirit like himself. The danger of contact with the objects is 'imaginary,' if you like, but it is spiritual; that is, it is the feeling that experience— sense-experience—is not the sole source or final test of truth, and that the things which are seen bring man daily into relation with things unseen. For, once more, the essence of taboo is that it is *à priori*, that without consulting experience it pronounces certain things to be dangerous. These things, as a matter of fact, were in a sense not dangerous, and the belief in their danger was irrational, yet had not that belief existed there would be now no morality, and consequently no civilization."

Principal Jevons has, it seems to me, said the profounder thing; but I am not satisfied with either of the two interpretations of taboo. This institution is really a complex thing. Sometimes it is nothing but superstition, and in such cases it is to be explained as any superstition is explained by man's natural fear of anything he deems supernatural. At other times taboo rises into the realm of the spiritual *must* and *must not*. And here, in the upper region of the institution, there are manifested two very different things: 1. On the surface, the taboo item—the blood, the corpse, the babe; and, 2. The taboo principle, namely, that some things are not to be done because they cannot be done without an inner, spiritual peril. And when I try to analyze this sense of spiritual peril I find not a mere fear of the supernatural as mystery, but a fear of the supernatural as making a masterful demand upon man's life. And such a fear of such a master in spiritual demand is, I am quite sure, the first movement in moral distinction—"the sunrise of the term Ought." Then, the expression of this taboo principle in the taboo item is determined in all sorts of ways; now, as Mr. Lang says, by the tribal counselors and clairvoyants and ministers of mystery; and now by pure accident worked over in individual imagination. But the reason why there can be any taboo item, the reason why it can be manufactured, the reason why it can be accepted at all, is that the intuitive experience of the savage has already yielded the taboo principle. In other words, I discover in savage life precisely what we find in higher human life, an intuitive, empty moral notion made concrete in manufactured items.

Conscience Analyzed and Related

In conscience proper there are three features only, namely: 1. Moral distinction; 2. Moral obligation; and 3. Moral settlement.

Moral Distinction. As already stated, every man makes an intuitive distinction between the right and the wrong. In doubt he may be, or completely misled, as to what is right or wrong, but ever is he personally sure that something is right and its opposite is wrong. Notice that I say "personally sure," for by this I wish to limit the certainty. This distinction is possible to man not as a conscious individual, but only as a self-conscious person. I claim simply this much, that no man in a normal condition is ever fully self-conscious without feeling moral distinction; that no normal man is ever sure of himself without at the same time being sure that there is a right and a wrong. In another connection the notion of the right will be more profoundly considered; here it must suffice to say that to the ordinary man this notion is an ultimate notion, like the notion of being itself, incapable by him of further analysis and definition. To him the right is right not because it is useful, not because it is beautiful—the right is right simply because it *is* right.

Moral Obligation. Nor can a person, in a normal condition, have this intuition of moral distinction and not also have a sense of obligation toward the right. The instant the right says to a man, "I am," it also says, "*You ought.*" When we most searchingly analyze this sense of moral obligation, we find in it three *momenta*, the obligation of allegiance, the obligation of search, and the obligation of action. In an ample moral life the person feels that it is not enough to join the right when seen; he should search until he finds out what is right, and then express his discovery in the finest moral conduct.

Moral Settlement. After any personal volition under the sense of moral obligation, there is always an inner ictic settlement with the person. If he has willed against his obligation, he has distress of spirit; if he has been true to his obligation, he has a flash of moral content. The transient and partial nature of this settlement needs firm insistence, for no man can come to abiding moral peace by doing one right deed, however heroic that deed may be.

The Coworkers with Conscience. With conscience there are two coworkers, namely: 1. The judgment, by which the man decides whether a given matter is right or wrong; and, 2. The will, by which the man makes a choice among the possible courses of action. In popular speech the judgment is considered a part of conscience; but, strictly speaking, there is no moral quality in the judgment; it is moral only in the loose sense that it is now dealing with moral matters. A man does not have two faculties of judgment, but merely one faculty performing two kinds of task. To make the judgment an integral feature of conscience is no more reasonable than it would be to regard the will as an integral feature because it makes volition in moral relations.

The actual coworking in a typical situation would be essentially like this: The man would come to his case thinking, "There is a right course here somewhere, and I must find it and take it." Then in search he uses his judgment and sooner or later decides, "That is the right course." The moment he makes this decision he feels an inner moral urgency as definite as this, "You ought to take that course." Then he wills one way or the other, and the ictic settlement follows.

CONSCIENCE AND EDUCATION

The question often comes up, Can conscience itself be improved by education? If by the term education the questioner means mental development, enlargement in knowledge, and the refinement of taste, the answer must be, "Not directly." We do not, simply by intellectual progress, simply by knowing more and more, simply by access of culture, get a clearer moral distinction, a larger sense of moral obligation, and a swifter and sharper moral settlement. Always is it possible, alas! to have life filled with schools and libraries and science and invention and art—yes, and even with philanthropy "touching human suffering with its merciful hand"—and yet not have much moral concern. Civilization and morality are by no means interchangeable terms.

But conscience is strengthened or weakened under the

law of use; and for use there must be motive; and motive is entangled with opinion; and opinion is often most vitally related to the peculiarities of our educational environment. For example, there can hardly be any serious question but that the modern man is losing the most delicate sense of moral obligation; and I am very sure that this loss is closely connected with the fatalistic teaching of our time. Such books as Der alte und der neue Glaube and Die Welträthsel have been published in popular form and sold by the thousand; our colleges and universities have made attractive those theories in natural science, and those theories in ethics, which do not leave even a clinging-spot for any personal responsibility; and the theologians and preachers have, some of them, added an atmosphere of unethical impotence by their ceaseless doctrinal mitigations. As to that masterly work in superficiality, "the new psychology," it is difficult fairly to estimate the sum total of its influence. There are students who are not harmed by it in the least; there are other students, however, who cannot live so continuously in the physical scene and not lose regard for the spiritual springs of moral life. As one teacher has wittily said: "Many a man feels himself discharged from responsibility when once he can describe himself."

But in relation to education, the more important feature is the judgment. So thoroughly is a man's judgment in moral matters a result of the educational influences about him that we could almost say, "Show us fully a man's history and his immediate environment, and we can point out the peculiarities of his moral judgment." We cannot quite say that, for even in moral judgment there is sometimes "a personal equation" of large account.

Now we are ready, I think, to appreciate the full consequence of this analysis by which the moral judgment is separated from the elements of conscience proper. With such a separated judgment, not only does a more precise and fitting psychology become possible, but also we relieve the moral side of man's nature from the charge of being a shifting, worthless indicant, and place the inherent weakness in his mental life where it belongs.

DEFINITIONS OF CONSCIENCE

Analytical Definition.

Conscience is the entire moral sense of the moral person, consisting of three features, namely:

1. The power to distinguish between the right and the wrong as two eternally antagonistic principles. This feature is moral distinction.

2. The power to feel a personal obligation to join the right, to find the right, and to do the right. This feature is moral obligation.

3. The power to feel self-blame, or moral content, in consequence of personal conduct. This feature is moral settlement.

Concise Definition.

Conscience is the power to feel the right and the wrong, with a sense of personal responsibility, both before and after conduct.

Popular Definition.

Conscience is the moral voice in a man which says, "*You ought.*"

FREEDOM, PERSONAL AND MORAL

From all this, there results the conclusion that without free volition there can be no justice, no satisfying the moral sense, no retributive system, no moral government, of which the creature can be the rightful subject, or God the righteous Administrator. The existence of a system, and the existence in the soul of man of a demand for a system combining these elements, demonstrates the reality of volitional freedom. Either there is no divine government or man is a non-necessitated moral agent.—*Daniel D. Whedon*, last words in his work on The Freedom of the Will.

Freedom, then, is a point upon which we can allow no shuffling or juggling in argument. It is unique, but it is self-evident; and every attempt to explain it away can be shown to involve a *petitio principii*, or begging of the question.—*J. R. Illingworth*, Personality, Human and Divine, Bampton Lectures, 1894, p. 107.

The truth, I think, is simply this: All determinism, strictly construed and logically carried to its issue, ends in materialism. Why should its advocate be afraid or ashamed of the issue he has himself forced? Surely, the last thing to go, in any system or practice of morals, should be that honest manliness which stands upright in the positions which have voluntarily and deliberately been assumed. And to fear being called a name which one merits is as cowardly as to call another an opprobrious name which is not appropriate or deserved.—*George Trumbull Ladd*, Philosophy of Conduct, p. 180.

Why, then, if law and order are only intelligible as the outcome of intelligence, may we not regard each individual subject, everything that is anything for itself and in itself, as a living law, or if you will as an active essence or character, interacting in its own peculiar manner with other subjects equally determinate? With experience in the concrete, we can deal satisfactorily in no other way, and no competent thinker dreams of interpreting the history of the world by means of a scheme of universal laws. . . . Such a view you will say is incompatible with the scientific conception of law, for that postulates necessity, whereas this lets contingency into the very heart of things. It is true: I not only admit it, but contend that any other world would be meaningless. For the contingency is not that of chance, but that of freedom; so far as everything that is, is a law in itself, has an end for itself, and seeks the good. . . . No sane man resents as constraint normal laws of thought, normal laws of conduct, normal laws of taste; or demands that truth, goodness, or beauty should be other than they are. Real freedom consists in conformity to what ought to be. For God, whom we conceive as essentially perfect, this conformity is complete; for us it remains an ideal. But were we created of a blind mechanical necessity, there could be no talk of ideal standards, either of thought or of conduct; no meaning in reason at all.—*James Ward*, Naturalism and Agnosticism, ii, 280, 281.

IV. FREEDOM, PERSONAL AND MORAL

PERSONAL FREEDOM

PERSONAL freedom is implicit in personality itself. By personality I always mean the power of self-conscious decision; and such decision is, in the very nature of the case, free decision. In other words, in full self-consciousness a man is thoroughly cut free, in thought, from the overriding of nature, and can now make an original decision from the standpoint of self-realization; and this being thus free from coercion, and so enabled to deal freely with all motives and to make a choice in the very center of selfhood, is precisely what I understand by personal freedom. But let us come closer to the process by which freedom is achieved.

THE ACHIEVEMENT OF FREEDOM IN THE PERSONAL PROCESS

Motive. A motive is anything which urges one toward volition. Usually many and fine distinctions are made at this point, but they are not necessary in our discussion, and are, moreover, likely to create confusion. The so-called "strength of a motive" is nothing but the charge of sensibility by which a motive gets its peculiar degree of urgency. It is the pushing power of the motive in feeling; or, to use Jonathan Edwards's exact words, "some sort and degree of *tendency* or *advantage* to move or excite the will." That is, the pressure of any given thing toward volition is simply the amount of interest one has in that thing. And so, what is a strong motive to one man may be a weak motive to another man, inasmuch as one man may have an intense interest where another man is not

beyond indifference.   Let us, then, hold this much fast:
not a motive's origin, not its position in a rational classification, not its force in the soul of a saint, but just its
urgency in this one particular man, is the really important
matter.   A man now loves what he loves, likes what he
likes, feels what he feels; and out of this present interest
he gets all the pressure he has toward volition.   Neither
rational quality nor moral quality adds an atom to the
strength of a motive, if a man cares for neither.   And so
you never can tell what the strength of a motive is by
abstract comparison and estimate under rational rule.
You must see the motive quiver and lift and urge in the
heart of the individual man.

The Blockade of Motive.   This place is crucial.   When
we feel the urgency of our present motives—when all
our clashing interests are pushing the will—why are we
not, as the necessitarians claim, driven by the strongest
motive irresistibly on to an immediate choice?   Why is
it not necessary for a person to will the thing in which at
the moment he has the greatest interest?   I answer:
Because in the protective action of personality under
pressure there is a complete blockade of all motive.
Personality is inherently obstinate.   It is made to resist
all destructive influence.   Whenever we are conscious of
self and are urged to make volition we first of all tighten
self-grasp, and this for an instant holds all inclination in
check.   Stated in another way, I hold that any pressure
toward self-decision first so intensifies self-consciousness
that the vision itself blocks the urgent motive.   Dr.
John Miley, in his discussion of the freedom of choice,
calls this blockade of motive "the rational suspension of
choice."   He has a strong hold of the fact, but he so uses
the word "rational" that it is misleading.   The suspension does render rational action possible, but the pause
itself is, I am convinced, as automatic as the instant,

instinctive spring of a man to save himself in a physical emergency. Indeed, the worth of the pause to the cause of freedom lies altogether in its automatic necessity. It is like holding an excited child quiet by sheer force. The person is automatically held steady against the onrush of feeling until he can get his bearings, until he can be rational, until he can make a truly personal decision.

But, it is asked, can the power of habit be explained in harmony with this view? Easily enough. No person is ever swept away by a habit *when he is conscious of self*. In any self-conscious mood he gets an opportunity to will against habit, and he can will against it, however strongly fixed, provided that after the blockade any motive urge him toward such volition. The difficulty is in carrying out the man's free decision. And why is that so difficult? Because personality itself may have become so weak that the man cannot remain long enough in a self-conscious state. The practical efficiency of reform is very largely a matter of vitalizing personality itself. Right here we can begin to understand why philanthropic schemes are so often ineffectual; they lack the appeal to a supernatural power that alone can energize the entire person.

The Uplift of Self-supremacy. This blockade of motive yields normally a potent result in consciousness. At a glance it can be seen that if we are to make any self-decision we need something more than the negative possibility, something more than relief from coercion; we need courage. Motives might be blockaded forever, and yet if the person did not appreciate the fact he would not do anything; he would loiter in a hopeless mood. Indeed, this experience of loitering indecision is often found among weary, discouraged men. They resist and resist, but they do not value their resistance; they do not believe in themselves; they do not rejoice in their manhood; they get no uplift from realized self-supremacy; and then they become so tired of the triumphant stagnation that they welcome almost eagerly the old, wrong motives again. Is this not a true account of an experience which men sometimes have? Do they not return to sin, sometimes, not because they cannot resist the temptation, but because they are exhausted and hopeless? Never can we comprehend men, never can we help men profoundly, until we understand the dreadful impotence of this ennui of negative, half-personal victory. Could a man hold an avalanche in check, and just do that and no more; never once feel the joy of such resistance; never once feel that he could do other things and greater things because the avalanche could not sweep him away—we would hardly expect him to stay there forever just holding an avalanche in check!

The worth, then, of self-consciousness lies not entirely in the way it creates resistance to motive and so protects a person from coercion, but in that protection together with the hopeful uplift which comes to the man in his new sense of self-supremacy. This uplift psychologically amounts, of course, to a new motive; but it is a motive which must follow the blockade *when self-consciousness is full*, a motive which is inherent in the personal process when that process is normal. And we need ever to bear in mind that the personal process is not always normal any more than the moral process in conscience is always normal.

The Self-selection of Motive. In the uplift of this experience of self-supremacy the personal selection of motive becomes possible. The person is now supreme, all his motives have been restrained, and his consciousness is astir with confidence, and he can look his motives over to choose and use any motive he has. He cannot create a motive, he cannot act without a motive; but in this state of self-conscious supremacy he can select any motive, high or low, weak or strong, which lies within his range of conscious interest. The motive does not seize the man, but the man seizes the motive. And let it be said repeatedly, he seizes it not because it is the stronger, or the strongest, motive. Such may be his practical reason for the selection in a given case, but the practical reason is not causal, is not coercive. It is not true that a person must always will to do that which he has the greatest immediate interest in doing. Again and again, especially at the beginning of a moral struggle, a man uses a weak motive when the antagonistic motive is so strong as to be actually violent.

But we have not touched bottom yet. There is a profounder sense in which it is true that a person always, even in free action, uses his strongest motive. When a man has that uplift of self-supremacy he begins to care most for just that supremacy, and this new interest now becomes his supreme motive. But this supreme motive does not urge him toward any one of his definite inclinations, but simply toward original action in selection. Thus the person's very freedom is under the very law the determinists constantly emphasize.

The Enlargement of the Circuit of Interest. We are now come to one of the most interesting and valuable features of the entire process. The self-selection of motive granted, still the range of motive would often be narrowly limited, and a man's personal life exceedingly barren, were there no way to enlarge immediately his circuit of interest. Some of the most painstaking students of the will have failed to discover how there is made perfect psychological provision for such enlargement; and yet the method is entirely patent in ordinary human experience, namely, *we borrow motives.* While it always holds true that we cannot actually create a motive, yet the motives we have we can use in new combinations, new applications, new adjustments to the will. To make personal volition in a certain direction, it is not necessary to have a direct interest; it will answer quite as well to have an indirect or transferred interest there. Thus, one large motive is often made to urge on many uninteresting items. Probably not one day of your life passes in which you do not do some things under the urgency of larger concern. You not only "hitch your wagon to a star," but all sorts of uncoveted drudgeries are drawn along, with some appreciable speed, by one motive, splendid up there in your little sky. That great Christian phrase, "*For Christ's sake*," what does it mean but that a Christian man can always get a personal motive for a difficult deed by transferring some of his love for his Lord?

Summary of the Entire Process. The achievement of personal freedom can be summarized as follows: When a person is self-conscious he meets all pressure upon his will by instant and automatic obstinacy which amounts to a perfect blockade of motive. Thus, there is secured a suspension of choice. Resulting from this suspension of choice there is normally in consciousness a personal uplift, an inspiring sense of self-supremacy. With this uplift into courage there comes into possibility the original choice or the self-selection of motive. Now, any motive in the conscious range can be selected, because it is not the quality or strength of the motive, but simply the choice of it, which satisfies the person's paramount interest in self-supremacy. "It is not the motive, but the motive as it bulges with the originality of the man!" And even the range of motive itself can be forced out of fixture and enlarged, because the person is able to borrow and combine and readjust motives to the will. Such is the process by which a man is cut away fully from the coercive tangle of nature and achieves what we term personal or volitional freedom. And is it not as evident as sunlight that every movement in the process is but an implication of the personal process itself? The automatic obstinacy is the precise thing which renders final self-decision possible. And the self-selection of motive, the borrowing of motive, the original adjustment of motive to the will, is the initiative and quick nerve of self-decision. Technically, in discussion, the terms personality and freedom are not exact equivalents, inasmuch as in personality the emphasis is upon decision from the standpoint of self-consciousness, while in freedom the emphasis is upon decision from the standpoint of motive; but in either case there is both a practical and a psychological implication of the other. In its very nature personality is the power of volitional freedom, and this freedom is actually achieved in the personal process.

DEFINITIONS OF FREEDOM

Analytical Definition of the Actual Process.

In the actual process of freedom there are four features, all implicit in the personal process itself, namely:

1. The blockade of motive, or the suspension of choice by such a grasp of self as amounts to a complete automatic resistance of all motive-pressure.

2. The uplift of self-supremacy, or the new realization in consciousness that the person cannot be overwhelmed.

3. The self-selection of motive, or the original choice, for direct or indirect use, of any motive in the person's circuit of conscious interest.

4. Self-conscious decision, or the preparatory self-selection of motive together with the full volitional use of the motive selected.

Concise Definition of Inherent Freedom.

Personal freedom, inherently considered, is the power to use uncoerced any motive given in self-consciousness.

Popular Definition.

Personal freedom is the power to will to do anything in which one has interest.

MORAL FREEDOM

As personal freedom is the volitional freedom of a person, so moral freedom is the freedom of that person regarded as moral. That is, the question of freedom is now to be related to the standard of right and wrong. First let us be sure that we all understand the practical contention. Dr. James M'Cosh says: "It is implied farther that the choice lies within the voluntary power of the mind, and that we could have willed otherwise, if we had pleased." The expression "*if we had pleased*" is pliable and can be made to lend itself to sheer necessitarianism. We could say of a fishhawk swooping at a trout, "He could have willed otherwise, if he had pleased." The trouble is that with the trout in sight the hawk could not be pleased with anything else. So in the case of a man, the first question is not, Could he have willed otherwise, if he had pleased? but, Could he have pleased to will otherwise? Could he, with crossing pleasures, have made a choice uncoerced? And, then, what we insist upon is precisely this: A self-conscious person, under moral demand, can decide to do right, or decide to do wrong, when in the same personal situation, with the same range and condition of motives, he could will to the contrary. Or this way: Given here and now any self-conscious person under any appreciated moral demand, he can, *just as he is*, will either way, for the demand or against it. To keep Dr. Whedon's terse expression, the man has "either-causal power."

Moral Responsibility. Moral freedom and moral responsibility are so inextricably connected that neither is possible without the other. It is axiomatic in morals that no man can be held responsible for that which he could not help. In one case there is a seeming exception, namely, where the volition automatically springs out of habit; but we must remember that habit itself is fixed by a long series of volitions. A man may be responsible for even an automatic manifestation of habit, if the habit itself is a rut of inability superinduced by self-conscious, intentional action. As Dr. Whedon says, "A servant may not cut off his hands and then hold himself innocent for not laboring."

Responsibility for Personal Character. This reference to habit opens up the way for the discussion of the larger responsibility for personal character. The principle here is that a person is responsible not only for what he freely does, but also for all he himself is as a consequence of what he has freely done. Our personal deeds not only tend to fix those physical and mental habits which play such a large part in external conduct—these deeds also tend to fix the great inner habit of personal bearing in indorsement. A man, as we usually find him, has two kinds of character: First, he has his character as a bare individual. This individual character comprises all his individual traits, the entirety of his native characteristics. For this individual character as such no man is responsible any more than a walrus is responsible for having tusks. All argument to the contrary is a contribution to chaos in ethics. Second, a man has his character as a person. This is his personal character; or, if we are regarding it from a moral standpoint, it is his moral character. Personal character does not necessarily comprise all of a man's individual traits, but comprises those traits merely to the extent of their actual personalization; or only in as far as they have been indorsed by the person when self-conscious. Soon we shall see how all self-conscious action tends to fix the state of motivity; here I wish only to make the point that a man gets at last an habitual responsible personal bearing toward his individual characteristics.

This difference between a man's individual character and his personal character I wish more earnestly to urge upon you. Do you not see that a man may inherit characteristics which he himself condemns in every self-conscious mood of his life? For example, take the generous temperament. Oftentimes it is an inherited thing purely and has no organic relation whatever to personal character. Here are two men. One of them is a saint, and that by the testimony of every man, woman, and child living about him; and yet he says: "I never give away money joyously, seldom easily, and at times it costs me positive torment." The other man is, by his own confession, a scoundrel, and yet he is so generous that it was said of him, "Only look at him, and he will get his check book." The niggard, in spite of his natural disposition, has, I say, moral worth in personal character, while the scoundrel's easy generosity is no more moral than the dropping of a ripe pippin into the grass. Matthew Arnold was never weary of reiterating that "conduct is three fourths of life." I object to the phrase. It is ethically shallow. Conduct is of large moment when, and only when, it truly expresses personal intention. Most seriously I say it, conduct full of flaw, with a man behind the conduct hating the flaw, means more morally, and so means more ultimately, than the finest combination of native traits instinctively used without any personal adoption. Browning somewhere says it is "not what man *does* which exalts him, but what man *would* do!" It is not the deed as mere performance; but the deed as an exponent of a man's purpose, the deed as related to a man's longing, the deed as an indication of a man's ideal. Nothing could be more densely unfair than to sum up a man's inherited items, and then to regard that irresponsible bundle of characteristics as the precise *quantum* of his personal character,

THE CHRISTIAN FAITH 49

when there may not be one item in the whole bundle which the person really wants or which he will finally possess.

An Old Allegory Revamped. In an Eastern country a young man was sitting by the sea, when there fell out of the sky into his hands a basket full of various threads. "Some were silk and some were cotton, some were stout and some were rotten." Soon he heard a voice, low but distinct, saying, "Spend the day weaving, my son." And all day long the young man wove, taking one thread and rejecting another. At sunset a storm came up from over the sea and blew wildly through the night. At dawn the young man was still there by the sea, and with a woven mantle; but all the loose threads the wind had blown away.

How Moral Character is Fixed. To complete our discussion of moral character, we need to see how such character can be absolutely fixed by the free use of motives. I will state the case as concisely as possible.

1. In the motivity of every moral person there are, at the beginning of test, two antagonistic groups of motives, the good and the bad. That is, any personal interest which can be related to conscience at all is necessarily either good or bad.

2. By using any motive in either group, the motive so used is made stronger, and also the opposite motive, if there is one, is made weaker. Or, by rejecting a motive, it is made weaker, and also the opposite one is made stronger. That is, if you have an interest, and express it in specific volition, you will increase that interest and diminish any opposing interest; or vice versa.

3. In this way, under the law of use, a motive can be emptied of all urgency. Thus unurgent, it is what some writers term "an objective motive"; but I prefer to call it an exhausted motive.

4. The exhaustion of any one motive tends to exhaust all the motives in the same group. The moral life is so related that if you touch it anywhere you must influence the whole. For example, no man can lose all interest in honesty and not begin to lose his regard for truth.

5. When the group *entire* of good motives, or of bad motives, is exhausted, then the person's moral character is fixed beyond any possibility of change. In other words, when a self-conscious person has no interest in *any* good thing he is unalterably bad. The other side should be stated in a slightly different manner, thus: When a self-conscious person has no interest in anything which does or *can* antagonize the good he is unalterably good.

This rationale of the ultimate stability of moral character need not be modified in the least to fit the fact that motive can be borrowed; for no motive can be so borrowed as to create a moral interest where the entire group is exhausted. Some hold, I know, that these exhausted or "objective" motives can again become personally operative as long as they are conceptions remaining in the mind. For example, a man has lost all concern for chastity, but he still has a clear idea of virtue, and even remembers what the feeling was like when he himself was chaste: can this man, merely because he retains this clear conception and this vivid remembrance, will himself back into personal virtue? I answer: He cannot, unless he have remaining in him *some* moral feeling, *some* sense of moral obligation, a spark at least of kindred concern.

The Proofs of Freedom

Volitional freedom is, as we have seen, bound up with the personal process itself, but beyond all this there are convincing proofs that man is free. Let us notice the most important of these proofs.

1. *The Intuitive Sense of Freedom.* Whenever a man is self-conscious, he has an immediate, an intuitive sense that he is free. Certainty as to this fact does not depend entirely upon one's own experience, although that personal experience alone must end, does end, all practical question. There is objective confirmation in the universality of deliberation over opposite courses of action, for to explain such deliberation is impossible unless we grant to men an inner consciousness of freedom. "An intuition of freedom is the very nerve of deliberation." Think of a citizen, for instance, trying to decide which way wisely to vote and yet never once feeling that he is able to make a free choice. Even such a fatalist as Spinoza says, "They think themselves free."

In his work The Methods of Ethics, Professor Sidgwick says: "I hold, therefore, that against the formidable array of cumulative evidence offered for determinism there is but one argument of real force, the immediate affirmation of consciousness in the moment of deliberate action." Commenting upon this statement, the writer of a recent book says: "Now, if it were really true that we have a consciousness of being free, in the sense in which this term has been used, this feeling would have as little weight, as a scientific proof, as the feeling that the sun moves around the earth has for astronomy." Passing by the false assumption concealed in that expression, "scientific proof"—an expression which lives an opulent life on extremely slender means—anyone looking closely can see that the analogy made by the writer is altogether misleading. The two things, the crude belief about the sun and the feeling about freedom, are not fundamentally alike. In one case there is an *inference* from appearance; in the other case there is a personal *intuition*. No man ever had an intuitive "feeling that the sun moves around the earth." Observing certain phenomena, he drew a

quick inference from the look of the thing. Surely the
inference was naïve, almost as naïve as a baby's finding
a playmate in a looking-glass; but the principle used was
the same as that constantly employed, not only in ordinary affairs, but also in scientific investigation. Now
and then, indeed, we find even among scientists an
exceedingly hasty inference which needs to be corrected.
Mr. Darwin himself once drew precisely such a precipitate
inference as to the sternum in poultry, and it was corrected by George John Romanes. But man's intuitions are
never corrected by a larger experience or by a later search.
A savage immediately feels that a half is less than the
whole, and the most civilized man to-day has the same
instant, inner throb of certainty. Even our higher, our
moral intuitions, while they may be lived out of vitality,
are never corrected as our inferences are corrected. We
correct our opinions, our theories, our fine schemes of
harmony, our systems of theology, of philosophy, and of
science, but no man ever has or ever can correct a personal intuition. Were it worth the work, it would not be
extremely difficult to search the writings of that great
agnostic and heroic man who has now passed out into the
silence beyond us, and show that either by intention or
by accident he has expressed every intuitional feeling
which can be found in an Omaha Indian.

Our contention is that man as a person has an intuition
of freedom; that whenever he is conscious of self, and by
just the strength, just the vividness that he is conscious
of self, he is conscious of freedom; that only by destroying
or mutilating personality itself can he escape from this
intuition of freedom; and, further, that the very men who
deny this fact for which we contend do, in spite of all
their finesse in argument, evince, in all the practical
matters of their life, the most unbounded confidence in
their own personal freedom.

If, now, man as a person has such an intuitive sense of freedom, we should regard it *as founded in integrity*. To say with Spinoza that men have such a sense, but they are deceived, is not truly philosophical; for philosophy must fairly explain life, and such a fatalistic impeachment of the basal integrity of man's experience leads to no just explanation of anything. In fact, if such unfaith were carried out to the utmost consistency, it would wreck not only all philosophy and all science, but also every practical department of human affairs. If we are to sail at all, we must trust the bottom of the ship!

2. *The Intuitive Sense of Responsibility.* I cannot agree with Professor Sidgwick that against determinism we have "but one argument of real force, the immediate affirmation of consciousness in the moment of deliberate action." After the action is all over, and oftentimes long after the action is over, there is a sense of personal responsibility for the action. Now, the bare testimony of self-consciousness is in adjustment with conscience, and the man regards himself as a free person under moral obligation. We are told by Professor Wundt and other psychologists of his school that the extent of the inner testimony is "that we act without restraint." But such is not the testimony at all; self-consciousness testifies to "either-causal power," or that, in the given situation, we can will in either direction. Allowing, though, this dubious inexactness to pass, these mediating psychologists should be criticized because they fail to realize that the full testimony of self-consciousness is seen most clearly when related to moral concern. Here, in this moral situation, a person feels that he is free unto—all the way unto—personal responsibility. Most tersely said, it is this: *A man feels responsibly free.*

And now again our own isolated experience is reën-forced when we look out upon societary life and try

rationally to explain that life. Study the entire matter
of blaming men or praising men for their conduct; seek
a rationale of public opinion; try to discover an adequate
foundation for criminal law; and very soon it will become
evident that in judging men for their deeds society but
expresses, however imperfectly, an innate sense of man's
responsible freedom. It may be true, as the utilitarians
claim, that the purpose of a criminal law is the protection
of society. It matters not, though, what the purpose
may be, the possibility of such law lies in the fact that
a criminal may be justly punished because he is responsible, and he is responsible because he, this very man
under these very circumstances, might have done
otherwise. Once prove that he could not have done
otherwise, that he was not personally free, that he was
insane or in any manner completely overwhelmed, and
whatever the technical outcome might be in the court,
the higher court of public moral sentiment would hold
the man as blameless. And every necessitarian on the
face of the earth would also hold the man as blameless!
And so we are come to this point: Not merely is volitional
freedom essential to the integrity of man's personal
experience; it is essential to the integrity of that experience as it is related to his higher moral experience.

3. *Freedom and Personal Loyalty.* In a passage frequently quoted as one of Professor Huxley's brightest
and most characteristic utterances he says: "I protest
that if some great Power would agree to make me think
what is true and do what is right, on condition of being
turned into a sort of clock and wound up every morning
before I got out of bed, I should instantly close with
the offer." There chances to be chiming at this very
moment a clock which makes quite an approach toward
Professor Huxley's ideal. In perfect conformity to a
number of physical laws, it does exactly certain very

intricate things. And it is altogether conceivable that "some great Power" could exalt this mechanism into something higher and more marvelous, so that the clock would be forced to think and to will; and forced so to think and so to will as everlastingly to keep in adjustment with reality; yes, and forced so to think and so to will as actually to coöperate with the moral plans and movements of the "great Power," and thus "like a planet take sides with God." And yet this perfected clock, in its precise, automatic expression of its Maker's purpose, would lack one thing, and this the very thing which Professor Huxley himself had in large measure, namely, *personal loyalty.* Who would not rather have Huxley as he was, loyal to the last fiber of manhood, writing to Charles Kingsley, "Still I will not lie!" than to have this Huxleyan clock, wound up every morning, mechanically indicating truth and necessarily chiming moral maxims? With the perfected machine there would be no costly staying by the truth in self-conscious sacrifice; no taking sides with righteousness when one could take sides against it; no indorsement of an ideal in a free personal bearing —in short, no loyalty, and so no true moral heroism. Volitional freedom is not merely bound up with the integrity of self-consciousness and man's sense of personal responsibility; it is absolutely necessary for the achievement of any heroic moral character.

4. *The Fact of Error.* Hardly can it be necessary to provide any elaborate evidence that there is error in the world somewhere. Probably even our necessitarian theologians would be willing to admit that their opponents are mistaken! Look where you will, in society, in politics, in philosophy, in religion, and you will find almost countless opinions and convictions which cluster into contradiction. As to the fact of error, then, there can be no question; but how can we explain the fact?

If determinism have the truth, then all error is automatic. Men are coerced into fallacy, yes, and into falsehood, too. Our search for truth thus becomes "a mock drama on a mimic stage," where every puppet acts as the wires move. In such case there could be no standard of truth. "All we could do would be to take a vote now and then over the question, *What is truth?* and even the ballot would be automatic." Indeed, volitional freedom is just as necessary for the explanation of man's rational life as it is for his personal life and his moral life. As Professor Bowne has said in his convincing chapter on "Some Structural Fallacies": "The only escape from the overthrow of reason involved in the fact of error lies in the assumption of freedom."

A Final Question. Inasmuch as personal freedom is intuitively affirmed in self-consciousness considered alone, and is again affirmed by self-consciousness when the person is under moral demand; inasmuch as freedom is essential to loyalty and moral character, and is just as essential in the explanation of our relations to truth and error—in a gathering word, inasmuch as personal freedom is vitally conjoined with every fundamental feature of man's being and is the only commensurate explanation of his experience, our final question amounts to this: Is our whole life as men a phantasmagoria with cunning deceptions everywhere, with cosmic equity nowhere? Determinism is really a scheme of unfaith, unfaith in man and unfaith in God.

PERSONAL MORALITY

To affect the quality of the day, that is the highest of arts. Every man is tasked to make his life, even in its details, worthy of the contemplation of his most elevated and critical hour.—*Henry David Thoreau*, Walden.

> Go, and demand of him, if there be here
> In this cold abstinence from evil deeds,
> And these inevitable charities,
> Wherewith to satisfy the human soul?
> —*William Wordsworth*, The Old Cumberland Beggar.

For it is to be remembered that moral qualities reside not in actions, but in the agent who performs them, and that it is the spirit or motive from which we do any work that constitutes it base or noble, worldly or spiritual, secular or sacred. The actions of an automaton may be outwardly the same as those of a moral agent, but who attributes to them goodness or badness? . . . Many actions materially great and noble may yet, because of the spirit that prompts and pervades them, be really ignoble and mean; and, on the other hand, many actions externally mean and lowly may, because of the state of his heart who does them, be truly exalted and honorable.—*John Caird*, from a sermon preached before Queen Victoria; text, Rom. 12. 11.

A feeble unit in the middle of a threatening Infinitude, I seemed to have nothing given me but eyes, whereby to discern my own wretchedness. . . . And yet, strangely enough, I lived in a continual, indefinite, pining fear; tremulous, pusillanimous, apprehensive of I knew not what; it seemed as if all things in the heavens above and the earth beneath would hurt me; as if the heavens and the earth were but boundless jaws of a devouring monster, wherein I, palpitating, waited to be devoured. . . . I asked myself: What *art* thou afraid of? Wherefore, like a coward, dost thou forever pip and whimper, and go cowering and trembling? . . . Thus had the EVERLASTING No (*das ewige Nein*) pealed authoritatively through all the recesses of my Being, of my Me; and then was it that my whole Me stood up, in native God-created majesty, and with emphasis recorded its protest.—*Thomas Carlyle*, Sartor Resartus.

V. PERSONAL MORALITY

BEFORE we can wisely discuss intrinsic morality, we need to eliminate formal morality, or those empty forms of conduct which look moral but do not spring from right motive. In a sweeping way morality can be defined as conformity to the moral law as that law is understood in a given community. With this comprehensive definition in mind, readily we can see that there is possible a merely external conformity; and when we closely study human life we find actual instances of such conformity. Of these superficial forms of morality there are at least two distinct kinds:

1. Morality based upon self-advantage. A purpose of utility does not necessarily poison the quality of conduct. Utility may sometimes, indeed, furnish our only reliable test as to whether a course of action be right or wrong. But when the personal aim is to obtain self-advantage by using moral forms without having any moral intention, then the conduct, however noble in appearance, is ethically worthless. For example, a short time before a close and important election in one of our cities, certain party managers yielded to public sentiment and checked a crying vice; but we now know that their moral alacrity was nothing but a political device. Not a man of them really cared for the moral law.

2. Morality based upon inherited disposition. Already we have seen (in the discussion of Moral Freedom) that a man inherits many traits and that these traits do not always express what he is in personal and moral bearing; but the point is of such practical moment that I wish to touch it from another angle. One may inherit a dis-

position, I say, which in its very nature is a formal moral bias, rendering it difficult for him not to conform at a particular point in moral demand. A man, for instance, might inherit a disposition so extremely gentle as to make it well-nigh impossible for him to commit murder. Wendell Phillips, as I once heard him tell it, tried one day to shoot a plover, and the act made him suffer so that never again would he engage in such sport. "That little, wounded, fluttering, helpless thing just looked at me and said: 'When did I ever do you any harm?'" Cannot anyone see that a native disposition like that would practically prevent certain kinds of wrongdoing? Surely. But what we are not so sure to see is that under this very gentleness a man might not be truly kind and noble in person. He might be not only selfish, but actually malicious, and even cruel in some subtle manner. Wendell Phillips himself was a moral hero; but even in his case his natural gentleness was not a reliable index of his personal character. Any opponent relying upon that mild disposition would have been subject to disabusement sudden and dire. Why, some of the worst women in all history have been in disposition like the saints of God, and because of this very fact they were the more dangerous. Again and again (and you must be made to feel this) the most noble features of individual character have been utilized to get a victory for some ignoble cause. And thus both kinds of formal morality can be combined, conduct based upon inherited disposition becoming conduct based upon both disposition and self-advantage.

The Intrinsic Moral Deed. This deprecatory emphasis has been placed upon formal morality for two reasons: First, that we may be more discriminating in our estimate of the morality about us; that we may not be deceived and think that we are getting on in morals when we are only getting on in respectability. But, second, that we may appreciate the intrinsic moral deed when we have it before our eyes. Whenever a deed, whatever its form, is done, not because it is the point of least resistance, not because it receives commendation in society, not because it gains money or votes or influence, but directly and only because to us it is right, that deed is intrinsically moral. This statement I refuse to modify by so much as a stroke. Ethical teachers are constantly telling us that deeds are moral when and because they conform to standards of experience and contribute to human welfare. These standards and contributions, however, have to do with manifestation and not with spirit. They are societary, but not personal. They are important, but not profound. Deeds are moral, personally moral, intrinsically moral, only when they express a man's own conception of duty, or his own feeling of moral love, as he has the conception or feeling when self-conscious.

This distinction between spirit and manifestation is of the utmost practical importance also. Given the moral spirit, and you are certain finally to have the best expression of it, for it is deep in the nature of the moral spirit to seek better and better ways of getting out among men. But the appearance can be had without one spark of the spirit; and when this is the fact—when you are working merely for individualistic ends, or for a frictionless society, or for an æsthetic paradise, or even for a socialistic brotherhood—when you are working for anything short of fundamental personal righteousness—you are not doing one abiding thing either for the individual or for mankind. Man is too great to live on your utilitarian schemes of makeshift.

Continuity in Moral Bearing. This intrinsic moral deed has not, though, as an isolated point in conduct, any sufficient ethical worth. It is not enough to be true once in a lifetime. Perhaps no wreck of a man ever lived who had not in some flashing instant won a real moral victory. Nor is sporadic morality, or the doing of intrinsic moral deeds now and then, of large ethical significance. The deeds *are not joined*, and so they do not express any continuity of personal intention. They are like some summer nights when the scene is intermittent with lightning. Now it is so light that one can pick up a pine needle, and then it is so dark that he cannot find the turnpike. In some way we must get out of our piecemeal luminosity. If we are to make any moral headway we need to have continuity in our moral bearing.

Allegiance to the Moral Ideal. We can, I am quite sure, discover the steps by which a man passes out of sporadic morality. In the first place, he gets *a vision of right as a totality*. The earliest moral possibility in performance is to do right at one definite point. Then, as the developing person keeps on doing right, here and there, at definite points, there comes to him sooner or later a vision. He sees that to be honest and to tell the truth express the same fundament; he sees that rightness is one and whole. All this was in his original notion, was in the first beat of moral intuition, but it was infolded, and only now, in this new vision, does the full import open out. In the second place, the man obtains *a moral ideal*. When he gets a vision of right as a totality he realizes that it is not enough to do right here and there, now and then, on concrete demand; he ought to be everlastingly committed to this total right. Thus he obtains a lofty moral ideal. In the third place, there is the actual commitment in *personal allegiance to the moral ideal*. Now the man passes out of sporadic morality. No longer is he satisfied with unjoined items of worthy conduct—with trying to-day not to lie and then tomorrow not to steal; his aim is to be loyal to the right all the time. This bearing of personal allegiance to the moral ideal is the only thing worthy of being termed personal morality.

ANALYSIS OF MORALITY

1. *Morality*.

   In widest speech, morality is the individual conformity to the moral law as that law is understood and expressed in the ethical standard of a given community.

2. *Formal Morality*.

   Wherever there is such individual conformity without right motive the morality is only formal.

3. *The Intrinsic Moral Deed*.

   Whenever there is conformity with right motive at any point of moral demand there is an intrinsic moral deed.

4. *Sporadic Morality*.

   Intrinsic moral deeds done, without continuity in moral bearing, only to meet the demand of the immediate occasion, constitute sporadic morality.

5. *The Passage Out of Sporadic Morality*.

   A man passes out of sporadic morality by three steps: First, the realization that the right is a totality; second, the realization that a man's ideal moral life is nothing less than absolute and everlasting loyalty to the right as a totality; and, third, the actual, personal surrender to this ideal.

6. *Personal Morality*.

   When a man aims to be perpetually loyal to all moral concern, in deed, in word, in principle, and in spirit, his bearing is personal morality.

THE EXPANSION OF THE MORAL TASK

This is a place of extreme difficulty. But the difficulty springs, not from the subject, not from any failure in fact, but altogether from the incapacity of the audience. We live in a Christian atmosphere; and with many the natural moral process has been taken up into the swifter Christian process, and so the moral movement, as a peculiar and complete movement, does not stand out in memory. It is as though we attempted to describe the final scenery of a long highway to a man who had traveled the first third of the distance on foot and the remaining two thirds by express train. To him our account would be too minute and clearcut to be convincing. And, again, of the men about us who are not greatly influenced by Christian teaching, only a few ever grant the moral ideal full play in their life. Quickly they hide away from the searching flame. This retreat, this personal flinching under severe moral demand, is fostered by the spirit of the time. We live in an age of externality. In many ways the age is magnificent, but its standards are conventional, its tests objective. We no longer expect any great inner things of men. And this externality, this sheer conventionality of mood, means badly for the intrinsic moral life because it pays a premium for moral cowardice.

The Servant of the Moral Law. If we try to find the dominant feature of personal morality we shall most certainly perceive it to be the realization that one is the servant of the moral law. And the most extraordinary emphasis should be placed upon that word *servant.* The man is not, like Goethe, seeking to enlarge, to perfect himself. He does not regard mankind as tributary to his own supreme development. He does not even say with Emerson, "That can never be good for the bee which is bad for the hive." If you take personal morality in any individualistic or in any utilitarian manner, you will entirely miss the noble fineness of its spirit. It is directly and constantly the spirit of service, the absolute service under moral concern.

The Deepening of the Moral Deed. As a servant of the moral law, the person demands that his deed shall express the very spirit of righteousness. This does not mean— at least, usually it does not mean—that the man must reject the societary commonplaces as to ethical action. Rather is it likely to mean that he must reinterpret, that he must deepen these commonplaces. For example, honesty in business cannot now be expressed by a transaction of scrupulous legality, while within the transaction there is concealed a plot to create an artificial stress in the market which will ruin a score of men. No profoundly moral man can plan the financial wreckage of a fellow trader, no matter what the law may say, and no matter what the societary view of it may chance to be. All this covert manipulation of stocks into arbitrary values; all this strategic campaigning to crush small merchants; all this building up of huge fortunes without regard to the daily needs of men, women, and children—yes, many things which are sanctioned in the business world and praised in the social world are to the servant of the moral law positively immoral.

The New Test. In getting a deed adequate to express the very spirit of righteousness, the servant of the moral law must have a new test. Of course, he still uses his own moral judgment, as he used it in doing his first, isolated, intrinsic moral deed; but he uses it in this new spirit of service; with a most righteous ambition, namely, to glorify the totality of moral concern, to make the moral law absolutely supreme among men. In this spirit and with this ambition he feels what Immanuel Kant termed "the categorical imperative." In various ways Kant was wont to affirm that the one perfect test of moral performance is that the embodied principle shall be meet for universal legislation. "How would this maxim, if universally adopted and executed, affect the moral welfare of men?" Thus Kant appropriated the only valuable thing (almost) there is in utilitarianism to deepen the moral deed; but he appropriated it without dropping any of his emphasis upon moral intuition.

There is need here, however, of a word of close discrimination. The regard for men by the servant of the moral law is not a philanthropic passion for humanity,

nor a Christian love for men because our Lord has redeemed them; no, it is precisely a regard for men as the
best method of serving the cause of righteousness.   The
new test is to be related to all men because nothing less
comprehensive will fully express and exalt the spirit of
moral concern.   Once catch this distinction, and you can
easily understand why, now and again, there is a great
moralist who will live for men and make constant sacrifice
for men, and yet not have any real sympathy for men.
Not every abolitionist loved the negro.   To some of them
he was "a strange, tormenting incubus"; but the spirit
of righteousness was violated by slavery; the principle of
slavery was not fit for universal application; and so the
negro must be set free.   With this discrimination in mind,
it becomes possible to utilize the statement made by John
Stuart Mill: "A morality grounded on large and wise
views of the good of the whole."

The New Conception of Motive.   But even Immanuel
Kant did not see the profoundest feature in personal
morality.   The moral loyalist has now not only a new
conception of the moral deed, and a new test to use in
deepening the deed, but also a new conception of motive
itself.   In the old piecemeal life it was enough, if the
initial motive-drive of an action was right, even if the
main motive did take on imperfect accretions.   The man
never lit a lamp and held it steadily through the winding
caverns of his deed.   He was hesitant of any introspection.   But now his consuming ambition is to serve
righteousness, and it never can be completely served
when a deed starts in the right and ends in the wrong.
The ethical demand upon him now is to keep the whole
complex motivity of his action as clean as blowing snow.
This is saying no more than that he must be loyal to his
ideal through the entire reach of his personal intention.
For illustration: Suppose that I tried to rescue a man

from debauchery, and my original motive was to make him moral, but in the days of effort there came, as an accretion, the desire to make out of the rescue ten thousand dollars; would that deed as a total satisfy the ideal in personal morality? The question requires no answer.

But we are not done. This new demand as to motive really means an absolutely righteous man. To have a perfect moral deed, motived in purity from end to end, there needs to be behind the deed a perfect moral man; or, at least, a man whose entire motivity is so organic in relation to his personality that it ever works for moral concern. Here I barely touch the point to indicate the merciless sweep in the expansion of the moral task. In a word, I maintain that no man can pass through the moral process to the end—that no man can follow his moral leadings unflinchingly—and be personally content with anything short of absolute inner righteousness. Instead of being an easy thing of palliation, real morality is a thing of the most strenuous exaction.

The Expanded Moral Task Impossible for Man

Steadily we have been moving from the beginning of personality on through man's moral life, until now we reach a task for man which we instantly pronounce impossible. But can we precisely locate the cause of the impossibility? Why is it that a servant of the moral law cannot satisfy his own ideal? Why is it that he cannot be a righteous man through and through? The theologians are ready with an answer. The failure, they say, is due to inherited depravity. Later we shall see that this answer has some truth in it. But this truth lies on the surface and does not expose the deep root of the failure. Another answer sometimes given is essentially this: In a complicated situation the moral loyalist, truly to serve the cause of righteousness, needs a moral judgment as nearly perfect as possible; and he cannot be certain that he has such a judgment. Again and again in his anxiety he says: "Can I rely upon my judgment? Is my judgment what it ought to be? Have I so lived in all my past, have I so sought all light, have I so used every ray of light which has come to me, that my moral judgment is at its best?" If the questions can be answered by the anxious moralist at all they will be answered in the negative, and so moral content to him becomes impossible. This answer is quite worth while, for it does explain some of the ethical distress of the servant of the moral law. Still it does not explain the fact that he never comes to peace; that even when there is no question as to the adequacy of the moral judgment, he has moral unrest. The flaw must lie deeper.

In speaking of the new conception of motive which arises as the moral task expands, we really caught a glimpse of the profound flaw in personal morality. *This flaw is the accretion of imperfect motive.* Our initial motive may be splendid in its purity; but as we use it accretion after accretion is formed until our deed comes into port like a ship out of the tropics incrusted with barnacles. There are, in man's natural experience, few things so utterly impossible as to do a great moral deed and keep it clean in all its relations to self-consciousness. In spite of all you can do, your mood will slip and some taint will steal in, and the very man who launched his deed in righteousness will sail it with a lower purpose. Leaving out the one motive of love, which will be considered soon, never in all my life have I severely scrutinized a good deed and been sure that it expressed from end to end my ideal of righteous conduct. Good deeds are of large value in several ways, but as a means of securing rest under a lofty standard of duty they are simply worthless. They may for a period keep a man so busy that he has no time to live with his own soul; but the first hour he looks his whole manhood squarely in the face he is bound to have distress. There are, I know, those who cultivate this ethical busyness and call it peace; but it is not *personal* peace. It is as superficial as the quiet and sense of health a sick man may obtain by taking an opiate. Let it be ever understood that sooner or later a man must face his own soul and face it in the most searching mood. He was not created to live merely an objective life, and he cannot always be satisfied with bare busyness.

In his Philosophy of Religion, speaking of the contradiction between the lower and the higher elements in man's nature, John Caird says: "But morality is, and from its nature can be, only the partial solution of that contradiction; and its partial or incomplete character may be said, in general, to arise from this, that while the end aimed at is the realization of an infinite ideal, the highest result of morality is only a never-ending approximation to that ideal." This is true, and yet it does not strike the definite reality. Man's moral weakness does not, exactly speaking, spring from his finitude, nor from his finitude under an infinite requirement; but precisely from this: *Man cannot become an organic moral person under the moral law.* As a self-conscious moral person, a man keeps yielding to conscience until he has a moral ideal to which he gives allegiance. With this personal allegiance, his task expands until he must, to satisfy his own standard, be righteous through and through. He tries to meet this demand, *but he cannot organize himself about his main intention.* He cannot control the deeps of his individuality. He cannot gather all his moods, all the flying moments of desire, all the dim, basic longings of his nature, all the subtle interlacement of body and soul—*he cannot get together.*

The Taproot of Moral Concern in Man. But why can-

not the servant of the moral law organize himself about
his main intention?   To answer this question, we must
greatly deepen our discussion.   We have analyzed conscience, and we have brought to light the process by
which the loftiest moral ideal is reached; but now we must
do more, we must dare to ask the radical question, Why
does a man have any concern whatever for this inner
demand we call moral?   To this most radical question
all sorts of answers have been given.   What is perhaps
the most popular answer to-day amounts to this: We find
in ourselves this "narrow and easily worried organ," conscience, and simply try to make terms with it, try to get
a bit of comfort under the tormenting peculiarity, very
much as one might make frantic and idiotic gestures to
relieve the cramp.   Then, there are various answers which
play a fugue about a thematic *summum bonum*.   Fairly
to treat all these answers and sift out the grains of truth
would be necessary in a work of pure ethics, but is neither
necessary nor helpful here.   The positive path is better
for us.   The taproot of moral concern in man is, as I see
it, this: *His intuitive sense of belonging to the supernatural
overmaster*.   Whenever a man becomes self-conscious of
moral distinction he spontaneously feels that the right
owns him beyond all natural claim.   It is out of this
sense of being owned that the definite feeling of obligation springs.   If we try to analyze the whole mood we
shall find in it the following features:

1. There is a sense of the supernatural.   What this term
supernatural really means to a man I will more closely
consider in another connection.   Here it is sufficient to
say that every unsophisticated man projects a supreme
mystery beyond the realm of nature.   His initial attitude
is dualistic.   He does not feel that the mystery beyond is
"one with blowing clover and falling rain."   He has two
worlds.

2. There is a sense of fitness. The word fitness is not quite adequate, but it must be made to serve. The man feels that this supernatural, this transcendent mystery is *his own place*. I would say his own home, but the word home is friendly; and the man does not feel, in his primary mood anyway, that the supernatural is friendly. No, it is just this and no more: "I fit into that; I was made for that; my place is over there." Precisely as a dolphin may feel that he is in fitness with the sea, or as a petrel may instinctively feel that the wild fling of the spray suits him, so a normal man intuitively feels that he fits into the vast mystery beyond nature, that the supernatural is in vital and necessary and everlasting conjunction with his being.

3. There is the sense of the supernatural overmaster. Both of the feelings, that of the supernatural and that of fitness, are gathered up into one feeling, namely, that this non-natural mystery owns him, and so has a boundless, unyielding claim to all he is and all he can do. *Ecce deus fortior me, qui veniens dominabitur mihi.* That this feeling has both a theistic implication and a theistic trend seems to me to be evident; and yet it is a mistake to teach that all men recognize in conscience the imperative of a personal God. Some men feel only a solemn presence or power, something in them and yet above them, an unpliable overmaster.

Another thing should be noted: This feeling that there is an overmaster with absolute claim upon us is not the feeling of dependence, but a feeling many reaches loftier. In the sense of dependence one feels *need*, but in the moral mood one feels *authority*. It is not that I require something, but that my overmaster requires something. Homer says: "As young birds ope the mouth for food, so all men need the gods;" and the sentence would make a suitable text for a large part of the moral and religious discussion since Schleiermacher. But the conception is superficial and leads to sentimental weakness in the religious life. Surely we do need God and the gifts of God. Surely we have this sense of need and should give it large place later. But (and I must urge this upon you!) the fundamental moral feeling is that of *authority*, and the supreme moral action is that of *obedience*.

If now we can succeed in keeping this taproot of moral concern free from Christian and theistic interlacing, we can, I think, perceive that the primary moral feeling is essentially a feeling of *fear*. Under recognized supernatural authority the truly moral man fears to do wrong. But we must be extremely discriminating here, or we shall plunge into a cheap utilitarianism. This moral fear is not like the animal fear of pain. (Remember our discussion of Conscience.) It is not, primarily, an associational fear of results. *It is an intuitive fear of the supernatural authority.* The man has no reason for it. He is made to fear conscience, that is all. The fear is just as immediate, just as constitutional, as the sense of moral distinction itself. Inasmuch, then, as the simple, unenriched moral bearing is one of fear, the man of bare morality is a *slave;* a slave not in the sense that his volitions are necessitated, but in the sense that his motivity is charged with fear. "The crack of the moral whip never ceases." Personal morality never can be anything better than the most noble slavery.

Now we are prepared to come back to the question of the accretion of motive. I said that under the moral law no man can become an organic moral person; and I now add the reason. The impossibility lies in the fact that the main motive of personal morality—fear—*is not an organizing motive.* Indeed, fear is a motive of disintegration. Make any creature afraid, and the result is a scattering of all its forces like an army in flight. The profoundly moral man, then, who is merely moral and nothing more, is in this anomalous condition, namely, the best thing in him, his motive enthroned, is all the time rendering it less and less possible to bring all the elements of his manhood into moral unity. Were there nothing beyond morality—and I say it deliberately—it would be much better to have no moral life at all, yes, much better to have no personal life at all. An eagle, or a tree, is a success, for there is organic life in small range; but a moral man is a failure; never deeply at peace with himself; constantly afraid of an abstruse, sublime something with which he dare not fellowship; a shivering slave without a dream of freedom; an inorganic man never once bearing toward the universe in personal triumph. Moral loyalty is of large value; but the value is not that of a finality, it is that of an increment in a spiritual process. Praise the moralist as we will, glorify his heroism as we should, still we are to say unto him, "Go on! the end is not yet!"

Only one motive is there which is capable of organizing a man, and *that one motive is holy love.* We must have love. It is not enough to have "morality touched by emotion." Many a moral man can take fire at bare thought of the supremacy of righteousness. It is not *any* emotion, it is not any *great* emotion which we need, but the one peculiar kind of emotion, the creative passion of love. This—love in the heart—is the organizer paramount. It will dominate every mood, make all idiosyncrasies coalesce, bring every wandering element of manhood into organic simplicity and beauty. It is not merely love's power of fusion, the fire, the intensity of the passion by which other emotions are transformed into blended urgencies, all driving toward the same object; neither is it the fullness of love, its oceanic occupancy of self-consciousness; it is these, fusion and fullness, with the addition of psychic endurance, the staying-power of love in consciousness—it is these three qualities which make love the organizer it is. But, further, it is not any sort of love which can organize a man. He must have *holy* love. Man is a moral person, and he can be fully organized only under moral terms. The love must be just as ethical as that great fear which the moral loyalist has. You must not throw that fear away. You must take that very fear and make it over into a holy love, a boundless passion for all moral concern, a passion so ethical that it would be an awful fear were it for an instant to stop throbbing with the joy of personal fellowship. But how, pray, can this be done? how can moral fear be made over into moral love? In some way *the moral law itself must be transformed into a personal Friend.*

From Personal Morality to Religion. As a matter of fact men do not to-day very commonly pass into religion from personal morality. They are, as said before, too cowardly to try to meet fully and patiently the requirements of their own ideal; and so they go back into sporadic morality, or into formal morality, or into a life immoral out and out. But whenever the loyalty is steadfastly maintained the man is certain sooner or later to realize the impossibility of his expanding task, and with this realization to experience ethical despair. An instance we have in the life of Thomas Carlyle. It is, I am aware, quite the fashion to depreciate Carlyle as "a dramatic exploiter of abnormal emotions"; but with sanity and verity he wrote out his own experience. And his own experience was typical—was the experience common to every soul morally in earnest.

The First Glimmer of Repentance. With serious purpose I have termed this despair of the hopeless moral loyalist an ethical despair. It is ethical because the ethical ideal is exalted by the very despair itself. The hopeless man cares more and more for his ideal, cares more and more for righteousness, in every moment of his distress. And so his consciousness is flooded with ethical quality. It is, I believe, this brave moral insistence, this unflinching purpose rather to perish than to cheapen one's life, which opens up the way for supernatural help. Anyway, a wonderful change takes place. The fierce determination turns into a personal sorrow for failure, perhaps the most beautiful thing in the universe. Yes, and, strangely enough, a hopeful thing, too; for the despair begins to break up like a clearing storm. This is not by any means so profound as is Christian repentance, but it is morally the same kind of an experience. I call it the first glimmer of repentance—and the dawn of religion.

RELIGION

Were one asked to characterize the life of religion in the broadest and most general terms possible, one might say that it consists of the belief that there is an unseen order, and that our supreme good lies in harmoniously adjusting ourselves thereto.—*William James*, Gifford Lectures, p. 53.

The origin of religion consists in the fact that man *has* the Infinite within him, even before he is himself conscious of it. . . . Whatever name we give it—instinct, or an innate, original, and unconscious form of thought, or form of conception—it is the specifically human element in man, the idea which dominates him. He gives it precedence over the finite. . . . Even primitive man, as soon as he comes to apprehend the finite, regards it as perplexing and unnatural.—*C. P. Tiele*, Elements of the Science of Religion, ed. 1899, Criticism of Max Müller, ii, 228–233.

There is necessarily present in us, in virtue of the very fact that our inner and our outer lives stand in constant relation to each other, the consciousness of a Being or Principle which is above both and revealed in both. . . . A human consciousness cannot exist without some dawning of *reverence*—of an awe and aspiration which is as different from fear as it is from presumption, from slavish submission as it is from tyrannical self-assertion. And it is this reverence, this sense of a subjection which elevates us, of an obedience that makes us free, this consciousness of a Power which curbs and humiliates us, but at the same time draws us up to itself, which is the essence of religion and the source of man's higher life.—*Edward Caird*, The Evolution of Religion, ed. 1899, i, 79, 80.

I have never seen a satisfactory definition of religion. The idea is too complex for a brief logical statement. . . . The past year or two I have given my class two or three statements, partly introductory, partly in the nature of a summation. . . . In different text connections they are as follows: *In its highest sense, religion is the normal personal bearing of men in and toward God, the ground of all finite existence. In a wider sense, it includes all actual or historic endeavors after such a bearing, however far short of the ideal they may come. . . . A personal bearing over against the divine, true in its intellectual presupposition, genuine in its ethical presupposition, complete and symmetrical in its forms of expression, is entitled to the name of absolutely normal religion. In the perfect love of the perfect God is found the flower and perfection of such religion. It presupposes a true knowledge, a right impulse, and issues in a well-balanced expression toward God and man.* Should you desire to quote any or all of these statements, I should prefer that you would not call them my definition, as that would imply that I believe it possible to frame a satisfactory, logical definition of the term.—*W. F. Warren*, from a letter dated Boston, January 26, 1903.

VI. RELIGION

THE conclusions in our discussion of religion have been reached under a general method which may be indicated in a few words. Three questions I have asked, in the following order: 1. What are the intrinsically significant things in man's life, individual, personal, and moral? 2. Taking it for granted that the Christian faith is the highest manifestation of religion, how can we philosophically relate that faith to the full life of man? And, 3. Having thus secured a Christian-anthropological standpoint, how can we explain all known religious data from that standpoint? No claim is made that this method is suitable for a science of religion; but surely it is the only method feasible for an introduction to systematic theology.

The Supernatural. Before we try to analyze religion, though, we need to come somewhat closer to this tempest-tossed term, *supernatural.* What is the supernatural as man understands it? I answer: The infinite mystery beyond the organism of nature. This answer, however, but leads to another question, What is nature as man understands that? John Stuart Mill says: "Nature means the sum of all phenomena, together with the causes which produce them; including not only all that happens, but all that is capable of happening; the unused capabilities of causes being as much a part of the idea of nature as those which take effect." This definition does not at all express the conception of the average man. Men do not regard nature as including all that happens and all that is capable of happening. The conception is much more limited. Nature includes only what happens within the range of common individual seizure.   Men call a thing *natural* when it appeals only to their individual apprehension, or when it appeals to any part of the man that falls short of moral personality.   Thus it is that the range of nature is not the same to all men.   The men are different and so the appeal is different.   And thus it is that as men change, the contents of their natural world may change also.   A man may say, "Why, that is natural, but it did not seem so before."   In other words, the idea of nature is a relative and not an absolute truth.   For their development, men need to be dualistic; they need two worlds; although, as a matter of ultimate fact, the two worlds make one organism and not two.   And yet, as we shall see later, men are not deceived.   A relative truth is not an untruth; it is truth in circumscription.   A man on the deck of a steamship sees the ocean in circumscription, but he does see the ocean and not a mirage.   "Reality strikes him full in the face."   If we bear in mind this relative significance, this educational value of the idea of nature, we can see that it is not important that there should be precise agreement as to what things are natural.   But it is important that every man, in all his development, should keep the idea of nature as a background over against which he can sanely and distinctly realize his higher world—the supernatural.

In analyzing the idea of the supernatural as conceived by the ordinary man, we find in it several elements: 1. The supernatural is *beyond* nature.   The thought here is not that it is further away, but rather that it is less seizable, less subject to common apprehension, more transcendent.   2. Involved in this transcendence is the full notion of *mystery*.   And this notion of mystery is very peculiar.   It is not at all the notion of a puzzle, that now baffles us, but some day may be guessed out, or worked out.   No man ever expects to solve the mystery of the supernatural. He may apprehend it a little better, but never can he master its depths, never can he comprehend it. In fact, this sense of mystery is probably nothing other than a special mood of man's inherent sense of finitude. He feels that he is "a speck in the center of the Immensities." 3. Involved in this sense of mystery, or at least starting in it, is the *notion of the infinite*. Out beyond nature there is not only a mystery, but a *boundless* mystery. The supernatural is without limits. In other words, the common man has the practical beginning of that tremendous conception which the philosopher protects and partly expresses by the term *absolute*. To some men, this infinite is an infinite person. To a few men, it is an infinite law or order. And it would seem as if instances had been found where the conception is so vague that it should be called merely the notion of a presence. But to the majority, in all the history of mankind, the infinite has been an infinite power. The infinite mystery out beyond nature has, in the end, its own way, can do all things—is almighty. To cover fairly, though, the entire range of human experience, we may say that to man the supernatural is the infinite mystery beyond the total system of nature; and nature includes all those things which can be seized or apprehended by the individual without the help of moral personality. Some question there may be as to my right to use, in this connection, the term system, or the term organism. But I have such a right; for the common idea of nature is that of a realm, or kingdom, and never that of unrelated confusion. The average man has no philosophical conception of an organism, but he has a practical view which, if fully analyzed, clearly amounts to the same thing. Indeed, every fundamental notion of the common man has a truly philosophical root. All men are philosophers, whether they recognize the fact or not.

The Origin of Man's Sense of the Supernatural. There now arises the question which I deem the most crucial in the discussion of religion, namely, How does this sense of the supernatural originate in man? or what enables man to fling out beyond nature a supernatural world? The answer lies truly in our view of what the supernatural means to man; but let us draw out the infoldment. And it may be helpful to note with more emphasis the peculiar conception we have of man, a conception underlying many of our discussions and cropping out again and again. *A man is an individual creature lifted out of animal automatism only in those moods which are personal or moral.* A man is first of all an individual and has the automatic experience of an individual. There are moments, hours, even days, when his life rises no higher than that of a most wonderful animal. Again, a man is a person, able to treat his individuality self-consciously, with uncoerced volition. Now he is above the automaton, and yet there is no moral quality *necessarily* in his experience. Not every instant of self-consciousness must be an instant of moral distinction and demand. There may be in certain degenerate men, or in certain abnormal situations, or in certain fragmentary moods, a quasi personal experience which is no higher. And again, a man may live the full life of a moral person, not only conscious of self, but also conscious of self under moral requirement.

These distinctions in mind, then, we affirm that man's sense of the supernatural originates only in the experience of the moral person. As an individual animal alone, he would have no more sense of the supernatural than there is in a zebra. Neither am I willing to grant the claim of Edward Caird, that "there is necessarily present in us, in virtue of the very fact that our inner and our outer lives stand in constant relation to each other, the consciousness of a Being, or Principle, which is above both and revealed in both." If I catch his meaning, it is that in the bare experience of personality itself we bind the subject and the object, the inner and the outer world, together by means of our sense of an overarching infinite. But I do not so understand man's personal experience. In the experience of bare personality, the person is entirely occupied with himself. Nor do I think that a man is able to spring this arch of the infinite even when he compares his personal experience with his individual experience. The more I study men, the more thoroughly I am convinced that the human sense of the supernatural is created by a movement in the moral life; and had man no conscience, he never would have such a sense at all. My own view may be stated in this manner: In man's conception of the supernatural world there are really two things: First, there is *an intuitive moral center*. This lies in conscience. When, in conscience, a man first feels the ultimate authority of the moral overmaster he gets his first idea of the supernatural. To the man the overmaster is beyond nature, is a transcendent mystery, is infinite—*is the supernatural*. Second, there is *an arbitrary augment*. Because a man is a person he can treat this moral center with originality. Never could he obtain the idea of the supernatural in any mood less than the ethical; but he can keep it when once he has it, and he can apply it, in any mood whatsoever. In this manner he comes to regard all sorts of things, even non-moral things, if mysterious, as supernatural, and projects a great realm beyond the laws of nature.

Before we take our next step, I wish to call your attention especially to the extreme valuation which I have placed upon man's sense of the supernatural by centering it in the moral life. Auguste Comte, and many who do not accept *positivism* as a philosophy, look upon this sense of the supernatural as a crudity temporary in human development; but I look upon it as the loftiest and most abiding feature of man's spiritual constitution. Imperfect and abnormal expressions of this sense will pass away, precisely as imperfect and morbid expressions of moral distinction itself will pass away. All crass superstition will disappear. Dante will not forever plan to use " the mystic number nine." Samuel Johnson will not forever be anxious "to go out or in at a door or passage by a certain number of steps from a certain point." But man's sense of the infinite mystery will not pass away as long as he has a moral nature at all. He will, as he develops, exchange mysteries, that is all. In truth, man's appreciation of the wonder of the supernatural is to be counted as his supreme dignity; it is this which, as a being made in the divine image, he "brings trailing from afar"; and it is this which, when all its implications are worked out, renders possible his full and final fellowship with God.

The Religious Process in Man

Superstition. When in any stage of life, or in any passing mood of his inner experience, a man separates the moral center of his supernatural world from the outlying augment of mystery his bearing is one of superstition. He feels sheer mystery and is afraid of it. In the folklore of Brittany we are told that when a fisherman is drowned the gulls fly crying and beat their wings against the casements of his house. Here we have an instance of mere superstition. If we study this and like instances we discover three things: a sense of mystery, a fear of mystery, and a lack of all moral quality. This lack, however, is entirely unlike the deficiency in an animal, for at any moment it may change and express moral concern. Again and again has a man's feeling begun in superstitious dread and ended in the torture of conscience.

Morality—Is It Religion? Often it is said that J. H.

Fichte taught that morality and religion are one and the same thing; but I do not so understand Fichte. In his Ethik he says: "Religion is conscious morality, a morality which in virtue of that consciousness is mindful of its origin in God." Probably Fichte means as much here as Kant meant in defining religion as "the recognition [Erkenntnis] of all our duties as divine commandments." If he did mean as much as Kant meant, then his conception of religion is beyond anything possible within the scheme of mere morals. But, in any case, I must regard morality as a much lower experience than that of religion. Both superstition and morality are, I grant, in the religious process, but neither of them reaches a point in the process beyond fear. And surely it is not economy to squander the noble term religion upon any sort of slavery.

Bare Religion. The principle of economy, though, is not my only reason, nor, indeed, my main reason, for lifting religion into a range beyond morality. The main reason pertains to my chosen method of studying the subject. Under this method chosen I study Christianity itself, to discover the fundamental religious characteristic, and find that characteristic to be not fear, but faith. I therefore hold that the first thing in the religious process worthy to be termed religion is a personal bearing of faith toward the supernatural. Man naturally fears the supernatural wherever he finds it, but because he is a free person he can do a greater thing than to create the arbitrary augment, he can master his fear by a venture of trust. This personal venture we call faith. With such faith a man no longer dreads the supernatural, he reverences it. And so fear is turned into awe, and the act of true worship becomes possible. If now we note, in the religious process, the lowest situation where there can be this venture of faith, we shall find the lowest kind of religion. At once we perceive that this lowest situation is at the point of the augment. Separate the augment from the moral center, and there is the supernatural as sheer mystery. Toward this supernatural as sheer mystery there is possible to man not only the bearing of fear, or superstition, but also the venture of faith. This is religion, but inasmuch as it is without moral quality, I term it *bare religion.*

Of this bare religion there are many instances, not only in heathen lands, but even in Christendom. Be sure to understand me fully here. I mean that there are men who maintain a brave bearing of confidence toward the awful mystery surrounding them, and yet their confidence has resulted from a purely personal venture, and not from a profoundly moral struggle. The self-decisions of such men never burn with serious moral intention; and their whole bearing toward the supernatural is, justly speaking, nonmoral. Having in mind Emerson's famous address before the divinity school at Cambridge, Professor William James said: "Now it would be too absurd to say that the inner experiences that underlie such expressions of faith, and impel the writer to their utterance, are quite unworthy to be called religious experiences." Surely that would be too absurd! Readily I grant that Emerson's experience was *religious*, but what I fail to discover in his experience is a Christian element, or even any vitalizing ethical element. He had large courage, large trust, and achieved a kind of content, precisely the kind Littré achieved; but to call Emerson's placidity moral peace would be to leave no worthy term for religious experiences more noble and more profound. Take Emerson's Threnody (almost the greatest lament in the English language), which reaches its climax of personal faith in these sublime words:

"Revere the Maker; fetch thine eye
Up to his style, and manners of the sky."

Study this poem from the beginning to the climax, and
you will find in it not one touch of Christian faith, and not
one touch of that moral atmosphere so evident in, say,
Sartor Resartus. The Threnody is religious, yes, extremely religious, but it expresses only the personal daring,
the venture into confidence of bare religion. And, in
this connection, I need to say one more thing: A religious faith which is not steeped in moral passion is an
exceedingly fragmentary and an exceedingly dangerous
thing. It would hardly be an exaggeration to say that
such faith has done more injury to men than any style of
mental aberration. Inherently, in the deep nature of
health, in the working out the full plan of human life, no
man has a right to any content which was not born in
moral concern. To be easily religious, to be religious
without earnest moral intention, is as much out of plan
as it would be for an eagle to fly with only one wing. If
the eagle can do it at all he may reach a higher crag; but
he was not made to fly with only one wing, and in such a
crippled state he never can fly high enough and long
enough to find his true home among the mountains.
*Religion is intended to help a man to reach the loftiest
moral life.*

The Religion of the Moral Person. Already, in our
study of morality, we have glimpsed the fact, but our
conclusions there we now need to place in larger relations.
What does a person do to get an experience which is both
moral and religious?—that is our question. He first
treats the supernatural, his entire vision of it, from the
standpoint of right and wrong. To him, that infinite
mystery, whatever else it may be, is ethical. It "makes
for righteousness." Then, the moral person treats himself from the same standpoint, right and wrong. And
this leads to self-blame and ethical sorrow over himself.
The man's mood here is not defensive—is not discrimi-

nating—he does not know and does not try to find out to
what precise degree he is at fault.   He makes no excuse
before men and no plea in the inner court.   He simply
feels that he has failed and that he himself is to blame
and that he is profoundly sorry.   This ethical sorrow is
the first glimmer of repentance.   Let us call it *initial
repentance*.   Such repentance makes a complete cleavage
between bare religion and the religion of the moral person,
just as it makes a complete cleavage between the most
noble morality and the religion of the moral person.   We
are wont to associate repentance with the Christian faith
alone; but before a man can have moral faith of any kind
he must repent.   Again, in the third place, the person
ventures out into a moral faith toward the supernatural.
For two reasons the faith is moral, namely, because it is
made with full emphasis upon the center of the supernatural, and because it is made in the spirit of repentance.
I doubt not that there is in this faith, just as there is in
the faith of bare religion, a large appreciation of personality.   Indeed, I do not see how any faith can be possible
without an intense appreciation of personality.   For to
have faith one must perceive the intrinsic worth of a
personal bearing over against any amount of external
performance.   But, and this is the heart of the matter,
the loyal moral person is all the time, even in his faith,
testing himself under an ethical standard, and so his
valuation of himself never misses an ethical tone.   It is
not what he means that is important, but what he means
under his moral ideal.   Therefore, when Professor Seth
affirms that a religious approach is possible "only in a
person, in a relatively independent or self-centered being,"
I quickly allow it; but must add, that such an approach,
to have large significance in the religious process, must be
made with moral faith.   The route to a worthy religious
experience is only by way of the moral law.

We can now clearly see that in the religion of the moral person faith can never be antinomian. Certainly he does make substitution for conduct. He does substitute spirit for letter, a personal attitude for external deed. To his own soul he dares to say, "What I want to do, what I love, is of more worth than what I can accomplish now, here, under my ideal of duty." Note this, though, he makes this substitution in his passion of concern for the moral law; and so, as a matter of daily fact, his new moral faith keeps him striving as never before, to get his inner purpose out into faultless conduct. The merely moral man cannot live, even before men, a life so stringent in noble service as is rendered possible to a person by moral faith.

The Enrichment. Even this religion of the moral person, this religion of moral faith, is not, however, "a finished product." It is capable of vast enrichment by means of love. Psychologically considered, this love exists when personal faith turns into awe. There can be, indeed, no faith without a lift of the heart, and no awe without a certain eagerness toward the object of it. But practically considered, this affectional movement in faith and awe do not amount to love. Nor is the affection involved in moral faith worthy to be, in and of itself, termed love. The word love should be economically, sacredly kept for that definite feeling which the religious man may have toward God as a Person in reciprocal response. The possibility of love involves the possibility of full reciprocity. You cannot *love* a mere *thing*.

The Consummation. But love itself is not the final word in a complete discussion of the religious process. Love is certainly the ultimate religious motive, but motive is only one, the central, element in the ultimate religious experience. Thus far we have intentionally placed the most tremendous emphasis upon personality, and more especially upon moral personality. The individual we have cast out into insignificance. Now we must bring him back! Religion is intended to satisfy not merely the moral person, but the individual as well. It must, to realize its plan, gather up into perfect satisfaction the total man with all his longings, even those which are the most subtle and vague. The individual man, deeper than any self-consciousness, has an instinctive craving for God. As the person feels authority, so the individual feels need. If you have ever watched a half-frozen animal, wandering about, not knowing what he was after, but restless until he found the fire, you have at hand an analogy for an individual's automatic craving after God. The moral person wants God, but he wants to have an active relation to him, he wants to know him, to obey him, to serve him. But the individual wants to have a passive relation to God, to be nothing in him, to rest in him forever. This individual side of religion is seen not only in every form of pantheism, but also in every form of mysticism. And the Bible itself, in some of the Psalms, in Saint John's gospel, and in Saint Paul's epistles, has many a trace of mysticism. Outside of the Bible, we could find the mystical temper not only in the writings of those men known as "the mystics," but also in the writings of some of the most famous teachers of the Christian faith. Furthermore, even in this age of externality and sensible performance, some of the finest poetry is either charged with mysticism or at least alive to the large significance of the mystical spirit in the deepest religious life. One striking passage I will give, from Johannes Agricola in Meditation:

"For I intend to get to God,
  For 'tis to God I speed so fast,
 For in God's breast, my own abode,
  Those shoals of dazzling glory passed,
  I lay my spirit down at last."

In the consummation of religion the two sides, the personal and the individual, the assertive and the quiescent, must equally find place, and must be entirely harmonious in their coincidence. How, though, can there be a joining and blending of such antipodal features? The question can, I believe, be fully answered. After the individual life is thoroughly personalized the probational struggle is over, and the person's condition of motivity has become such that he can and does yield his whole being to God. This final and absolute yielding is the culmination of a long series of personal decisions, and is itself a self-conscious act, a veritable self-commitment. The response to this final and absolute self-commitment is an inrushing, an enswathement of the man by the divine life, so that every fiber of his being is penetrated and vitalized. For the first time in his existence the entire man *lives*. He is in organic adjustment to the Infinite. He thinks God's thoughts, he feels God's emotions, he wills God's volitions—in finite measure, he lives God's life. And yet the man as a person is not overwhelmed. He grasps himself, knows himself in every peculiarity, and fills out ceaselessly every inherent indication of the plan of his own being. In all the eternities he will never cease to be his own personal self, will never come to be precisely like any other creature in the universe. In individuality the man is conjoined with God; in personality he is separate in self-consciousness, and yet also conscious of his union with God. As a mote floats in the sunbeam, so this bit of manhood quietly rests in God; but he rests there as a person who has deliberately chosen his everlasting home. True it is that he will remain, that "he shall go no more out"; yes, true it is that he *must* remain; but he must remain, not because he is established by coercion, but because he himself has freely exhausted every motive to go, and nourished every motive to stay.

And even his present establishment in rest is personal and not automatic, for ceaselessly it throbs with the supreme joy of self-consciously choosing to live forever in God.   In this manner, the two antipodal features of man's nature find at last their harmonious coincidence. Absolute personal unification with the Infinite God— this is the consummation of religion.

ANALYTICAL SUMMARY

I. The Supernatural

1. The fundamental thing which renders religion possible to man as a person is his intuitive sense of the infinite mystery beyond nature, or his intuitive sense of the supernatural.

2. This intuitive sense of the supernatural is moral in its origin. When a man first glimpses moral concern in its otherness, its supremacy, and its boundlessness, that is to him the supernatural.

3. Then the man himself arbitrarily enlarges his supernatural world until it includes many things having no moral quality and no moral relation.

4. Thus there are in the average man's conception of the supernatural two things which should never be confused: (1) The moral center, where the mystery is a voice in moral demand.   (2) The arbitrary augment, where the mystery is nothing but mystery—a vague other world without moral distinction and urgency.

II. Bearings Toward the Supernatural

1. Whenever a man is in a nonmoral mood his bearing is one of spontaneous fear toward the arbitrary augment of sheer mystery. As this fear has in it no moral quality, never yields any pressure toward duty, we place the bearing low in classification and call it superstition.

2. Whenever, on the other hand, the man is in a moral mood, his bearing is one of spontaneous fear toward the moral center, or toward the total mystery with his emphasis upon the moral center.   His fear now is vibrant with moral quality, yields constant pressure toward duty, and so we place the bearing higher in classification and call it morality.

3. But it is possible for a man to overcome fear by venture, to bear toward the supernatural in personal faith.   This venture of faith, this "personal leap into confidence," is so intrinsically unlike fear, so much loftier than fear, so much more fruitful than fear, that we place the bearing still higher in classification and call it religion. Not only so, but to term it religion also fits into our analysis of Christianity itself.

III. Religion

Definition.

Religion is a personal bearing of faith toward the supernatural.

Analysis.

1. Religion is a *personal* bearing. Religion is possible only to a person, for it involves self-conscious decision.

2. A personal bearing of *faith*. The personal bearing must be one of trust.

3. A personal bearing of faith toward the *supernatural*. It is man's sense of the supernatural which renders religion possible to him as a person. Sometimes a high mood of æsthetic sensitiveness is regarded as religious, but it is not religious unless the man deem beauty itself supernatural.

Kinds of Religion.

1. The religion of mere faith, or bare religion. This is but a personal venture of confidence toward the supernatural conceived as sheer mystery.

2. The religion of moral faith, or the religion of the moral person. This is a personal venture of confidence toward the supernatural conceived as centering in moral concern. The moral faith is consequent upon repentance.

3. The religion of love. This is the religion of moral faith enriched by love toward the supernatural now conceived as a responsive person.

4. The ultimate religion. This is the religion of love consummated by absolute personal unification with God.

THE THEISTIC ARGUMENT

I hold, then, it is true, that all the so-called demonstrations of God either prove too little, as that from the order and apparent purpose in nature; or too much, namely, that the world is itself God; or they clandestinely involve the conclusions in the premises, passing off the mere analysis or explication of an assertion for the proof of it—a species of logical legerdemain not unlike that of the jugglers at a fair, who, putting into their mouths what seems to be a walnut, draw out a score yards of ribbon—as in the postulate of a First Cause. . . . All this I hold. But I also hold that this truth, the hardest to demonstrate, is the one which of all others least needs to be demonstrated; that though there may be no conclusive demonstrations of a good, wise, living, and personal God, there are so many convincing reasons for it, within and without, a grain of sand sufficing, and a whole universe at hand to echo the decision!—that, for every mind not devoid of all reason and desperately conscience-proof, the truth which it is the least possible to prove it is little less than impossible not to believe; only, indeed, just so much short of impossible as to leave some room for the Will and the moral election, and thereby to keep it a truth of religion, and the possible subject of a commandment.—*From Coleridge's Aids to Reflection*, Works, i, 220, 221.

I am aware, of course, that among a large number of advanced minds at the present time nothing is considered more absurd and out of date than what is called anthropomorphism, or the endowing of the Great Cause of things with human attributes. To believe that the Deity is constructed after the model of our own mind is considered as ridiculous as to believe that the earth is the center of the universe, and human beings the objects for whose special delectation the whole galaxy of suns and planets and stars have been created. Nevertheless, in spite of the agreement and weight of opinion on this point, I shall venture to affirm, on the contrary, that to believe that the cause of the universe can be conceived of in terms other than those of our own personality (or a part of our personality) is as hopeless an hallucination as to believe that by any effort whatsoever one can jump off one's own shadow. . . . I will undertake to show in any system of philosophy whatever that has a coherent scheme where the author's conception of the cause of things is drawn from theories or experiences of the human mind.—*John Beattie Crozier*, Civilization and Progress, pp. 192-194.

Now, to the plain man it will always seem that if our very notion of causality is derived from our own volition—as our very notion of energy is derived from our sense of effort in overcoming resistance by our volition—presumably the truest notion we can form of that in which causation objectively consists is the notion derived from that known mode of existence which alone gives us the notion of causality at all.—*George John Romanes*, Thoughts on Religion, pp. 117, 118.

VII. THE THEISTIC ARGUMENT

THE word demonstration, when exactly used, means an argument of such cogency as to compel anyone who understands the process to accept the conclusion. In this exact sense the theistic argument is not a demonstration. A man of sanity, intelligence, and entire honesty can follow the process step by step and yet not be convinced that there is a personal God. In truth, there are to-day many such men, men who are not carried by any or all the proofs of theism, genuine agnostics who say with Mr. Darwin, "I am conscious that I am in an utterly hopeless muddle." And yet the theistic argument has real value as an explanation of the universe. When we become more modest and look upon the universe as a problem to be explained, then the theistic argument grants us the most rational explanation of that problem from the standpoint of our personal experience. In the first place, because man is a free person, he dares to assume that his problem *can* be explained—that the universe is "not a farrago of nonsense," but is amenable to rational search. Then, he further dares to take for granted the reliability of his own personal experience and to explain his problem in the terms of that experience. What these terms are we will now try to discover.

Causation. Hume, it seems to me, never understood the principle of causation. It is not, as he held, an outcome of habit, a thing founded on the observation of an invariable sequence of events. Time and time again there is such sequence (as when day follows night), and yet we do not regard the events as cause and effect. The two ideas, indeed, that of sequence and that of cau-

sation, are altogether different. One is a surface relation,
and the other is an efficient connection. A mere precedence may be inactive and even impotent, but a cause
must have inherent efficiency and must bring something
to pass. The pith of the idea is the idea of power. A
cause is *power at work*. But where does this idea of
power come from? How do we ever get the notion at
all? We get it from the experience of self-assertion, and
self-assertion in check. We ourselves make an effort to
do something, and it is done. Then we try again, and,
meeting an obstacle too great for our strength, our self-
assertion is in check. It is this double experience of doing
things and failing to do things which gives us the idea of
power and the idea of power at work. Thus, by means of
personal experience men obtain the notion of cause and
effect. Causation is the first term of personal experience
by which men explain the problem of the universe. The
universe is to them an effect produced by power at work.
And in the very nature of the case they regard this power
at work as will-power, for all the power they profoundly
know is will-power.

Personal Intention. One of the most peculiarly interesting speculations in theistic discussion is John Stuart
Mill's "argument for a first cause." In the cosmos he
finds, he says, not merely a feature of change as events
come to pass, but also two abiding features, namely, force
and matter. In the feature of change, the events are caused
by the abiding, impersonal force acting upon the eternal
matter in fruitful junctures of collocation. This "collocation" reminds us instantly of "the arrangement and
position" (τάξις καὶ θέσις) of Democritus; and, given
in brave English, it means that the universe originated
in haphazard. Concerning such fortuitous origin Lord
Kelvin has said: "Is there anything so absurd as to
believe that a number of atoms by falling together of

their own accord could make a crystal, a sprig of moss, a microbe, or a living animal?" And the same absurdity we must associate with Mill's most ingenious statement of fortuity. But why is it so absurd? Why might not a great, abiding, impersonal power, with a certain amount of good luck in collocation, do everything? such a power would be a cause, for the eternal force is at work behind the events which take place. And perhaps Mill would allow us the idea of will-power if we were able to chasten it of true personal content. Let us, then, generously state the question thus: Why may we not believe that the universe is an effect produced by an impersonal will-power acting in fortunate chance-combinations? I answer: Because such a conception is in violation of man's second term of personal experience, the experience of personal intention. We ourselves not only do things, but we also do things which we intend to do—things which unequivocally express our personal intention. These things have often unmistakable marks of design. Not bare intelligence, but intelligence in such complicated combinations of effect as surely to manifest self-conscious purpose. Who, for instance, could examine a telescope, and not be altogether certain that it was made by personal intention? Such a combination can be interpreted in no other way without violating a fact of our own personal experience. Precisely so in regard to our interpretation of the world about us. In nature we discover countless marks of purpose. Some say that these marks have been obliterated by modern scientific study; but this is not so. Science has not even obscured the marks. If it has, here and there, taken away an item, it has given us a more purposeful combination than we ever had. What does it matter if the theist lose the web-foot of a duck, if he find about the duck a vast and complicated movement which ceaselessly manifests personal intention? With a few unimportant modifications, the argument from design can be made to-day much more effective than it was in the time of Paley. I say, then, that in nature we discover plain marks of purpose. And these marks we treat in harmony with our own experience as persons. To the charge that this is a plain case of *anthropomorphism*, our reply is, that is just what it should be. It is only a doctrinaire who would expect men to explain the world from any standpoint other than that of their own fundamental experience.

The Term of Unity. Following Kant, many writers on theism have pointed out the inherent weakness in the argument from design. With this argument, you can show that the great cause of things probably is personal, but you cannot make it evident that the personal cause is *one* person. In the marks of purpose, superficially examined, there is no trace of unity. To clearly bring out the point, let us go back to our telescope. To explain the making of the telescope, we do need power at work with personal intention, but we do not need one person alone. There might be several, or many persons, connected with the making, and even with the designing, of the telescope, and still it would express personal intention. Just so when we try to explain the cosmic problem, we do not require monotheism to account for apparent design. Thus we reach the question, Why may we not posit a polytheism to explain the problem of the universe? In our day the trend in science and philosophy is so monistic that our question is academic rather than practical. And yet it should be thoroughly answered.

In Professor Everett's valuable lectures, The Psychological Elements of Religious Faith, he says: "What reason have we, then, for believing in a unity which cannot be proved by induction? The only answer is that we cannot help believing in it. We cannot think of causation without thinking of unity, we cannot make large generalization without going beyond them to universal assumption. We receive a new thought, and we must at once bring it into relation with all our former experience. But no chain can support anything unless it is attached to something; an endless chain of reasoning is powerless, and we cannot help recognizing unity as that to which all reasoning ultimately attaches itself." This is well said, but it does not express more than a part of the truth, as I understand the matter. The first idea of unity we certainly do get from our own personal experience. Not only so, but because of our inner experience in self-consciousness we have what may be called a proclivity for unity, we want unity, we seek unity, we never rest until we find unity. Even were there no moral condition involved, no polytheism could ever seriously dominate the convictions of men. It is not natural for men to be satisfied with a crisscross of power and purpose at the bottom of things. But it is not true that in the world itself there are no indications of unity. When we more closely scrutinize the marks of purpose; when we note how things enter into intricate combinations and exist in relations of harmony and reciprocity, we discover trace after trace of underlying unity. No one can watch a storm gather and burst, or a gull fly against the wind, or a child grow into manhood, and not perceive a fitness in things. And from this idea of fitness to the idea of unity in a cosmic plan is not a long journey. I would not say, though, that by induction alone we obtain or could obtain a belief in unity. The two things I have said must be joined. From our personal experience we have the idea of unity and the bias toward unity; and with these two alive and alert the marks of unity appeal to us convincingly. Then we add these marks of unity to our data, and explain our problem by means of a unitary, personal cause.

The Transfer of the Infinite. There is one more question: When we have explained our cosmic problem by positing a unitary, personal power, why does the principle of causation not demand a cause behind this posited cause, and then cause behind cause, until we have an infinite series? To this question several answers have been given. One answer is that with our finite limitation we find an infinite series unendurable. As a tired land-bird in mid-ocean will light on the mast of a ship, so we in our mental weariness must have a resting place. Another answer is that in the experience of personality we ourselves make an original beginning in causation. We are, to that extent, out of causal connection; and so there is a sense in which every free person is a first cause. The longer I study the case the less am I satisfied with either answer. The true answer is profounder, I believe. We make at last a transcendent addition to our personal cause. There is an effort to satisfy the whole man, and so we utilize our sense of the supernatural. Already, as we have seen, there is in all our moral and religious life the conception of the supernatural as the infinite beyond nature. This infinite is to us a necessary stopping place, an almighty finality. No man can or needs to urge his thinking on beyond his sense of the infinite. I do not claim that to all men the infinite means as much as the absolute means to the philosopher; but it does mean as much as the first cause means to the theist. There is nothing beyond it, and it is self-sufficient. Having, then, this great conception in his own experience, it is natural for a person to use it in dealing with his cosmic problem; and so he transfers the infinite to the Creator of the universe, and now he has a cause that is potent, personal, unitary, and uncaused.

REVELATION

And I have felt
A presence that disturbs me with the joy
Of elevated thoughts: a sense sublime
Of something far more deeply interfused,
Whose dwelling is the light of setting suns,
And the round ocean and the living air,
And the blue sky, and in the mind of man:
A motion and a spirit, that impels
All thinking things, all objects of all thought,
And rolls through all things.   Therefore am I still
A lover of the meadows and the woods
And mountains; and all that we behold
From this green earth.
      —*William Wordsworth*, Tintern Abbey, July 13, 1798.

Men can as well subsist in a vacuum, or on a mere metallic earth, attended by no vegetable or animal products, as they can stay content with mere cause and effect, and the endless cycle of nature.   They may drive themselves into it, for the moment, by their speculations; but the desert is too dry, and the air too thin—they cannot stay. —*Horace Bushnell*, Nature and the Supernatural, p. 66.

Let us go still farther; nature is immoral, thoroughly immoral, I may say immoral to such a degree that everything moral is in a sense, and especially in its origin, in its first principle, only a reaction against the lessons or counsels that nature gives us. . . . There is no vice of which nature does not give us the example, nor any virtue from which she does not dissuade us.   This is the empire of brute force and unchained instincts—neither moderation nor shame, neither pity nor compassion, neither charity nor justice,—all species are armed against one another, *in mutua funera;* all passions aroused, every individual ready to oppose every other.   This is the spectacle that nature offers us.—*Ferdinand Brunetière*, Art and Morality.

That this personal will is benevolent, and is shown to be so by the facts of the universe, which evince a providential care for men and other animals—this is just one of those plausibilities which passed muster before scientific method was understood; but modern science rejects it as unproved.—*Sir John Robert Seeley*, Natural Religion, p. 11.

VIII. REVELATION

The Cosmos and the Individual. To understand the attitude toward the natural world of a man like Wordsworth, to appreciate his "fellowship with the fields," we only need to remember that he was the deputy of the individual as surely as Browning was the deputy of the person, the moral person. But is this attitude of Wordsworth legitimate and useful and wholesome? Certainly it is. At times man needs such a deputy, some one who can give utterance to all the cravings of his individuality. As an individual, a man is a part, and a very important part, of the natural universe. The cosmos becomes complete only in him. And so man is sensitive to even the most hidden currents in the cosmic life. Indeed, there is, I sometimes think, a secret cosmic force, not yet caught by science, perhaps never to be caught by science, which binds together every created thing, and makes us all from men to rocks into one vast mystic organism. And as a factor, a responsive atom, in this mystic organism, every man, not only the poet, but even the most ordinary man, has a cosmic life, cosmic impressions, cosmic moods, which are nonpersonal, and sometimes even contra-personal. As a ranchman expressed it: "Often when I camp here it has made me want to become the ground, become the water, become the trees, mix with the whole thing; not know myself from it; never unmix again." Keep this cosmic life of the individual in mind, and we can explain the fact that when men are exhausted with work, or baffled by temptation, or overwhelmed in sorrow, they turn with a pathetic eagerness toward nature. Men may come and go, friendships may wear to shreds, all the personal conditions of life may change; but our great cosmic mother is out there yet with all her land and sea and sky. She will not fail us. She will not misunderstand us. She will not become weary of our importunate sorrow. She will swell our lament into volume with her wildest winds. "Nature never did betray the heart that loved her." Yes, there are times when a man needs a mountain much more than he needs a person. And if you insist upon calling this impersonal, mystical help from nature a revelation, your usage is improvident; and yet I have no unyielding objection to it, if we can only agree to limit the meaning and worth of the revelation.

The Cosmos and the Christian. Another thing is necessary in clearing the way for the point at issue: we must eliminate the Christian interpretation of the cosmos; for, in any searching discussion of natural revelation, that interpretation is of no significance whatever. Already the Christian has had supernaturally given to him the full divine message. Ever does he have in mind the facts and doctrines and principles of the Christian faith; ever does he have in heart a positive, a triumphant manifestation of grace; and with such realities and vitalities in him, surely it is no wonder that to him the heavens "declare the glory of God."

The Point at Issue. Let us, then, see precisely what our real question is. It is not whether the cosmos affords theistic indication. That question we have answered affirmatively. Nor is our question whether nature does not grant an uplift of solace to the individual in his cosmic moods and needs. That question we also answer affirmatively. Nor is our question whether nature does not express to the Christian believer much of the majesty and wisdom and purpose of God. That question is not pertinent and should be entirely eliminated. The point at issue is definitely this: whether there is in the cosmos, for the moral person, such a revelation as is necessary to enable him to move on in the religious process of his life.

A Frank Word Concerning Nature. A most striking passage in the most forceful plea ever made for the adequacy of nature is this: "The creation speaketh a universal language. . . . It cannot be counterfeited; it cannot be lost; it cannot be altered; it cannot be suppressed. It does not depend upon the will of man whether it shall be published or not; it publishes itself from one end of the earth to the other. It preaches to all nations and all worlds; and this Word of God reveals to man all that it is necessary for him to know." This passage from The Age of Reason I quote to show how completely the assurance of deism has passed away. In point, compare these words of Thomas Paine with the last published words of Herbert Spencer. The fact is that the more men know about nature, and the more they rely upon nature, the more agnostic and hopeless they become. For one thing, men need to be told a few plain things about themselves, about their origin, about their spiritual condition, and about their destiny. And in nature there is no perspicuous anthropology. Even the few natural hints are so dubious that they must be treated by religious faith and coaxed into meaning.

This dubiousness in anthropology, though, is not nature's main flaw, by any means. Her main flaw is that she nowhere manifests righteousness. Of course, if with many of the rationalists we regard the human conscience as natural we can find a moral imperative in nature. To me, however, man's moral life is supernatural. But were we willing to pass over this difference of view the practical question would remain, namely, Can a man discover in the external world any supplement, or even any indorsement, of his own moral concern? To this practical ques-

tion I must, without hesitation, answer, No. I do not go
as far as Ferdinand Brunetière goes when he declares that
"nature is immoral, thoroughly immoral." I am not
altogether satisfied with that bitter indictment in which
John Stuart Mill says that "nearly all the things which
men are hanged or imprisoned for doing to one another
are nature's everyday performances." I simply hold that
nature is nonmoral, that she pays no tribute to righteousness, that from her works alone no person could ever learn
that the Creator has any ethical interest. Sometimes we
are told, I know, that immorality is overtaken and punished under natural law; but the opinion is very superficial. Strictly considered, the punishment falls, not upon
the immorality, but upon the incautious manner of it.
In discrete ways moral principle is constantly violated,
and yet the transgressor escapes as far as any cosmic law
is concerned. Nature ever says, "Thou shalt not bun-
gle." But she never says, "Thou shalt not do wrong."

I was intending to stop here, but I cannot; I must go
farther and almost agree with Mill and Brunetière. There
is no equity in nature. She knows nothing of what is
meant by that noble English phrase, "Give him fair
play." She will herself cripple a man with all kinds of
weaknesses and then crush him because he is weak. Not
only so, but sometimes these weaknesses are a result,
under natural law, of the action of some other man for
whom the cripple is in no degree responsible. That is,
nature is so indifferent to equity that *she strikes the wrong
man*. Once study heredity in connection with the doctrine of the survival of the fittest, and there comes to
view a mass of irresponsible suffering and failure which
antagonizes every human idea of equity, and even moves
us to moral indignation by its pitiless cruelty. But we
are urged to expand our horizon and take a larger look at
life. A certain journalist has written these words to

stimulate joy: "There is great consolation in realizing that even though we go to the wall it is by a great and impersonal law, and just as surely as we do go something better survives by our overthrow." To this I instantly answer that to make inequity impersonal does not turn it into equity; and if we go to the wall unjustly, nothing better can survive by our overthrow. There can be no progress, no universal gain, by any procedure which is intrinsically unfair. The only goal, yea, the only cosmic goal, worth reaching must be expressive, absolutely expressive, of moral concern. There is no more expanded horizon; there is no larger look at life. We will be intolerant of any evolutionary scheme which tries to substitute increase of potency and perfection in adjustment for perfection in ethical quality. If we try to explain the mystery of existence at all, let us begin by refusing to explain it in any way which violates our intuitive sense of justice and debases our moral manhood.

A Perilous Crisis. This inequity of nature, or this nonmoral attitude of nature (if you prefer the more moderate contention) leads to a crisis of very great peril; and the crisis is precipitated logically in this manner: To obtain a belief in the supernatural Person we make use of our moral personality on the one side and of the theistic indications of the cosmos on the other side; but the instant we have these two sides in juxtaposition there stands out a pronounced contradiction. Our whole sense of the supernatural, our whole moral constitution, demands a God who is absolutely righteous, and yet we are unable to discover even one trace of righteous intention in the very cosmos which we believe he himself has made. And so, after all our long effort to be thoroughly true to our inner being, we are suddenly flung into a pit of confusion. *It is perilous.* And when I call the situation perilous I am not merely noting the dire logical outcome,

I am not using the language of theoretical fright, but the language of actual human experience. With many men this crisis is the precise point where they have lost their theism, their religious faith, and even their former confidence in the reliability of their own moral intuitions. Indeed, there is probably no strain so severe upon a sensitive soul trying to live a profound life as that strain which he experiences in trying to harmonize his moral ideal with the brutal facts of the universe. More than six tenths of all aggressive pessimism, like that of Schopenhauer, and a smaller fraction of that dumb despair which has been called "the ache of modernism," have originated, I believe, in the awful shock of the realization that the holy of holies in man's nature is not only not indorsed, but is even positively violated from pinnacle to crevice by the natural methods of the cosmos.

The Religious Process in Stoppage. This apparent inequity of nature results, further, in a total stoppage of the religious movement in man's life. Let us see how this blocking comes about. Before studying religion we examined, you will remember, the moral process taken alone; and we concluded that it had no possible outcome in personal peace; and this simply, or mainly, because the moral man had no organizing motive of ethical love. Thus, even in morality, we discovered a basic need of love. Then, taking up our task in larger relations, we passed into the more comprehensive religious process; and there, in the religious process, we at last came to a personal bearing of faith toward the supernatural which was so charged with ethical quality that we named it the religion of moral faith. But even this, although truly the religion of the moral person, we found to be an unfinished thing—an ineffectual fragment straining toward the ultimate religious experience. And here again the lack, the one thing essential to progress, was the motive

of love. The religion of moral faith must be enriched
by love. Emphasize, then, this point: that man, to
organize his entire life as a moral, personal individual,
and to advance in religious experience, must have something more than ethical intention and personal trust—
he must have ethical love, he must actually love the supernatural as the moral infinite. How, then, is such a love
rendered possible? First of all, there needs to be a change
in man's conceptions. His supernatural, his moral Infinite, must drop its vagueness and become to him a real
supernatural Person. And in our examination of the
theistic argument we saw how this important change
might fully and legitimately take place; we saw how man,
by being deeply true to himself as a person and a religious
person, could, in his effort to explain the problem of the
cosmos, obtain a belief in the existence of a personal God.
Right here, though, we enter, I say, a situation which
is both perilous in its staring contradiction and a total
stoppage of the religious process. Why is it such a stoppage? Because it is a situation absolutely uncreative
of love in man for God. Why so? Because there is on
God's part no revelation of an ethical love for man. It
is a waste of time to argue with the extra-optimist whether
in the cosmos there are not evidences of divine love as a
barely personal interest in man and consequent care for
man—say, some such interest and care as an artist or an
author has for his creations—for were there the largest
amount of such love, it would not have even the slightest
worth for the religious movement. The important matter is not the existence of interest and care, but the *kind*
of interest and care which exist. They must be moral.
The interest must kindle in the very heart of righteousness
and then burst out like leaping flame into a real care to
secure the moral welfare of man. Allow me to tear the
situation open. Man is trying to complete his life by

reaching a perfect religious experience. To move on toward that consummation, man must love God. To love God, God must be to a man a Person. To love this supernatural Person, man must be convinced that he, man, is loved; yes, the Person must show such unquestionable interest in man as to overcome all the inherent fear of the supernatural. But this is not enough. And just here theologian after theologian has gone astray. This revelation of divine love must itself be moral. The love must not flinch away from supreme moral concern. Man is a moral person, and he cannot love a God who is less than a moral person, and the God indicated by the inequity of nature is less than a moral person. Therefore man's entire moral and religious movement is in total stoppage—unless, in some extraordinary way, there shall come *help*.

THE INTRODUCTION

PART SECOND
THE CHRISTIAN RELIGION

καὶ ἶρις κυκλόθεν τοῦ θρόνου

THE CHRISTIAN RELIGION AND THE MORAL
PERSON

Die Offenbarung Gottes in Jesus Christus, auf welcher die christliche Religion beruht, ist also nicht so zu verstehn, als handelte es sich um ihn als eine isolirte Erscheinung in der Geschichte. Es handelt sich vielmehr um den grossen geschichtlichen Zusammenhang, in dessen Mittlepunkt er steht.—*Julius Kaftan*, Dogmatik, s. 39.

If Christianity is found to be matched to human nature as no other system can pretend to be, and as cannot be accounted for by any wisdom of which man of himself is capable, then we are justified in referring it to God as its author. In the proportion in which this fitness of Christianity to the constitution, the cravings, the distress, of the soul, to man's highest and holiest aspirations, becomes a matter of living experience, the force of the argument will be appreciated. It will be understood in the degree in which it is felt.—*George Park Fisher*, The Grounds of Theistic and Christian Belief, revised edition of 1902, p. 89.

When two religions say the same thing, it is not always the same thing.—*F. Max Müller*, Preface to collected works.

But the true originality of a system of moral teaching depends not so much upon the elements of which it is composed as upon the manner in which they are fused into a symmetrical whole, upon the proportionate value that is attached to different qualities, or, to state the same thing by a single word, upon the type of character that is formed. Now, it is quite certain that the Christian type differs, not only in degree, but in kind, from the pagan one.—*W. E. H. Lecky*, Rationallism in Europe, i, 313, 314, revised Appleton edition.

IX. THE CHRISTIAN RELIGION AND THE MORAL PERSON

BEFORE taking up those discussions which, in our plan, are definitely to lead up to the system of doctrine, we should note and emphasize the profound connection between the two parts of the Introduction. Let us, therefore, relate the Christian religion to man, the moral person.

THE WORK OF THE HOLY SPIRIT

This is not a fitting place in which fully to consider the work of the Holy Spirit; but something needs to be said, because the Holy Spirit is the real dynamic of the Christian religion. Surely there are historic facts and mental conceptions which the Holy Spirit utilizes, but these facts and conceptions are but useful pivots of power and not the power itself. The power itself is the energizing will of the Holy Spirit. Without him, the Christian religion would be, at the most, but an empty intention to rescue men. The rationalists, some of the extreme ones, are wont to say that we need more truth, that truth will lift men out of all their failure. We do need truth, more and more of it; but under all that need is the paramount need of a vitalized moral personality.

The Holy Spirit and Personality. First of all, in this new and extraordinary Christian dispensation, the Holy Spirit affects personality itself. The Christian religion is most intensely personal. As some one has said, "The Christian message has a personal pronoun at each end of it—it is, 'I say unto You!'" But the full fact is finer yet—that personal *You* is so empowered by the Holy Spirit as to be quite another person in possibilities.

"Arouse man," Schelling once said, "to the consciousness of what he *is*, and he will soon learn to be what he *ought*." This is about half true, true in its appreciation of the worth of full self-consciousness, false in its lack of appreciation of the significance of personal freedom. You cannot make any man right by intensifying his self-consciousness. But it is true, and momentously true, that no man can have a profound moral life until he has a profound personal life. And the Holy Spirit does give to man a profounder personal life. He invigorates self-grasp, clarifies self-estimate, and enables a person to remain longer in self-conscious experience. Many a man before the Spirit awakened him was constantly dropping down into the individual, was constantly at the mercy of the automatic overrush. He was, in fact, a person only by right of classification, for hardly for a moment could he stay in personal vision. His self-consciousness was like the moon on a night when the whole sky is tossing with clouds. Now and again, for an instant, there is a flying gleam of gold, and then it is all lost in the overrush of clouds.

The Holy Spirit and the Conscience. In the closest psychological relation with this vitalization of personality is the greater influence of the Holy Spirit upon conscience. I myself believe that all the features of conscience are not a natural outcome of the personal process—although they do give teleological eventuation and significance to that process—but rather the immediate work of the Holy Spirit. Conscience is God's living relation to man, mediated by the Holy Spirit. In any case, though, it can hardly be practically questioned that conscience is quickened under the Christian dispensation. Moral distinction is probably not changed; but moral obligation, and especially moral settlement, are affected by what may be called the Christian exertion of the Holy Spirit. Perhaps I had better briefly give my full view: The Holy

Spirit does something for every man; but he will do more
for the moral person who, in any time, or in any place,
makes his best personal response to the initiative moral
pressure; and he will do still more for men in any situation
where the Christian message is declared; and he will do
still more for men where the Christian message is declared
in a situation which is quick with the faith and love and
sacrifice belonging to actual Christian experience.

THE CHRISTIAN RELIGION AND MORAL LOVE

The most unwholesome thing in the teaching of the
mediating theology is its unqualified assertion that the
dominating feature of Christianity is the love of God for
man.   Here is a statement of the type to which I refer:
"The possession in Christ of the supreme revelation of
God's love and purpose constitutes the distinctive mark of
Christianity."   In a general way, this statement is the
truth, and might be adequate in certain parts of a popular
sermon; but once placed and emphasized in theology it
becomes as harmful as poison.   In the person and work of
Christ there is no manifestation of a divine love which is
nothing more than a personal interest, nothing more than
a going out of the heart toward men.   There is love, infinite love, manifest, but it is moral love.   It is love in,
though, and because of, perfect righteousness.   Man is
loved as a moral person capable of moral response.   He
is loved for moral ends.   His only joyous outcome is
moral, moral, moral.   The Christian religion begins, continues, and culminates in moral concern.

The Indirect Preparations.   I have spoken of the significance which nature has for the individual; and I have
also indicated the educational value of man's conception
of nature over against his conception of the supernatural;
but now there is more to be said.   Nature, by the very
fact of her failure to show moral concern, makes it im-

possible for the moral person to stay in nature. The individual, the animal, could stay in nature forever; but the moral person must find another world. "He must fly the awful vacuum." Thus, nature tends to create an urgency in man's need of another revelation of God, which shall fully manifest moral love.

This is also the point of view, I think, from which we may see the true Christian interpretation of the heathen religions. With certain exceptions, or at least with certain hesitations in decision, I cannot regard these religions as mere combinations of superstition. Doubtless there is in them much superstition, but to the superstition are joined many elements which are truly religious. Considered psychologically, and not historically, and not practically, they are like some of the debased forms of the Christian religion itself, say like the Roman Catholic. But, as far as I know, there is not in any one of these heathen religions a conception of divine love as moral. Speaking of the beliefs of men living under the ethnic religions, Professor Seeley has said, "They have believed in gods that were beautiful, powerful, immortal, happy, but not benevolent." As he uses the word benevolent, he means a disposition to help men, to secure their well-being; and this disposition must have a moral origin. And yet I prefer to say that the gods of the ethnic religions have no righteous concern for men. If they show any interest in men it does not spring from moral concern, and does not amount to a righteous passion. And, when I study these religions in a comprehensive spirit, with a purpose to relate all things, under the providence of God, to the Christian faith, it becomes evident that they, like nature, are an indirect preparation for the ultimate manifestation of God's moral love toward men. Here, again, the moral person gets an urgency; he cannot rest, he must find another world.

The Direct Preparation. Of far greater importance, though, than these indirect preparations, in nature and in the heathen religions, is the direct preparation in the history of the Jewish people. Even with the large place the Old Testament has come to hold in Christian scholarship, how few there are who realize its fundamental importance to the Christian religion! For example, think of a man so alert and open-minded as is Professor Adolf Harnack saying this: "Jesus Christ's teaching will at once bring us by steps which, if few, will be great, to a height where its connection with Judaism is seen to be only a loose one." Could any utterance made by responsible Christian scholarship be more careless, more superficial, more deeply untrue? One would suppose that even an ordinary examination of our Lord's own attitude toward the Old Testament would lead to a conviction that his teaching had close connection with the dispensation which he came to fulfill. The ethical ground of the gospel of Jesus Christ comes almost entire from the Old Testament; and the daring emphasis upon grace is made wholesomely expedient by that long, unflinching, tremendous moral imperative in the history from Abraham to Amos. In truth, those very severities which we now pronounce unchristian were for an ethical and preparatory end, for they tended to shut out Jehovah's people from all the insidious fascination of the deadly immorality about them. How can any student of comparative religion fail to realize that the mighty ethical momentum of Christianity comes from the life of the Old Testament? That moral law, given in such definiteness and yet in such forceful grandeur that it penetrates all our civilization; that poetry in the psalms which always burns, and sometimes blazes, with the enthusiasm of righteousness; and those towering prophets of moral insistence who stand out like a range of mountains in a flat world—what, I ask, could Christianity be or become or accomplish without that direct preparation? A loose connection! Why, the connection is so close that it is more than external, more than historical, it is an historical connection made spiritual in an organic plan, it is a connection through which the Holy Spirit to-day brings Christian things to pass. There is, probably, not a typical Christian conversion in which the Old Testament is not effectively involved; nor a typical Christian experience which is not by the Old Testament nourished and balanced and enlarged.

The New Conception of God. In connection with this direct preparation for the revelation of moral love, there arises a new conception of God, a conception far beyond anything possible in bare theism. God is regarded as a person, holy, in action, for the moral rescue of his people. The God evident in the Old Testament is not an "Eternal Somewhat," but an Eternal Someone, with personal plan and self-conscious volition. The contention of Matthew Arnold at this point is really not worthy of serious notice. And, further, this personal God is holy. Later we will try to find out just what is meant by holiness; but, in any possible interpretation, holiness can be relied upon to protect every moral interest. Again, this holy God is conceived of as in action. He is in earnest even unto the actual deed. It has been said that the God of the Old Testament is no other than the God of deism. But the God of deism is an infinite idler. "He sits forever doing nothing in the sky-parlor of the universe." On the contrary, the Lord God of Israel is ever intensely concerned with events and ever strenuously doing deeds. Again, in the center of all this interest and activity, we find the first note of a divine redemption. God is active, God is in earnest, to rescue his people unto righteousness. And when this redemptional idea is augmented by the Messianic idea there is a very direct and a very complete preparation for the comprehensive plan of redemption as unfolded in the New Testament.

The Christian Object of Faith. However much we may make of this revelation in the Old Testament, it cannot provide the true Christian object of faith. The Messiah himself, as a Redeemer to appear on somewhere in the years, is not able to meet man's entire need and to complete the religious process. Nor is Jesus Christ as man, or as an exalted creature, the Christian object of faith. Nor is Jesus Christ as God, or as God-man, the Christian object of faith. If we pause with only the person, we shall altogether fail to catch the potent Christian peculiarity. The new object, the Christian object of faith, is Jesus Christ, the incarnate Son of God, as *the actual Redeemer.* The conception is two-ply: First, there is the person who is God incarnate in man, who is therefore both human and divine. On the one side, Christ is so truly man that he is our own Brother, *we own him;* never can he get beyond us, never can he escape our humanity. And precisely because he is our own we have no dread of him. Even in our sins he can get at us. Thus, the terribleness of the naked supernatural, and the isolation of the God of bare theism, and the ethical rigidity of Jehovah, are taken away. And yet, on the other side, Christ is so absolutely God to us that he is our finality in power, in authority, and even in moral ideal. All the moral concern there is we find in him. Beyond him there is no demand whatsoever. It is the wonder of wonders, but the moral law now looks toward us in friendship, without dropping an iota of moral requisition. Second, this divine-human person is our actual Redeemer. He is not out there in the realm of expectation—*he is here!* The only Son of God has actually come and has actually completed his redemptional work. By his death he has literally made full atonement for the sins of all mankind. The Christian object of faith, then, is Jesus Christ, God and man in one person, with the finished work of redemption in his victorious hand. The person and the atonement must be woven into one assertion—"*Jesus Christ, and him crucified.*" Thus, in the Christian religion, we obtain the perfect revelation of moral love.

The Response of the Moral Person. Probably no two men ever reach the Christian experience by the same combination of features; and yet we can, I think, discover the main features which are combined in any typical case. They are these: 1. A profounder sense of moral responsibility. This is the psychological start and is entirely the work of the Holy Spirit. When he empowers personality, the man is lifted out of the automatic slavery and there is a keener sense of personal freedom. But the result is not, as we might at first suppose, a feeling of self-sufficiency. For the man's moral nature is vitalized at the same time, and so the keener sense of freedom is over against a severer moral demand; and the total result is a profounder sense of moral responsibility. 2. A greater dissatisfaction with all the inadequacies. In this profounder moral mood not only nature and morality, but all religious bearings and endeavors, if less than Christian, seem to the moral person as empty and useless. 3. A conviction of sin. Grant this moral person, empowered by the Holy Spirit, and restless under all he has found and all he has done, the new and severely ethical conception of God; allow him a swift vision of the awful holiness of God, a holiness which searches like lightning and never condones any wrong thing; show him how intensely angry God is over unrighteousness, how he personally takes it to heart, and grieves over it, and actively uses all the resources of the

Godhead to destroy it—let the man once *see* God, and the result is a torturing sense of sin. It is much more than a feeling that conscience has been violated; it is a feeling that in our wrong we are against God, that we are in willful antagonism with the Holy One himself.   4. Christian repentance. This, too, is very much deeper than that initial repentance which we found to be possible as a passage out of morality. It is thus deeper for two reasons: In the first instance, because it begins in the conviction of sin, and so gets a tremendous moral momentum. In the second instance, because it is a response to the revelation of moral love in our Lord's person and death. 5. Christian faith. This is like and yet unlike that moral faith which we found to be possible in the religious process. The likeness lies in the fact that the Christian faith is also a bearing of trust; and in the further fact that the trust is moral in its nature. The unlikeness lies in the fact that the Christian faith keeps a hatred of all sin, in a peculiar ethical poignancy which originates in Christian repentance; and in the further fact that the heart-interest belonging to any kind of faith has now become a positive personal love with a definite object. No man, in sorrow over his sin, can trust Jesus Christ without beginning to love him. 6. Moral love. This Christian love for the Saviour, however, demands separate and most emphatic treatment. There are four points which should be carefully noted: The first point is psychological. The love is inherent in faith itself; is, indeed, but a personal accentuation of the heart-thrust of faith. You would almost say that Christian love is moral faith made perfect. In any case, Christian love means the largest appreciation of man's heart-life. Thus Christianity keeps insisting that the greatest thing in a man is not his head, but his heart. The second point is ethical. This Christian love is *moral* love. Not only does it express the

consummate endeavor of the moral person over against
his ideal; but also it will, when once perfected, when once
fully enthroned, organize a man, make him one harmonious being, a satisfied and passionate lover of righteousness.   In all the universe there is nothing more absolutely moral than the perfect love of a Christian man
for his Saviour.   The third point is religious.   By means
of this Christian love the whole religious process is lifted
out of stoppage.   The last point is Christian.   This
moral love which enables the moral person to move on in
his religious life is purely a Christian thing.   For it there
have been various kinds of preparations, to it there have
been various kinds of contributions; but the one thing
which has actually rendered it possible is God's revelation
of his own moral love for man in the person and death of
his only Son, Jesus Christ our Redeemer.

THE ESSENTIAL NATURE OF CHRISTIANITY

We are now ready, I think, to gather into compact
statement the essential peculiarity of the Christian
religion.   The most striking book about Christianity
which has been published in recent years is Professor
Harnack's Das Wesen des Christentums, really a series
of sixteen public lectures delivered in Berlin University
during the winter semester of 1899–1900.   Nothing could
more fully indicate the theological drift of our day than
the fact that this book has received, in almost all quarters,
an unstinted meed of praise.   "At last a true prophet has
appeared, and we have a voice of authority."   To me,
however, the book is not so remarkable for what there is
in it as for what is left out of it.   You can, in these
lectures, readily recognize Christianity; and yet, after all,
it is not Christianity, at least it is not fundamental Christianity, which you recognize.   It is as if a very skillful
artist had painted the contour of the body of a man so

perfectly as to make recognition instant and indubitable, but had left out the man's face altogether, never once suggested by so much as a stroke that the man had any face.

What, then, is Christianity? Not in its accidents, not in its passing historical forms, not in its special applications to definite tasks and problems, however important they may be; but in its intrinsic nature, in its basal *Wesen*—when the Christian religion is laid bare to its ultimate peculiarities, what are they? The true answer, I believe, springs quickly from our discussion. They are three:

1. A Peculiarity in Revelation. God has revealed his moral hatred of sin and his moral love of man in the incarnate person and atoning death of his only Son, Jesus Christ our Saviour.

2. A Peculiarity in Response. The Christian response to this revelation is in a profound repentance which culminates in faith in Christ as a personal Saviour, a faith that is quickened by moral love.

3. A Peculiarity in Life. The Christian religion is a life of moral love. The whole being of the Christian man is organized about the central motive of love. First of all, and through all, and under all, he loves his Redeemer and his God; then he loves all men, not as a philanthropist loves all men, but as Christ loves all men, seeking their moral salvation, and their everlasting rejoicing in the kingdom of God. The Christian man has much work to do, many tasks to meet, and many problems to solve; but in all work and tasks and problems his perpetual purpose is to express his moral love for God and man. This peculiarity of life, together with the peculiarity in response, together with the peculiarity in revelation, is the one convincing Christian apologetics. The true religion is that one which fits into man's nature and completes his life.

THE CHRISTIAN RELIGION AND THE HUMAN
RACE

There is such a natural principle of attraction in man toward man that having trod the same tract of land . . . becomes the occasion of contracting acquaintances and familiarities many years after; for anything may serve the purpose. Thus relations merely nominal are sought and invented, not by governors, but by the lowest of the people; which are found sufficient to hold mankind together in little fraternities and copartnerships: weak ties indeed, and what may afford fund enough for ridicule, if they are absurdly considered as the real principles of that union; but they are in truth merely the occasions, as anything may be of anything, upon which our nature carries us on according to its own previous bent and bias; which occasions, therefore, would be nothing at all, were there not this prior disposition and bias of nature. . . . And therefore to have no restraint from, no regard to others in our behavior, is the speculative absurdity of considering ourselves as single and independent, as having nothing in our nature which has respect to our fellow creatures, reduced to action and practice. And this is the same absurdity as to suppose a hand, or any part, to have no natural respect to any other, or to the whole body.—*Joseph Butler*, Sermon upon the Social Nature of Man.

As the conditions of men become equal among a people, individuals seem of less, and society of greater, importance; or, rather, every citizen, being assimilated to all the rest, is lost in the crowd, and nothing stands conspicuous but the great and imposing image of the people at large.—*Alexis DeTocqueville*, Democracy in America, ii, 357.

Fraternity is undoubtedly a Christian idea, come into the world with Christ, spread abroad in it by Christian agencies, and belonging to the ideal that hovers perpetually over Christian society.—*John Rae*, Contemporary Socialism, p. 219.

This is the fundamental truth out of which comes the regulative law of Jesus about social life. Society does not exist for itself, but for the individual; and man goes into it not to lose, but to find, himself. . . . Nowhere do we find on earth that picture of society reconstructed by the idea of Jesus, society around the throne of God, which shines out upon us from the mysterious promises of the Apocalypse; the glory of which society is to be this—that while the souls stand in their vast choruses of hundreds of thousands, and all chant the same anthems, and all work together in the same transcendent duties, yet each bears the sacred name written on the flesh of his own forehead, and carries in his hand a white stone on which is written a new name which no man knoweth saving he that receiveth it. It is individuality emphasized by company, and not lost in it, because the atmosphere in which the company is met is the idea of Jesus, which is the Fatherhood of God.—*Phillips Brooks*, The Influence of Jesus, the Bohlen Lectures, 1879, pp. 98, 99, 100.

X. THE CHRISTIAN RELIGION AND THE HUMAN RACE

HAD our aim been comprehensively anthropological we should, in the first part of the introduction, have studied man not only as an individual moral person, but also as a social person. But our aim was narrowly economic, yes, jealously economic; the single intention being to emphasize man's moral life in such a manner as to show, beyond the possibility of obscuration, the teleological connection which exists between this moral life and the Christian religion. But now that this economic work is done we need to bring into full view the social side of man's nature, for this social fact has very extraordinary consideration in the Christian system. It may be true, as Professor Ritschl has said, that "all religions are social"; but Christianity is peculiarly social —indeed, so thoroughly social that neither its doctrines nor its method nor its spirit can be understood and expressed in the terms of individualism.

THE SOCIAL FACT

Of all of Emerson's Orphic sayings, the one most arbitrarily untrue is this: "Man is insular and cannot be touched. Every man is an infinitely repellent orb and holds his individual being on that condition." Exactly the opposite is the truth. Every man is planned for human fellowship and can live his normal, his deepest life only in relations of such fellowship. He must give and take. He must divide his spoil with other men. He must rob men of their experiences, their sorrows, their joys, until his soul is like a camp full of captured treasure.

Just as the individual needs and craves nature—the trees, the fields, the sky, the ocean—so the human person needs and craves men. And the greater the person is in pure humanity the more men it takes to satisfy his inner craving. A man like Charles Sumner, unless enlarged as Sumner was by a generous philanthropy, can get on quite contentedly with a few cultured friends; but Abraham Lincoln had to have all sorts and conditions of men, and thousands of them. Sometimes, in selfishness or by necessity, a man will isolate himself, perhaps will dare to believe that his soul can better ripen, or that his work can better be done, without any human fellowship; but the days become more and more sapless, and finally his whole being springs into violent protest. In 1851 Thomas Arnold (the younger) wrote to his mother as follows: "I think the greatest mistake I have ever made was that of fancying that an honest man was sufficient society to himself, and that the growth and vigor of the intellect was compatible with loneliness. I remember well the first practical check that this feeling received. It was at Otago; I had made up my mind to go on foot a journey of three or four days into the unknown interior. I could get no one to accompany me, and I did not care for anyone. . . . As I struggled back over the mountains, almost sick with hunger, I could not help remarking within myself a longing to get back to the settlement and the haunts of men equal to the desire which I had felt a day or two before to penetrate deep into the silence and solitude of the bush. 'No,' I said to myself, as I leaned on a great bowlder at a spot whence the eye commanded a far-stretching plain, on which not the faintest curling smoke told of the presence of man, 'thou wast not made to be alone!' A sort of horror fell upon me, the might of Nature seemed to rise up—irresistible, all-pervading—and to press down upon my single life.

From the hour that I reached the settlement I became, I think, a wiser man."

Personal Loneliness. One of the most significant things connected with man's inner life is his experience of loneliness. This experience is one of those commonplace matters which we take for granted, just as we take bodily weariness for granted, but which on close examination becomes indicant of a deep cause. Why is a man ever lonely? Some writers have answered the question in this way: A man, like certain animals, has a gregarious instinct; and so when he is separated from men he simply is restless because the gregarious instinct is not satisfied; this restlessness is what we mean by loneliness. This answer might possibly be adequate to explain our loneliness when we are away from men; but how can it explain our loneliness when we are with men? On a city street, in a throng of people, a man may be as lonely as he would be if alone in the Black Forest. No, the cause of human loneliness is not a gregarious animal instinct, but is rooted in the very nature of personality itself. What a lonely man seeks is not so much the superficial human contact; the touch of a man's hand, the look of his eye, the word of his mouth—these are but means to an end. The end is personal companionship. The lonely man wants a reciprocity in personality. He wants to enter the life of another self-conscious being who can understand him and "trade experiences." As a man in trouble said to his faithful dog, "Yes, yes; but you cannot help me, for you do not know anything about it." So the need is personal; but now we must go further. Why does a man need this personal reciprocity? I answer: Because the process of personality is a lonely process. In self-consciousness a man is necessarily flung into isolation. And in this personal isolation there are two experiences: One of these, the first experience, is that joyous sense of freedom which we have termed "the uplift of self-supremacy." This first experience, though, is speedily followed by another which is not joyous, namely, the initial realization of personal isolation. It is in this second experience, when in self-consciousness a man stands out to himself like one slender, separate match burning under the vast expanse of the night-sky, that the lonely soul cries out for men. Still we are not done. Why does a man, in this mood of personal isolation, feel such a need of fellowship with men? Because one feature of self-consciousness is self-estimate, and when a man comes, with any degree of thoroughness, to place estimate upon self he perceives his own fragmentariness, his own need of supplement. He feels as a self-conscious leaf might feel blowing about away from the tree. And a man feels in this way because his incompleteness is a fact. He is an unfinished item, a splinter of a comprehensive plan. And it is not merely that he is finite and needs to be filled out by the Infinite God—that is a larger point to be placed fully in another connection; no, it is that every man is made for other men—is purposely created jagged so as to fit into other men—is planned to be a reciprocal factor in a great social organism. And this great social organism is the human race.

The Human Race

First of all, if it is possible, let us lift our conception of the human race out of that crass and materialistic realism which has ruined so much theology, and vitiated so much philosophy, and colored the theories, nearly all of the theories, of modern science. Realism is of large worth as rhetoric—as the poetry of impressive speech—but in fundamental thinking it is nothing but pernicious error. The human race has no solidarity in the realistic sense—it has no cohesion in entity—no actual coalescence like that of a body of water where the individual drop is swallowed out of meaning and even out of existence. All the various and sliding forms of realism cannot be noted here; but this does not matter, for realism is so essentially false that there is not one sly form of it which has any reality whatsoever. It must be cleared out of theology root and branch. Mankind is solid simply in the sense that all men belong to one special divine plan where the design is to build a multitude of self-conscious, responsible fragments into one mighty organism socially and unselfishly interlaced. A man is not a racial thing, but a racial person.

Nor am I willing to allow the racial idea to be entangled with monogenism. There are to-day orthodox champions who seem to think that without Adam and Eve there could be no unity of the race. I do not so understand the matter. That the race originated in one human pair is a view in fitness with the doctrine of racial unity, and a view essential to any fair and wholesome interpretation of the Bible; so much I myself must hold. But the idea of the unity of the race is profounder than monogenism. Indeed, it is not only conceivable that men might make one organic race and yet not come from one pair; but also conceivable that men might come from one pair and yet not make an organic race at all. And the apologetic entanglement of racial unity with monogenism is harmful because it tends to destroy Christian perspective.

The Racial Organism. To understand the method and meaning of the racial organism, there are four points to be considered: 1. The common experience. Inasmuch as all the members of the race are persons, they have in common a personal experience, their entire inner life being interpreted through self-consciousness. Thus it is that men can understand each other, and can act upon that great principle, "Put yourself in his place." 2. The personal service. Add to this common experience personal freedom, and we at once get the possibility of personal service among men. If I so understand another man that I can really enter his life, and am free, I can enter his life with a purpose to help him, and can turn my appreciation of his situation into actual service. 3. The individual supplement. But, again, men are not only persons, they are also individuals. And as individuals they are unlike. Even if the elements of individuality are the same, the combination of the elements is so different that the result is unlikeness. And so no two men are ever entirely alike. Nor do they tend to become alike. Under the stress of certain external circumstances, men may take on an unvarying crust of conventional likeness. It is, however, nothing but a protective or imitative mannerism. Once crush the crust, and you will find a man underneath as original as Plato. Even the most commonplace man, "if you can only catch him," will turn out to be a fresh wonder of individual peculiarity. Thus it is that no living thing in the universe is so exhaustlessly interesting as a man, just a man. For sheer tonic, one common man is, to anyone with patience, and especially to anyone with a purpose of service, of more worth than all the artificial excitements in existence. But the value of this individuality in the racial organism lies not mainly in the fact that it is intensely interesting, but rather in the fact that every man can, by means of his own peculiarity, add something to the size of another man's life, and so actually help to complete that life. That is, we now have the principle of individual supplement or complement. Most deeply said, every man may become a larger being by the sympathetic capture or social reception of another's peculiar experience. Let us pause for a moment and try to realize what a glorious law of compensation we have here. It is one special operation of that greatest of spiritual laws, he that loseth his life shall find it. Because a man is a free person he can purpose to lose his own interests and ambitions in the service of a fellow man; but when he renders this service, when he enters the life of his fellow, he not only helps him, but also is himself enlarged by all the peculiarity of the man whom he has helped. Thus by unselfish service one can add to himself man after man until verily he lives the life of the entire race! Is it not, then, very clear that in such a personal interlacing, that in such a tangle of social reciprocity, we have a better basis for a racial organism than is anything which realism has provided? Have we not a complex of members? Is not every member essential to the largest life of every other member? and also essential to the meaning of the total race? 4. The racial plan. But our racial organism is not yet complete. The common experience and personal service and individual supplement are but features in a racial plan under which humankind gets all its intrinsic significance; under which the race is created, and redeemed, and providentially protected and guided, and made to move on toward a distant goal. Thus there is an end in view, a purpose in the organism, for which every racial feature has been designed, and to which every racial member may lend constant contribution. With this racial plan noted, we have every element necessary to form a racial organism.

CHRISTIANITY AND THE RACE

The Christian Method. In its method the Christian religion is social. Sight is never lost of the fact that a man is an individual, separate in personality and moral responsibility. And probably, on the whole, the responsible individual person is the more impressively in the forefront of the Christian message. But this responsible person is ever treated as a social person, needing other men for service and development and joy. Sometimes, it is true, the Christian leader has been individualistic, exclusive, ascetic; but in this he has gone far afield from the teaching and practice and spirit of our Lord and his apostles. Other things being normal, the truest Christian is the greatest friend-seeker, but his friendships cannot be merely personal, or merely philanthropic. They must "let one anchor drop into the eternities."

Again, and more definitely, in the Christian church there is the one supreme provision to meet all personal loneliness. A man's social need may overlap his home and all his special friendships, but never can it reach beyond the efficiencies of a real Christian church, organized about the gospel and the two sacraments, dominated by the Holy Spirit, and glorified by the transcendent presence of our Lord. Take one item, the fellowship in Christian experience. How quickly men having that experience can understand each other, and how thoroughly they can commune with each other, and how intensely they can love each other! In such company no man can wander "lonely as a cloud." The personal process goes on—indeed, it goes on more profoundly than before—but all its loneliness is broken up by personal fellowship. It is like exploring Mammoth Cave with a company of intimate friends. The caverns and tortuous passages are there as aloof and subterranean as ever, but they are made friendly by the torches and faces and voices of those you love.

The Racial Nexus. One of the most singular turns in the history of opinion is the modern Christian depreciation of man's bodily life, a depreciation which is, I am convinced, an indirect inheritance from heathen philosophy. In extreme and pathetic inanity, this depreciation is manifest in that vagary which has been deftly named "Christian science"; but none the less unmistakably evident is the depreciation in some of the prevailing forms of belief and sentiment in the Christian church itself. For example, one can hardly find a popular book bearing upon death and the future life, or even attend a funeral service (leaving out the fixed burial service), and be made aware that there are such Christian doctrines as those of the intermediate state and the resurrection of the body. In fact, judging from my own large experience with preachers, they are rapidly coming to reject these doctrines altogether or so to vaporize them that they lose all Christian meaning.

That in the Christian view of man his body is placed under emphasis is so fully apparent as to require no discussion. The emphasis is seen in almost every fundamental doctrine. Our practical concern is with the reason, the rationale of the emphasis. In finding this rationale, we need no metaphysical discussion. Whatever the body may be in its final entity, we now have to do with it merely as the fixed instrument of man's objective life. Without a body a man could be a person; but without a body a man could not be a social person. The philosophical significance of the body is that it is the machinery of personal expression. By means of his body a person breaks isolation, and goes out, and gets a community. This view, I am well aware, plows under all the forms of spiritism; but they should be plowed under, for in no one of them is there an atom of Christianity. Indeed, the few grains of indisputable fact which they possess are so interpreted and so related as to become positively antichristian.

Further: Man's body is not only social, but also racial in its significance. The human body is the racial nexus. It connects the individual human person with his race.

A man is not granted what I may call a generic body—a body to enable him to have social intercourse with any person and every person who may live somewhere in the outer spaces of the universe of God. No, he is granted the body of a man, a special body which nicely and precisely enables him to get at men. Now, we can see the relation which the body has to the racial organism. It is by means of the human body that the racial organism can be actualized. It is by means of the human body that all those principles of social interlacing—the common experience, the personal service, and the individual supplement—can, under the racial plan, be utilized. The strength of this view lies in two things, namely, in the way it fits into Christian doctrine, and in the way it catches the Christian spirit. Let us say, then, this: The Christian religion places extreme emphasis upon man's body because his body was designed of God as the special instrument to secure a racial brotherhood.

The Racial Brotherhood of Moral Persons. Only at the end of the system of doctrine can we fully apprehend the Christian plan concerning man, but we can glimpse the plan now in its connections with our introductory discussions. Man is a moral person, and the Christian religion ever regards this fact as of supreme importance. Not only is the plan so adjusted to every stage of the moral process that it forcefully meets a man wherever he may be in his development as a moral person, but also its perpetual aim is to protect the moral law and to complete man as a creature responsible under that law. Every part of the Christian salvation is ethical through and through. But when we come to method, when we consider how it is that the moral person is rounded out into peace and joy, there comes to view a most wonderful piece of social strategy. The one man, the individual person, is saved, but not alone—he is saved with others,

by means of others, for others, *into others*—he is saved
in brotherhood.   When his own entire life is at last organized about the motive of moral love, this love is not
for God alone, but for God and man; and so the individual
event bursts its boundaries and becomes a racial event.
In a word, the Christian aim is to save separate men in
such a way that the final result will be a racial brotherhood of moral persons.

Now and again the question is asked: Is the man
created for the race, or is the race a mere method of
completing the man?   In a full Christian answer neither
the man nor the race will be sacrificed.   The race is
planned to complete the man.   In the final racial brotherhood there will be, as Phillips Brooks says, "Individuality emphasized by company."   But there will also be
company emphasized by individuality.   The man is
created to exalt the race just as truly as the race is designed to complete the man.   The race itself has a teleological meaning and will as an organism finally express in
a peculiar manner the glory of God.

CHRISTIAN CERTAINTY

So, then, Reason rode fast on the straight highway, as Conscience showed him, till they came to the King.—*Langland*, Vision of Piers the Plowman.

Le cœur a son ordre; l'esprit a le sien, qui est par principes et démonstrations; le cœur en a un autre. On ne prouve pas qu'on doit être aimé en exposant par ordre les causes de l'amour: cela seroit ridicule.—*Pensées de Pascal*, xxv, liv.

It is of slight importance for the person of the observer, whether this physical object which I see before me is in truth just as I see it, or other than I see it. But the whole constancy and strength and worth of the personality depends upon the question whether this moral good which I acknowledge as reality, or this moral demand which I experience as real, has an actual existence or not; the personality cannot free itself therefrom without the innermost basis and the supreme aim of its life being lost. . . . Whether the sensuous objects, upon which the moral action shows itself, or upon which the moral idea appears, are that which they seem or something else, does not touch the truth of the moral relation in which I stand to them and they to me, does not prejudice the reality of the moral facts which by them become manifest for me; nay, it may happen in the reverse way— and this (as we shall afterward see) is the case with Christian certainty—that precisely the abiding moral certainty forms the basis for the certainty as to the reality of historic, thus external and in the first place sensuously perceptible, facts. But this is yet only the one side, which the moral certainty presents to the observation. Along with it stands the other, that that certainty by no means bears the character of universality and necessity in the measure and in the manner which belong, for example, to the mathematical certainty.—*Fr. H. R. Frank*, The System of Christian Certainty, pp. 104, 105.

Umgekehrt darf der Konsensus der gläubigen Gemeinde seiner eigenen Gewissheit die stärkste Stütze sein. Wie nur innerhalb der Gemeinde der Glaube des einzelnen entsteht, so ist das übereinstimmende Zeugnis der Gemeinde dem Christen fortgehende Bürgschaft für die Realität und Normalität seiner Erfahrung.—*L. Ihmels*, Die christliche Wahrheitsgewissheit, u. s. w., s. 286.

XI. CHRISTIAN CERTAINTY

KNOWLEDGE AND BELIEF

ECONOMICALLY to reach the heart of the matter, we will begin with the most simple forms of knowledge. A teacher in a primary school, holding up four apples, two in each hand, asks, "What are these?" A child answers, "Apples." "How many in each hand?" "Two." "How many in both hands?" "Four." "Why four?" "Because two and two make four." In these answers the child touches the two great realms of which man may have some knowledge, namely, the realm of reality and the realm of truth. The realm of reality comprises the entire range of *being*, or everything which actually is. The realm of truth is more limited, lying within the realm of reality, and comprising the entire system of rational principle. To be *real*, a thing must exist, and exist according to its nature. This expression, "according to its nature," however, is merely a protective redundance, for a thing can *exist* only in accordance with its nature. A picture of an apple, for example, is a real picture, for it has the nature of a picture; but it is not a real apple, for it has not the nature of an apple. Likewise, a remembrance of an apple, or a dream of an apple, is a real remembrance, or a real dream, but not a real apple.

To be *true*, a thing must express rational principle. That two and two make four does express rational principle, and for that one reason it is true. If you wish to inquire how the child gets this rational principle, I will say that it is parcel in the fundamental make-up of the child. He finds it insistent there just as he finds moral distinction insistent there. And so he takes it for granted

as a finality. If it be urged that the principle is a resultant of experience, we need not object to the point,
provided that the experience be regarded as *necessary*
and not accidental, that is, as an experience which is
intrinsic in the normal unfolding of the child's life. If
yet further you wish to inquire why this, or any rational
principle is a finality, I will say that the reason is in God
himself. He thinks rationally; rational principle is inherent in his holy organism. And we, made in his image,
affirm constitutionally some of the divine finalities after
him. Thus any rational principle is both universal and
eternal. Two and two make four, precisely four, here, now,
anywhere, forever. Mr. Mill's world where two and two
may make five is not a possibility in sane supposition.
Or, as one has cleverly said, "If there is a world where
two and two make five, the inhabitants do not mean by
two what we mean by two, or they do not mean by five
what we mean by five."

Unyielding we should also be concerning the child's
relation to reality. Probably to many it will seem to be
overweening, but I hold that he has knowledge of a real
apple just as certainly as he has knowledge that two
and two make four. Impressively we are told that
the child's apple is a mere phenomenal apple, and the
reality is hiding in behind like a timid sprite. But this
sprite, this lurking "thing in itself," we do not need. It
explains nothing. It is a dreamer's luxury. And it
cannot itself be consistently explained. And so it becomes a perplexity and a growing burden in philosophy.
Why not, then, in the name of sensible economy, away
with it? Inasmuch as, sooner or later, we must regard
the phenomenon as objective, as a point beyond us
where the work is done, let us fix the reality at that point
and in that point. Let us say that the very core of the
thing comes out in its attributes. Let us allow no idler

in behind the action. In other words, I hold that the activity of a thing is never to be separated from the thing itself. Every phenomenon *is a reality—manifested.* The child's apple is the real apple.

Constantly we are reminded that our senses are imperfect, and therefore our seizure of an object must be imperfect. Certainly this is a fact, but it does not weaken our contention. The claim is that we know reality and not that we know *all* reality. When a blind man, for instance, touches a hot piece of iron, he does not get all the reality, but he does most surely get some of it. Even in the case of the child, it is not necessary to affirm that he knows an apple *totally.* The entire apple-reality may greatly overpoise what the apple is to him. Nevertheless what the apple is to him is reality and not fantasy. Nor does the further fact that there is a subjective function, that the child adds to the external object, that he "treats" the apple, weaken our contention. The apple is made on purpose to be so treated, it is a part of a system of reality; and, out of the system, unrelated to the subjective side of the system, it has no significance whatever. Alone, it would be as meaningless as one blade of a pair of shears.

The question as to the method of connection between the subjective function and the objective item is one which has called out some of the most interesting and some of the most curious speculation in philosophy. As far as I am able to see, there is only one way adequately to conceive of the connection, and that is in the terms of what I will dare to call a Christian monism, such as is suggested by Saint Paul when he says, "For in Him we live, and move, and have our being." If we can first avoid all pantheism, by affirming both the personality of God and the personality of man, and then avoid all deism, by affirming the divine immanence, looking at all objective things as mere "causal points" where God is and where God works in relation to mind, we can obtain one system in which all the forces and connections are by and in God himself. The only serious objection to this view is a practical one. Our average man, whom we aim to help, constantly "thinks in pictures," and it is extremely difficult, if not impossible, to make the monistic view lend itself wholesomely to that superficial style of thinking. "What! do you mean to tell me that these dangerous things and these obnoxious things and these comical things are all activities of the living God?"

Personal Belief. The realm of reality is vaster than the range of coercive objects, and the realm of truth comprises many rational realities which cannot be demonstrated. As one has said, "God thinks beyond geometry and wills existence beyond our cornfields." It is even doubtful to me whether in our final, eternal life all that is true or real to God will be coercive to us. In any case, there can be no question as to our condition now. In this life there are many things, necessary to our highest good, which must be seized by belief if they are seized at all.

The main peculiarity of belief, as contrasted with knowledge, is that it always involves personal decision. Some of the higher forms of knowledge are personal to the extent that they are interlaced with self-consciousness, but they are never direct resultants of self-decision. Indeed, the worth of knowledge lies largely in the fact that it comes by coercion. You cannot, whatever may be your character, stand out against a demonstrable truth. If you try to resist the multiplication table you will be given shelter in an asylum. Belief, on the contrary, is very largely a personal creation. Whether you will have any belief or not depends, in the last issue, upon yourself, upon how much you care for your ideals, upon

how much you are willing to venture in the name of a
finer manhood. And so in belief there is a daring, a
militant spirit, a resolute purpose to fling one's whole
being beyond the dusty commonplace of the surface experience. As James Russell Lowell says:

"Experience is a dumb, dead thing,
The victory is in believing."

It is, therefore, belief and not knowledge which indicates a man's personal character—yes, and helps to form
his personal character as well. Consequently, in a man's
development, in his movement toward perfect manhood,
belief is of the greater concern. The most momentous
thing (at least in this period of probation) is not one's
hold upon axiomatic truth and coercive reality, but one's
bearing toward his ideal. Not truth in the mind; but,
as Lessing said, the love of truth, truth in the heart,
what a man is ready to do or to suffer in behalf of truth—
it is this personal attitude which is the one extremely
significant matter. Even if a belief at last turns out to
be untrue, in part or altogether, it may not be an entire
waste, provided it expresses the longing and striving of a
person after a lofty life.

At this turn of our discussion, however, we need to be
most discriminating. Belief is never an arbitrary vagary.
Belief is never at all like presumption. It does not even
look like presumption. In presumption a man is willful,
egotistic, self-sufficient. "He is not loath to fool with
facts." Presumption is enormously selfish, wanting
things for self at any cost. "Even in prayer, it is only *his*
crop which must catch the miracle." In belief, veritable
belief, on the contrary, a man is a humble and reverent
servant of all reality. Toward men he may be as com-
manding as Martin Luther, but toward a fact he is as
docile as a child. He says, "If that is so, then I will

yield my point." Often, indeed, belief is but knowledge idealized. It is thus in friendship and in patriotism. And even in religion, belief (now called faith) begins in real self-knowledge and then springs toward the sky to live an ampler life.

With all this firmly said and iterated, still we should never lose sight of the limitation to which all belief is necessarily subject. For the very reason that belief is so largely a matter of self-decision, it lacks that power of swift and universal conquest which knowledge has. With any rational chance, my knowledge can gain dominion anywhere, for its truth can be exactly demonstrated. But belief cannot make use of demonstration. The best it can furnish is a probable argument of persuasive appeal; and before such an argument men are always likely to hesitate. "Ah!" they say, "who knows how much caprice may be snugly concealed in this belief?" That is, my belief must, among men, pay the tribute of my personal freedom. I cannot be free without some expense. I cannot be free and yet expect men to treat me as if I were a thoroughly reliable automaton. Nor does the individual personal character afford an unfailing proof of the verity of a man's belief. Who, taking only one case, would be convinced by Count Tolstoy's nobility of character, of the truth of any one belief in his most astonishing collection? "But think of his long self-sacrifice." Certainly, but his self-sacrifice shows his sincerity, that is all. Almost every kind of error beneath the sun has been sincerely held. And sometimes, for reasons which can be discovered, a most erratic and a most dangerous religious leader has the most noble character in an abnormal situation. But, remember, we are now considering the character of the isolated person. Once add, in a large enough measure, the element of social confirmation, and the evidential import is entirely changed. When we find a definite and adequate moral character, typically evinced in an abiding community, we possess, in such a character, forcible evidence for the truth of the belief which lies fundamental in the life of that community. But even this evidence, however forcible, does not amount to a compelling demonstration.

The Rationale of Christian Certainty

Having made this preliminary study of knowledge and belief, we are prepared to consider the philosophy of Christian certainty. We will deal with its intention, its method, and its sufficiency.

The Intention. The Christian intention is not, as many seem to think, to make provision for knowledge. Everyone, though, will surely understand that the term knowledge is used here not in the loose manner of popular speech, but in the narrow sense of our own previous discussion. Precisely speaking, we *know* a truth, or a reality, only when it carries us simply as rational beings beyond all possibility of sane dispute. As a rationalist once stated the point, we know a thing when it is "so clear and distinct that it cannot be doubted." And he means when it cannot be doubted by any rational mind. In this narrow, philosophical use of the term, Christian truths and facts are not and cannot be *known* by men. Christianity is not an exact science, aiming to force assent by an irrefragable mathematical process. There is not one Christian doctrine, not one Christian event, not one Christian reality, securely beyond the possibility of some man's personal rejection. Not only so, but this possibility of personal rejection is the key to the entire worth of the Christian religion. Were men coerced into a knowledge of God and Christ and all the mighty matters of redemption, personality would be overwhelmed and there could be no personal repentance, no personal faith, no personal peace, no personal loyalty—no personal service. No, no, the Christian intention is not to make provision for knowledge, not in any fashion to compel the mind—not even to satisfy the mind as an isolated fragment, as a mere instrument of rationality. The Christian plan is to meet the whole man with his mind, his personality, and his conscience. More closely yet, the Christian intention is to take a moral person who dares, under the stress of his moral needs, and with his ideal beckoning in the distance, to believe in Jesus Christ and his atonement for sin—to take, I say, this venturing Christian and satisfy *him*—make him certain, in every crevice of his manhood, that whatever of person or event or doctrine is vitally coherent with his experience is grounded in reality or vibrant with truth.

The Method. In the process of Christian certainty there are four important features, as follows: 1. The feature of self-knowledge. This is the basal start. In self-grasp a man obtains the necessary fixed point; and in full self-consciousness he obtains the realization of his Christian experience. Often this self-knowledge is called knowledge, and sometimes it is called personal belief; but, in a searching discussion, neither name is entirely satisfactory. The knowledge is of self, and differs from ordinary knowledge in two respects: first, in that it is possible only in the high, self-conscious mood; and, second, in that it cannot be transferred by means of demonstration. Your Christian experience may be very rich and very profound, but you cannot, to another man, make it resistlessly cogent that you have such an experience. The reality is not an object for universal knowledge, but merely an object of self-knowledge. And, again, self-knowledge also differs from personal belief; for, inasmuch as the knowledge of self is a result of coercion and not a result of self-decision, it is not fully personal. It pertains to the personal process, but it does not reach to the end of that process. 2. The feature of moral concern. The certainty is ethical through and through. And here I mean much more than that the steps leading up to a Christian experience are thoroughly moral. I mean this: A central reason why the Christian man is sure of this or that is its fitness with his moral ideal. No Christian, for example, accepts the fact of the Incarnation on bare rational grounds. As an isolated event in history, I doubt whether anyone could, in these scientific days, believe that God had actually become man. It is so out of range with rational expectation! It is so in violence with the practical modern temper! How easy, how supremely sane, it is for the *Zeitgeist*, in all his robust health, to fling the miracle aside as "one of those infantile myths"! But to a man with a profound Christian experience the Incarnation is not an isolated event in history. It is a related event in moral history. It is "an ethical deed of God." It is a necessary part of a far-reaching moral plan to save man. The miracle, stupendous as it is, is, for the Christian believer, lifted into complete rationality by means of its ethical significance. In truth, not only is he able to accept the entire doctrine of the Incarnation, but also he craves it as a starving man craves bread. 3. The feature of personal belief. With all this start in self-knowledge and all this influence of the moral ideal, there is still a personal venture, an actual self-decision involved in all Christian certainty. The process (up to this point) by which the certainty is obtained is this: The man knows himself; gathers the deep richness of his Christian experience into self-conscious realization; instantly perceives that a certain fact or doctrine is in living conjunction with his inner experience (as a man once said, "I myself need the virgin birth almost as much as I needed pardon"); as instantly perceives that this fact or doctrine fits into his moral ideal; and then makes the venture, yields his whole being in personal belief. This venture is not *rationalistic*, but it is *rational;* for surely a man has the right to take some risk to satisfy the demands of his personal and moral life. 4. The feature of social confirmation. Robert Browning once wrote to a friend, "I want you to give my conviction a clinch." The two words, conviction and clinch, suggest the philosophy of certainty in belief. First there is a personal element, the person himself gets a conviction; then there is a social element, the personal conviction is clinched, or confirmed, by other men. You believe in your country, in her history, in her constitution, in her institutions, in her people, in her significance among the nations. Your belief amounts to such a conviction that you could gladly die to express it; and yet every other patriot makes you a little more certain that your country is worth dying for.

In the Christian faith this principle of social confirmation has its finest and largest application. A Christian is not a hermit. He is not alone either in his experience or in the expression of his experience. He has a community, he lives in a testing and supplementing and confirming community. In every crisis of his life, in every new turn of public opinion, in every phase of self-knowledge, in every look at his moral ideal, before and during and after every self-decision, he is *bounded by a brotherhood*. And this brotherhood is singularly adapted to the needs of the Christian man. It is made up of moral persons, all trying to complete their life in truth and reality; all these moral persons have had the initial moral and Christian experiences; all have now the same profound relation to Jesus Christ and his death for their salvation; and still all these redeemed moral persons come together with countless differences in individuality, in mental training, in position and occupation, in influence over men, and in present religious attainment. Thus, this brotherhod has mighty resources in social service and confirmation. It is too much to say that this confirmation is coercive, turning conviction into knowledge; but it is not too much to say that it gives to personal assurance such ratification that the Christian consciousness is full of certainty.

The Sufficiency. As the personal process is gathered up and continued by the moral process, so the moral process itself is gathered up and continued and completed by the Christian process. Thus the Christian process is one of synthesis and culmination. It is from the standpoint of this synthetic, culminating process that Christian certainty has sufficiency. It makes sufficient contribution to that Christian process. The certainty is, in the first place, sufficient for the ongoing of the process. At any point, a man can have *confidence enough to move on.* Whatever of fact or doctrine he needs for moral progress, he can be sure about. And so, inertia is never a necessity in the life of the moral person. Right here I must take exception to a view often implied, and sometimes deliberately taught, namely, that one can begin the Christian life, or go on to the richer kinds of religious experience, *by making experiment under doubt.* As though a man should say to himself, "I am not at all sure about this thing, but it's worth trying; and if nothing comes of it I will be as well off as I was before." In a recent book this view of Christianity, taken by hazard, is even given apologetic significance: "I conclude, therefore, that the true source of religious confidence is not primarily the objective Christian evidences, but the Christian experience obtained through a voluntary trust in the gospel when doubt is possible, or, what is substantially the same thing, by acting in a state of some uncertainty as if the religion were known to be true. In other words, Christianity is offered to the human race, not as a mere contribution to religious knowledge, but chiefly as *a body of directions for a moral crisis*, and is therefore to be used like everything else of the same class, that is, it is to be proved by making trial of it." These words touch reality in several places, but, taken together, they are extremely misleading. Not one genuine movement toward Christianity, or within the Christian life, can be made "by acting in a state of some uncertainty as if the religion were known to be true." To act in such a way is to pretend, and such pretension would violate the ideal of any moral loyalist. It is precisely this sort of teaching which lends support to the superficial evangelist, and fills our churches with powerless imitations of the Christian experience. Think of a man trying to become a Christian, or trying to reach a higher plane of Christian life, by means of a false personal attitude, and an attitude which any true moralist would despise! "But did you yourself not insist upon taking some risk, upon personal venture?" Yes, but the personal venture which I insist upon originates in regard for reality and is in the name of the moral ideal and not against it. The personal venture which I insist upon is not a dubious experiment— not an arbitrary and desperate leap at a passing possibility. A Christian is not like—a *real* Christian is not like a restless and reckless adventurer, who gambles with opportunity, who sails for an unknown shore in a spirit of hazard, thinking, "There may be gold there!" Rather is the real Christian like an immigrant who has shown both confidence and courage. In the land where he was born he experienced poverty and tyranny. He learned of another country where there was work and liberty and appreciation of simple manhood. He made the venture, crossed the sea, built a new home, and obtained a new citizenship. And now, in his ample life and perpetual intercourse with his neighbors, he is more and more certain that in his confident venture he has made no mistake.

The certainty is, in the second place, sufficient for the completion of the process. The Christian life, as you will readily remember, is to eventuate in a social organism, in a racial brotherhood. In this organism neither the significance of the moral person nor the significance of the entangled community is to be lost. The one man stands out as personally emphatic as though there were no other man in existence; and yet the community has a peculiar and an everlasting importance as a community. With this plan for a double outcome in mind, notice the nicety with which the Christian certainty makes contribution to the outcome. On the one side, the man, as an individual, moral, responsible person, is exalted by his free venture under his ideal. His certainty has come to him by a method most intensely personal. Not for an instant has his own independence, his own volitional freedom, been overwhelmed. As he stands there now, satisfied in every fiber of his manhood, he is more of a person, less of an automaton, than ever before. His personal mood has more vitality, more endurance; he can stay longer in self-consciousness. But, on the other hand, this satisfied man has a larger and more wonderful interlacing with his brethren, for his certainty has come to full bloom only in a social soil, and his certainty is complete only in their organic confidence. He is sure with the strength of their total satisfaction. His self-consciousness is filled by the entire community-assurance of truth and fact. Thus, even the final mental life of the Christian man is to be a life in fellowship. Not one opinion will he have which is not, while fully his own, a part of the Christian consensus of opinion. An ultimate Christian doctrine, therefore, is more than a personal belief—it is the belief of the social organism of redeemed moral persons. It satisfies, not the mind in isolation, but the whole man; not one man alone, but a vast number of men; not merely a vast number of men, but all these men, with individual difference, and personal likeness, and one common relation to Jesus Christ and his death for their sins, coming together in a perfect reciprocity of thought and feeling and service. Herein lies the philosophy of the stability of the Christian faith.

ESSENTIAL POINTS IN DEFINITION

Knowledge.

When a man is made certain by coercion of any truth or reality, such certainty is knowledge. An unfailing mark of knowledge is its capability of irresistible and universal transfer from mind to mind.

Belief.

When a man makes a venture under an ideal of any kind his confidence in the truth or reality of the object of his venture is personal belief. Unlike knowledge, belief is incapable of any irresistible transfer from mind to mind.

Christian Certainty.

This is a peculiar sort of belief. It is a personal belief, socially reinforced, under a moral ideal. A full definition may be given thus: Christian certainty is that personal, moral assurance which a Christian man, in organic relation with the Christian brotherhood, more and more profoundly has, first and most vitally of the reality of his spiritual life in Christ, and then of the reality or truth of the objects and events and doctrines bound up with that life in Christ.

THE CHRISTIAN BOOK

Weil denn Eure Kaiserliche Majestät und Eure Gnaden eine schlichte Antwort begehren, so will ich eine Antwort ohne Hörner und Zähne geben diesermassen: Es sei denn, dass ich durch Zeugnisse der Schrift oder durch helle Gründe überwunden werde—denn ich glaube weder dem Papst, noch den Konzilien allein, dieweil am Tag liegt, dass sie öfters geirrt und sich selbst widersprochen haben—so bin ich überwunden durch die von mir angeführten heiligen Schriften und mein Gewissen ist gefangen in Gottes Wort; widerrufen kann ich nichts und will ich nichts, dieweil wider das Gewissen zu handeln unsicher und gefährlich ist.—*Martin Luther*, Sein Leben und Seine Schriften, Julius Köstlin, i, 452.

You easily observe, I therein build on no authority, ancient or modern, but the Scripture. If this supports any doctrine, it will stand; if not, the sooner it falls the better.—*John Wesley*, from a letter dated February 5, 1756.

When it comes to be a question of psychological analysis, no doubt the distinction of subjective and objective is a difficult thing. Still, we can as a rule tell in a rough and rude way what is our own and what we owe to others. And if ever there was a case in which there was clearness of conviction on this head it was in the case of the prophets and apostles. They knew perfectly well, and they make the distinction perfectly clear, when they are speaking their own thoughts, and when they are speaking thoughts and delivering a message which is not their own.—*W. Sanday*, from a sermon preached before the University of Oxford, October 21, 1894.

We are Christians and therefore occupy a position with regard to Holy Scripture quite different from that which we take toward the Homeric poems, the Nibelungen, or the treasures of the library of Asurbanipal. Holy Scripture being the book of the records of our religion, our relation thereto is not merely scientific, but also in the highest degree one of moral responsibility. We will not deny the human element with which it is affected, but will not with Hamitic laughter discover the nakedness of Noah. We will not with vandalic delight destroy that which is holy. We will not undermine the foundations of Christianity for the sake of playing into the hands of Brahmosamajic, that is, of Brahmanic or Buddhistic, rationalism. For the notes that are struck in German lecture halls and books are at last reëchoed from distant Asia, and make vain the efforts of our missionaries. We will not give up what is untenable without replacing it, wherever possible, by that which is tenable. We will interpret Genesis as theologians, and, indeed, as Christian theologians, that is, as believers in Jesus Christ, who is the end of all the ways and words of God.—*Franz Delitzsch*, from the Introduction to his New Commentary on Genesis.

XII. THE CHRISTIAN BOOK

The Miracles of the Bible

OUTSIDE the range of conservative theology there are three pronounced attitudes toward the miracles of the Bible:

1. The attitude where all miracle is regarded as impossible. The whole case is settled beyond recall by an *a priori* assumption. The criticism of Hume by Professor Huxley is sometimes quoted to show that Huxley did not deny the possibility of miracle, but merely demanded adequate evidence. Such, however, was not his position. What he did not deny was that any given thing might exist, or any unusual event might take place; he only asked for sufficient evidence; but had you furnished the sufficient evidence, he would have said that the thing or event proven was not miraculous, but purely natural, only formerly not understood.

Within the province of biblical criticism, this first attitude toward the Scripture miracle is represented by Professor Wellhausen, who, in his crude, frank rationalism, often reminds us of Paulus. Here is a passage taken from the Sketch of the History of Israel and Judah: "The Hebrews, compelled to abandon the direct eastern road (Exod. 13. 17, 18) turned toward the southwest and encamped at last on the Egyptian shore of the northern arm of the Red Sea, where they were overtaken by Pharaoh's army. The situation was a critical one; but a high wind during the night left the shallow sea so low that it became possible to ford it. Moses eagerly accepted the suggestion, and made the venture with success. The Egyptians, rushing after, came up with them on the

further shore, and a struggle ensued.   But the assailants
fought at a disadvantage, the ground being ill-suited for
their chariots and horsemen; they fell into confusion and
attempted to retreat.   Meanwhile the wind had changed;
the waters returned, and the pursuers were annihilated."

2. The attitude where the miracle is obnoxious to the
person.   Some of the Ritschlians belong to the first class,
but some of them do not hold that a miracle is impossible;
and their extreme hesitation can be fairly explained, I
think, by saying that to them the miracle is obnoxious.
Of course, we shall be required, sooner or later, to explain
our explanation; for some one is sure to ask: "Why is
the miracle obnoxious to them?"   Even in answering
this question, though, I am not willing to call these men,
as some have called them, "rationalists in disguise."
Rather would my own answer be this: Like a large number
of other thinkers who are alert and sensitive to modern
tendency, they are dominated by the scientific conception
of natural law, and they feel that a miracle is incongruous,
out of keeping with the quiet, steady majesty of the
universal order, an event unlike God, an event which can
be tolerated only by an immature mind—in short, miracle
means to them lawlessness, and so it is an offense to their
scientific habit of mind.

3. The attitude where the miracle is considered burdensome in Christian apology.   There are men who have
not themselves given up the miracles of the Bible at all;
but they are looking for something "strategic in apologetics."   At the front as teachers or writers or preachers,
they feel the reality and sorrow of the fact that faith
after faith is yielding, that man after man is going down
into hopeless skepticism.   They thus come to a full
realization of the entire strain upon thoughtful men in
this, the most critical period in Christian history.   And

they try to relieve this strain; they try to see how much they can give up, and yet save the essential content of the Christian religion. As one writer stated it, in an editorial on "The Recession of Miracle," "We still hold to the miracle, but we are looking for our lines of retreat." Once filled with this apologetic purpose, it is not strange that the Christian miracle seems burdensome to these men. And once burdensome it is not strange that the miracle is rejected outright or refined away.

The first of these three attitudes does not merit the serious consideration of any real Christian theist; for if there is an infinite personal God the question of miracle cannot be one of inherent possibility, but must be merely a question of method, or divine intention. The second attitude results from a failure to appreciate the ethical dignity of a Christian miracle. It is not incongruous for God to break the universal order, if such a rupture can be made to contribute to righteousness. There is majesty in the natural law, but there is still greater majesty in the moral law. As Cardinal Newman once said, "Miracles, though they contravene the physical laws of the universe, tend to the due fulfillment of its moral laws." The third attitude is a most serious misapprehension from several points of view: First, it is a misapprehension of the present situation. The stress of the situation is not caused by science, but by a superficial ethical life, which has no force sufficiently to *ethicalize* the lordly demands of science. Given a profoundly moral situation, and the Christian miracle would not be burdensome in the least. Science has not proven anything which tends in any way to weaken man's *moral* openness toward the literal resurrection of our Lord's body. Again, there is a misapprehension of man's nature. A man is a moral person, and he wants a great personal task. Arrange your accommodations, plan out your compromises, exhibit

your mediating theologies, and at last they will be rejected
by men. The very hope of the Christian faith, in relation
to conquest, is the enormous demand it makes upon personality. Again, and last, there is a misapprehension of
the Christian religion itself. The miraculous cannot be
taken out of Christianity, for the simple reason that it is
fundamental in the Christian structure. Christianity is
an organized miracle. Suppose you could get rid of the
smaller miracles, you would still have to deal with the
Incarnation and the Resurrection. And if you tried to
get on without these, there would be remaining the peculiar person of Jesus Christ, and he is the most stupendous
Miracle of all, "the Grand Miracle of Christianity about
which all the others play as scintillations only of the
central fire."

The Christian Conception of the Supernatural. In our
discussions of morality and of religion we treated the
supernatural superficially, from the standpoint of man's
nature and development. To man, in his development,
that is supernatural which belongs to the infinite mystery
beyond nature, that is, beyond the realm of ordinary
individual seizure. In the Christian conception there is
no contradiction of this purely anthropological view; but
there is a deeper interpretation of the facts. To obtain
this deeper interpretation, the standpoint is changed
from man to God. Both the natural and the supernatural now have significance only as expressions of the
divine will. In one sense, the old dualism disappears,
for there is but one universe, of which God is creator,
upholder, and ruler. At the bottom of things, there is
one organism, working out one sublime intention. "The
one God shines in a star and whispers in a conscience."
All this can be readily and eagerly admitted. And even
more can be admitted. Had sin never come into the
world, the divine bearing in the universe, and toward

men, would be ever one, and that one bearing normal,
natural. But sin has come into the world, and that
awful event changes everything. God's relations with
us, his plans for us, all are no longer entirely normal.
With sin once a reality, there comes into God's method
a kind of dualism. There are now two divine bearings,
one toward the lower individual, and one toward the
higher moral person. Thus, God makes, in a perfect
manner, precisely the same distinction that man (as we
found) makes in an imperfect manner. These two
bearings of God may properly be called the natural and
the supernatural. Whatever comes by the ordinary
volitions of God, whatever expresses the divine *habit*,
is natural; and whatever comes by the extraordinary
volitions of God is supernatural. The Christian supernatural, therefore, is not a bare expression of the purpose
of God, but is an expression of his unusual volitions in
carrying out his purpose. This point is of extreme importance. Sometimes the saint so easily finds God everywhere, so clearly discovers the larger intention of God
even in the most common objects and events, that he is
quite inclined to obliterate the distinction between the
natural and the supernatural, and to seek a philosophy
which recognizes such obliteration. But the moment
such obliteration is lifted into a philosophy of life, not
only is the philosophy practically unwholesome in relation to the religious experience, but also it fails to make
adequate provision for the costly feature of divine self-
sacrifice in redemption. If the Incarnation was normal,
if there was behind it only an ordinary volition, that
grants an event as philosophically inexpensive as the
making of a continent. But if the Incarnation was
beyond the normal unfolding of God's relation to man,
if there was behind it an extraordinary volition, that
grants an event which can be charged with a sacrifice

ethically and intrinsically costly to God. It is because of this moral and redemptional bias that we must regard the supernatural as much more than a mere wonder, as much more than that which is temporarily extraordinary to man. Forever will it be extraordinary to man, for it is extraordinary to God himself. "*It is extraordinary at both ends.*"

The Christian Miracle. It remains to place the Christian miracle. It is not only supernatural, but also a peculiar kind, we might say a peculiar degree of the supernatural. When God so wills beyond his habit that his volition is contrary to his habit; when the ordinary volition is not only outclassed but actually held in abeyance; when the habit must yield to make way for the extraordinary volition—then the result is a miracle. Thus, a miracle is intrinsically, and may be ethically, the most expensive action possible to the Infinite God. The more important features of my entire view can be gathered up as follows: The supernatural is to be considered only from an ethical standpoint, if we are to understand its meaning in the Christian system. For moral ends, a man's conscience is extraordinarily vitalized and protected—this is the first degree of the supernatural. For further moral ends, for definite Christian experience, a believing person is converted and assured and sanctified —this is more extraordinary, is a higher degree of the supernatural. Up to this point the action is beyond the divine habit, but in no instance a contravention of that habit. Now we come to the miracle, and we will first take one which is as meager ethically as a Christian miracle can be. To make his personal influence more immediately efficient, and thus prepare the way for his redemptional message and work, our Lord turns water into wine. This is not only supernatural, but also contraventional—it is actually *against* the divine habit to make wine in that manner. To urge, as so many timid apologists do, that the miracle was done under a "higher law" does not touch the reality of the miracle at all, for this "higher law" is nothing whatsoever but a contravening action for higher ends. Now we can sweep on to the Incarnation. To render possible the moral salvation of mankind, the only Son of God actually becomes man. This is beyond the divine habit and against the divine habit, but it is more than all that—it is a continued contravention, a breaking forever of the normal life of the Godhead, an everlasting miracle. The whole ethical intensity of Christianity can be expressed in a sentence: The redemption of man has cost God a miraculous sacrifice which is never, never to end.

THE AUTHORITY OF THE BIBLE

The possibility of the authority of the Bible lies in the fact that a need for an objective standard is created by the process under which the Christian experience is reached and enlarged and completed. This need is an important feature of the development of the moral person himself. The nature of biblical authority, therefore, is not arbitrary but inherent, not artificial but intrinsic. The Bible, in a word, is in authority because it is a moral dynamic.

The Dynamic Element in the Obtainment. When we examine the steps by which we have obtained the Bible we find a dynamic element in every step.

First step: Our Lord himself started the Christian community, but he did not do this in any arbitrary, artificial way. He made himself morally necessary to a number of men who were open to his spiritual influence. His relation to his disciples was that of a moral dynamic, constantly enlarged, until it mastered their total manhood. In this spiritual manner the authority of Christ became at last for the Christian community, exactly and in all matters, the authority of God.

Second step: After the death of our Lord a peculiar authority fell to the apostles. In a sense they were, in the Christian community, to take the place of Christ. They were regents in authority. They were chosen and inspired, not mainly to organize the church, but to interpret and apply the message of redemption from the standpoint of a finished work, that is, from the standpoint of our Lord's death. It is an evident mistake to teach that the entirety of Christian doctrine may be seen in the blessed words of our Saviour. Before his death only germs, hints of the full doctrine, could be wisely revealed. The Sermon on the Mount should always be supplemented with the deed of atonement and its interpretation by the apostles. But their interpretation, all their teaching, was dynamic. The ultimate reason why it *took hold* of a Christian man was that it vitally entered into, and fitted into, all the Christian experience the man had. Of course, there was often shown a formal authority; but without the inner dynamic little power would formal authority have had in any time of test.

Last step: It was the death of the apostles which made the Bible necessary to the Christian community. In the profoundest sense the apostolic office was not continued. Since the close of the apostolic interpretation not one, not even the smallest item, has been added to the biblical organism. The apostles completed once for all the body of fundamental Christian truth; and, through all the complications and upheavals of the coming centuries, this body of truth was to take their place. Notice, for a moment, the profound method which is suggested here. Christianity is to triumph by reaching and satisfying and mastering the free moral person. But with such extreme recognition of personal freedom there needs to be some objective check—no coercion, but a check—or there will appear vagaries as individual and countless as the grains of sand. The needed check is provided in precisely the suitable strength. The moral person is to live under the check of a brotherhood, and the brotherhood is to live under the check of the inspired Word of God. The fullness and efficiency of the Christian life depend upon the perfect interplay of these three features, the personal, the social, and the biblical. Now the obtainment. The Bible was not obtained in any arbitrary manner. The criterion of canonicity was essentially spiritual. It is true that there was, in considering any given writing, the question of historical connection; but the historical question was really a means to an end. What the Christian church was after all the time was to discover and sanction those writings which to the Christian consciousness revealed the person of Christ and the doctrines and facts of redemption. Had any writing whatsoever antagonized Christian experience, had any book failed to win the inner Christian amen, such a book would have been rejected. Therefore we can affirm that every step in the obtainment of the Bible was not arbitrary but dynamic.

The Dynamic Stages in the Authority. A thorough treatment at this point would take us over the ground already covered in our discussion of the Christian religion in its relation to the moral person. We will, therefore, barely outline the case. In reaching full authority for the Christian man and the Christian community, the Bible passes through three stages; and just as each step in the obtainment of the Bible was essentially dynamic, so here each stage in the process of influence is dynamic. These stages are, we say, three in number: 1. The stage of moral experience. The Bible, by its revelation of God and

Christ, by all its tremendous ethical insistence, by its vista of final things beyond the grave, is precisely adapted to effect man's conscience. "*It burns a man.*" No moral person can read the Bible and hide away from moral requirement.   There is no other instrument which lends such ethical opportunity to the Holy Spirit.   To any moral person, at whatever place he may be in moral development, the Bible is absolute authority as to his immediate moral life.   And it is to him thus absolute in authority, not because some man, or some church, has declared it to be so, not for any artificial reason, but simply because it creates a moral urgency, because it urges the man along the very course he was planned to take.   It is always to be granted that the moral influence of the Bible can be augmented by true men, and especially by a true church; but what is done by the men, or by the church, is to furnish an opportunity for the normal working of the influence of the Bible.   In any situation the greatest moral thing which can be done is to give the Bible a fair chance at men.   2. The stage of Christian experience.   I am now thinking of the isolated fact of Christian experience.   Why is the Bible authority to the one man who has been converted?   The answer is three-fold: First, the Bible is profoundly involved in the whole process by which the man has come to moral peace; second, the Bible is the supreme means by which the Christian experience is now nourished; and, third, the Bible is the expression, the objective capture, of man's entire subjective life.   This last point needs, perhaps, a word of amplification.   Our inner world is subtle and flashing; our finest moods are often as evasive as the delicate perfume of a wild flower; after they are gone, we can hardly believe that we had them at all.   But when we read the Bible we are certain that we had such moods, for there they all are, caught in God's Word as minutely as a mirror catches the lines of a face. Thus, the Bible serves not only to urge the moral nature, not only to connect the Christian experience with all our moral development, not only to nourish that experience with rich facts and doctrines, but also as a sort of *Christian memory*, to hold, and keep real to us, all that has taken place in our inner life. 3. The stage of Christian experience in brotherhood. This is but a social enlargement of the second stage. In his new relation to his brethren, the Christian man looks at the Bible through their combined experience, and its dynamic influence upon him is increased by them. If the Bible is dynamic in authority to one man with a Christian experience it is more comprehensively so to two men bound together in Christian fellowship and service. The total philosophy of Christian certainty springs in here. A doctrine might not carry one man alone; but to two men, in their conjoined experience, it might appeal; and to a thousand men it might be morally self-evident. Once lift the social Christian organism out of formality and secularity, and the Bible will take care of itself. But we have not said enough. The Christian brotherhood itself is not a thing merely of to-day. It has, under the operations of the Holy Spirit, a most vital connection with the past. We have not only a Christian experience, but also a Christian inheritance. Could we bring together all the men, in this world and in the other world, who form the one Christian kingdom, the one organic brotherhood in Christ our Saviour; and could we secure a perfect expression of their Christian consciousness in its relation to the Word of God, we would find that consciousness to be a deposit of all the Christian experience of all the Christian centuries.

The pith of the matter can be given as follows: The Bible is an ultimate authority to men because it appeals to

them with spiritual cogency.   This is the basal principle.
This appeal is cogent to the moral person, because it fits
into and stimulates and enlarges his own moral ideal.
This appeal is cogent to the Christian man, because the
Bible, as used by the Holy Spirit, has largely produced
his Christian experience; and also because the Bible now
nourishes and expresses that experience.   This appeal is
more widely cogent to the Christian man in actual
Christian fellowship and service, because he now ap-
prehends the Bible through the combined experience of
his brethren.   The Bible is ultimate authority to the
Christian church for several reasons: first, because it has
come down to the church by a cogent spiritual method;
second, because it is authority personally to every real
member of the church; and, third, because it has been
made a part of the Christian organism.   This last point will
be more clearly seen in another connection.   Here I wish
only to glimpse the idea that the Bible is something more
to the organic Christian church than it can be to an
isolated Christian, or even to all separate Christians
added together.   To have the profoundest relation to
the Bible, Christians must so come together in Christ as
to live in full communion with him, in full fellowship
with each other, and in full service for mankind.

The Extent of Biblical Authority.   In the very nature
of the case, if our dynamic view is the true one, the extent
of the authority of the Bible is not the same in all situations.   To a moral seeker the authority is not the same
that it is to a converted man.   To a converted man
with a meager religious experience the authority is not
the same that it is to a saint.   To a saint living in holy
isolation, like some of the famous anchorets, the authority
is not the same that it is to a saint giving his whole being
to the joys and sorrows and activities of the church.   To
a formal church, half breathing under endless ceremonies

and ecclesiastical ambitions and worldly conceits and
compromises, the authority is not the same that it is to a
church with a present Christ and a penetrating Holy
Spirit. Not to waste our time in these situations of
spiritual poverty, let us say at once that to the real
Christian brotherhood, or to any man in organic relation
to that brotherhood, the Bible is ultimate authority on
precisely four things, namely: 1. On Christ. The Bible
is reliable in its account of our Lord, as to his character,
as to his teaching, and as to his deeds. The Christian
consciousness can and does take this reliability for
granted. 2. On the facts of redemption. The Old Testament preparation for Christ, the redemptional integrity
of its history, the actuality of its prophecies; the miracle
of the Incarnation; the death and resurrection and ascension and session of our Lord—all these redemptional
facts are given in the Bible in absolute finality for the
Christian brotherhood. 3. On the doctrines of redemption. But we must ever remember that a biblical doctrine is not the scientific doctrine of systematic theology.
The biblical doctrine is merely a practical statement of
the significance of a redemptional fact. For example,
the Bible has much to say about the necessity for an
atonement, to render possible the forgiveness of sin; but
the Bible does not try to furnish a scientific theory of the
atonement. Were we to work out this point completely
you would see that Christian certainty may, as the
Christian community develops, reach much further than
biblical authority reaches; but the two, the authority and
the certainty, can never be in conflict. The Bible must
always supply the data for any doctrinal enlargement
of which the Christian consciousness becomes certain.
4. The principles of conduct for the daily Christian life.
The application of these principles is purposely left open;
but the principles are binding, and they are so plainly

taught that one can easily make out of them a practical system of Christian ethics.

In a compact statement of the practical significance of our view, we would say this: *The scope of biblical authority exactly coincides with the scope of the biblical purpose; and the purpose of the Bible is to furnish in moral cogency all the data necessary to understand, to accept, to assimilate, and to preach the entire plan under which God redeems mankind.* In a word, the Bible is authority on redemption. And let us complete the matter by adding—*to every moral person who is willing to be redeemed.*

As to Science. It follows from what has been said that the Bible is not a final authority upon any scientific question. The opinions of the author of the book of Job on natural history are not, and, in the nature of the case, cannot be, binding upon the Christian church. There is, however, one clear exception, it seems to me: If a scientific question, like that of the origin of the race, has a real Christian entanglement, is bound up with a fundamental Christian doctrine (in this instance with the doctrine of sin), then the Christian doctrine must be protected. I will be plainer. As a man with a self-conscious Christian experience, in full and open relation with Christian men, I can allow no abiding antagonism between a Christian doctrine and a scientific theory. Always I have the right to reconsider the case, and I may be able to change my interpretation of the doctrine. But if I cannot change it, if the antagonism still remains, if one view or the other must go down, then for me the scientific theory must go down. For the theory, however generally held, is nothing but probability, and my experience in Christ is absolute self-certainty. For me, as one person, the experience is an ultimate, like self-consciousness itself. I am, first of all, not a scientist, but, first of all, and last of all, a man redeemed by our Lord and living a life of

unspeakable reality in him.   A Christian man should ever
be open to all scientific discussion, but he will not empty
out the content of his faith any more than he will try to
stop breathing.

As to Inerrancy.   Even on matters not scientific,
absolute inerrancy in the Bible is not required, provided
the portrait of Christ, the facts and doctrines of redemption, and the principles of Christian conduct are supplied
in sufficiency for the Christian consciousness.   For example, it is a matter of no great Christian moment what was
the precise wording of the superscription of the cross.
On the other hand, such an arbitrary and rationalistic
reduction of the sayings of Jesus as that made by Professor Schmiedel is a serious modification of the portrait
of Christ in the gospels and can therefore never be allowed
by the Christian church.   "But how are we to draw the
line?"   Christian consciousness, simply grant it time for
comparison and practical test, will draw the line with unfailing clearness and firmness.

The Regions of Liberty.   In biblical discussion, within
the Christian brotherhood, there are four regions of
liberty: 1. That of the canon.   The question here is,
Does this book really belong to the Bible?   2. That of
the text.   The question here is, Does this text belong to
the book? or, Does this word belong to the text?   3. That
of the literature.   The questions here are several: Who
is the author?   Is this passage or book composite?   What
is the style, poetry or prose?   Is this quotation used
precisely?   What is the historic setting?   4. That of the
interpretation.   The question here is, What does this
text, or passage, or total writing, mean?   These four
regions belong largely to Christian scholarship, which
always in the Christian church is to have a place of appreciation and untrammeled service.   Only we must insist that the scholarship be *Christian*.   A Christian

scholar is a scholar with a Christian experience, in full relation with Christian men, who does all his work with the profoundest sense of responsibility toward every other man with a Christian experience. With such an experience and with such a relation, and with such a spirit, the Christian scholar is constantly under a double check: First, the check of the entire brotherhood; and, second, the check of the Bible as a whole, or of the Bible taken as a redemptional organism of fact and doctrine.

Saying all this, still I have not given you any just appreciation of the steadiness of the biblical situation. Not merely is the Christian scholar under perpetual check himself; but his scholarship is a check upon the haste and crudeness in the thinking of the common man. It is this endless crossing of brotherly checks, this building a consensus of opinion out of every kind of a man—it is the vast democracy of Christianity which makes a general Christian attitude so reliable. Thus, while the regions of liberty are never arbitrarily closed, they are practically closed in just the degree that we have Christian agreement.

THE INSPIRATION OF THE BIBLE

The inspiration of the Bible as a subject is often confused with that of the authority of the Bible; but the two involve very different questions, and very different discussions, the discussion of authority being much the more important, inasmuch as it presupposes the philosophy of Christian certainty itself. The question of inspiration is really this: How can we explain the power and peculiarity of this Christian Book which is final authority on Christ, and on the facts, the doctrines, and the moral principles of the Christian salvation?

The Typical Theories. The theories of biblical inspiration have become so numerous that they can be properly classified, and fully discussed, only in a history of doctrine.

We can spare the space for only the bare mention of the four theories which are typical; and even with these we must save time by avoiding their incrusted terminology: 1. The theory that an inspired man is simply one with a natural genius for religious insight and leadership. According to this theory John Wesley was as really inspired as was Saint John. 2. The theory that an inspired man is simply one with an overflowing Christian experience. According to this theory, many an unknown man to-day is as really inspired as was Saint Paul. 3. The theory that an inspired man is one who is coerced by the Holy Spirit into a precise utterance. According to this theory, an inspired man is nothing more than a phonograph of God. 4. The theory that an inspired man is one who receives from the Holy Spirit extraordinary dynamic help, but without any violation of the integrity of individuality and without any interruption of the action of personality. According to this theory, the inspired message comes from the Holy Ghost and the free man in psychic conjunction—God speaks through the entire peculiarity of a man raised to a higher power.

The Probability. There is, I am convinced, no worthy reason for holding one of these theories to the exclusion of the remaining three. The probability is that the Word of God was given by a combination of all four methods; but it is not now possible for us to decide in every case precisely what took place. The data are not sufficient.

The Indorsement Theory. With this probability in mind, I will suggest a more comprehensive view of the inspiration of the Bible, as follows: 1. The standpoint is the process of redemption as an historic movement, beginning with the preparation for the coming of our Lord, culminating in the death of Christ, and completed by the work of the apostles. 2. In this long historic process men were chosen, each one in his own peculiar situation, to speak, or to write, or to do, whatever was essential to further the redemptional movement. 3. For this furtherance, these chosen men received only such divine help as was needed. At one time it was necessary only to emphasize a common moral fact before the people, and any brave soul could do it. At another time it was necessary to lift a commonplace into spiritual ideality, a work which only genius can do. At another time it was necessary to organize a nation, and it required the highest order of statesmanship. At another time it was necessary to have a Christian testimony, and it could be given out of any overflowing Christian experience in the early church. At another time it was necessary to catch and to express a doctrine of grace entirely beyond the possibility of natural discovery; and for this work a man was extraordinarily helped, raised to a higher power, without being erased as a free person. At another time it was necessary for the man of God to have an absolutely transcendent experience, an experience to which he could make no individual or personal contribution whatever; and he was, for the occasion, actually coerced by the Holy Spirit. He had no more freedom than the sky has in accepting a sunset. Perhaps he is a prophet, and he looks down the centuries, in the swift, clear vision of God himself, until he can see "a man of sorrows"—"smitten of God," "wounded for our transgressions." Or perhaps he is an apostle, and he is transported into a realm of immeasurable glory, and hears "unspeakable words, which it is not lawful for a man to utter." There are, too, some places in the Bible where the best explanation of the very phrase is that it came directly from God. And when I say the best explanation, I mean the explanation which naturally grows out of the Christian conception of God's relation to man in redemption. How extremely absurd

it is for any Christian thinker to hold that God could not
or would not, in the furtherance of redemption, give a
prophet or an apostle a message as definite as human
speech.   Even the most incipient Christian theist should
be ashamed of such fundamental inconsistency.   4. This
psychology of inspiration, however—the precise psychic
connection between agent and word or deed—is not the
important thing.   The important thing is that the Holy
Spirit accepted the word or deed, and actually made use
of it in the historic process of redemption.   *By indorsing
it the Holy Spirit made the thing his own.*   It was inspired,
or inblown, with his intention.   As an illustration of my
meaning, take General Washington's orders when Alexander Hamilton was on his staff.   The psychology of
those orders is a very interesting study.   Closely we
examine this order and that, to decide whether it came
from Washington's mind entirely, or only in part, or not
at all; and again and again we find it impossible to tell.
But the question is purely academic; for the one supremely
important thing, in relation to the struggle for independence, is that Washington was there, with a plan,
under which he considered every order and then signed
it.   It is the indorsement which makes the orders significant.   5. But there is more than this first indorsement
by actual use in the history of redemption.   The Holy
Spirit was the deeper Will of that entire dynamic process
by which the Christian church accepted and rejected
writings and so gradually formed the canon.   The formation of the canon of Holy Scripture is a second indorsement.   6. And there is also a third indorsement.   For,
profoundly regarded, the present relation of Christian
consciousness to the Bible is an indorsement by the
Holy Spirit.   7. The Bible, therefore, is the Word of
God, because all the parts of it were actually used by
the Holy Spirit in the historic process of redemption,

because he brought these parts together into an organic record of redemption, and because he lives in the whole Bible to-day, richly relating it to the Christian consciousness. Holding this comprehensive indorsement theory, we never say, "The Bible *contains* the Word of God." We say, The Bible *is* the Word of God. Just as parts of the human body are less significant than other parts, and yet all are required to make a complete bodily organism, so portions of Scripture are less important than other portions, and yet all come together to furnish to the brotherhood in our Lord a full expression of the heart and mind and will of God in the salvation of man.

THE SYSTEM OF DOCTRINE

We conclude that though it is always easy for thoughtless men to be orthodox, yet to grasp with any strong practical apprehension the theology of Christ is a thing as hard as to practice his moral law. Yet, if he meant anything by his constant denunciation of hypocrites, there is nothing which he would have visited with sterner censure than that short cut to belief which many persons take when, overwhelmed with the difficulties which beset their minds, and afraid of damnation, they suddenly resolve to strive no longer, but, giving their minds a holiday, to rest content with saying that they believe and acting as if they did. A melancholy end of Christianity indeed!—*John Robert Seeley*, Ecce Homo, pp. 89, 90.

Do I then utterly exclude the speculative reason from theology? No! it is its office and rightful privilege to determine on the negative truth of whatever we are required to believe. The doctrine must not contradict any universal principle; for this would be a doctrine that contradicted itself. Or philosophy? No. It may be and has been the servant and pioneer of faith by convincing the mind that a doctrine is cogitable, that the soul can present the idea to itself; and that if we determine to contemplate, or think of, the subject at all, so and in no other form can this be effected.—*Samuel Taylor Coleridge*, Aids to Reflection, Works, i, 222.

Biblical or New Testament theology deals with the thoughts, or the mode of thinking, of the various New Testament writers; systematic theology is the independent construction of Christianity as a whole in the mind of a later thinker. Here again there is a broad and valid distinction, but not an absolute one. It is the Christian thinking of the first century in the one case, and of the twentieth, let us say, in the other; but in both cases there is Christianity and there is thinking, and if there is truth in either, there is bound to be a place at which the distinction disappears.—*James Denney*, The Death of Christ, p. 5.

XIII. SYSTEMATIC THEOLOGY

IN our Introduction the aim was to secure an anthropological foundation for Christian theology, by showing that man's personal and moral development can be normally completed only under the terms of the Christian religion. With that foundation laid, there now comes to us a greater task, namely, to construct a system of Christian doctrine. In using the term systematic theology the emphasis is to be placed upon the word *systematic*. It is not enough to discuss the doctrines separately. It is not enough to show precisely what the Bible, on the surface, teaches concerning every doctrine. The doctrines are all interlocked at the root. Between them there is an underlying philosophical connection. This philosophical connection must be revealed. Not only so, but the connection must be brought out in such a way as gradually to exhibit the Christian faith as one mighty organic whole.

This systematic view of Christianity, seeing it as a coherent doctrinal total, is important for several reasons: First, because it has an *apologetic* value. Dr. William F. Warren once said, "An adequate system of doctrine is the only adequate Christian apologetics." It is only when one catches a vision of the Christian organism, from an inside doctrinal standpoint, in such a work, say, as Martensen's Christian Dogmatics, that he can begin to feel the tremendous force of Christian evidence. And yet we must at this point note a caution. Systematic theology should never be an *intentional* apology. There ought not to be in it even the tiniest trace of mediation tactics. Rather should it be so steeped with the Chris-

tian severities—with all those Christian peculiarities
which tax the natural man—as to be positively obnoxious
to any man who is not straining himself in moral endeavor.   A negative test of a worthy systematic theology
would be that its important message had incurred the dis-
like of two sorts of men, those who have a slender ethical
purpose, and those who are trying to make Christianity
"easier for this scientific age."   But the man who is
morally open to Christian appeal, the man whose heart
is breaking under an impossible moral burden, the man
who prefers to confess that his life is a moral failure
rather than to compromise with any utilitarian makeshift—if *that* man can be led to perceive the doctrinal continuity, the undersweeping granite ledge of the Christian
system, he will find the apologetics he needs for conviction.   Second, because it has a *biblical* value.   Systematic
theology is almost as necessary to any comprehensive
biblical theology as biblical theology is necessary to any
worthy systematic theology.   Often the profounder understanding of the Bible teaching involves a philosophical
grasp of all Christian truth.   Who, for instance, could
ever master the Epistle to the Romans without such
philosophical grasp?   There are in that epistle single
statements which are in root-relation to almost every
primary doctrine of the Christian system.   Third, because
it has a *practical* value in balancing and steadying the
Christian life.   A Christian experience which is nourished
by isolated, unrelated doctrine is likely to lose all balance,
and to become an exceedingly unwholesome thing.   Take
the great doctrine of personal faith itself and tear it out
of its moral and Christian connections, and what a dangerous transformation it undergoes!   It was faith, but
now it is presumption of the most perilous degree.   Can
you not see that systematic theology tends to prevent this
exaltation of the fragment at the expense of the whole?

Had that Christian man who has so eagerly accepted "Christian Science" only once been able to see Christianity stand out in its total meaning and in all its bearings upon life, could he, think you, have taken, in place of Christianity, a weak trituration of pantheism?

In constructing a system of Christian doctrine the source for all the data is the Bible, and the Bible alone. The data, however, are not obtained by making a collection of "proof-texts." Whether a text is to be used or not depends upon its relation to the entire biblical organism. One text may tersely express a gospel trend, and so may have the utmost worth, while another text may express but a passing phase of the historic movement, and so may contribute nothing to the final system. First of all, the systematic theologian must have, as a basis, a genuine biblical theology. And I mean here something far beyond the fragmentary works which are often published in the name of biblical theology. The whole Bible must be philosophically grasped as a Christian unity which is manifested in variety. The moment this is done there will be seen a *center* to the Bible; and without doubt that center is the death of our Lord. There is no possibility of any profound biblical study without instant and constant recognition of that center. But even this is not enough. Not only must all biblical values be determined from the center; but also the result must be regarded afresh over against the consciousness of the Christian church. All the doctrinal struggles in the past, all the great creeds, all the great works in theology, all the Christian biographies, everything which expresses Christian experience, must be studied by the systematic theologian to get at the Christian consciousness. This Christian consciousness is not a source, it furnishes no data; but it lights up the data, it unfolds the norms, it helps one to see the biblical truth *more Christianly*. "A man's eye is not authority on an elm tree, but it enables him to *see* the tree." But even this is not enough. The systematic theologian must study his own age day and night, until he can distinguish between the real Christian consciousness of his own time and the *Zeitgeist*. The *Zeitgeist* is a spirit of the world always rationalistic, never Christian, and seldom even profoundly ethical. Surely that theologian is extremely unfortunate who ever needs to say to the *Zeitgeist*, "What will you allow me to believe?" But if the assertion in the real Christian consciousness of our day is beginning to change; if men are now actually converted, if they grow in grace, if they possess the richest joys in Christian experience, if they have large consolation in their sorrows, if they are in constant Christian fellowship, if they are giving their lives in self-sacrificing service—and yet in all this experience and fellowship and service they manifest no interest in this or that doctrine, no need of it, no certainty about it—we here have a Christian situation which demands the most serious attention of the systematic theologian. But even all this is not enough. The systematic theologian has something himself. He too has a new life in Christ. He has a new conception of God, of man, and of the universe. "Old things are passed away; behold, all things are become new." He has personal certainties which speak in his consciousness with the urgency of thunder. He has a vision in which the Christian total stands out like the outline of a continent. Can he throw all this experience away? He dare not. By all the moral worth and spiritual majesty of this new life which God has given to him he must be absolutely and sacredly true to himself. His task, then, is to take his own Christian consciousness, together with that of the present time, together with that of all Christian history, and with the aid of all these so to interpret and relate the normative biblical data as to reveal the whole organic plan of redemption.

Now an admission should be made which may tend to increase the prevailing prejudice against systematic theology. No systematic theology, worth the making, can be constructed without more or less tentative speculation. The practical man has such a dread of speculation that when the word is mentioned he instantly thinks of the doctrinaire. But every great step in practical invention and discovery, and even in the sciences, is made by speculation. Professor Huxley called it "the scientific imagination"; but he meant exactly what I mean by tentative speculation. You have the unyielding data in the various facts. To all these facts you must tenaciously hold. Then you must imagine harmonizing connections; you must fling bridges from fact to fact until they are all interrelated. There is a test of the worth of your work in its social confirmation; that is, in the actual use of your bridges by other men. Or, coming to Christian thinking, suppose that we can make a philosophical connection between future punishment and the integrity of moral personality, protecting every statement in the Bible, and make this connection in such a manner that every converted man responds to it, we will have in this response a Christian confirmation of the reality of the connection made by speculation. And there is further confirmation if our speculative work at this point suggests deeper meanings for other Christian facts, or tends to bring out more sharply the significance of redemption as a totality.

If you have fully caught my conception, you can readily see that a genuine systematic theology is a work having no formal authority whatever. It is a mistake, I think, to call it *dogmatics*, or to give it any ecclesiastical position, or in any way to relate it to doctrinal lordship.

It is not your ruler, but your friend, trying to make Christianity satisfy your entire manhood, by bringing out all the profound moral connections, and by showing that the redemption in Jesus Christ's atonement is the one key to all there is in the universe.   Saint Paul himself began to indicate the province of systematic theology, for he could not keep from philosophical thinking in his greater epistles; and he expressed the real spirit of the matter when he said, "Not that we have lordship over your faith, but are helpers of your joy."

ESSENTIAL FEATURES OF THIS BOOK

THE INTRODUCTION

1. Man as a moral person related to the Christian religion.
2. Man as a social and racial person related to the Christian religion.
3. The philosophy of Christian certainty.
4. The Bible as the basis of a system of doctrine.

THE SYSTEM

1. *The Conception of Systematic Theology.*

    The interpretation of the doctrinal data of the Bible, from the standpoint of Christian consciousness, with the purpose of revealing the plan of redemption as an organic whole.

2. *The Central Note.*

    The redemption of man as a racial brotherhood of individual moral persons.

3. *The Doctrinal Divisions.*

    First Division—Man's need of redemption.

    Second Division—Jesus Christ, our Lord and Redeemer.

    Third Division—Our Lord's redemptive work.

    Fourth Division—Redemption realized in the new man.

    Fifth Division—Redemption realized in the new race.

    Sixth Division—The Triune God revealed in redemption.

THE FIRST DOCTRINAL DIVISION
MAN'S NEED OF REDEMPTION

Starting, then, with the being of a God (which, as I have said, is as certain to me as the certainty of my own existence, though when I try to put the grounds of that certainty into logical shape I find a difficulty in doing so in mood and figure to my satisfaction), I look out of myself into the world of men, and there I see a sight which fills me with unspeakable distress. The world seems simply to give the lie to that great truth of which my whole being is so full; and the effect upon me is, in consequence, as a matter of necessity, as confusing as if it denied that I am in existence myself. If I looked into a mirror, and did not see my face, I should have the sort of feeling which actually comes upon me when I look into this living, busy world and see no reflection of its Creator. . . . To consider the world in its length and breadth, its various history, the many races of man, their starts, their fortunes, their mutual alienation, their conflicts; and then their ways, habits, governments, forms of worship; their enterprises, their aimless courses, their random achievements and acquirements, the impotent conclusion of long-standing facts, the tokens so faint and broken of a superintending design, the blind evolution of what turn out to be great powers or truths, the progress of things, as if from unreasoning elements, not toward final causes, the greatness and littleness of man, his far-reaching aims, his short duration, the curtain hung over his futurity, the disappointments of life, the defeat of good, the success of evil, physical pain, mental anguish, the prevalence and intensity of sin, the pervading idolatries, the corruptions, the dreary, hopeless irreligion, that condition of the whole race, so fearfully yet exactly described in the apostle's words, "having no hope and without God in the world"—all this is a vision to dizzy and appall; and inflicts upon the mind the sense of a profound mystery, which is absolutely beyond human solution.

What shall be said to this heart-piercing, reason-bewildering fact? I can only answer, that either there is no Creator or this living society of men is in a true sense discarded from his presence. Did I see a boy of good make and mind, with the tokens on him of a refined nature, cast upon the world without provision, unable to say whence he came, his birthplace or his family connections, I should conclude that there was some mystery connected with his history, and that he was one of whom, from one cause or other, his parents were ashamed. Thus only should I be able to account for the contrast between the promise and the condition of his being. And so I argue about the world; *if* there be a God, *since* there is a God, the human race is implicated in some terrible aboriginal calamity. It is out of joint with the purposes of its Creator. This is a fact, a fact as true as the fact of its existence; and thus the doctrine of what is theologically called original sin becomes to me almost as certain as that the world exists, and as the existence of God.—*John Henry Newman*, Apologia Pro Vita Sua, pp. 241–243.

XIV. THE CREATION AND FALL OF MAN

The Scripture Account. By a number of mediating theologians this biblical account of the creation and fall of man is regarded as a myth. The term myth itself is not precisely fixed in its meaning; but it may mean something far beyond an intentional fiction, it may mean even a crude expression of real belief. It is in this higher sense that the term is used by the more conservative of these mediating theologians. If they are evolutionists, as is usually the case, the myth is to them the distinctive mark of a necessary period in man's normal development, "an inevitable product of the human mind in certain stages of culture." Holding this higher view, they never throw a religious myth away; rather do they study it with large seriousness, expecting to discover important data for anthropology. Belonging, as a choice inner circle, to this conservative group, there are a few writers who add a further and most important point, namely, that the biblical myth, although it has no historic worth, does have a Christian worth, inasmuch as it teaches such moral and religious truth as tends to prepare the mind for the full appreciation of the later Christian spirit and doctrine. In all fairness it should be said that this view possesses much apologetic force and is capable of an extremely conservative exposition. Possibly it is the only view which now can be honestly held by a great many thoughtful Christian men. And yet I cannot accept it. It seems to me to be nothing but a restless pause on the way to rationalism. There is a better view, I am sure—a view which is reasonable, and which has in it the soul of the Christian contention for the supernatural. Doubtless we have here, in this Scripture account, a world-tradition which is not to be taken in bald literalism; but I can see no forcible reason why it may not be a picture-narrative of actual fact. Why may it not be solid history in naïve drama? Neither the word poetry nor the word symbolism is nicely adequate, for both these words suggest a purpose too deliberately idealistic for this chapter of the childhood of mankind. Could we hear an American Indian (one not yet sophisticated by civilization) describe an event of great importance to his tribe, an event perhaps involving war, his whole power in single aim to tell the exact fact, we would certainly understand the dramatic naïveté of this biblical account. The rib, the tree, the apple, the serpent, are a picturesque way of talking, that is all, and just the kind of language men would everywhere use had we dared to keep close to the glory of our childhood. That there may be no chance for misunderstanding, I will give an analytical statement of my full view: 1. This scriptural account of the creation and fall of man is a record of historic facts. 2. These facts are given in naïve dramatic form—"the primitive style of narration characteristic of the age in which it was written." 3. The account was handed down from the beginning as a world-tradition based upon an original revelation from God. 4. This world-tradition was, at last, under the inspiration of the Holy Spirit, *cleansed* (an examination of the traditions in the ethnic religions will show how necessary such a cleansing came to be), *cleansed* for a redemptional use. 5. As thus cleansed this world-tradition was established in the canon by the Holy Spirit. 6. Thus, what we have is a world-tradition cleansed and indorsed by the Holy Spirit for its redemptional meaning.

The Significance of Man. If, with this conception of the account, we examine it closely, we shall find that it teaches certain things which are, from a redemptional standpoint, of the utmost importance in bringing out the significance of man: 1. God himself made man. Man is of divine origin. 2. Man was made as the summit of creation. The whole universe is but a getting ready for man. 3. Man was created in "the image of God." That is, man has moral personality like God himself. The exegesis which makes this "image of God" to mean man's delegated rulership over the animal kingdom is exceedingly superficial. He was placed over the animal kingdom because he was a moral person at the summit of creation. 4. Man was created a social being under a racial plan.

The Purpose of Creation. By noting all these items of significance the divine purpose in creating man becomes evident. God purposed to have not a higher animal, not a more consummate automaton, but a moral person, a creature free under supreme moral demand; not an isolated moral person, but a race with the most intricate social entanglement. Bringing together the three features, the personal, the moral, and the racial, we may concisely state the purpose of creation thus: The aim was to obtain a racial brotherhood of moral persons.

The Motive of Creation. To hold, as many do, that God's motive in creating man was love is perilously insufficient. If we keep in harmony with the conclusions reached in our Introduction, the least we can say is that the divine motive was moral love. But even in saying this we do not quite touch the root of the matter. To touch this root, I need to make reference to a basal principle which will come up again in a most serious discussion, namely, the principle of personal self-expression. It is inherent in the very nature of personality to seek objective expression. Personality must get out in some manner, or violate its own law of structure. Pure subjectivity is a primal personal experience, but it is far from being the entirety of a person's normal life. Nor are we passing into what we considered under man's social urgency. The need of self-expression is not a part of that need of companionship which arises from personal loneliness. Give a person all the companionship his nature craves, companionship of the greatest variety and of the finest quality, and still he will keep trying to express his inner life. Again I say, and, if possible, a little more emphatically, that a person is fundamentally a creator. The moment he has self-knowledge of an inner world he wants to make an outer world. This imperious law, or principle, of self-expression is the very nerve of great exploits, great art, great literature. I do not say that utilitarian motives may not be added, I do not say that utilitarian motives may not help. But the initial thrust for any great creative work is the personal longing for self-expression; and there are instances where this personal longing furnishes the entire motivity. Recently I heard, with increasing wonder, Beethoven's Fifth Symphony. And after coming out of the rapture of the bewilderment I said: "There is only one way to explain the enormous prodigality of this symphony: Beethoven was trying to fling out every thought and every feeling of his soul! He wanted to express himself."

This principle of self-expression must ever be kept in mind, to understand the divine prodigality in creating the universe. There are countless things in the world which burst the bands of all economy. "Every flower is useful, if we only know enough to find it out." Yes, useful as a part of the vast creation made to express something of God's inner life. And this cosmic expression is a preparation for a later and more sublime expression of God's inner life. In that one comprehensive way I can allow you to preserve the idea of utility. Now we are perhaps open to the important point: *The race of mankind is, in plan, a brotherhood of moral persons created to express the love of God which is both social and holy.* In our final discussion of the Trinity we shall try to see all that this statement means. Now it is enough to affirm that it is only from the standpoint of the full Christian doctrine of the Trinity, as one organism of three self-conscious persons with interrelations of holy love, that the creation of man can be explained without yielding to the philosophy of pantheism. From this Trinitarian standpoint, we can discover perfect divine motive, and still not swamp the motive in a divine necessity. In the words of Bishop Martensen: "In a certain sense one may say that God created the world in order to satisfy a want in himself; but the idea of God's love requires us to understand this want as quite as truly a *superfluity.*"

AN ANALYTICAL INTERPRETATION OF THE FALL OF MAN

1. With the New Testament teaching in mind, one should, I think, give Satan historical position and emphasis in any surface interpretation of the Scripture account of the fall of man. But in any deeper philosophical interpretation he has no significance other than that of method in test. Man fell as a moral person responsibly free, and the external form of the temptation, whether this or that, could make no essential difference. Satan could create no motive; he could simply bring to pressure motives which man himself must sooner or later feel.

2. Looking closely at the case of Eve, we discover three essential motives for sin, namely: first, physical craving; second, cosmic curiosity; third, the personal spring toward self-assertion.

3. "And when the woman saw that the tree was good for food, and that it was a delight to the eyes." This

surely means that the senses were involved, that the bodily life was bound up in the temptation. And this is precisely what we would expect, for man can have no bodily life, with a conscience, and not be tempted at some time. Even our Lord did not escape this test which comes from the body. There are several sorts of physical craving, but, philosophically considered, they are all equally significant. They, all of them, are natural urgencies which are to be controlled under higher concern. To have any worthy moral character a person must master his entire body in the name of his moral ideal.

4. "And that the tree was to be desired to make one wise." The thing meant here is not that larger wisdom which is charged with moral quality, but rather that experience which one gets by finding out for himself what there is in the world. It is just the experience which Goethe was ever seeking; to find out all there is, whether high or low—to exhaust the cosmos. The eager curiosity which urges a person to make this quest I have called cosmic, or world, curiosity. As a motive it is even more fundamental than physical craving, and is very essential to man's development and to the progress of civilization.

5. "Yea, hath God said, Ye shall not eat of any tree of the garden?" This plainly means that the temptation was an appeal to the spring of self-assertion, which is in our personal makeup even more profoundly than is cosmic curiosity. Personal freedom itself implies not only the power for self-assertion, but also the spring, the leap of the person toward it. Take any boy, however noble, and tell him that he must not do a certain thing, and even if he submits to natural or moral authority his first healthy impulse is to resist the command. The entire psychological movement is gathered up by that phrase of the common people, "It wasn't easy, but he gave up."

6. The most convincing line in Milton's epic is this: "From thy state mine never shall be parted." Of course, this is, on the surface, a poet's large license in dealing with the Scripture words: "And she gave also unto her husband with her, and he did eat." But, in the depths, Milton has found the fact of social influence, an influence which often operates with the three inherent motives already mentioned. If your wife, or any friend, or even any associate, does wrong, it is harder, other things being normal, for you yourself to do right. No man, in personal health, wants to be holy all alone. Thus, when any person sins, or when any person resists sin, the whole psychological situation is suddenly changed. No new cause of personal volition is produced, but the *occasional background* is changed.

7. There are now two things which should be lifted into the utmost emphasis: First, these four motives— physical desire, cosmic curiosity, the personal spring toward self-assertion, and social influence—are, in and of themselves, not only good, but absolutely essential to the development of the man, and to the progress of society. Second, every one of these four motives becomes at once bad when it urges a moral person to disobey God, or to violate any moral ideal. In other words, the possibility of sin is necessarily involved in the fact of moral personality itself. There cannot be a free person placed under a moral demand without his having both the volitional ability and the personal motive to violate that demand. Either the universe must be altogether automatic, with no opportunity for moral character, or there must be granted the possibility of personal sin. This endless discussion of "the mystery of evil"—how superficial, how lacking in all moral acumen, it is! In any serious home, in the upbuilding of the moral life of any child, there is seen, again and again, the clue to this

"mystery beyond all our wisdom." Let a father once say to a child, in the name of higher concern, "Thou shalt not!" and there will be the personal battle of Eden all over again. God did not want transgression, but *he did want the possibility of it*, because he wanted personal sainthood. *All evil in possibility is the awful price which had to be paid for any personal sainthood.*

But, it is often urged, the Edenic test was unfair because our first parents had no knowledge of the dreadful consequences of their disobedience. "Had they only known they would have obeyed." This objection also reveals a lack of moral grasp. Every moral conflict is a personal conflict under an ideal; and never can the personal significance of the struggle be changed by knowledge of any sort or amount. Excepting this: There are times when complete knowledge of results creates such an overwhelming fear that all personal action, and so all moral meaning, becomes impossible. In such cases, the moral probation must be shifted to another point where there is less knowledge.

The first sin was a personal act of disobedience. It was a taking of self in place of God. In the startling words of Philippi, "Man's self-assertion to Godhead was his fall." Personal sin is the supreme egotism of a moral person. It is getting one's own way over against duty. *It is selfishness.* One of the characters in Tennyson's Becket is made to say, "If I had been Eve i' the garden I shouldn't ha' minded the apple, for what's an apple, you know, save to a child?" Every such treatment of the account (and there are many) misses in the accidents the supreme selfishness of the scene. Man did not care enough about God to do his will. That was the fall of man.

XV. THE DOCTRINE OF SIN

THE term *sin* is used in so many ways that it is, in systematic theology, especially important to secure a more rigid classification of phases under the general term. The underlying idea of any kind of sin is that of lawlessness, or ἀνομία. In the widest sense a sinner is anyone who does not measure up to God's perfect law. Taken in this generic meaning the Westminster definition is perfect: "Any want of conformity unto or transgression of the law of God."

Personal Sin. But when John Wesley said that sin is "a voluntary transgression of a known law" he was not thinking of sin in this sweeping manner, he was thinking of a *responsible* violation of God's law. For such violation it is evident there must be knowledge of what the law is, and a personal intention to break it. Why may we not say, then, that under generic sin there is personal sin, or that sin for which the moral person is accountable? Precisely analyzed, in relation to ethics, there are three features in all personal sin, namely: 1. A moral standard; 2. This standard in actual grasp by the personal judgment as to right and wrong; 3. Personal intention. Surely you can see that this personal sin cannot be inherited? No man can inherit another man's personal bearing toward moral judgment. In fact, no personal act, or activity, or experience, can be inherited. Strictly speaking, nothing personal can ever be passed from being to being. And inasmuch as the personal deed, or attitude, cannot be inherited, it is inconceivable that the personal responsibility for such deed or attitude can be inherited. The theological conception of "an

inherited guilt" results from a full failure to understand
what personal life is, on the one hand, and what moral
life is, on the other hand. With a few verbal changes, I
would adopt Bishop Foster's words: "Sin is something
which the individual man does; it is an act. There is no
sin where there is not a sinner; and there is no sinner
where there is not an act committed by him which constitutes him a sinner."

Individual Depravity. In considering depravity we
need to bring up again the distinction made in this work
between the individual and the person. Under the fact
that man is a person is the fact that he is an individual
being with body and soul. Before a babe comes to self-
consciousness he has a fundament of being with a complex of characteristics which are some of them physical
and some of them psychical. The sum total of such
characteristics I call the individuality of the child. This
individuality is developed, and even modified, as the
child grows. Indeed, the whole complex of native characteristics is at last treated from the standpoint of self-
consciousness. And the ultimate man is, as I have said
before, the individual *personalized* by the self-decisive
rejection and indorsement of original traits.

By depravity we mean that this basal individual life
of a man is *inorganic.* The native characteristics are a
clutter of items as unrelated as the odds and ends one
finds in an attic. The term *total depravity* is one of those
unfortunate phrases with which the scholastic theologian
is fond of weakening his message; but there is a profound
sense in which a man is, as he comes into the world,
totally depraved. The point was brought out in our
study of morality, and is this: No man can organize his
individual life under the demand of conscience. He is
totally unable even to start an organism. And the greater
his development in moral personality the greater the

impossibility of that adjustment which secures wholeness and peace in manhood. It is this inorganic condition of a man's fundamental, individual being which I understand to be depravity. Every man comes inorganic into the world. Concerning this inorganic condition of depravity, there are two things so patent that they require no proof whatever: The first is the fact that depravity is *universal*. No organic man is ever born. The second thing is that depravity is *inherited*. The person is a new creation, personality is never repeated, no man receives ability for self-consciousness and self-decision from his ancestors. But the individual has his complex of traits under the law of heredity. In other words, individuality is a racial matter and personality is not. Thus, inorganic individuality is inherited.

This, though, only raises a larger question: "Why is it that the free moral person cannot organize his individual being under his moral ideal?" This question, you will remember, we answered thus: The natural moral life is one of fear, and fear is not an organizing motive; the man needs to have for organization the motive of moral love. In a simple word, no man can be complete unless he actually loves the Holy God. Now we must push the discussion into a further recess. Why does man have this fear under moral authority? Because, I say, man now lives under the dominion of conscience *alone*, and he was not made so to live. Conscience itself is a ragged, unfinished item. Man was planned to live in constant personal intimacy with God, and to have his moral life perfectly saturated with that blessed holy fellowship. Just as one of our children is born into a home, and gradually, as the little human life opens into personality, comes to the personal grasp and regard for the father and mother, so it was intended that a man should be at home with God. But now man is an outcast from the personal vision and intimacy with God. No wonder he is afraid all alone out there under that vast, vague, ever-growing, absolutely pitiless moral demand. "So he drove out the man; and he placed at the east of the garden of Eden the Cherubim, and the flame of a sword which turned every way, to keep the way of the tree of life." This, then, is my understanding of depravity: Man's entire individual being is inorganic in its relation to the moral person. It is thus inorganic because the moral person lives under moral fear. And he lives under fear because he has been banished from the divine fellowship and is but a lonely slave under moral law.

The Broken Brotherhood. In the Arminian sense (responsible transgression) there can be no such thing as racial sin; but the race can be racially ἀνομία, it can be out of joint with its under plan, it can be a failure. This is what we should mean by racial sin. Let us urge the meaning for a moment. The human race was designed to be an organic brotherhood of moral persons, in which every member would fit into the life of all, and minister to the progress and joy of all, and receive stimulus and social companionship and positive supplement from all. But this great plan has been defeated by sin. Precisely as the individual man is inorganic, so the race is inorganic. The brotherhood is broken. Here and there we have a pathetic group of men trying to help each other, but often a large part of their effort is sheer waste. Of course, it is easy enough to contribute to the surface comfort of men; but to enter their real life, to understand them, profoundly to enlarge them and bless them, is an extremely difficult matter. Now think of doing this for all men, and you will begin to realize the awful extent of our racial failure! The cause of this racial failure is twofold: First, every individual member of the race is born depraved, and many members of the race

are living in personal sin. Thus, the racial members
are not capable of racial coalescence. And, second, the
race has lost its center of organism. That center was to
be God in immediate personal companionship with all
men. To say that the race now exists only through the
omnipresence of God is to miss the point altogether. The
point is not that God is needed as a present power, but
that God is needed as a present personal companion.
Men need to enjoy the actual vision of God as their supreme Friend. And all aims should begin in this vision,
and all activities should feel the warmth of this vision
even as in a cloudless day every growing thing feels the
warmth of the sun. This conception is so sublime that
we are timid before it, but we must dare to seize it.
Never can we understand the work of our Lord until we
can see that the original purpose was to have a brotherhood of men made complete by fellowship with God.

God's Hatred of Sin. When we try to explain this
recession of the divine personal companionship from the
race and the individual man there are several halfway
things which can be said in the spirit of euphemism; but
it is much more wholesome to state at once, and with
plainness, the final fact. The recession is due to God's
hatred of sin. But this hatred must be carefully related
to our sentiment; for this is one of those places where the
Christian feeling is fully as important as the Christian
idea. We must not go to the one extreme of holding
that the divine hatred is arbitrary, is a thing merely of
God's naked and unrelated will. We must not feel that
"God *could* have a different attitude toward sin, if he
only *would*." We must realize that God could not be
God, that he could not exist at all, without hating sin.
But we must not go to the other extreme of holding that
this divine hatred is but an intense smiting by an impersonal law, and that there is no personality involved. If

in any way you drop the personal element out of the hatred, you will lose, altogether or in part, its mighty ethical stroke. In the deepest sense, no impersonal bearing or performance can be ethical. No, we are to think (and then to feel it) of the law of God's holiness as plunging eternally into his absolutely exhaustive self-consciousness, and there furnishing motive for an active, personal hatred of all sin as a violation of that fundamental holiness. Thus, God not only hates sin, but *he means to hate it*.

This divine hatred of sin is expressed not only in depravity and the broken brotherhood, but also in the natural world. I have said several partial things about nature, but it is now necessary to give a thoroughly Christian view. The reason why nature is such a bewildering jumble—now declaring the glory of God, and then becoming as voiceless as the sphinx; now as gentle as a mother, and then as cruel as a monster; now suggesting the most noble mood, and then actually violating every known moral principle—the reason for this bewildering jumble is that nature also is a broken organism. In a low sense, it is an organism still, it is organic as a physical system, and it appeals to the individual. But the world of nature is no longer competent for man as a moral person. God has not withdrawn from the cosmos as its cause, its present force, its life, its beauty; but as a divine revelation, as a word from the Infinite, Moral, Personal Being, the universe has been cast aside. Just as the individual man and the whole race are broken, so the home of man and the race is broken. Consequently the cosmos is to be finally destroyed. There is to be not only a new man, and a new race, but also a new universe. Redemption is to cover the person, the race, and their perfect home.

Even now we have not exhausted the expressions of God's hatred of sin. There is one more expression and that the most dreadful of all—*death*. In relation to the death of Christ it will be necessary to bring out the full Christian interpretation of death; but a general, tentative word should be spoken in this connection. A most striking evidence of the success with which science has eaten into the very vitals of Christian opinion is seen in the typical modern Christian view of death, and even of the death of Christ. If one ever could die of a broken heart he might, I think, be justified in doing so after reading some of those popular poems and sermons and books which try to show that death is almost, if not quite, the most useful and the most beautiful event in human experience. But if I understand, even in the smallest measure, the substance of the Christian faith, death should be to the Christian consciousness an abnormal event, a monstrous action of physical law against man, to express in every movement of its loathsome and appalling process God's boundless hatred of sin. The race is a failure, and therefore it is to be destroyed. Beyond the grave there will be no Adamic race, but a new race in which our Lord will take the place of Adam. This racial destruction is by the method of death. The body, the old racial nexus, is to be torn from the man, and then to be made the starting point for another body, a new and a glorious social nexus. The entire divine bearing in death and depravity can, I think, be expressed in this way: God so loves man that he will himself pay the most costly price for man's salvation; but he so hates sin that he must secure, at every step of the way, a most extraordinary and even abnormal expression of his holy hatred. Man can be saved, because God loves him, but the path of salvation must be one violently out of course. Thus, we may say that depravity, and the broken race, and the wrench in nature, and the death of men—culminating in the death of our Lord—all manifest God's hatred of sin, but they manifest that hatred as an awful background from which stands out the infinite love of God toward men.

The Peril of Sin. Depravity in and of itself has no peril. As related to the work of the Holy Spirit, all depravity can ever do is to change the form of the conflict of the moral person. Nor is the peril of sin in a habit of vice. Vice is really a superficial thing, and, at its worst, but an expression of depravity or of personal sin. The peril of sin lies in the fascination of personal sin, in that extreme self-assertion which is selfishness. In the very nature of the case, every untested, every unsubdued person wants his own way. And if you place this untested person under a moral law he will have instant interest in breaking the law. Personality itself must be chastened by free choice into the enjoyment of lawfulness. But let the free person once break the law, once get the taste of lawlessness, once have wildly throbbing in consciousness the experience of an immoral freebooter, and the untrammeled self-assertion is endlessly fascinating. And just here lies the dreadful peril. For this personal bearing in selfishness will soon stiffen into personal habit; to endure any moral restraint will become more and more irksome; until finally there will be no motive to submit to moral demand. This means, indeed, that the moral demand itself has been emptied of all urgency. And that means nothing less than everlasting moral death.

DEFINITIONS

1. *Sin.*

In the most comprehensive generic sense, human sin is any nonconformity on the part of man to God's law. Most tersely, sin is lawlessness.

2. *Individual Depravity.*

When this nonconformity to God's law is an inherited inorganic condition of the individual man, the sin is individual sin, or depravity. Most tersely, depravity is irresponsible lawlessness in individuality.

3. *Personal Sin.*

When the nonconformity to God's law is an intentional violation, in act or bearing, the sin is personal sin. Theologically,
personal sin is responsible lawlessness in self-decision. Ethically,
personal sin is a self-conscious violation of the moral judgment.
Practically, personal sin is selfishness.

4. *Racial Sin.*

When the nonconformity to God's law is in the rupture of the
racial plan for solidarity in human fellowship, the sin is racial
sin, or race depravity. Most tersely, racial sin is lawlessness in
social life.

MAN'S NEED OF REDEMPTION

Man needs redemption in three ways:

1. As a moral person, a responsible sinner before God,
a man needs to be forgiven, and united with God.

2. As a disrupted man, individual, personal, and moral,
he needs to have his entire being reorganized and harmonized and made complete.

3. As a shattered brotherhood, mankind needs to be
made over into a new race, with a divine center, and a
membership of perfect coalescence in love and service.

THE SECOND DOCTRINAL DIVISION
JESUS CHRIST, OUR LORD AND REDEEMER

At last the weapon which they had been seeking, to cut off the head of their enemy, was suddenly drawn from his own scabbard. A letter was produced from Eusebius of Nicomedia, in which he declared that to assert the Son to be uncreated would be to say that he was "of one substance" (ὁμοούσιον) with the Father. . . . The letter produced a violent excitement. There was the very test for which they were in search. The letter was torn in pieces to mark their indignation, and the phrase which he had pledged himself to reject became the phrase which they pledged themselves to adopt.— *Arthur Penrhyn Stanley*, Eastern Church, p. 228.

. . . And in one Lord, Jesus Christ, the Son of God, begotten of the Father, only begotten that is to say, of the substance of the Father, God of God, Light of Light, very God of very God, begotten not made, being of one substance with the Father, by whom all things were made, both things in heaven and things in earth—who for us men and for our salvation came down and was made flesh, and was made man, suffered, and rose again on the third day; went up into the heavens, and is to come again to judge the quick and dead.— *Translation of the passage as first read at Nicæa.*

XVI. THE DEITY OF OUR LORD

THERE are five methods by which it is possible to construct an argument for the deity of our Lord; but I shall not make exact use of any one of these methods. Indeed, my aim is not to build a formal, logical argument of any kind, but rather to show how closely our Lord's divinity is related to his work in redemption.

A word should be said concerning the use of Saint John's gospel. To trace all the windings of the criticism of the fourth gospel is not feasibly within the scope of the plan of this book. A bald personal assertion must suffice. A Christian scholar can master the entire range of critical discussion down to the latest contentions of Abbè Loisy, and still have unshaken confidence in the Johannine authorship and in the reliability of the fourth gospel as a record of the words and deeds of our Saviour. The best Christian scholarship will never give up this invaluable, this greatest gospel. I shall, therefore, in my discussion, make not even the slightest discrimination in favor of the synoptic gospels. Perhaps, however, it may be well to add that the force of this discussion would be essentially the same, even though not one passage were quoted from Saint John.

THE CONSCIOUSNESS OF OUR LORD AS RELATED TO REDEMPTION

His Mission.

1. It is clearly in the consciousness of our Lord that his mission was to save men. His full conception of his work is gathered up in these words, recorded by Saint Luke (19. 10): "For the Son of man came to seek

and to save that which was lost." If it be urged that he
came to establish "the kingdom of God" the answer is
that his very conception of that kingdom (as related to
men) was not merely philanthropic but actually redemptional. The personal entrance into that kingdom
was only possible by being born anew (Saint John 3. 3).
And sinners were called to repentance (Saint Luke 5. 32).

2. For this mission of redemption he had given up all
the glory of his preëxistent state. (Read all of the
seventeenth chapter of Saint John's gospel and compare
it with the passage in the Epistle to the Philippians,
2. 5–11.)

3. In carrying out this mission of redemption he is
to lay down his life for men. In the tenth chapter of
Saint John's gospel read the comparison of himself with
the "Good Shepherd."

4. More definitely, this laying down his life was to
be a ransom paid—a ransom for many. "For the Son
of man also came not to be ministered unto, but to
minister, and to give his life a ransom for many" (Saint
Mark 10. 45; also Saint Matt. 20. 28; and compare with
Saint Matt. 26. 28).

If we now put together these four points, surely we
must affirm as much as this: It was clearly in our Lord's
self-consciousness that he had, in a spirit of self-sacrifice,
given up the glory of his original estate and come into
this world with the one purpose to ransom men from sin
by means of his own death.

His Relation to Men.

5. Jesus ever regards himself as the final authority for
men. Notice the tone of authority in his forms of speech:
"Verily, verily, I say unto you;" "Ye have heard how it
hath been said, but I say unto you." Sometimes the
strangest thing in his speech is not its content, but its
manner, the way it manifests an absolute consciousness

that he himself is the last court of appeal. (See Saint Matt. 5. 18–39 and Saint John 14. 2, 3.)

6. Jesus regards himself as the supreme Master of men. As supreme Master he demands *obedience*. "And why call ye me, Lord, Lord, and do not the things which I say?" (Saint Luke 6. 46; compare with Saint John 21. 22.)

7. As a further revelation of the consciousness of mastership over men, notice our Lord's claim upon their love. "He that loveth father or mother more than me is not worthy of me; and he that loveth son or daughter more than me is not worthy of me" (Saint Matt. 10. 37; and, as a significant background, read the passage in Saint Matt. 22. 37–39).

8. In relation to man's spiritual needs, Jesus regards himself as the ultimate and perfect supply. "Jesus answered and said unto her, Every one that drinketh of this water shall thirst again: but whosoever drinketh of the water that I shall give him shall never thirst; but the water that I shall give him shall become in him a well of water springing up unto eternal life" (Saint John 4. 13, 14; compare with Saint John 10. 10).

9. Jesus regards himself as *the Race-Man*. Of all the discussions bearing upon the term "Son of man," in its meaning as used by our Lord, the discussion by Professor Stevens, in his Theology of the New Testament, seems to me to be the most nearly satisfactory. But, for my purpose, this term "Son of man" has no large importance; and for the sufficient reason that we already have, in the four facts noted in this connection, a clear revelation of our Saviour's consciousness of his peculiar relation to men. When we try to state this peculiar relation in a compact word we can do no better than to say that Jesus Christ is conscious of being the Race-Man. On the one side, he owns the race. It is his race in such a final way

that he has the absolute right to make his claim upon
all men.   No man, high or low, rich or poor, this or that,
can escape him.   In his consciousness there is a great
racial grasp.   And, then, on the other hand, he belongs
to the whole race.   Every man has a property in him.
It is his supreme business to live with men and for men,
all men.   Therefore, there is a fitness in his redemptive
work.   It is not extraneous.   It does not come at men
from the outside.   Our Saviour is not a stranger.

His Relation to the Moral Law.   Now, holding fast to
what we have, namely, our Lord's consciousness of the
redemptive purpose of his mission and of his peculiar
relation to mankind, it becomes exceedingly important
to discover the content of his moral consciousness.   How
was he, in consciousness, related to the moral law under
which man must be redeemed, if redeemed at all?

10. The first thing to be marked here is that Jesus
Christ never manifested any consciousness of being himself
a sinner.   This point does not in the least depend upon
the minute exegesis of such a text as that in Saint John's
gospel (8. 46), where our Lord exclaims, "Which of you
convicteth me of sin?"   It is a matter of personal bearing.
Read the record in the gospels from end to end, and you
become positive that Jesus felt perfectly free from sin.

11. Even as the separate texts are overarched by the
general bearing of Jesus, so his general bearing is overarched by the one fact that he claimed to have the moral
authority to forgive sin.   "But that ye may know that
the Son of man hath authority on earth to forgive sins"
(Saint Matt. 9. 6; read the entire passage in Saint Mark
2. 5–12).

12. But all—the separate texts, the general bearing,
and the forgiveness of sin—are overarched by our Lord's
assertion that he alone is to be the final Judge of men.
"For neither doth the Father judge any man, but he hath

given all judgment unto the Son" (Saint John 5. 22). "For the Son of man shall come in the glory of his Father with his angels; and then shall he render unto every man according to his deeds" (Saint Matt. 16. 27).

With these three cumulative points before us, we cannot say less than this: In his mission of redemption Jesus Christ regarded himself as the embodiment of the moral perfection and authority of God's absolute law. His bearing and utterance were precisely as if in consciousness he felt that he himself and the moral law were interchangeable equivalents.

His Relation to God. This surprising discovery of the content of our Lord's moral consciousness leads us to dare to ask a most crucial question: Did the consciousness of Jesus, in carrying out his mission of redemption, affirm any peculiar relation to God? If so, what was that relation?

13. Jesus regards himself as alone able to understand God the Father and to reveal him. "All things have been delivered unto me of my Father: and no one knoweth the Son, save the Father; neither doth any know the Father, save the Son, and he to whomsoever the Son willeth to reveal him" (Saint Matt. 11. 27).

14. Jesus regards himself as the one and only way unto God the Father. "Jesus saith unto him, I am the way, and the truth, and the life; no one cometh unto the Father, but by me" (Saint John 14. 6).

15. Jesus regards himself as so essentially one with the Father (ἐγὼ καὶ ὁ πατὴρ ἕν ἐσμεν) that having seen Jesus one hath seen the Father. "Jesus saith unto him, Have I been so long time with you, and dost thou not know me, Philip? he that hath seen me hath seen the Father; how sayest thou, Show us the Father? Believest thou not that I am in the Father, and the Father in me? the words that I say unto you I

speak not from myself: but the Father abiding in me doeth his works" (Saint John 14. 9, 10; 10. 25–33). The Ritschlian view that Christ was conscious of merely an ethical union with God, an agreement with God in moral purpose, seems to me to be superficial even as isolated exegesis. But we cannot rest in any isolated exegesis, the passage must be treated in harmony with all the other claims of Jesus. So treated, it is evident that Jesus held in consciousness such a fundamental relation to God the Father as to be able to be, in the redemptive work, a complete equivalent of the Father's authority and nature. Jesus does not regard himself as a mere delegate from God, but as the actual presence of God to accomplish their salvation.

16. In Christ's estimate the Holy Spirit is peculiarly related both to our Lord's redemptive ministry and to our Lord himself. Not only does the Holy Spirit wait for the end of that ministry, but he is to be *sent* by Jesus himself. "Nevertheless I tell you the truth: It is expedient for you that I go away; for if I go not away, the Comforter will not come unto you; but if I go, I will send him unto you. And he, when he is come, will convict the world in respect of sin, and of righteousness, and of judgment" (Saint John 16; read the entire chapter). Godet's comment here is so penetrating that I will quote it: "His departure was the condition of his restoration to his divine state, and this would enable him to send the Holy Spirit. It is the same idea which we meet with in 7. 39: 'The Spirit was not yet; because Jesus was not yet glorified.' That Jesus might send the Spirit, he must possess him as his own personal life, and that as man, since it is to men that he is to impart him." This, though, is deeper than we now need to go. What I wish to emphasize is that Jesus Christ, while on the earth, working out his redemptive

plan, was conscious of being the condition of the redemptional activity of the Holy Spirit and also of being the personal authority to start that activity.

His Consciousness After His Resurrection.

17. We have caught glimpses of our Saviour's redemptional consciousness, here and there, during his active ministry; but the inquiry naturally arises, After his resurrection, does he manifest the same consciousness, the same conception of himself? "And when they saw him, they worshiped him; but some doubted. And Jesus came to them and spake unto them, saying, All authority hath been given unto me in heaven and on earth. Go ye therefore, and make disciples of all the nations, baptizing them into the name of the Father, and of the Son and of the Holy Spirit: teaching them to observe all things whatsoever I commanded you: and lo, I am with you always, even unto the end of the world" (Saint Matt. 28. 17-20; compare with Saint Mark 16. 14-16; also with Saint Luke 24. 44-49; also with Acts 1. 6-8). The rationalistic contention that this passage reveals an altogether different attitude from that of Jesus before his crucifixion is such a contention as we would expect from men who have never caught the spirit and progressive method in our Lord's mission of redemption. But I am quite sure that to the real Christian consciousness this most extraordinary passage effectually appeals as an indorsement, in succinct expression, of the same redemptional consciousness which our Saviour had during his active ministry. The passage is neither more nor less than the conjoining, for the establishment and future work of the Christian church, of all the tremendous claims which our Lord had ever made.

By an examination of our Lord's miracles and of his conception of his relation to Old Testament prophecy we could enlarge our study of his consciousness; but we have done enough to show three things: First, he regarded himself as on a mission of redemption; second, this mission to be accomplished by self-sacrifice culminating in his death; third, this sacrifice having peculiar significance from his racial relation to man, from his self-identification with the moral law, and from his self-identification with God. As the Son of God, as the embodiment of all moral concern, and as the Race-Man, he, having sacrificed his original estate, will now die that he may redeem mankind —that is the intrinsic veinage of the self-consciousness of Jesus Christ.

The Apostolic Consciousness

For our limited plan it is not necessary to consider every expression in the New Testament of the apostolic mind; it is quite sufficient to note the beginning and then the fullness of the consciousness. In each instance, the question would be, When this apostle became conscious of self, what were the important, the characteristic things, he held? Or, more simply, what were his primary convictions?

The First Trace in Saint Peter. In looking at Saint Peter in the book of Acts, we should not expect too much. He was a great apostle, but he was in a fever. He had been well-nigh overwhelmed by the rush of mighty events —the trial and death of Jesus, the resurrection, the appearance of Christ, the ascension, the "tongues parting asunder, like as of fire," on the day of Pentecost. His very boldness is a hot, violent thing almost certain to obscure the inner vision; and no utterance of his at this time is likely to contribute much to Christian doctrine. And yet for this very reason, for the very reason that he is in such agitation, his consciousness is to us of large worth. For we want to find out the characteristic inner seizures of an apostle in all the upheaval at the very beginning of the Christian church. The points which stand out clearly are these:

1. While Saint Peter blamed the Jews, he regarded the crucifixion of Christ as no accident, but a part of the divine plan. "Being delivered up by the determinate counsel and foreknowledge of God" (Acts 2. 23). "But the things which God foreshowed by the mouth of all the prophets, that his Christ should suffer, he thus fulfilled" (3. 18).

2. While Jesus is "a man approved of God" (2. 22), yet Saint Peter sees in Christ's name the authority, the divine power, the dynamic finality of redemption from sin. "And Peter said unto them, Repent ye, and be baptized every one of you in the name of Jesus Christ unto the remission of your sins; and ye shall receive the gift of the Holy Spirit" (2. 38). "And in none other is there salvation: for neither is there any other name under heaven, that is given among men, wherein we must be saved" (4. 12).

3. But there is more. In Saint Peter's consciousness there is more than that Jesus Christ is a man approved of God and chosen beforehand to suffer and die as the one potent means for the salvation of men. Saint Peter calls Jesus "the Prince of Life" (3. 15). Also he calls him "both Lord and Christ" (2. 36). Saint Peter works miracles only in Christ's name. "In the name of Jesus Christ of Nazareth, walk" (3. 6). The gift of the Holy Spirit he connects with the name of Christ (2. 38, already quoted). And, finally, Saint Peter thinks of Jesus as exalted by the right hand of God: "Him did God exalt with his right hand to be a Prince and a Saviour, to give repentance to Israel, and remission of sins" (5. 31; 2. 33).

Not for a moment would we assert that we find in these three points any more than a moiety of what we found in the consciousness of our Lord. But is it not clear that we have here *the beginning of the same thing?* Was Saint Peter not beginning to realize that Christ's mission was the redemption of man by self-sacrifice, culminating in death; and that this sacrifice was not made by a mere man, but by one peculiarly related to men and to right-eousness and to God? May we not say that Saint Peter's consciousness was, at least in prophetic outline, a copy of his Master's consciousness?

The Fullness in Saint John. Leaving out Saint Paul, whom I wish to reserve for our discussion of the atone-ment, the fullness of the apostolic consciousness is best seen in Saint John. And if we take Saint John as revealed in the book of the Revelation we find a certain maturity, a certain richness and ripeness in Christian conviction, not to be found in any other apostolic writing. The book of Acts might be called the spring of apostolic experience, Saint Paul's epistles the summer, and the book of the Revelation the autumn—when ripe fruits drop as "gentle airs come by." I will make a brief analysis of Saint John's doctrine of the Lamb of God.

The Lamb Slain. The figure of the Lamb was not, as many seem to think, selected mainly to suggest the gentleness of Christ. Indeed, this conception of a gentle Christ is, just now, a reality so overemphasized as to be almost lifted into unreality. Saint John is thinking, not so much of a lamb, as of a lamb *slain.* "And I saw in the midst of the throne and of the four living creatures, and in the midst of the elders, a Lamb standing, as though it had been slain" (Rev. 5. 6).

The Blood of the Lamb. The conception of the Lamb slain is involved also in the expression "the blood of the Lamb"; but "the blood of the Lamb" is most definitely related to the salvation of men from sin. Such a con-nection is established even in the first chapter—"Unto him that loveth us, and loosed us from our sins by his

blood" (1. 5). And then of those before God in white
robes the elder says: "These are they that come out of
the great tribulation, and they washed their robes, and
made them white in the blood of the Lamb" (7. 14).
And speaking of the conquest over "the accuser of our
brethren," Saint John says: "And they overcame him
because of the blood of the Lamb" (12. 11).

The Lamb and the Book. As to the meaning of this
"book written within and on the back, close sealed with
seven seals" (5. 1), many opinions have been given; but,
with any possible view, Saint John is paying an extraordinary tribute to the power of the Lamb. He alone
can open the peculiar book. And I think we may safely
say more, even that Saint John himself furnishes the
clue to his meaning. A little later, in the ninth verse of
this fifth chapter, we read: "And they sing a new song,
saying, Worthy art thou to take the book, and to open
the seals thereof: for thou wast slain, and didst purchase
unto God with thy blood men of every tribe, and tongue,
and people, and nation." This, to me, means, when put
into simple phrase, that the Lamb of God alone has power
to save men, and he has this power because he died for
their sins. That is, the strange, difficult book was the
problem of human redemption. And, further, the elaborate description of the book is but a figurative way of
saying that the moral difficulties of redemption were
almost insuperable. In fact, all through Saint John's
peculiar imagery, there is a most intense moral emphasis. His throne of God is nothing whatever but the
moral law.

The Lamb and the Redeemed. The first thing to note
as to the redeemed is that they do not come out of the
twelve tribes alone. "After these things I saw, and
behold, a great multitude, which no man could number,
out of every nation and of all tribes and peoples and

tongues, standing before the throne and before the Lamb" (7. 9). Thus, redemption is lifted out of ethnic locality and given a racial extent. Again, these redeemed men are in a relation of loyalty and fellowship with the Lamb. "These are they that follow the Lamb whithersoever he goeth" (14. 4). And, again and again, we have the idea that the redeemed absolutely belong to the Lamb by purchase. They "were purchased from among men" (14. 4, etc.).

The Lamb and the Throne of God. In almost every part of the entire book the Lamb sustains a peculiar relation to the enthroned God. And the emphasis of this peculiar relation culminates in the ascription of worship "unto him that sitteth on the throne and unto the Lamb": "And every created thing which is in the heaven, and on the earth, and under the earth, and on the sea, and all things that are in them, heard I saying, Unto him that sitteth on the throne, and unto the Lamb, be the blessing, and the honor, and the glory, and the dominion, for ever and ever" (5. 13).

If now we are willing to make due allowance for the difference in style of speech, I am sure that we can see in this doctrine of the slain Lamb an expression of essentially the same redemptional consciousness which was manifest in the life and sayings of our Lord. To Saint John our Lord's mission was redemption; this redemption was accomplished by a sacrificial death; our Lord's relation to men, in this redemption, was as wide as the human race itself; and the redeemed will treat their Redeemer with precisely that worship which they will pay to God upon his throne. At the end of this short study of the apostolic consciousness the one point which I most care to lift up is that the apostles, from first to last, did not look upon Jesus mainly as their teacher, their master, but rather as their Saviour from sin; and because he was

their Saviour their natural tendency was to exalt him
into the moral power and absolute nature of God himself.
They did not get at the deity of Christ philosophically,
but redemptionally. They did not even try to explain
redemption theologically by calling Christ divine. It
was much more simple. Jesus Christ had saved them
from sin, and in all the glory of the new life in Christ
their whole being rushed out to him as to their God.
This explains why we have no more in the apostolic utterance; and it also explains why we have so much. The
absolute deity of our Lord is surely in the message of the
apostles, but it is in that message not as systematic
theology, but as a redemptional experience.

The Problem of the Early Church

Now let us come down to the beginning of the fourth
century and see if we can make real to our minds the
Christian problem. At the very start we need to remember that the Christian church had inherited the rigid
monotheism of the Old Testament. That "Jehovah our
God is one Jehovah" (Deut. 6. 4) was to the typical
Christian as authoritative as ever it was to any man of
Israel. Indeed, it can be shown that a basal monotheistic conception runs all through not only the writings
of the Greek fathers, but also the New Testament itself.
Profoundly considered, the New Testament is as monotheistic as is the Old Testament. Therefore, with such a
didactic inheritance, the early Christian church, to exalt
Jesus Christ into the Godhead, must have had a motive
forceful enough to overcome a most positive natural inclination. Let us, then, instantly banish from our minds
the notion that we are dealing with men who are pre-
occupied with a doctrinal readiness to deify Jesus
Christ.

But with this monotheism they had inherited precisely what we have been considering, that is, our Lord's conception of his own mission in its aim and method and relations; and this conception essentially repeated in the manifest consciousness of the inspired apostles. Of course, the apostles could not, for the leaders of the early church, add anything to the authority of their Lord; but the apostolic teaching could and did make them more sure in their interpretation of the real meaning of Christ's life and words. Had no apostle ever reaffirmed, so to speak, the consciousness of Christ, the psychological situation, and the practical situation, would have been somewhat different for the early church. It would have been Martin Luther's situation, only many times more perplexing.

Their relation to the Scripture was, however, not artificial, but dynamic. It was mediated through their own Christian consciousness. And their Christian consciousness was resultant from their Christian experience. And the center of their Christian experience was a vital relation to their risen Redeemer. When now we search out their own personal bearing, in this vital relation to Jesus, we find it to be not merely one of faith, but also one of actual worship. There can be no question about this. Worship of Christ was so common to the Christian daily habit of life that Tertullian, in writing his Apology, deems it necessary to defend the practice (xxi). Canon Bright says: "All through the antenicene period, Christians who knew as well as any Jew could have told them that the Divine Unity was the root-truth of true religion, did one thing which spoke decisively as to the purport of their creed. With equal deliberation and fervor, habitually and as a matter of course, throughout life and in the face of death, clergy and people, learned and unlearned, alike and together, *worshiped* the crucified, risen, and glorified Jesus as their Lord and their God."

"The sea was heaving as if in the hours before a storm!" And when the storm burst, it was, for the Christian faith, the most crucial moment in the entire history of the church. Every Christian man should be trained to understand the conflict with Arianism just as every citizen of the republic should be trained to understand the Declaration of Independence. Allow me to lift the struggle out of its confusing nomenclature. Essentially the situation was this: First, the one nerve of the whole matter is that these Christian men had been saved from sin. Seize that fact with all your strength, or you will never comprehend this mighty battle. Second, this salvation from sin they absolutely associated with Jesus Christ and his atonement. Third, they had inherited their Saviour's own interpretation of the relation existing between his redemptive work and the intrinsic peculiarity of his person. Fourth, this consciousness of our Lord they found essentially repeated in the whole body of apostolic experience, the repetition gaining in force and completeness from first to last. Fifth, this inheritance from Christ and his apostles exactly fitted and satisfied their own Christian consciousness which was resultant from their own Christian experience. Sixth, out of this combination of features they had gained a conception of Christ which they spontaneously expressed by worshiping him even as they worshiped God. This is a fair practical statement of the inner situation; and it all can be gathered up into a sentence: While up to this time they had no metaphysical view (the most of them) of Jesus Christ, yet, in their redemptional experience, they so regarded him that their hearts went out to him in full worship. Now, Arianism offered to these redeemed men, worshiping Christ—what? *A creature*—a being who actually had *commenced to live;* a being *made* by a swift, potent volition of Almighty God;

a being that could be *duplicated*—yes, duplicated as often as God might wish to will it—duplicated as easily as archangels or men or planets can be duplicated— Arianism offered to these redeemed men worshiping Christ *that creature!* Surely they had to reject the offer. In the name of all they had inherited, and all they had experienced, and all they had done, they had to reject the offer. Their rejection of all creaturehood in Christ was not only a redemptional consistency, but also a redemptional necessity. It was not so much their theology which was in danger as their Christian experience itself. Indeed, I myself believe that had Arianism been triumphant the Christian faith would have been swept entirely away. Our experience with later depreciations of our Lord's person indicates what would have taken place on a large scale, namely, the gradual devitalization of personal experience in Christ, and then, with this devitalization, the rapid yielding to rationalistic demand until every Christian doctrine was emptied of its original meaning.

Now we can understand why the Athanasians were obliged to go into metaphysics. The Arian offer was too fundamental in its relations, and too subtle in its statements, and too ingenious in its scriptural defense, to be met on the surface in a practical way. There is nothing so slippery as a heresy trying to enter the church. To check it, the practical mind and the Scripture method have ever been completely helpless. There is not one Christian truth which can be fully defended against heresy, save by using more or less of metaphysics, for every final meaning lies deep in metaphysics. Every Arian contention had an important metaphysical implication. The very idea of creaturehood itself is at last a metaphysical idea.

Let us, then, come at the pith of this metaphysical

work of the Athanasians, and try to make it clear to our
modern way of thinking. The pith of the matter is in
these few words: "Very God of very God, begotten, not
made, being of one substance with the Father." The Greek
reads thus: θεὸν ἀληθινὸν ἐκ θεοῦ ἀληθινοῦ, γεννηθέντα, οὐ ποη-
θέντα, ὁμοούσιον τῷ πατρί. The Latin reads thus: *Deum verum de Deo vero, natum, non factum, unius substantiae cum
Patre.* To bring out the significance of these words, I will
make a somewhat arbitrary analysis of them. There are
two statements, and then each statement is briefly explained by a peculiar phrase. The first statement is that
Jesus Christ is "very God," or, as a theologian to-day
would say, absolutely God. The explanation of this first
statement is in the peculiar phrase "being of one substance
with the Father." Upon this term *substance* a surprising
amount of learned research has been expended with a
small amount of philosophical insight. The instant
meaning of the word is of little concern, for it was nothing
but a weapon, and an accidental weapon at that, to
protect an underlying and extremely important idea,
namely, that the Father and the Son are what they are
by means of one and the same organism; that they are,
therefore, structurally necessary to each other, so that
neither can exist at all without the other.

The second statement, indicating the method of this
organic divine life, is that Jesus Christ, the Son, is "of
very God." The explanation of this second statement
is in the peculiar phrase "begotten, not made." This
explanation is really twofold: First, there is the term
"begotten," which evidently had come from Saint John's
"only begotten." (See Saint John's gospel 1. 14, 18;
and 3. 16; and 1 John 4. 9.) Then this term is itself
further and negatively explained by the expression "not
made." As if they had said: Jesus Christ is of God, but
not in the sense that a creature is of God by optional

creation. Christ is begotten, but not made. Here again
they were compelled to use the weapon at hand, but it
is plain enough what they meant. They were trying to
say that our Lord has *a derived being, but the derivation
is necessary and without beginning and without resultant
inferiority.* The Father is the causal ground of the Son's
existence, but the Father does not *choose* to will the Son
into existence; he *must* eternally do so by the very process
of his own eternal life. This causing the existence of the
Son is the method by which the Father *is* the Father,
and without being the Father he could not exist at all.
It is loose speech to call this process of begetting the Son
creation, I think; but we may do so, if we are only careful
to insist that it is *necessary and eternal* creation. Many
times, and even in recent years, we have been told that
this eternal generation, or begetting, of the Son of God
is empty verbiage, a sort of theological rhetoric, incapable
of conception by the human mind. I entirely fail to
respond to the objection; and I fail to comprehend how
any thinking man, familiar with the struggle over the
Athanasian contention, can ever have even the slightest
difficulty in clearly grasping the meaning of Athanasius.
Surely we may conceive of two real persons; both of them
without beginning; both of them alike in attributes, so
that neither one of them is inferior to the other; and yet
one of them is the *cause*, furnishes the power by which
the other one has all his life; and then we may conceive
that the *causal person lives only by giving* just as the
caused person lives only by receiving; and thus they exist
by means of one and the same organism. And, now that
I am at the point, I will dare to affirm that this eternal
generation of the Son is not only conceivable, it is also
one of the most fruitful conceptions in all Christian
thinking. It helps us to understand all those sayings of
Christ where, at one stroke, he insists upon both his

equality with the Father and his dependence upon the Father, for these sayings reach widely beyond our Saviour's temporary condition of humiliation. And not only this, the Athanasian conception helps us to enter into the very atmosphere of the plan of redemption. Devotionally, to a Christian man, this supreme Christian creed is of more worth than The Imitation of Christ.

The problem of the early church, given in a word, was to protect, under perilous attack, the whole significance of their redemptional experience in Jesus Christ. And they did this, in full consistency with all their Christian opinions, by maintaining that our Redeemer, Jesus Christ, is, in his own person, eternally, necessarily, and absolutely—*God*. It was the greatest piece of work ever done by uninspired men.

THE MODERN CHRISTOLOGICAL PERIL

The Arians are gone, but their equivalent is still here. The modern agnostic movement in Christology I can but regard as a most serious attack upon the deity of our Lord, and, through that, upon the entire significance of redemption. And the extreme peril of the attack lies in two things: First, that our leaders in the practical work of the church are so occupied, so busy with large affairs, that they do not realize the nature of the attack; and, second, that some of our greatest teachers and writers have honestly made up their minds, under the pressure of the new demands of science, that the old Christology is now untenable, even if it ever had any reality to the Christian mind. It is one of those critical periods when a small man can be pardoned for wishing there were some process by which he could for a few years become Athanasius.

Fairly to bring before you this agnosticism in Christology, I will quote a passage from an editorial in one of our influential, nonsectarian, religious journals, a passage which I have selected out of a large number of statements equally pertinent, because it is perfectly steeped in genuine spiritual quality. That is, I want you to see the agnostic bearing in its loftiest spiritual mood. The passage reads as follows: "I will not and I cannot enter into polemical discussions about him [Christ]; I will not and I cannot enter into metaphysical analysis of him. I have no capacity to define with fine phrases his relation to the Infinite and the Eternal God, and I have no wish to do so. I rejoice in the mysteries of his being which I cannot solve. But to be like Jesus Christ is my deepest and sincerest desire, to have some share in the work he is doing is my supremest ambition; in his teaching I find the sum of all spiritual truth, in his spirit the secret of all life, and in himself an object of love and reverence such that all I have is too little to give to him. If I try to put this experience into a form of words, I can find no better phrase than to say that I believe that *the Eternal Presence, whom no one can see or comprehend, manifested himself in this one human life that all might see and comprehend him, and that through him all might come to be sharers of his life and conformed to his image*" [italics mine]. Any student remembering Professor Ritschl's remarkable chapter on "The Doctrine of Christ's Person and Lifework" will note at once that in this editorial utterance we have an expression of one side of the Ritschlian view of "the Godhead of Christ." The Ritschlian view, very briefly stated, is this: Christ is divine in the sense that he has the value of God in the Christian experience. When we analyze this value we find two things, namely, that Jesus is "the manifest type of spiritual lordship over the world" and "the perfect revealer of God." That is, we ascribe deity to Christ because he shows us how to master the world and because he is to us in our religious experience a perfect revelation of God. Concerning the last point Ritschl says: "As Bearer of the perfect revelation, Christ is given us that we may believe on him. When we do believe on him, we find him to be the Revealer of God." But when we ask for more, when we ask what Christ really is in fundamental relation to God the Father, or what Christ is in himself, say, whether he is a creature or not, then Professor Ritschl gives us such an agnostic answer as we already have in the editorial quoted. It is true that the Ritschlian answer has, to many, a profounder appearance because it is related by manipulation to the Kantian theory of knowledge. But this Kantian theory of knowledge actually adds an extra burden to the agnostic position, for the theory is weak in itself. To make hiatus between the action of a thing and the thing in itself is nothing but gratuity in philosophy. It is much more reasonable to hold that when we have the work of a thing we have the thing at work. In spite of the great name of Kant behind it, this positing a ground of action which is not actually in the action is a purely arbitrary performance. To meet the Ritschlian Christology from the standpoint of a theory of knowledge, I would contend that if Jesus Christ has for men the complete value of God, either he must be a sheer automaton, a projected theophany, or he must be God himself. He could not be a free man, he could not be a creature, for no creature, however inspired, however helped, can remain in self-consciousness and act beyond the range of the finite. Either the free personality of Jesus must be given up or his absolute Godhead must be maintained.

But my main concern is not with the Ritschlian theory of knowledge, nor even with the Ritschlian theology by itself, but only with this agnostic Christology, however and wherever manifest. And I am concerned with this agnostic Christology, not as a scientific theologian, looking at its bearing upon this or that speculation in a system of doctrine, but as an ordinary Christian man, looking at its bearing upon the Christian experience in redemption. You cannot transform our Saviour into an interrogative and not do violence to the whole extent of the redemptional consciousness, from that of the man who has found forgiveness and peace in Christ to-day, back through the Christian centuries, back through the apostles, to our Lord's own conception of his mission and his person. This, though, is not all. This agnosticism tends to empty the atonement for sin of its profoundest ethical and sacrificial meaning. This meaning is deeper than any of our theories, and more important than all our theories—it is the root-peculiarity of the Christian faith— and it is this: God, in his awful holiness, so loved men that he gave, out of his own being, his eternal, uncreated Son to save them from sin unto everlasting life. Therefore, our salvation has come only by the most costly self-sacrifice on the part of God the Father. And in this expensive self-sacrifice in the name of moral regard and love lies the ethical quality as well as the evidence of infinite love. But once hold that Jesus Christ was a creature, and you have thrown all this holy costliness away. And this agnosticism says that it cannot tell whether Christ was a creature or not. *We must have a Christology that can tell, or violate, and then vitiate, the Christian experience in redemption. It is not systematic theology, but the vitality of the Christian life, which is at stake.*

XVII. THE INCARNATION OF THE SON OF GOD

THE central idea in the doctrine of the Incarnation is this: *The Son of God given as man, for the redemption of man.* This means that we are to *start*, not, as many theologians do, with the man Jesus, but with the Son of God living personally, self-consciously, in the glory of the Godhead. Jesus Christ is God become man, and not man become God. We must instantly reject this view of a very peculiar man, or even of a miraculous man, gradually coming nearer and nearer to God, gradually being more and more filled with divine potency, gradually being more and more conjoined with God, until at last Christ is very God ("ganz und schlechthin Gott"—Rothe). "And the Word became flesh, and dwelt among us (and we beheld his glory, glory as of the only begotten from the Father), full of grace and truth" (Saint John 1. 14).

In recent years the question of the virgin birth has become one of "the points of fire" in theological discussion; and there are some who hold the miracle still, as a veritable New Testament teaching, and yet say it is "only a minor matter connected with the Incarnation and should have a subordinate place in the doctrine." I do not think that this apologetic treatment is wise; nor do I think that it represents the real Christian consciousness concerning the matter. It is true that the miracle of the virgin birth is not necessary, philosophically speaking, to the accomplishment of the Incarnation. There are several other conceivable ways by which the Son of God might have become truly man. The virgin birth is also entirely unessential (many famous theologians have taught the contrary, however) in securing our Lord's freedom from depravity. Becoming man in anyway whatsoever, our Saviour would have been able to organize his whole being about his moral ideal, with the supreme motive of moral love, and the real companionship with God his Father. All this we may admit; but the virgin birth, nevertheless, belongs to the process of the Incarnation by *the most inherent fitness*. To have the stupendous miracle of the Incarnation itself actualized by a natural method would be as much out of place as to have the sun rise without manifesting its nature in heat and light. The nature of the miracle should come out; the method should express the inner nature of the event. Not only so, but the virgin birth is in fitness with the great miracles at the close of our Lord's earthly ministry, the resurrection and the ascension. The profoundest Christian consciousness will, I am very certain, more and more intensely do two things, namely, banish all miracle after the apostolic period, and demand every biblical miracle which tends to emphasize the extraordinary ethical meaning of our Redeemer's sacrifice for sin. The question for Christian men is not a scientific question in the least, but only a question of moral emphasis, a question of redemptional ethics. We will at last have everything which renders more real, more glorious, our salvation through the Incarnation and Death of our Lord.

Although we start with the preëxistent Son of God, yet as a result of the virgin birth we come in our thinking to the proper manhood of Christ. But this is the precise point where we must begin to avoid even the faintest color of humanitarian thinking. We should not allow even the chill of the climate of that thinking to penetrate our hearts. The humanitarian conception of Jesus Christ is wrong, not only in theory, but in feeling also. And the feeling is more poisonous than the theory. The manhood of Christ is not that of a human person. All the personality of our Lord he brought with him into human existence. He takes on an addition, a human addition, to his individuality, that is all. The manhood is ever impersonal, never anything but a lower coefficient for the abiding person of the Son of God. The Christian value of this view is very great, for it means that the human nature of our Lord will never come to personal emphasis, never come to triumph, so to speak, but will always stand out for the Redeemed as evidence of the sacrifice the Son of God made for man's salvation. The dignity of man, man's worth in God's sight, is not to be found in the humanity of Christ, as if our nature were so wonderful that even the Infinite One might be proud to wear it. That method of magnifying man is humanitarian and not truly Christian. No, the worth of man is to be found in the one fact that God cared enough about us to redeem us at such awful cost. Thus, the best place for a man to discover his inner value is not at Bethlehem, but at Mount Calvary. The manhood of Jesus Christ is ever to be regarded as a part of the humiliation of the Son of God.

This prepares the way plainly to ask the question: Had there been no sin, and so no need of salvation, would the Son of God have become man? Bishop Martensen says: "Are we to suppose that that which is most glorious in the world could be reached only through the medium of sin? that there would have been no place in the human race for the glory of the Only Begotten One but for sin?" This conception of a cosmic meaning of the Incarnation—that the universe itself could be made complete only by God's Son becoming man; that sin is but an accident which gave a peculiar occasion for the carrying out of a great original plan—is fascinating to every Christian theologian having Martensen's philosophical cast of mind; but the splendid thing should, however we may cling to it in our dreams, be given up. For it is out of emphasis with the New Testament teaching as to the appalling nature and consequences of sin; and it tends to obscure the divine costliness of redemption. Indeed, this cosmic conception, once fully held, would entirely change the Christian mood, for it would lift Christianity out of its tragedy by giving the Incarnation place among the normal and majestic processes. The ethical stress, the abiding moral sorrow, in the Christian life must be preserved in the most jealous manner. No grander view in philosophy shall be allowed to entice us away from our rejoicing sorrow in our Lord—*rejoicing*, that he so loved us as to rescue us; *sorrow*, that the rescue cost so much—cost even the breaking up of the normal plan of the divine life.

In his exceedingly helpful work, The Christian View of God and the World, Professor James Orr has made a suggestion with a purpose to mediate between the cosmic conception and the purely redemptional conception of the Incarnation. The passage reads as follows: "It seems to me that the real source of difficulty in thinking on this subject lies in not grasping with sufficient firmness the fact that, however we may distinguish from our human point of view between parts and aspects of the divine plan, God's plan is in reality one, and it is but an abstract way of thinking which leads us to suppose otherwise. In our human way of apprehension we speak as if God had first one plan of creation—complete and rounded off in itself—in which sin was to have no place; then, when it was foreseen that sin would enter, another plan was introduced, which vitally altered and enlarged the former. But if we take a sufficiently high point of view we shall be compelled to conclude, I think, that the plan of the universe is one, and that, however harsh the expression may sound, the foresight and permission of sin was from the first included in it." I do not discover any worth in Professor Orr's suggestion. Under all our imperfect language about two divine plans, there is a reality which is not affected in the least by "the foresight and permission of sin." The reality is this: *Sin is contrary to God's ideal.* Sin is foreseen and permitted as a second best rather than to have no personal creatures at all. The present plan, although from all eternity, is not what Infinite Holiness wanted, but even this plan is better than to have the whole universe automatic. And when we speak of two plans we are thinking of the actual plan over against the divine ideal. And, coming to the point at issue, the Incarnation, the real question is: Does the Incarnation of the Son of God belong to the divine ideal, does it express the normal relation of God to the cosmos, or is it a part of a plan which is the divine ideal modified by the certainty of sin and the purpose of redemption? My only possible answer has been given to this question. No Christian man should allow any touch of Hegelian philosophy to place the Incarnation in the divine ideal, in the normal life of God; for so to place it gives it cosmic majesty at the expense of intense redemptional import.

THE HUMILIATION OF THE KENOSIS

The Teaching of Saint Paul. The Scripture passages involved are four: Saint John's gospel 1. 14; 2 Cor. 8. 9; Heb. 2. 17; and Phil. 2. 5–8. Inasmuch, though, as the great passage in Philippians more than covers the other texts, it is necessary to discuss that one only. Saint Paul's words are: "Have this mind in you, which was also in Christ Jesus: who, existing in the form of God (ἐν μορφῇ θεοῦ ὑπάρχων), counted not the being on an equality with God (τὸ εἶναι ἴσα θεῷ) a thing to be grasped, but emptied himself (ἑαυτὸν ἐκένωσεν), taking the form of

a servant (μορφὴν δούλου λαβών), being made in the likeness
of men (ἐν ὁμοιώματι ἀνθρώπων); and being found in fashion
as a man (σχήματι εὑρεθεὶς ὡς ἄνθρωπος), he humbled himself,
becoming obedient even unto death, yea, the death of
the cross."

Fully to understand this passage, one first needs
firmly to grasp the distinction between the term μορφὴ
and the term σχῆμα, a distinction so convincingly
brought out by Bishop Lightfoot in his commentary.
The term μορφὴ is the deeper term, meaning the *essential form of being*, while the term σχῆμα means merely
the fashion of actual life. As a most simple illustration,
let us take an ash tree, say a mountain ash. The μορφὴ
of this tree is the entire combination of essential characteristics which are necessary to constitute and manifest
that individual thing we call a mountain ash. Take
away even one of these characteristics, and it would not
be a mountain ash, but something more or less different.
Thus, the μορφὴ of the tree is the tree's typical or
mountain ash individuality; that is, all the peculiarity
which constitutes the tree just that sort of an individual
which is classified as a mountain ash. But this tree also
has a σχῆμα, or fashion of life, which has no necessary
connection with the fact that it is a mountain ash. It
is crowded, or it stands alone in the clearing; it has a
suitable soil, or an unsuitable soil; it is bathed in the sun,
or struggles upward in the shadow—such things make up
the tree's σχῆμα. The discussion is not complete here,
but it is full enough to suggest all that we now require.

To Saint Paul, God himself has an essential form of
being and a fashion of life. The divine μορφὴ comprises
all of God's essential characteristics—all the interlaced
attributes which are necessary to make God what he is
and to express what he is. The divine σχῆμα, on the other
hand, is but the manner of God's life, or, as he is per-

sonal, we may say, more closely, the manner of God's experience. It is, I think, precisely what Saint John means by δόξα, that "glory" which the Saviour had with the Father before the world was. If you say that this "glory" is also essential to God, I answer, It is necessary from the standpoint of inherent fitness in a perfect divine experience, but it is not necessary to the very existence of God himself.

Keeping in mind this distinction between the essential form of being and the more superficial fashion of actual life, we are prepared to study Saint Paul's conception of our Lord's humiliation. Of what did our Saviour, the Son of God, empty himself? Of that thing, surely, which he counted not a thing to be grasped, as one holds fast to a great prize, whether or no, namely, the τὸ εἶναι ἴσα θεῷ, "the being on an equality with God." It is plain enough that the Son of God, according to Saint Paul, gave up being on an equality with the Father. Right here it has been urged, however, that originally our Lord was on an equality with God in two ways: one way as to the form of being, the other way as to the fashion of life. If so, which of these two, the form of being or the fashion of life, did he give up? Or did he (keeping to the exegesis) give up both? Canon Gifford has, as far as I am concerned anyway, forever settled the grammatical question at this point, showing that the Greek cannot mean that the μορφή, or essential form of being, was surrendered. And we also reach the same conclusion under the principle of exegetical economy. The aim of the passage is to teach a deep humiliation; and to protect that aim completely we need to hold no more than that the fashion of life was given up. In other words, the ineffable glory of God's experience is enough, certainly, to make a full contrast with the limitation of a human life ending in death upon a cross.

And, further, this double exegetical conclusion would be confirmed were we to press the question into a philosophial consideration. And, last of all, we have the consciousness of our Lord, as given by Saint John, that to redeem men he had given up the glory of God and not the Godhead.

What did our Saviour, the Son of God, take on? "The form of a servant." The word μορφή is again used here, and it means precisely what it means in the verse before. Our Lord took on the attributes of a servant, or that essential form of being which pertains to the cramping existence of a slave. Not the accidental experience of a slave; but, profounder than all that, the very μορφή, the essential form, the fundamental being of a slave. The idea here is not that Jesus Christ lived, suffered, died *like* a slave, but that he *was* a slave. He had the whole essential structure of a δοῦλος. And now Saint Paul tells us the exact kind of a servile μορφή which our Lord took on, the exact kind of a servant that he became. "Being made in the likeness of men." The word used here is not μορφή, but ὁμοίωμα, of which Bengel says that it "denotes a relation to other things of the same condition." Saint Paul means that the Son of God became, not only a servant, but also that special kind of a servant which men are. He was a *human* δοῦλος. It is simply saying that our Lord became a man, but saying it in such a way as to put extreme emphasis upon the servile limitations of manhood. Even this is not all. The humiliation is still greater. Our Redeemer not only became man; he also took the actual experience—the σχῆμα—of a man; and a peculiarly humiliating σχῆμα, one that ended in death, and even in the shame and torture of the death of the cross. "Being found in fashion as a man, he humbled himself, becoming obedient even unto death, yea, the death of the cross."

Analytically given, the teaching of the apostle Paul as to the humiliation of the kenosis is as follows: 1. Being originally, and continually subsisting in the essential form of God, our Lord had an inherent right to enjoy the actual manner of life, or the transcendent experience of God.   2. But this transcendent divine experience he would not cling to regardless; but gave it up as an act of redemptional humiliation.   3. This impoverishment of himself was not all.   There was a second stage of humiliation in the further fact that he took on the servile essential form of being which men have; and then lived the actual life of a man.   4. And there was a third stage of humiliation; for our Saviour obediently lived this actual life of a man down to the experience of death.   5. And this third stage of humiliation was emphasized by the suffering and ignominy of crucifixion.

The Teaching Transferred to Systematic Theology.   By making a few changes in the words, the Pauline conception of the kenosis can be expressed in the spirit and form of systematic theology: As a preëxisting person our Lord had two things, namely, first, a divine nature with all the attributes of the Godhead; second, a divine personal experience equal to that of God the Father.   The divine nature he did not give up, but has it eternally. But the divine experience he could and did give up in redemptional humiliation.   And, further, he not only surrendered this divine experience, but also had, in place of it, a servile human experience of the most humiliating extreme, reaching down to death, and that death even by crucifixion.   The possibility of this servile human experience was due to the fact that to his original and eternal divine nature he had added a human nature which is the nature of limitation and dependence.

A Deeper Study of the Kenosis.   If we are ever to appreciate the profound significance of our Lord's humiliation our discussion of the kenosis must be deepened. This study is all the more important because the doctrine of the kenosis has been so manipulated as to *seem* to impair the supreme authority of Jesus Christ; indeed, has been so manipulated as to be made to lend itself to a purely humanitarian view of him.

What do we mean by the term *nature* when we are speaking of an individual? Some writers seem to think that an individual's nature is a sort of inner pulp out of which qualities are extracted as literally as pins are taken from a cushion. Toward such a crude, materialistic conception there is no worthy mood short of impatience. The fact is that there are many Christians who are materialistic, not as to man's destiny, but as to man's constitution. By the nature of anything I understand neither more nor less than *that structural law by which the thing is precisely what it is*. With Professor Bowne's idea of being as active, one would say that this structural law is the law of the thing's action: "Now, this rule or law which determines the form and sequence of a thing's activities represents to our thought the nature of the thing, or expresses its true essence." This view is, I am convinced, the only full stopping place; but for our present purpose it is quite enough to say that under every individual existence there is a basal plan or law which determines all individual difference in characteristics. Coming again to Saint Paul, I would say that his μορφή is the individuality which expresses this structural law. But we need to be cautious here. The μορφή is not *a separated consequence*. The nature, the structural law actually appears in the μορφή. The common people come quite close to the fact when they say, "It's the very nature of the thing to be that way."

Making now our application to the kenosis, we can hold that the original structural law of our Lord's being is exactly that law which makes God what God is—self-existent in organism, omnipotent—in short, having all the divine attributes. Then, we can make a distinction between this law as actually in the attributes and the attributes as actually in self-consciousness. Holding fast to this distinction, we can, I think, at least begin to apprehend what took place in the Incarnation. The divine life as a personal experience—as "glory over glory streaming"—our Lord could and did give up; but he did not, and he could not, give up the original structural law, the basal plan of his being, that intrinsic fundament by which alone he had the possibility of the ineffable experience of God. Our Saviour did not achieve manhood by a reduction of his deity. Truly he became man, but after he became man he had every divine capacity, every divine power, every divine attribute. I well know how impossible it seems, at first, that a person can have a complete attribute and yet not seize it in self-consciousness; but perhaps I can convince you not only that such is the fact, but also that the fact is quite common in human life. Here is a mother, for example, who has the full attribute of love. By this I mean that she has the habit of love fundamental in her womanhood. Her capacity for love, we will say, has been gathered up into a definite habit of love for her child. If you take away this habit of love for that child, what remains will not be the same individual woman at all. The attribute of love belongs to her very nature. Indeed, we can go further; for this habit of love may have been so personalized, so indorsed by crucial self-decision, that the mother must love that child forever. The habit has become a part of her everlasting individuality. And yet, basal as the attribute is, it does not always appear in the woman's self-consciousness. The child may be sick unto death, and the mother, in sheer exhaustion, may have fallen asleep. Would you in such case say that she had lost out of her nature her love for her child? Not a man of you would say such a thing as that; you would say, She has lost the love out of her consciousness, but she has it still deep in her heart. If it be urged that the mother is only a finite creature, I answer, That fact does not change the other one, namely, that it is possible for a person to have an attribute in the individual nature and yet not to have the attribute in self-consciousness.

But some brother, who is thinking of the present biblical situation, says: "You would not claim, though, that Jesus Christ was, in his earthly life, omniscient?" That is precisely what I do claim. By the attribute of omniscience I understand the inherent power for the perfect intuition of all reality and all possibility; and I believe that our Lord never for an instant even lost that structural feature out of his being. But this does not mean that the attribute of omniscience was aplunge in self-consciousness all through that period of humiliation. As men, we ourselves have the inherent power for some intuition—for instance, that a half is less than the whole. Do we drop the power out of our nature every time we drop the intuition out of consciousness? Or take even acquired knowledge, as we term it—does a learned man need to carry in self-consciousness all the time, day and night, every item which he has acquired? May he not dare to take some rest from his terrible burden? Sir William Hamilton, I have read, could banish from his consciousness all his vast erudition, and live for hours at some one delicate point in philosophy; but I have never read that when he came out of his mood of abstraction he discovered that he had lost every other truth and every other fact which he had ever acquired. In my own thinking I have considered not only omniscience, not only love, but also all the remaining divine attributes, and my firm conclusion is that our Lord emptied himself of no divine thing save the transcendent personal experience of God.

What we have said now makes it necessary more closely to study our Saviour's humanity. When we say that our Lord took on a human nature, precisely what do we mean? I mean this: He added to the original structural law of his being another law, namely, the law of a finite, dependent creature such as man is. Under this new law man's limited existence could be real to him. Under the law of his divine nature he had an infinite intuitive knowledge of man, but he could not have human life as an actual personal experience. In the absolute God there is no normal capacity for the finite. This is not an imperfection in God any more than it is an imperfection in the sun not to be small enough for a candlestick. Or, take this illustration in suggestion: John Burroughs knows much more *about* a snow-bird than the "little, nervous, fastidious" Junco knows about itself; and yet the great, kindly naturalist cannot without a miracle have the actual limitations and peculiar experience of the bird. The miracle of the Incarnation, as I lay hold of it, is the conjoining of two structural plans of being so that the incarnate Son of God has now two inherent capacities, one for divine experience and the other for human experience. For example, he can actually be a δοῦλος in spatial limitations, as when, on the way to Emmaus, he "drew near, and went with them"; or he can override these limitations, as when he "vanished out of their sight." If it be objected that all this took place after his resurrection, I answer, first, that the resurrection simply made fitting a revelation of capacity which was in his nature all the time; and, second, that the same philosophical significance belongs to the scene on the

Mount of Transfiguration, or to the scene at the grave of Lazarus. Indeed, time and time again, our Saviour plainly showed a double capacity in nature.

Before thoroughly testing my conception of the incarnate person of the Son of God I wish to state it clearly and succinctly. After the Incarnation our Lord was one person, living under two abiding structural laws of being, and thus having two kinds of capacity, one kind divine, the other kind human. His impoverishment, therefore, was not as to nature but as to personal experience. And the degree of this impoverishment was due to his redemptional aim to live a typical human life "down to its dregs of death." For to live such a life there must be either an erasement (as in infancy) or a modification (as in the temptation) of his original seizure in self-consciousness.

The Infancy of Jesus. Under this theory that the kenosis applies only to self-consciousness, what is our conception of our Lord's human infancy? There can be no severer test than to answer this question. That babe was not a human babe in a profound philosophical sense. Never under any possible conditions could that child have become a mere man, a human creature. We must instantly banish every trace of creaturehood from our conception. That babe was as truly God as when he was absolute in the glory of God the Father. The self-consciousness of the Son of God is now in total eclipse, but he himself is still organic in the Godhead and has still all the inherent divine capacity. Not one divine attribute has he lost out of his nature. And yet there is not an atom of docetic life here. He does not *seem* to be living the life of a human infant, he *is* living it. His dependence upon Mary, all the first tiny outreachings of a child's instincts, the first perceptions crawling slowly into clearness —all are completely real—why? Simply because the

structural law of a human being is at this time in supreme
dominion, and there is no personal experience of his divine
nature.

But not yet am I fully understood—some one is thinking, "Would you, then, say with John Milton, 'Our Babe,
to show his Godhead true, can in his swaddling bands
control the damnèd crew'?" Can this infant exercise
the prerogatives of his deity? Certainly not, for such an
exercise of prerogative would require self-decision, and
such self-decision would require not only a divine nature,
but also the self-grasp and self-estimate of that nature in
consciousness.

Repeated Personal Choice of Humiliation. As the child
Jesus grows the two structural coefficients of consciousness are less and less exclusive, and at last (we cannot be
sure as to the time) Jesus Christ is in positive seizure of
the structural law of his divine being. From this point
on he can at will overwhelm the human side of his life.
He has taken on the human nature for time and eternity,
but this does not mean that he may not banish it from
personal experience. The Son of God does not now *need*
to be hungry and weary and powerless, he *chooses* to be so.
Thus, there is a perpetual ethical quality in his humiliation; and just before his death this ethical quality reaches
its loftiest point. The death of Christ is not a humiliation
which was chosen once for all before the Incarnation, but
rather a humiliation chosen again and again, and at last
chosen in finality in Gethsemane. The death of Christ
was not necessary because he had a human nature; the
human nature merely rendered the experience of death
possible. The death of Christ was necessary only
ethically, was necessary only redemptionally. Even here
there is almost no Christian emphasis upon the fact that
Jesus was a man. The manhood was but a means to an
end. Because he was man he *could* die, and because he

was God he *would* die for an atonement. Thus, that cross itself is perfectly saturated with moral meaning.

The Temptation of Christ. This point of repeated personal choice naturally brings our discussion to the question of our Lord's temptation. And here we need to satisfy two kinds of men: First, there is the man who fears that we may destroy, or obscure, the *reality* of the temptation. This man says: "If you emphasize the Master's Godhead so greatly, you make, as far as I can see, his temptation into a mere deceptive exhibition. My own temptations mean life or death, and never can I allow you to take away from me the courage which has come to my heart from believing that my Saviour's victory was a real victory in a real conflict." The feeling expressed here is genuinely Christian, and it may partly explain the extreme modern emphasis upon the true humanity of Christ. I only wish that the entire humanitarian emphasis could be explained in this manner, for an error which grows out of a Christian sentiment is never deeply dangerous; at least, never so deeply dangerous as an error which grows out of a rationalistic root. But the man's fear is the result of a superficial understanding of the psychology of temptation. The reality of temptation, and the strength of temptation, too, depends simply upon *the consciousness of pressure in motive.* At this point the popular notion that a weak person has the greater temptation is altogether incorrect. The greater the person, the greater the clarity of self-consciousness, the greater the temptation, provided there is motive for wrongdoing. But, as I have already shown, the strength of a motive never can, in and of itself, mean the defeat of a free person. Our Lord had, at the time of his temptation, very great motives to keep loyal to his ideal and to his Father; but his human nature did furnish motives to violate that loyalty, and these motives were actual in consciousness, and were felt with all the mighty seizure of his personality. In short, our Lord was, in self-consciousness, under real pressure to reject the demand of his own conscience, and this made his conflict real.

Again, there is the man who is in theoretical fear of the very reality which the other man dreads to lose. In apparent desperation, he asks: "Suppose Jesus Christ *had* yielded to the temptation, what would have become of the plan of salvation? You dare not teach that his temptation was real in the sense that he could have become a transgressor!" And the strange thing is that scholastic ingenuity has laboriously tried to meet this theoretical fear, when the answer is as clear as a cloudless sky. *The premise of the whole plan of redemption is the omniscience of God.* Let a man once master the significance of redemption in its relation to personality and moral character, and he must premise omniscience; he can no more believe that God is nescient than he can believe that man is coerced. It was foreknown that when the Son of God took on a human nature and thereby came to have a human probation, because of the new motives in consciousness, he would in his personal freedom come off more than conqueror. Our Lord's temptation was real, his triumph was real; but the result was certain (not necessary), just as the final, total outcome of redemption is secure in the absolute omniscience of God.

The Authority of Jesus Christ. Some years ago I wrote, in another connection, these words: "Practically, the Incarnation has no bearing whatever upon the authority of our Lord; for he had, in his human life, instant access to the resources of his Father. With such resources at command he might choose not to know; but in such chosen ignorance he would never speak as if he knew. Surely the Son of God did not become man that he might

make false statements." Then I added a quotation from
Canon Gore's Bampton Lectures, which runs thus: "Let
it be said at once that we could not, consistently with
faith, hesitate to accept anything on any subject that
our Lord meant to teach us." The aim and spirit of this
former utterance satisfy me still, but the point of view
does not satisfy me. It is superficial. When we speak
of the authority of Jesus Christ we are not thinking of
his infancy, but of his manhood after he had obtained
his redemptional self-consciousness. And, I must hold
that this redemptional consciousness involved a self-
grasp of his divine nature, and therefore of all his divine
attributes, and therefore of the attribute of omniscience
itself. So much as to theory; now let us turn to the
gospel record. Those writers who emphasize the kenosis
with a humanitarian intention are ever eager to call our
attention to our Lord's saying that even the Son knew
not "of that day and hour," but why do they not call our
attention also to those places where, as in the case of
Peter's denial, our Lord evinced a vision of future events,
some of these events entirely contingent upon man's
freedom? The gospel account, I think, does not fit into
their theory, but does fit into mine. The record bears
out my contention that in his manhood our Saviour had,
and had in personal command, the attribute of omniscience, sometimes using it, and at other times refusing
to use it, in order that he might experience human life
to its limit. His humanity did render it possible for him
not to know, but his humanity did not render it impossible for him to know what he would and when he would.
With such a conception of our Lord, I cannot admit that
he ever mangled a fact. To a certain extent he might
accommodate himself to the ignorance of men and to the
imperfections of his time; to a certain extent he might
wish to have an inner world as poverty-stricken as their

own; to a certain extent he might wish to compel himself to live in the unopened scene of to-day; but it is too much to ask us to believe that Jesus Christ ever held a false opinion or spoke a false word.

The Question of Two Wills. "After the Saviour took on a human nature did he have two wills, one divine and the other human?" The very asking of such a question is indicative of crude thinking in psychology; but the question has some historical importance in theology, and is also troublesome to many students, so I will take the time to answer it. My answer must be: In one sense, No; in another sense, Yes. The will is not a thing *added* to a person, nor an item distinctive in a person, say as a mainspring is distinctive in a watch. When we say that a person *has* will, we mean, or should mean, nothing other than that he *can* will, that is, he has the inherent capacity for decision. The person is one all the time, now feeling, now thinking, now making volition, and now, perhaps, doing all three at a personal stroke. Our Lord, also, was not two persons, but a unitary personal being; and when he willed anything, he did not have, lying in behind, a second will like a machine's supplemental attachment which is kept in reserve to do a second kind of work. But inasmuch as our Saviour did have, added to his original divine nature, a human nature; and inasmuch as that human nature could at times dominate his consciousness, we should, it seems to me, call that volition human which was made under such domination. Taken in this manner, I could agree with men like Canon Liddon; but I would, of course, need to add that there were occasions when our Lord's decision was, exactly speaking, neither all divine nor all human, but rather divine-human. For there were occasions when both natures were explicit in self-consciousness. But the entire question of two wills, I apprehend, comes out of a blundering effort to protect the integrity of each nature in Christ; and I believe that such protection I have secured.

The Incarnation and the Cosmic Process. The theory of "the double life" is held by a number of Christian theologians who, like Bishop Martensen, do not find any way to provide for the ongoing of the universe without the constant volition of the Son of God. Thus the Incarnation is isolated from the cosmic process, and our Lord is conceived of as living two lives, one life as God absolute and the other life as God incarnate. At one and the same time he is (Proclus of Cyzicus) "in his mother's arms and on the wings of the winds." Professor Briggs seems to hold to this view, for he says: "The kenosis is conceived in its relation to the work of Christ Jesus for man in this world. So far as the Son of God has other relations to the universe, the kenosis here mentioned does not apply. As the Mediator of the divine government of the universe, in whom 'were all things created,' and in whom 'all things consist,' he continues in the form of God, at the same time as in the Incarnation he empties himself of the form of God." I can accept any miracle which is essential to the Christian faith, but this view of a "double life" is to me not so much a Christian miracle as a psychological monstrosity. It is like saying that a man can be himself and his own elder brother, and then calling it a miracle. In fact, there is in the view no serious consideration of the integrity of personality. And not only so, but I must regard the view as peculiarly dangerous. In consistent thinking, it is likely to mean no more than that Jesus Christ is the under and necessary agent of the Son of God, who remains intact in the glory of the Godhead. Held in this way, it would, equally with Ritschlianism, destroy the ethical import of the self-sacrifice in the Incarnation. And, equally with Ritschlianism, it would be likely, in unskillful hands, to drop into an unrecognized humanitarianism. And not only so, but the view is not even required to protect the cosmic process. For the ongoing of the universe only two things are necessary, namely, the organism of the Godhead in its entire integrity, and this perfect divine organism brought to volitional point by the infinite will. The organism of the Godhead is not, even during our Lord's human infancy, impaired in any structural way by the Incarnation; and this perfect divine organism is brought to volitional point by the will of God the Father. In fact, the will of the Father is always the primary efficiency, for the Son does not originate anything, but merely carries out in obedient love the Father's purpose. Whether the work is redemption or creation, the volitions of the Son are but the will of the Father accepted and made doubly personal in projection.

After the Ascension. Our Saviour never ceases to be both very God and very man. He never ceases to have the two structural laws fundamental in his being. But after the ascension his life is different from his earthly life. His body now is a glorified body (Phil. 3. 21), and his human nature is lifted out of the cramping limitation of the time process. And yet he has the memory of all the poverty and slavery and suffering of his earthly life; and he also has inherent capacity for all the finite experience which redeemed men will have after their own glorification. Thus, in the most literal sense, our Lord is "one of us everlastingly."

THE THIRD DOCTRINAL DIVISION
OUR LORD'S REDEMPTIVE WORK

Crucifixus est Dei Filius;
non pudet, quia pudendum est;
et mortuus est Dei Filius;
prorsus credibile est,
quia ineptum est:
et sepultus, resurrexit:
certum est, quia impossibile.
— *Tertullian*, De Carne Christi, v.

XVIII. THE HOLINESS OF GOD

In discussing the Christian religion as related to the moral person we glimpsed the subject of the divine holiness; but that glimpse is not enough for our coming discussion. Before trying to apprehend the supreme Christian doctrine of our Lord's redemptive work we need clearly to understand the root of that work; and the root of that work is surely the holiness of God. First, let us turn to the Old Testament.

The Moral Sovereignty of God. The most striking characteristic of the Old Testament is its perpetual consciousness of the fact of God. At every crisis, and even in every smaller turn of history, the scene is filled with God. You hear human voices and see human forms, it is true, but they merely emphasize the dominating presence of the Lord God of Israel. "God was the only force in the world." But when we would get behind this fact of God, when we would learn the exact conception of God held in the Old Testament, our task is not so quickly performed as one might at first suppose. There are very dim places where hardly two Old Testament scholars can agree as to the final meaning; and, what is more confusing still, there sometimes seems to be a shifting from one meaning to another. All this granted, however, yet there is a line of certainty. If we are willing to avoid the insignificant utterances and the sporadic moods, if we are anxious to catch only the general trend in teaching, there will sooner or later appear one mighty intention to urge upon men the moral sovereignty of God. In the Old Testament, God is, primarily, the Divine Ruler, who ever rules with the most strenuous moral regard. He does not, he will not, he cannot palliate sin.

This statement, though, should not be made without making another, a subordinate statement. The divine moral regard taught in the Old Testament, although inflexible, is never heartless. Again and again the ethical strenuousness is relieved somewhat by a note of loving-kindness. There are a number of passages which are to the point; but I wish you specially to note that "very surprising ancient passage" in the book of Exodus (34. 5–7) where Jehovah descends in the cloud, and passes by before Moses, and proclaims himself as "a God merciful and gracious, slow to anger, and abundant in loving-kindness." But even in making this subordinate statement we must preserve the ethical environment. About every gracious utterance in the Old Testament there is an atmosphere charged with moral lightning; and sometimes there is more than the atmosphere, there is the actual flash. Indeed, the actual flash appears in the instance just cited, for the passage, you will remember, closes thus: "and that will by no means clear the guilty, visiting the iniquity of the fathers upon the children, and upon the children's children, upon the third and upon the fourth generation." It has been said that such visitation is injustice, and so cannot be moral, cannot reveal the moral sovereignty of Jehovah. I admit without hesitation that such visitation is downright injustice; and were it in no corrective connection, were there no supplemental revelation, it would be clearly immoral. But in a crude situation, where free and sinful persons are being gradually trained toward a moral goal, injustice itself can be so related to that goal as to become urgent for it, and thus become moral, not in essence, but in effect. Practically considered, anything is moral which in its sum total of influence tends to make men hate sin and love righteousness.

What I hold, then, is this: The cumulating sweep of Old Testament teaching is insistent upon, not the majesty, not the supremacy of God, but his *moral* majesty, his *moral* supremacy. And, further, that the expressions of divine tenderness do not weaken this moral insistence. And, further, that the so-called "immoralities of the Old Testament" are not like the same cruelties and strokes of injustice left ambiguous, or uncorrected, in the natural world; but are so peculiarly connected, and so plainly supplemented, as ultimately to exalt the moral sovereignty of God.

The Fatherhood of God. It is not worth the cost to take sides on the question whether or not the doctrine of the Fatherhood of God is taught in the Old Testament. Even if it is taught there the teaching is out of the main current, and results in a very different degree of emphasis from that which we find in the New Testament. As Professor Sanday has said, "And yet the doctrine of the New Testament assumes such different proportions as almost to amount to a new revelation." Nor is it worth our time to try to analyze the New Testament doctrine of the divine Fatherhood to bring out exactly all the elements in their perfect combination. Indeed, after reading all the important special works on the subject I am far from certain that such an analysis can be made. The one thing essential to us in this discussion, however, stands out very clearly in the New Testament. That one essential thing is this: *God loves men as a perfect father loves his children.* The last word of revelation is not that God is a moral sovereign, but that he is a sovereign Father. Mr. Lidgett's phrase is an exceedingly happy one—God is "*the Father regnant.*"

There is no fundamental contradiction between the conception of the moral sovereignty in the Old Testament and the conception of sovereign Fatherhood in the

New Testament, but there is an extremely important difference in practical emphasis. In the one case, the emphasis is upon enthroned righteousness; in the other case, the emphasis is upon personal love. The righteousness has in it loving-kindness, and the love is thoroughly moral, and yet the change in emphasis creates another world. It is something like the difference between a bright day in January and a bright day in June. Both days have the shining sun; but in January plants freeze even in the sunshine, while in June they grow and burst into bloom. The Old Testament is essentially a world of moral sovereignty, and it is frigid. The New Testament is essentially a world of moral love, and it is creative.

Why is the emphasis in the New Testament upon God's love? There are two reasons which readily come to mind: 1. There is a reason in what may be called the method in the divine pedagogy. Man being what he is, a person, and as he is, a sinner, the first thing necessary to be done for him is to place the most tremendous stress upon the moral fact; but this tremendous stress is sure to generate despair in the sinful moral person. He has the ability to exercise faith, I admit; but the faith exercised under such circumstances cannot complete the man's religious life. Therefore, this extreme stress upon the moral fact is first modified by the Messianic expectation, and then transformed into dynamic gladness by the full revelation of the moral love of God in the gospel of the Son of God as actual Redeemer. 2. The second reason is profounder. The inspired authors of the New Testament are ever writing from the standpoint of the redemptional consciousness. And God's primary motive in redemption *is* love. In other words, God does not make an awful self-sacrifice to save men because he is a moral ruler, and as a moral ruler is seeking to obtain subjects for his kingdom. The point of view is not what *God needs*

rectorally, but what *men can experience*. Both in creation and in salvation God is profoundly thinking of men.
He wants them to have the possibility of moral character,
moral service, and moral fellowship; and then to have the
glorious experience in everlasting joy. True it is, and
we need to repeat it again and again, that God's total
interest in men is a moral interest. He does not care for
a man whether or no. But this divine moral interest is a
vast beneficence, and is not merely an ambition to get
a new colony of citizens.

The Holiness of God. Our discussion thus far has been
of some worth, and yet it has been all on the surface.
When we ask what is meant by *moral* love, the expression
which we have used so freely, we come upon a large
problem in harmony, namely, the fundamental har-
monization of God's personal love for men with his
infinite moral concern. It is easy enough to join the two
things in a phrase, but such verbal work does not shcw
the principle of harmony. And, as a matter of fact, this
principle of harmony has not been seriously sought by
the conventional theologian.

The solution of our problem in harmony lies, I am
convinced, in fully grasping the ultimate, basal meaning
of the divine holiness. First of all, though, let us turn
to the Word of God. The primary significance of the
term *holiness* as used in the Old Testament (קֹדֶשׁ) we
cannot determine beyond a doubt. Several times, in
the last fifteen years, I have been obliged to change my
tentative opinion, until now I am more and more inclined
to think that the word, in its earliest usage, had no distinctly ethical content. Probably it was merely a vaguely
reverent indication of the bare idea of Deity, and probably
the only definite thought *always* in the mind was this: *God
is unapproachable*. Just as in going into the presence of
royalty upon the throne, men would not rush at their

king, but would drop to the earth, or by some peculiar
gesture manifest their reverence, so in a higher degree
they regarded their God as not easily to be approached;
and the term holiness was (not "an otiose epithet")
the rhetorical index of their reverent hesitation before God.
But in the clearest personal moods there must have been
in the mind some reason for the divine unapproachable-
ness; and this reason would naturally correspond with
the conception of God which was held at the time.
Gradually, then, the holiness of God would itself come to
mean as much as the actual conception of God could furnish of content.   Then, as under the great ethical prophets, the whole view concerning Jehovah was charged with
moral quality and with moral intensity, the holiness of
God would, at last, mean nothing less than his absolute
moral perfection.   But, whether we accept this theory
or another, we can safely affirm that there are lofty places
in the Old Testament where the statement that God is
holy certainly means that he is absolutely and inflexibly
righteous.

The term holiness, as used in the New Testament
(ἅγιος, ἁγιότης, ἁγιωσύνη) is one of those words taken
over into Christian thinking and filled with a new
spirit.   Admittedly the word has a point of connection
in the old Greek usage, but in the New Testament it
gains ethical tone and fullness.   Professor Stevens says:
"The Christian use of the word lifted it into accord with
the highest ethical conceptions, and gave it the idea of
separateness from the sinful world, harmony with God,
the absolutely Good Being, moral perfection.   Thus
ἅγιος is, above all things, a qualitative and ethical term."
The prophets of the Old Testament were, I believe, the
teachers who made possible this final moral establishment of the idea of holiness.   In the Christian view the
holy man is the man whose entire being is organized under

moral concern. But when the term is applied to God the full Christian meaning is, I think, something more. It is that God is both absolutely perfect and absolutely moral. In God there is no blemish of any kind whatsoever; but this divine perfection is urged with the most intense ethical emphasis. God is perfect *and* he is righteous. The Christian conception *starts* with God's perfection and *culminates* in his moral life. It is not that God is perfect because he is moral, but rather that he is moral because he is perfect. Thus God's moral life obtains its awful unyieldingness, for it is rooted in the wholeness of the Infinite Being. This point I must insist upon, for it has, when we come to the doctrine of the atonement, the most vital importance. The final Christian idea is that God must be ethically satisfied, not because he bechances to have a moral standard, but because he has a moral standard *and*—AND this moral standard is the necessary expression of his absolute perfection.

This is the Christian view, as I understand it; can we give to it any clarity by philosophical consideration? I think we can in the following manner: The fundamental individuality of God himself is under law, in the sense that it is a complex of initial qualities made organic under an eternal plan of harmony. An attribute, say that of justice, cannot exist in God in isolated pulsation, but must enter into modifying relations. Justice must come to terms with all God is. Perhaps you will understand me better if we think for a moment of the most noble kind of a man. In fact, it was by studying such a man that I first found the clue to the point. This most noble kind of a man is never just, never absolutely just, for his sense of justice is always chastened by other noble qualities which he possesses. In truth, no Christian man could be merely just for even one day and not cease to be a Christian. No one thing in large manhood gets its

own way entirely. I will not say that lofty character
is a compromise, for the word compromise has taken on
a flavor of weakness, if not of positive unrighteousness;
but I will say that every lofty character is a modification
of many qualities into harmonious reciprocity. Much
more, then, it seems to me, is the individuality of God an
organic whole where many items of attribute are modified
and adjusted unto complete harmony. This underlying
plan of adjustment, determining precisely to what extent,
and precisely in what connection, an attribute is to have
force, is what I understand by the law of God's holiness.
Therefore, the law of holiness, or holiness in the divine
nature, is the finality, the fundament of all God's being.

Holding fast to this view of basal holiness in God,
we have a clear entrance into the significance of his
moral concern. God is a personal Being and so is
both self-conscious and self-decisive. The law of holiness appears in self-consciousness, and the result is
moral distinction with moral obligation. (This will be
considered under moral law.) Toward this moral distinction and obligation God bears in self-decision.
This self-decisive attitude toward the eternal distinction between right and wrong is the divine moral
concern. In intrinsic personal meaning this moral concern in God exactly corresponds to a man's loyalty to
righteousness. But in application to God the word
loyalty is unsuitable, for personal loyalty implies the
pressure of antagonistic motives, and the absolute God
has no antagonism in motive. And yet the divine adoption of the law of holiness is not mechanical, but a genuine
personalization of that law. Quickly you will catch my
meaning if you think of the life of a saint in the final
glory. He is established, perfectly fixed in moral character,
and so he has only one sort of motive urgent toward
volition; but nevertheless his decision is not an automatic

spring at a mark—it is a self-decision made in the full vision of self-consciousness.

We are now prepared to deal directly with our problem in harmony. Our question is this: How can we harmonize the moral concern of God with his love for men? Or we can state the question in another way: How can God have toward man a unitary bearing which has in it both personal love and moral concern? First of all, I must entirely reject the pantheistic view that the love of God has primary relation to man; that man, or at least some moral person, must be created to furnish an object for the divine interest as an inherent and original yearning. This view has crept into the very life of modern thinking, and the result is a sentimentalism which is most unwholesome. God had no intrinsic need of men, or of any created objects for his love. The love of God is eternally complete, eternally infinite as an actual experience in the triune Godhead, an experience belonging to the ineffable fellowship of the divine Persons.

Next, let us notice the wonderful relation which this eternal love of God sustains to the law of holiness. *Love is the dynamic of the law of holiness.* It is by means of this very love that the organization of the Godhead is effected. The law of holiness becomes personal in moral concern, but it becomes dynamic in personal love. Thus, love is the holiness of God absolutely actualized in personal experience. And thus, the eternal love of God is the most intensely moral feature in the whole life of the Godhead.

Coming now to God's love for man, what is it? exactly how much does it mean? It is infinite moral beneficence, neither more nor less. The love of God for man (whether we have in mind God the Father, or all the divine Persons in one individual organism) is but a moral longing to have all men achieve the everlasting experience in personality of moral concern made dynamic in the rejoicing fellowship of moral love. In other words, God's interest in men is an unselfish reflex of the divine manner of life. God wants men to have, in their finite capacity, the same kind of moral organism, the same kind of moral joy in fellowship, that the Persons of the Godhead have in their infinite capacity. Thus, our problem in harmony is solved by regarding the love of God for men as nothing other than an altruistic manifestation of his moral concern itself.

The Wrath of God. Already we have considered God's hatred of sin as expressed in depravity, in the natural world, in the broken brotherhood of man, and in the abnormal event of human death; but, if we are true to the whole message of the gospel, we must go further, and teach that this divine hatred of sin is also manifested in a bearing of wrath toward sinful men. Often in our preaching we say, "God hates sin, but he loves the sinner." The utterance is profoundly Christian in spirit, but it should never be taken to mean that the immediate divine attitude is complacent toward a man now in sin; as if the man himself could be actually separated from his action and motive. The plain Christian fact is that the immediate attitude of God toward any and every sinner is one of anger. While God will do all possible things to rescue a man from sin, he bears toward the man in positive wrath every moment of his sinful life, provided that the sin is personal sin involving moral responsibility.

Sometimes this wrath of God is regarded as so purely and so intensely personal that it amounts to hardly more than a self-determined, infinite, personal grievance against the sinner. And, again, the wrath is regarded as so impersonal, so much a consequence of law, that it amounts to hardly more than automatic fury. Bishop Martensen, in his Dogmatics, gives us an illuminating word when he says: The wrath of God is "a revelation of love restrained, hindered, and stayed through unrighteousness." His meaning is that God's love is like a torrent in mighty rush, and when you try to dam the rushing stream it beats in violence against the obstacle. But Martensen's conception requires a most careful treatment, or it, too, will drop all ethical quality in a mechanical movement. In some way the wrath of God must be first lifted out of all possibility of caprice and then filled with personal decision. It must be made a thing of both law and personality. As a protective enlargement of Bishop Martensen's conception, I will state my own entire view of the wrath of God:

1. The fundament of the matter is the law of the holiness of God.

2. In every situation the primary demand is that this law of holiness shall be expressed.

3. The objective expression of this law of holiness is always by the personal decision of God, and therefore the expression is a thing of both law and personality.

4. In a normal situation, where there is a response in the yielding of the moral person, the law of holiness is fully expressed by the unitary bearing of God in simple moral love. That is, God's entire interest comes out in one throb of infinite longing for the moral completion of the man's life.

5. In an abnormal situation, where on the part of the moral person there is actual resistance instead of a yielding response, the law of holiness can be expressed only by a twofold bearing, in which two things are emphasized, namely, a desire to rescue the sinner, and an inflexible regard for the law of holiness. It is a case where the freedom of man throws God's bearing out of normal tendency and makes necessary a separate emphasis upon moral concern.

6. In a situation which is not only abnormal, but also irrevocably so, the law of holiness can be expressed only by moral concern alone. In this hopeless situation God's only interest is in holiness. I well know how out of range it is with the temper of the *Zeitgeist*, but we should firmly say this: The holy God does not, and cannot, love a moral person who has in his freedom forever settled it that he will have no moral life. Such a man must be everlastingly under the full wrath of God. Moral love is not now beating against an obstacle, it has been finally rejected and flung back into the primary insistence upon the law of holiness.

XIX. THE MORAL GOVERNMENT

The Moral Law. As a starting point in rejection, I will analyze that view of the moral law which was given by Hugo Grotius in his famous Defensio, and which became the foundation of the pure governmental theory of the atonement.

1. There are two kinds of divine laws: First, those laws which are grounded in the nature of things; or *the absolute laws*, such as, for example, the law against bearing false witness. Second, those laws which were created by the naked will of God; or *the positive laws*, such as, for example, a ceremonial law.

2. An absolute law is fully irrelaxable. A positive law is not, in itself, irrelaxable, although it may be made irrelaxable by a divine oath, or by a promise of God, or by a special decree that it shall not be changed.

3. The law involved in the atonement is that sin shall be punished according to its demerit, or with a punishment "corresponding to the crime" (*pœnâ tali quæ culpæ respondeat*).

4. This law that sin shall be punished according to its demerit is not grounded in the nature of things, and is therefore a positive law, and is therefore by nature relaxable.

5. Now comes the question, Has this law, as to the punishment of sin, ever been made irrelaxable by a divine oath, or by a promise of God, or by a special decree? After a discussion of Scripture which is remarkably shrewd even for a consummate lawyer, Grotius answers, No; neither by oath, nor by promise, nor by special decree, has this positive penal law been made unalterable.

6. The law, then, that sin shall be punished with a punishment "corresponding to the crime" can be changed whenever God so determines. Thus, the way is prepared for the Grotian theory of substitution.

One is tempted to criticise this Grotian conception of the moral law from end to end, but we have no time to spend on such wasteful work. I will say only this much, If there is even the tiniest spark of *reality* in the view I have no ability to make the priceless discovery. In the one place where Grotius could touch reality (the idea that something is deeper than the volition of God as personal) his treatment of the place results in distinctions which are as unreal as they are ingenious.

But it is not enough to reject Grotius; we need to find a larger conception of the moral law. If we cannot lift the view of the moral law out of this atmosphere of the court of justice, there is not even the slenderest possibility of effecting any conviction in the Christian consciousness. The Christian man knows right well that the God of his salvation does not deal with men like a justice of the Supreme Court. In seeking this larger conception of the moral law our work is not a minute biblical exposition, but rather a philosophical study based upon the entire sweep of Christian teaching. Were we to consider Saint Paul alone, our final conclusion would be larger than any which could be exegetically drawn from his use of the term νόμος, although his use of that one word would surely, in some passages, carry us far beyond the Mosaic law.

Before stating my own conception of the moral law, there is one important thing to be done in preparation, namely, to trace moral distinction to its causal finality. We touched upon the matter in our discussion of the holiness of God, but the full consideration was, for pedagogical reasons, left over for this connection. Our question is this: Passing beyond the relative right, what makes any absolutely right thing *right*, or any absolutely wrong thing *wrong?* Where and what is the eternal fundament of moral distinction? where and how is the eternal fixture of moral fact? There are several answers which I must instantly reject. The causal finality is not arbitrary. It is not what Horace Bushnell once denominated "the bare almightiness of God." The sheer divine will does not create moral distinction, and then by naked volition fix one thing as right and another thing as wrong. Nor is there a law of moral distinction and fact beyond God, a law which can be conceived of as separate from God, "grounded in the nature of things." There is no "nature of things" outside of God and in eternal operation. God is the total ultimate. I will not try to thrust even a point of imagination in behind God. All this suggestion of "two Infinites," one of them being the personal God, and the other being an impersonal somewhat, can have no lodgment in my philosophy of the Christian faith. Nor is Dr. Dale's view that "in God the law is *alive*"—that "it reigns on his throne, sways his scepter, is crowned with his glory"—altogether satisfactory. Dale was, I am sure, on the track of the fact, but he did not quite clear up his thinking. He does not seem to be certain what and where this law is which comes to life in God. Sometimes the law appears to be placed in God, and then, again, outside of God. And then, again, the law is treated as if it were a pure abstraction, an economical point of departure in thinking. But the law which Dale needed, and which probably he was seeking, is the law of God's own organism, the law of holiness. This law of holiness is profounder than the personal life of God, and yet it does come to dominion only in that personal life. It has all the steadiness of a necessary impersonal Infinite; and yet it becomes ethical in personal experience and becomes completely effective in personal love.

In closer work let us now see how this law of holiness is personally ethicalized. You will remember that in our study of personality we made a distinction between the two beats in self-consciousness, self-grasp and self-estimate? The same distinction is of worth in clearing up the situation here. When in self-grasp God seizes the law of holiness, or the basic plan of his own harmonious life, he places an estimate upon it, and that estimate is the personal beginning of the whole moral world. In that estimate there are two features: first, moral distinction; second, moral obligation. That is, God both makes in self-consciousness an eternal difference between right and wrong and feels that the law of holiness insists upon the right. The feeling of this insistence is the *original* "sunrise of the moral ought." To this moral ought, expressing the law of holiness in positive demand, God gives himself in eternal self-commitment; and this self-commitment is moral concern, or the divine personal righteousness. Now we are on the watch for the definite moral fact. A moral fact, absolutely considered, is anything in harmony with the law of holiness thus personalized. For example, it is wrong to tell a lie, not because there is a law to such effect "grounded in the nature of things," and not because God has arbitrarily willed it so; but because God *must* will it so to satisfy the personalized law of holiness. God himself cannot will a falsehood, cannot will contrary to truth or reality, and not violate his own moral concern for the law of holiness as that law is grasped and estimated in the divine self-consciousness. Words are poor tools here, but through all their poverty you will not fail to note the important thing which I am trying to do for Christian ethics by tracing all moral life back to an unyielding fundament without sacrificing the philosophical and practical significance of the personal God of the Christian faith.   Of course, my analysis is sheer speculation, but it is a speculation which lends itself constantly to wholesome Christian thinking and feeling.   And, further, you will not fail to note that my view supplies a clue to every element in the conscience of man, and indicates how profoundly man has been created in the image of God.   In a final brief word, then, a thing is absolutely right, not because God wills it, but because God wills it in harmony with the plan of his own being as realized in his own personal life. Browning (as usual) is not far from the truth when he says:

> " I trust in God—the right shall be right
> And other than the wrong, while HE endures."

I will now state, as succinctly as may be, my full conception of the moral law.   It is nothing other than the law of God's holiness realized in his personal experience, and may be itemized as follows:

1. The law of holiness in the nature of God.   This is the bare plan of harmony according to which the entire Godhead is one individual organism.

2. The law of holiness in the self-consciousness of God. As the law is grasped it is estimated, and thence arises moral distinction and moral obligation.

3. The law of holiness in the self-decision of God.   As the moral obligation appears, God eternally yields to it in self-commitment, and thence arises the personal bearing of moral concern, and all specific volitions determining moral fact.   In moral concern, God wills every right thing to be a right thing.

4. The law of holiness in the personal fellowship of moral love.   The law of holiness is the plan of harmony; but the plan is actually carried out, the holiness is perfectly effected under the supreme motive of love which

the persons of the Godhead have in their fellowship. For example, the law of holiness requires that the attribute of justice shall be modified to a certain extent; but this modification is accomplished only under the impulse of moral love, not God's love for man or any creature, but that love which binds the persons of the Godhead together in blessed fellowship. Just as we found, in our study of the moral person, that moral love is the one motive powerful enough to organize completely his whole being, so the Infinite Being himself becomes an organism by means of moral love. I say here, too, *moral* love, for the love of God gathers up the entire moral process in personality and so has in it moral distinction, moral obligation, and moral concern. But these moral *momenta* are all transmuted into rapture by a personal love which is absolutely unselfish. In this way the divine moral life is lifted out of the frigid dreadfulness of mere duty, the moral ought is made a thing of rejoicing enthusiasm. In moral concern no person of the Godhead is thinking of himself; he feels that concern *in* his love for the other persons. Thus, we are able to conceive of an inflexible moral life which is also completely altruistic.

The Moral Law in the Moral Government. Again we come to that great principle of personal expression. When we urge this principle as a law inherent in the divine personal life it may look at first as if we were yielding a tribute, if not a full assent, to the pantheistic idea of the necessary development of Deity. But we are yielding no tribute whatever. According to our view, no manifestation unfolds in any way the individuality of God. Nor is any expression necessary to achieve, or to develop, the personality of God. Already, God is a Being absolutely perfect in both individuality and personality. The expression is purely personal. It is the normal activity, you might almost say the vocation, of personality. Personality cannot be idle, it must be doing something, it wants "to get out under the sky." This is a totally different notion from that involved in pantheism, different practically as well as theoretically. I will, however, admit this much: Were there only one person in the Godhead, this principle of expression would be entangled with a need of personal fellowship; and the solitary God would, in his awful loneliness, be driven to create persons to satisfy this social need; for it is simply inconceivable that any self-conscious being could live eternally alone. Even this would not lead (necessarily) to pantheism, but it would make the universe of created persons so fundamentally necessary to complete God's life that a most unwholesome sentimentalism would be the outcome in theology. But the doctrine of the Trinity saves us from the sentimental entanglement. Moral persons are created by the triune God of the Christian faith under the motive of beneficence united with the principle of personal self-expression.

The case as to the expression is, however, still clearer when we begin to consider the moral government; for the moral government deals with finite persons after they have been created; and there can be no question but that God must deal with them according to the law of his own inner life, and not according to an arbitrary plan prepared for the occasion. God must so act toward moral creatures as to express truly what he is in himself. God could not create even a wake-robin as a mere whim, much less could he be arbitrary in matters of moral destiny. There are to-day writers who hold (if I understand them) that the moral law was made by the will of God on purpose to govern moral persons. Such a view is entirely beyond my credence. The moral law is eternal from its base to its summit, from the basal plan of holiness to the crowning experience of moral love. There would have been the moral law, precisely the same, too, had the universe of things and persons never been willed into existence. But this eternal, this unchangeable law does find a new expression in the moral government of God. Indeed, the moral government is nothing other than the moral law itself now related, in a scheme of perfect economy, to all created moral persons. It is the holiness of God made active in actual administration.

The Goal of the Moral Government. In this administration the moral government has an end in view, has a definite goal which it is ever seeking to reach. This goal may be conceived under the figure of three concentric circles. The comprehensive outer circle is the *cosmic goal.* At last, under the moral government, the entire universe is to manifest the perfect holiness of God. Often it has been affirmed that such a complete cosmic expression of holiness requires that every individual moral person shall ultimately become holy. I do not see any force in the affirmation. What is required is this: The final universe must express all God is. And therefore every created person must at last be so placed and so treated as to reveal the moral law in its long reach from the law of holiness, on through moral concern, to moral love. But it is interposed, "A sinner forever unsaved could not evince the moral love of God." Why not, I ask, if God *had loved him and used all the resources of the Godhead to save him, and his everlasting condition and placement manifested all the facts?*

The middle circle is *the goal of the individual holy person.* I am now thinking of angels, and all individual moral persons, who have no racial connection. The outcome in this individual goal is more than a bare expression of divine holiness; it is such an expression in all the joy of actual fellowship with God. All holy persons are to be admitted into the presence of God, and to witness the glory of God. It will not quite answer to say that the δόξα is enlarged, but we can say that it is accommodated to the moral creature, so that he can, in a finite measure, take part in the ineffable experience of the Godhead. In no absolute sense can a creature ever be like God, whether in being or in experience; but a holy creature can live in the blaze of the infinite life and never be consumed; can gather into consciousness the supreme felicity and never be overwhelmed. The innermost circle is the *racial goal*. This innermost goal has all the significance of the other two, as to expression of holiness and fellowship with God; but it has, further, a peculiarity of its own. Both the expression and the fellowship are to be with a racial emphasis. The race of mankind is to be made a holy brotherhood; and in perfect social solidarity is to be taken into the divine δόξα, and is there to enjoy all God is and manifest all God is. Thus, the goal of the moral government is one goal, as to the expression of holiness; but three united goals, as to the manner of expression.

The fact of a goal to be reached implies *intentional movement* toward it; and this movement is the one key to all method in the moral government. God does this or allows that, all because he is trying *to move*. For the sake of economy, let us now keep man alone in mind, inasmuch as we are working specially toward man's redemption. Men are sinners and men are free persons, and therefore holiness cannot be expressed at a stroke, as omnipotence might be expressed. The full expression can be achieved only by means of a gradual movement which ends in the goal. *This movement is secured by augment in expression.* That is, in every situation the moral government is trying to get into concrete manifestation something more of God's moral law than was evident before. Connected with this principle of augment is the principle of crisis. Now and again the history breaks into great points of meaning where the moral law completely dominates the event; and the movement under moral government fairly leaps toward the goal. But the one supremely important thing to fasten in the mind, before we take up such details of moral government as penalty and moral requirement, is this idea of movement by augment toward the goal.

Moral Requirement. The moral requirement is what the moral government requires, as a moral demand, in any given stage of the movement on toward the final goal. In the Garden of Eden the requirement was: "But of the tree of the knowledge of good and evil, thou shalt not eat of it" (Gen. 2. 17). Whatever this was in fact, it was a temporary demand suitable to the childhood of the race; but still it was the beginning of a movement toward the goal, and never is it to be treated out of relation to that movement.

Another stage in moral requirement is expressed in the Decalogue, or the Law of the Ten Words, where morality and religion are knit together in "a charter of ethical piety." For our present purpose it is not necessary to discuss the relation this law sustains to the different codes of Hebrew law. (See article by Professor Driver in the Hastings Dictionary, vol. iii, p. 64.) All we need is to note the loftiest point in the Hebrew conception of moral requirement. On the one hand, we are not to regard the Decalogue as an unimportant matter of merely local significance; and, on the other hand, we are not to regard it as a finality. The Decalogue was fulfilled by our Lord. Following Turretin, some theologians have taught that the Decalogue needed no correction, and our Lord only brought out its real meaning. But our Lord's new interpretation amounted to a correction of the whole spirit of the Decalogue, and was a mighty movement toward the goal of the moral government.

As Professor Paterson has shown (Hastings Dictionary, vol. i, p. 580), it is quite "possible to construct with scarcely a gap the Decalogue according to Christ"; and at every point there is movement toward the larger ideal. Following the law of Christ, one does not cease to be a moral man; but he passes into the spirit of moral love, which now fills his consciousness and gives motive for the most noble conduct. It is somewhat as if a man having a lofty ideal of duty, but also having with this ideal of duty a spirit of sheer legalism, should suddenly find himself in active possession of a great heart throbbing warmly toward man and God. Would he not be surprised? The exact truth is in the utterance of Saint Paul when he says: "Love therefore is the fulfillment of the law." (Read Rom. 13. 8–10.)

Penalty. There are two very different views of the significance of penalty in the moral government: One view is that penalty is the automatic visitation of justice upon the offender in precise regard to his guilt. Just as fire will burn you to the extent of your exposure, so justice will reach you to the exact extent of your sinful exposure. According to this view, when extremely and consistently held, there is in penalty no reformatory aim and no deterrent office. The other and opposing view is that all penalty is really utilitarian—reformatory, or educational, or in some way protective of moral interests. In this connection Dr. John Miley did some wise work in trying to weld the two views. In his Systematic Theology (ii, 173) he says: "There are the two offices of justice. But they must never be separated. Penalty, as a means in the use of justice, has an end beyond the retribution of sin. But, whatever its ulterior end, it is just only as it threatens or falls upon, demerit. And only thus can it fulfill its high office in the interest of moral government. It is the failure first properly to discriminate the two offices of justice in the punishment of sin and the protection of rights, and then properly to combine the two elements in the one doctrine of punishment, that the rectoral atonement exposes itself to really serious objections, which yet have no validity against a true construction of the theory." This is a complete answer to those who claim that to hold the rectoral aim and worth of penalty is to have "no ground of punishment but the benefit of others." But my objection to the rectoral theory is not in the least like the objection of those represented by Dr. Charles Hodge. To me, the whole utilitarian conception, even if so modified that "the law of expediency [only] determines the measure of divine penalties within the demerit of sin," is not profound enough. It does perpetual violence to the *awful note of reality* in redemption. I am not satisfied with automatic penalty, nor with expedient penalty, nor with the two kinds joined together to express the office of justice. We must have, I believe, the larger conception that the aim in all penalty is so to express, not the justice of God, but the holiness of God, as to secure actual movement toward the final goal of moral government. This expression of the divine holiness is not automatic, and yet it is as *necessary* as though it were automatic. This expression of the divine holiness is not an expedient either, and yet it has more moral value in the moral government than any expedient could have. Penalty is for actual movement toward the holy goal. And so the only way to do without a given penalty is to procure such a substitute for it as will express more completely or more intensely the holiness of God.

XX. THE CHRISTIAN MEANING OF DEATH

BEFORE considering the teaching of the Bible which
bears directly upon the death of Christ, we need to determine what meaning death itself has from the Christian
point of view. My plan is first to indicate the non-
Christian conceptions of death; then to examine the Bible
in both Testaments; then to furnish a philosophy of death
adequate to express and protect the Christian meaning.

NON-CHRISTIAN CONCEPTIONS

The Idealization of Death. Death is idealized into a
friendly and even beautiful event by some of the modern
philosophical writers, but especially by the modern
poets. This poetic idealization is not to be explained
by the natural temper of the poet, which inclines him to
"transform a stump into a stairway," but rather by the
fact that he is (with notable exceptions) a heathen mystic
made superficially hopeful by a Christian atmosphere.
He is an easy optimist who has never paid the ethical
price of a profound optimism. A perfect example of
this class is Walt Whitman, who has influenced modern
poetry in a most subtle manner. In a poem, written as
a protest against the thoroughly Christian painting,
Death's Valley, by George Inness, Whitman says:

"Nay, do not dream, designer dark,
Thou hast portrayed or hit thy theme entire:
I, hoverer of late by this dark valley, by its confines, having glimpses
    of it,
Here enter lists with thee, claiming my right to make a symbol too.

"For I have seen many wounded soldiers die,
After dread suffering—have seen their lives pass off with smiles;
And I have watched the death-hours of the old; and seen the infant die;
The rich, with all his nurses and his doctors;
And then the poor, in meagerness and poverty;
And I myself for long, O Death, have breathed my every breath
Amid the nearness and the silent thought of thee.

"And out of these and thee,
I make a scene, a song, brief (not fear of thee,
Nor gloom's ravines, nor bleak, nor dark—for I do not fear thee,
Nor celebrate the struggle, or contortion, or hard-tied knot),
Of the broad blessed light and perfect air, with meadows, rippling
      tides, and trees and flowers and grass,
And the low hum of living breeze—and in the midst God's beautiful
      eternal right hand,
Thee, holiest minister of Heaven—thee, envoy, usherer, guide at last
      of all,
Rich, florid, loosener of the stricture-knot called life,
Sweet, peaceful, welcome Death."

The Scientific View of Death. This scientific view Dr.
Newman Smyth has gathered up, for popular service, in
his interesting apologetic, The Place of Death in Evolution. For our purpose here we do not require the
details of the discussion. The gist of it all is that, as a
result of scientific investigation, death is regarded as a
servant of life in the economy of nature. Death is not a
finality of failure, but a sacrifice to secure a higher process
of life. Death is a crucial feature in the normal movement toward the finest vitality. Dr. Smyth says: "As
life becomes more organized and complex, death pre-
vails. It comes to reign on earth, because it comes to
serve. At length in the history of life a living form arose,
so multicellular and so well organized that it ceased to
continue the course of life, simply by dividing and mul-
tiplying itself into daughter cells; it had acquired the
power of giving up its life for another; it died in order that
its offspring might continue its life in forms struggling to
still higher organization and better fitted to survive while

it must perish. One parent form passes away in order that others may catch up the motion of life, and in turn transmit to others life's rhythm and joy. Thus death comes in to help, and not merely to hurt; to help life further on and higher up, not to put a stop to life."

THE CONCEPTION OF DEATH IN THE BIBLE

In the Old Testament. By death the writers of the Old Testament usually mean what we mean by physical or bodily death—not annihilation, but the cessation of this existence on earth by the separation of the soul from the body. Professor A. B. Davidson says: "By death the Old Testament means what we mean when we use the word. It is the phenomenon which we observe. Now, all parts of the Old Testament indicate the view that at death the person is not annihilated; he continues to subsist in Sheol, the place of the dead, though in a shadowy and feeble form occasioned by the withdrawal of the spirit of life."

Sometimes the objection has been raised that *death* as used in Gen. 2. 17 ("for in the day that thou eatest thereof thou shalt surely die") could not have meant bodily death, inasmuch as Adam and Eve did not, according to the account, die a bodily death on the day of their disobedience. But the real meaning of the Hebrew is not fully brought out in our English Bible, not even in the Revised Version. The real meaning is (see Dillmann's Commentary *in loco*): "Death will be certainly for thee the consequence thereof." But even if the English translation were correct, the objection would have no force; for death is a long process which only culminates in the final separation of the soul from the body. As a matter of direful fact, a man begins to die as soon as he is born. Our entire relation to the natural world is one of death; and many of us have a hard fight of it to keep alive at all.

As Martin Luther said in his Table Talk: "Death peeps out at every limb."

I carefully examined about two hundred passages, where the term *death* is either used or implied, in the Old Testament; and I did not find one where the meaning was not (plainly or probably) that of bodily death. In some instances, though, it seemed to me that the whole meaning of the statement was not exhausted by the idea of bodily death. It was bodily death *and* a peculiar background.

In the New Testament. We have in the New Testament a much more complicated situation. But we can start with at least two certain points: First, that in the New Testament the usage is sometimes like the prevailing usage of the Old Testament, the term *death* meaning nothing more than bodily death; and, second, that in the New Testament the usage is sometimes most comprehensive, the term *death* meaning *the total present condition of the sinner*. Now the question comes up, Does the term *death* ever mean in the New Testament narrowly and precisely moral, or spiritual, death? So eminent an authority on New Testament words as Professor Hermann Cremer says, No (Wörterbuch, *in loco*). But I cannot be so certain. There are a number of places where, as in the second chapter of Ephesians, both text and context would seem to require a meaning sharply beyond the general idea of an abnormal total condition produced by sin, a meaning exactly corresponding to that disintegration of conscience which we are wont to call moral death.

Again we have, as a striking peculiarity of the book of the Revelation, the expression, "second death." Without doubt this means, not the annihilation of the wicked, but their everlasting punishment. In his Critical History of the Doctrine of a Future Life, Professor Charles says: "The second death is the death of the soul, as the first is the death of the body. It is not the annihilation, but the endless torment of the wicked that is here meant."

Death and Sin. As to the relation which sin sustains to the "second death," and to every phase of moral death, we need no argument whatever. Nor is it economy to spend out time in proving that in the Old Testament sin and bodily death are placed in a penal connection. Our crucial question is this: Does Saint Paul teach that bodily death is a penal consequence of Adam's transgression? The test passages are 1 Cor. 15. 21–22 and Rom. 5. 12. To economize, we will consider only the passage from Romans. It reads thus: "Therefore, as through one man sin entered into the world, and death through sin; and so death passed unto all men, for that all sinned." The matter is of such extreme importance that we will deal with it through exegetical authority:

Gifford on Romans (The Speaker's Commentary). "That death must here be understood in its primary sense as the death of the body, is clear from the connection with verse 14, where no other meaning is admissible, and from the unmistakable reference to the narrative in Genesis (Gen. 2. 17) and the sentence there pronounced, 'Dust thou art, and unto dust shalt thou return' (Gen. 3. 19)."

Beet on Romans. "We have no indication that the word *death* (chap. 5. 12–19) means anything except the death of the body. The argument rests on the story of Genesis; and there we have no hint of any death except (Gen. 3. 19) the return of dust to dust. The proof in Rom. 5. 14 of the statement in verse 12 refers evidently to the visible reign of natural death. And the comparison of Adam and Christ requires no other meaning of the word. Through one man's sin the race was condemned to go down into the grave; and through one man's obedience and one divine proclamation of pardon believers will obtain a life beyond the grave. The whole argument is but a development of 1 Cor. 15. 22."

Vaughan on Romans. "Natural death, primarily, and as the punishment specially denounced; *spiritual* and *eternal* death, incidentally and secondarily, as the necessary consequence of the severance of a creature from the service and love of the Creator."

Meyer on Romans. "The θάνατος is physical death viewed as the separation of the soul from the body and its transference to Hades. Had Paul taken θάνατος in *another* sense, therefore, he must have definitely indicated it, in order to be understood."

Godet on Romans. That the meaning is physical death Godet says "is confirmed besides by the obvious allusion to the narrative of Genesis (2. 17 and 3. 19) as well as by the explanation in the following verses (13 and 14), where the word death is evidently taken in the strict sense."

Orello Cone (Paul, the Man, the Missionary, and the Traveler). "That the θάνατος of Rom. 5. 12 is primarily physical death there can be no doubt, not only on account of the analogy of the Jewish theology, but also because the word is employed without any indication that other than its literal sense is intended."

Bruce (Saint Paul's Conception of Christianity). "When Saint Paul says, 'So death passed upon all men,' does he allude to the familiar fact of physical dissolution, or is death to be taken comprehensively as including at once temporal, spiritual, and eternal consequences? If my conjecture as to the Adam-Christ train of thought be correct, we must understand θάνατος in the restricted sense."

The Mood of the Bible. The exegesis of this or that passage of Scripture does not, however, furnish us with the full case. The Bible has a *mood* toward physical death. This mood is expressed, for instance, in the

ninetieth psalm, that "most pathetic description of the
drift of the generations of men into darkness." And
even such seeming breaks in the mood as we find in the
third chapter of the book of Job really only serve to emphasize the general attitude of the Bible toward bodily
death. In the Old Testament the mood is one of profound sadness; but in the New Testament the mood
changes and is intensified into the most unmitigated
hostility to physical death. Death is not regarded as
"my good friend death," but as man's relentless enemy
to be overcome only by the power of Jesus Christ, the
Son of God. And so, even if there were no definite text
in point, we would need to explain this mood from the
standpoint of redemption and the Christian consciousness; and such an explanation would require the precise
connection between bodily death and the divine punishment of sin. In one sentence, there is not the slightest
doubt but that the Word of God treats physical death as
an abnormal human event coming upon the race as an
immediate penalty for the Adamic disobedience of God's
command.

Conclusions. But our study of the teaching of the
Bible, more thoroughly gathered up, results in the following definite conclusions:

1. While the Bible sometimes teaches that the condition of the sinner is a state of spiritual death, and that
this spiritual death eventuates in everlasting punishment,
it nevertheless puts the most significant stress upon
bodily death.

2. Bodily death is not regarded as a friendly or useful
event, as a normal feature in a beneficial process of
nature; but is regarded as abnormal and hostile and
terrible.

3. The explanation of this biblical attitude toward
bodily death is to be found in just one thing, namely,

that this death expresses God's inflexible hatred of sin, is the penal stamp which he has fixed upon the entire human race because of man's original transgression.

4. The consequent Christian bearing toward bodily death is one of sorrow, dread, and hatred; and all this lifted into solemn triumph by means of the Lord Jesus Christ alone. Saint Paul has the exact, full Christian feeling when he bursts out: "*But*—thanks be to God, which giveth us the victory through our Lord Jesus Christ."

A PHILOSOPHICAL STUDY OF DEATH

What is Death? In practical speech death is the negation of life. Death is the absence of life. It does not carry with it necessarily the idea of total annihilation. Surely there might be death with annihilation, but usually there is no such entire destruction of the object in death. For example, here is a tree which has been entirely dead for months; but it still stands with trunk, branches, bark, and roots—the tree has not been annihilated, but it is dead.

What is Life? But when we say that "Death is the absence of life," what do we mean by *life?* In his First Principles, Herbert Spencer says, "Life is definable as the continuous adjustment of internal relations to external relations." But such adjustment is rather what life does than what life is. A better definition is that of Bishop Dahle: "Life is that force in an organism which places all other forces, working in it, in serviceable relation to its growth and preservation." This is very close to the fact, but not quite complete. Let us begin with the idea of an organism. An organism is a complex of essential parts, every part making contribution to the common end, and all the parts interdependent. That is the lowest organic condition. In a higher organism every part must be both means and end—by which I mean that every part gets as much as it gives. In the highest conceivable organism, like the personal organism of the Trinity, not only is every part essential to the organism, but also the entire organism is essential to every part; that is, the very existence of every part is possible only in and by means of the entire organism. Now, what I understand by life is this: *It is the power of organic action*. Or, it is the power which every organism has to act as an organism. That tree is dead because its power to act as an organic tree is gone. The parts of the tree are still in action as separate parts, change after change taking place, but the parts do not act together to accomplish a common purpose, and so the tree *as a tree* is dead. And the death of the tree began the very moment any smallest feature of the tree went its own way and no longer made contribution to the common task. Thus, life is the power of reciprocity in action, and death is the absence of that power. And so the inevitable mark of death is the breaking up of an organism. In the beginning of death the organism begins to break up; and in the completion of death the organism is entirely broken up. There is no need, with Bishop Dahle, to emphasize the ideas of growth and preservation, for the organism will take care of itself and exercise every organic function, if it only has the power of organic action.

The Organism of a Man. Already, in considering the racial nexus, I have called your attention to the fact that the human body has great importance in Christian doctrine; but here I wish to get at the same point from another angle. The organism of a man is not completed in the soul alone; full manhood requires both soul and body. But we must be careful at this point not to yield an inch to the materialists. The Christian conception is squarely between the two extremes: 1. That the soul is dependent upon the body for existence itself; and, 2. That the man is complete as a bare personal soul. Speaking of Saint Paul's teaching, Professor Charles says: "According to the apostle, on the other hand [over against Philo's idea that the body is the enemy of the soul], though the flesh is in antagonism with the spirit, there is no such antagonism between the body and the spirit. Nay, rather the body is indispensable to the completed well-being of the latter. A bodiless human spirit is 'naked,' is in a state of weakness and deprivation."

The biblical emphasis upon the importance of the body can be thus related to the conception which I have given of life and death: Man is a personal soul, or a spirit, in such vital fitness with a physical body that the two, soul and body, make in their plan one organism. When the organic relation is perfect, then there is the full manifestation of human life; when the organic relation is impaired, there is the first note of death; and when the organism is entirely broken up, then death is complete.

The Source of Life. Not yet, though, have we discovered the root of the matter. Underlying all the utterance and emphasis of the Bible there is one primal conception, namely, *God is himself the source of life.* It is not merely that life comes from God as Creator, it is profounder—*God is the life.* No created thing has any power to live. The organism does not create, but only expresses the power. Now, I think, we can see the bottom. Man as an organism is utterly dependent upon God. It is only when man is in absolute correspondence with God that he has the power of perfect organic action. But man is a moral person, and therefore he cannot have a purely automatic correspondence with God. The correspondence needs to be personal and moral. In swifter speech, a man, to live a full human life, must have constant companionship with God in moral love. Man, thus, by his disobedience snapped the vital relation—broke away from the very source of life—and so instantly the human organism began to break up—away from God man began to die. The whole case can be analyzed in this way:

1. The deepest fact of human death is that man is not in vital personal companionship with God.

2. Thus, death is first of all evident in man's moral nature, for right there is the point of personal rupture with God.

3. But death is not only moral, but also human, in the sense that it injures, and at last breaks up, that organism of soul and body which is essential to a full human life.

4. The extreme biblical stress upon bodily death is for two reasons: First, because bodily death has in its awful event the entire significance of death. A man's organism goes to pieces in death because he has not moral power enough to keep the thing together; and he lacks this power because the original vital connection with God has been lost. And, second, because bodily death is the consummate expression of God's hatred of sin—indeed, the penal mark against sin.

The Bodily Death of Man and Death in the Natural World. If we consider man's death as a consequence of sin the question arises, How can we relate man's bodily death to the universal and structural fact of death in the natural world? Different answers have been given, of which the most important are these:

1. The connection between death and sin is *proleptic.* Foreknowing man's sin, God provided a world to fit the fact.

2. The *tree of life* was intended to protect man, or to lift him beyond the operation of natural law. In commenting on Rom. 5. 12, Dr. Whedon says: "Adam's first organism seems to have been naturally dissoluble, and

its dissolution to have been prevented by the tree of life. His bodily immortality seems thus to have been properly supernatural." A view something like this was held by Professor Franz Delitzsch, who looked upon the tree of life as having a kind of sacramental efficiency.

Dr. Latimer, the dean of the School of Theology in Boston University, united the two views. In his lectures on Didactic Theology he said: "As to physical death, the difficulty is removed when we consider that it is likely that man was created mortal and the tree of life guaranteed his immortality. . . . Yet even this mortality was the result of sin, proleptically, so to speak, since God's foreknowledge of man's fall determined him to confer upon man a mortal constitution."

3. The answer, however, which best suits the temper and method of modern Christian apology is that sin merely gives a new moral content to a normal event. Death as a part of the process of natural law is a normal thing, but the entrance of sin into man's life transforms for him the event into a dreadful abnormal experience. The most convincing statement of this view has been given by Professor James Denney. I will quote a fragment: "*Conscience*, quickened by the law of God, has to look at death, and to become alive, not to its physical antecedents, but to its divine meaning. *What is God's voice in death to a spiritual being?* It is what the apostle represents it—death is the wages of sin. It is that in which the divine judgment of sin comes home to conscience." Of course, this view can readily be joined to the proleptic; and this connection is skillfully made by Professor Bruce in his Apologetics.

4. This last answer to our question, this conception of human death as a normal event filled with abnormal quality, I have most seriously tried to accept, for it affords the Christian preacher "the line of least resistance"; but

I am obliged to reject it as insufficient. *It is too easy.*
It does not penetrate the awful tragedy of sin. Sin, I
believe, has spoiled the whole universe. Everything
from the flowers to the planets is a failure—does not work
out the full ideal. Nature is like a limping king. He
gets along, but his movement is out of keeping with his
majesty. Let the scientist investigate and induce his
conclusions; I will in my thinking and feeling make no
terms with death. I hate death; I hate it everywhere—
in garden, and meadow, and swamp, and forest—everywhere; it violates every noble thing in me; I long for a
world where there will be no dead thing, where every
created thing will just live, live, live forever! I must,
therefore, begin with the proleptic view. Man is the
center in cosmic significance. This does not necessarily
require that our earth must have the importance now
assigned to it in the speculations of Alfred Russel Wallace.
It merely requires that our earth, and the whole regime
of nature under which man lives, has been created with
fitting reference to his peculiar probation, and to his
terrible rejection of God. The world ever manifests a
shattered ideal, and one feature of this sad manifestation
is the process of death. From the standpoint of the
divine ideal, death is an abnormal thing. All its waste
and foulness and (in the higher ranges of life) suffering
and positive cruelty are, in the deepest thinking, entirely
unnecessary. The fact that death is now made to serve
in many ways a useful purpose is a point of no force, for
sin itself is made to serve in many ways a useful purpose.
And, further, we are, according to the Christian faith,
finally to have a universe with no death in it from side to
side. If the Christian man can believe in the reality of
an ultimate universe having no process of death, surely
he can believe that such a universe is God's ideal; and
that this world with death all over it is but the eternal

ideal accommodated to the awful history of human sin.

This proleptic view will answer in application to the world as the environment of man's probation, and in application to man's constitution and placement in the world; but it will not answer as an explanation of man's own experience of death. For it is perfectly evident that the account in the Old Testament, and special references in the New Testament to that account, demand a definite historical connection between the first transgression and man's bodily death. This definite connection I would make in this manner: Man was created mortal; he was placed under the possible dominion of all natural law; but he was also created a moral person, with full freedom, in a peculiar plan of vital relation with God. From the very start, the intention, the ideal purpose, was for man to develop as an actual self-conscious companion of the living God. The realization of such vital companionship would not require a high degree of mental life, but it would require absolute obedience. Perhaps the *tree of life*, of which Whedon and Delitzsch and Latimer made so much, may be regarded as the picture-indication of this vital plan of companionship with God. Had man obeyed God, the companionship would have been maintained, and in such companionship man would have remained organic, could not have died. In other words, the higher possibility would have triumphed over the lower possibility. Precisely what would have taken place we do not know, but we can get a hint by thinking of the transcendent event of translation, and by thinking of the life of our Lord immediately after the resurrection. What I hold, then, is that for man to live in a world of death did not make it necessary for man to be a slave to natural law, and to pass out of this earthly existence by the rupture of the human organism. The possibility of this

rupture was proleptic, but the rupture was historical—
was entirely due to man's sin. Thus, there was a *fall* in
the most literal sense.

But it is urged, "The perfect saint now on earth must
die." Yes, the saint must die because he does not, in
all his holy life, get back the connection of vitality. He
may come to love God supremely, that I believe; and he
may organize all his motive life by means of that one
mighty motive of supreme love; but he has not a constant vital seizure of God in self-consciousness. That
he cannot have before his glorification beyond the grave.
Man's perfection in self-decision is possible in this life, but
his perfection in self-consciousness, and so his perfection
as an individual person, is not possible in this life.

The Personal Significance of Bodily Death. You will
remember what I have said as to the social meaning of
man's body—that his body furnishes him with the machinery of personal expression. Keep that point in mind,
and bodily death will begin to take on a large personal
significance. In the experience of bodily death a man is
for the first time *absolutely alone.* As long as he had a
body he had to see something, or hear something, or
touch something. A man may have no fellowship with
men, and may think that he has exhausted the torture
of loneliness. But he has not exhausted it. He can still
see the sun, or hear the thunder, or feel the wind in his
face. These things do not meet his personal need at all,
but they do occupy his attention, and protect him from
the solitude of profoundest introspection. But in death,
the body is torn away, and the man has no protection
whatever. He is naked in the silence. All he has is just
his own isolated poverty of person—a single, impotent,
self-conscious atom of being—a bare needle-point of quick
personality all alone in the long reaches of the Infinite.

The Moral Significance of Bodily Death. The most

dreadful feature of the isolation, though, lies not in the fact that the sinner has lost his world of persons and things; but in this fact together with the further fact that he has *not* lost his conscience. He is not only absolutely alone, he is also *alone with conscience*. Not one person, not one thing, can even for an instant shelter him from the violence of the moral smiting. Now, of all times, this lonely sinner needs the friendly presence of God; but his death is empty of the friendly God. His death expresses the holy anger of God. The man must now meet the insistence of God's moral concern closely and finally before the last door of destiny is forever closed. O God! if that isolated sinner had only yielded to his Saviour, and now had *him* in personal fellowship there in the solitude of death, how the whole situation would be transformed!

The Racial Significance of Bodily Death. As the human body is the racial nexus, the loss of the body in death must have racial significance. Not only does physical death isolate the individual person, it also breaks him off from his race. *He is now a man without a race.* The full meaning of his raceless condition will be brought out in other connections; but I want you to begin to hold the point even now. The Adamic race, as a racial ground-work of social solidarity, is gradually being destroyed by bodily death. One by one men are by death wrenched out of the racial relation, and flung out into the isolation of bare personal existence, to await as responsible persons the final judgment.

The Fitness of Bodily Death as Penalty. Although bodily death is a divine penalty, still we are not to think of it as an arbitrary penalty. It is not "a judicial execution, but a consequence involved in the nature of the transgression." But this statement must not be taken to signify anything automatic. God personally

indorses an expression of his hatred of sin which fits into
the nature of the transgression. You can see this intrinsic fitness the moment you bring to mind again the
essential character of personal sin. In personal sin the
normal independence and self-valuation of personality
are so extremely emphasized over against the demand of
the moral ideal as to become selfish egotism. The moral
person says: "*I* will do right." The sinner says: "*I* will
do wrong." In each case the free and majestic person
is at the front; but in one case there is submission, and
in the other case rejection of moral authority. Bodily
death is in consummate fitness with this supreme selfishness of personal sin. Bodily death is the strongest accentuation of egotism. It takes this egotist, this sinner,
wrenches him out of the protective physical scene, breaks
him off from his race, flings him into absolute isolation,
and compels him to inhabit his own selfish fragment of
being. Death says to the sinner, "You would not obey
God, you would not love your fellow men, you lived for
self, you wanted only self—THEN TAKE IT!"

Such an extreme accentuation of the inherent egotism
of personal sin is a most fitting end to a life of probation.
To see this point clearly we must note again the relation
probation sustains to personality, and especially noticing
the probational import of self-consciousness. Already I
have spoken of the fundamental motives which urge men
toward volition (in the analytical treatment of the fall
of man), one of these motives being bodily, one cosmic,
one social, and one personal. But while several of these
motives are not inherent in bare personality, yet it is in
the operation of personality that they all come to ultimate
deposit in moral character. For we must never forget
that moral character can only be achieved by positive
indorsement in self-decision. But for such self-decision
there must be self-consciousness. Now we are ready for

our point. This self-consciousness which is essential to self-decision, and therefore essential to the fixing of moral character, is a sporadic experience in our earthly life. It comes in broken flashes, now and then, here and there; and it is only in these blazing moments of self-vision that we have our strokes of destiny. But a man needs to review the whole history of self-decision, to behold in the flash of God's moral lightning all he has done, and all he now is as a result of all he has done. He needs one final crucial chance thoroughly to face his manhood, and, in this fullness of self-conscious opportunity, to accept himself, or to reject himself. Thus, death is the climax of probation.

There are in your minds, I quickly perceive, two rising objections to this large probational valuation of bodily death. The first objection is that death is often such an event of pain or confusion or lethargy as to be clearly unsuitable for such pregnant work in self-decision. My briefest answer to this objection is a personal one. My own experience has taught me that the *surface* of death, what the physician and the other bystanders observe, is no indication whatever of the personal event beneath the surface. The door of the inner chamber is shut. The second objection is that such a valuation of bodily death tends to discredit the sufficiency of life itself as a probation. My answer to this objection is again to call your attention to the significance of personal habit—I say *personal* habit, not automatic habit, but that bearing of the responsible person which results from repeated self-decisions and the continued narrowing of the range of possible motive. With this psychology of moral character clearly in mind, we see at once that, in any typical instance, it must be life and not death which practically determines destiny. But we can also see, I think, that the probational process is only fairly and fully completed by a last crisis in which the moral person is solemnly alone with his conscience and his entire history. In this last crisis the pressure toward righteousness is exhausted (if there be any possible pressure remaining), and another probation beyond the grave is philosophically inconceivable.

The racial fitness of bodily death does not require special discussion, as such a fitness is involved in what has been said concerning the racial nexus, racial sin, and the racial significance of bodily death.

XXI. THE TEACHING OF SAINT PAUL

A COMPREHENSIVE plan in biblical theology would require us to begin with the Old Testament, and then to study the New Testament entire, approaching it, not as many do through the gospels, but through the apology in the Epistle to the Hebrews. But for our work in systematic theology the teaching of Saint Paul furnishes all the more important data, and no further biblical study would essentially change the outcome.

Professor Denney has said: "The doctrine of the death of Christ and its significance was not Saint Paul's theology, it was his gospel. It was all he had to preach." Exception has been taken to Denney's view, and we have even been told that "Christ's death was but an incident in his life"; but Denney, beyond any other writer of our day, has understood the apostle Paul, and garnered the very life of the New Testament. Take out of the Pauline message the death of Christ, and every element of his teaching would become meaningless. Without his peculiar emphasis upon our Lord's death, you cannot fully appreciate even Saint Paul's practical opinions.

"*Made to be sin on our behalf.*" "Him who knew no sin he made to be sin on our behalf" (2 Cor. 5. 21). At the very start, we can be sure of one thing, namely, that ἁμαρτία does *not* mean *sin* in the first clause, and *sin offering* in the second clause. It means just *sin* in each place. We can also see at once that the entire expression "who knew no sin" is a perfect equivalent of this: *one not a sinner.* And we can keep the apostle's striking contrast completely, if we consider the expression "made to be sin" (ἁμαρτίαν ἐποίησεν) as a strong rhetorical equivalent of this: *one made or constituted a sinner*. Jesus Christ, then, according to Saint Paul, was one not a sinner and yet one constituted a sinner. This much seems to me to be entirely convincing.

Now, as to this seeming contradiction, is there any clue? Yes, the clue is to be found in the fourteenth verse, "because we thus judge, that one died for all, therefore all died." The idea here is that of substitution. Christ died *for* all, or in behalf of all (ὑπὲρ πάντων), and so it is really, potently, as if they died. That death of Christ *belongs to them all* as truly as if every one of them had died that death. They all have title-claim to the Lord's death just as one has complete right to the work of a substitute.

We are now thus far: Christ's death did not belong to him normally, but came to him as being a substitute for men, as standing in the place of men. Now we are ready for the sharp turn. In himself, Christ was *not* a sinner, but as a substitute, standing for men, he was a sinner. We can now touch the root of the apostle's conception: How could Jesus be—how was he—a substitutional sinner? Why, simply in the one fact that *he died*. Death, this bodily death, was the exact, historic, divine penalty for human sin; and this penalty of death came upon our Lord precisely as it strikes every human sinner. Christ was thus *treated as a sinner is treated;* by substitution he was "numbered with the transgressors"—he was placed in the category of sin. And so he was not a sinner, and yet at the same time he was a sinner—a *made*, a *constituted*, sinner.

"*A propitiation, through faith, in his blood.*" "Whom God set forth to be a propitiation, through faith, in his blood" (Rom. 3. 25). Saint Paul's surface meaning in this passage may be fairly rendered thus: Christ was set forth, openly, in his blood, to be a propitiation, available by faith. The crucial word is ἱλαστήριον. And as to the meaning of the word, the exegetes have not been of one mind. But for their scholarly discussions we have no concern here. Whatever they do with the word, they are unable to destroy the idea of propitiation. As Professor Sanday says: "The fundamental idea which underlies the word must be propitiation." But deeply, what is meant by propitiation? Surely a propitiation is *the means by which one is rendered propitious*, or favorable, or open to plea. Inasmuch, therefore, as Saint Paul says that Christ was set forth, openly, in his blood, to be a propitiation, available by faith, the apostle's full thought is, I am confident, this: The death of Jesus Christ is the sacrificial means by which God is rendered propitious to one having faith.

We can now get the connections in Saint Paul's mind, if we start with the twenty-fourth verse: "Being justified freely by his grace through the redemption that is in Christ Jesus: whom God set forth to be a propitiation, through faith, in his blood." "Being justified"—but how? "Freely by his grace"—how do we get this grace? "Through the redemption that is in Christ Jesus"—but, more closely, what is meant by this redemption that is in Christ? The meaning is precisely this: The death of Christ renders God so propitious toward us that when we have faith in Christ set forth in his blood we can be justified freely by his grace. Thus, Saint Paul's conception is that justification is explained by free grace; that this grace is explained as a feature of redemption; and that redemption is explained by the propitiatory death of Christ, made personally available only by faith.

"*Reconciled to God through the death of his Son.*" "For if, while we were enemies, we were reconciled to God through the death of his Son, much more, being recon-

ciled, shall we be saved by his life; and not only so, but
we also rejoice in God through our Lord Jesus Christ,
through whom we have now received the reconciliation"
(Rom. 5. 10, 11; compare with Col. 1. 21, 22, and with
2 Cor. 5. 18, 19). The word translated "reconciliation"
is καταλλαγή; and our first question is, Does it mean
reconciliation by means of a change taking place in men?
or is there an actual change which takes place in God?
From our English usage, it would, at first glance, seem as
if the reconciliation were by a change in men, God himself being favorable all the time. But our English usage
is altogether misleading. The change is primarily in God.
We know this conclusively for two reasons: First, this
reconciliation, Saint Paul says, was "through the death
of his Son." And, already, in this very epistle, as we
have seen, the apostle has taught that the death of Christ
was a propitiation, or means of changing God, or making
him propitious. That is, Saint Paul is but saying in a
new way essentially what he had said before. To say
that by the death of Christ God is made favorable to men
is essentially the same thing as to say that by the death
of Christ God is reconciled to men. And just as the
propitiation becomes available by personal faith, so the
reconciliation is completed by men becoming reconciled
to God. Second—but we do not need to go back to the
third chapter, for the decisive point is given in the passage
before us. Saint Paul here tells us that "*while we were
enemies* we were reconciled to God through the death of
his Son"; and then, a bit later, that we have "now received the reconciliation." In the first place, that is,
before men did a thing toward it, God became reconciled
to men by means of the death of his Son; and now we
accept by faith the divine offer of reconciliation.

In this connection there is one further item of important suggestion. The fact that the reconciliation of

God to men involves the bodily death of Christ is made emphatic in the Epistle to the Colossians (1. 21, 22) where we read: "And you, being in time past alienated and enemies in your mind in your evil works, yet now hath he reconciled in the body of his flesh through death." Bishop Lightfoot explains the passage in this way: "In Christ's body, in Christ's flesh which died on the cross for your atonement, ye are reconciled to him again."

"*That he might himself be just, and the justifier of him that hath faith in Jesus*." "To show his righteousness (δικαιοσύνη), because of the passing over of the sins done aforetime, in the forbearance of God; for the showing, I say, of his righteousness at this present season: that he might himself be just (δίκαιος), and the justifier (δικαιόω) of him that hath faith in Jesus" (Rom. 3. 25, 26). This remarkable passage is Saint Paul's nearest approach to a philosophical doctrine of the atonement, and so it demands our most careful consideration.

We notice at once that the apostle makes a distinction between God's forbearance toward sinners and his justification of sinners. This forbearance was best in times past; but it could not satisfy God, and so it had to be done away with by a very different thing, namely, by justification—justification by faith in harmony with God's being just. "That he might himself be just, and the justifier of him that hath faith in Jesus."

But why does God have this end of justification in view at all? Why does he *want*, under any conditions, to justify the sinner? No one familiar with Saint Paul's writings can possibly doubt what his answer would be— *Because God loves the sinner*. And so, in the divine depths, justice must be harmonized with love's demand. How is this profound harmony to be secured? Saint Paul's answer is this: By the manifestation of the righteousness of God in the death of Christ ("for the showing,

I say, of his righteousness at this present season: that he might himself be just, and the justifier ").

Now we reach the critical point. What does Saint Paul mean by this *righteousness of God*—this δικαιοσύνη θεοῦ? That he does not mean bare justice is evident for two reasons: First, a philosophical reason. God's purpose is to harmonize justice with the demand of love, and this harmony could not be achieved by expressing justice alone. Second, a biblical reason, a reason in the consistency of Pauline theology. Saint Paul's own usage is contrary to the view that the righteousness of God means bare justice. Turn, for a case, to 2 Cor. 5. 21: "That we might become the righteousness of God in him." We find here the same expression, δικαιοσύνη θεοῦ; and it cannot mean justice—that we might become the justice of God in him. Righteousness is, I am sure, a larger term than justice everywhere in the Bible. Sometimes it means moral concern; sometimes it means "the sum of all moral excellence" (Sanday); and sometimes it means moral love. Speaking of this very passage in Romans, Professor Stevens says: "Here δικαιοσύνη must mean the self-respecting attribute of holiness in God, the reaction of his nature against sin which must find expression in its condemnation. Holy love is the best definition of Paul's conception of the ethical nature of God." A full statement of the matter may be given as follows:

The righteousness of God is the holiness of God, sometimes in one bearing of emphasis and sometimes in another; but in the complete bearing, perfect moral love. And Saint Paul uses the term to express the complete bearing. With this understanding of the apostle's usage, the great passage in Romans can be paraphrased as follows: God cannot forever deal with sinners in a partial way. Sooner or later, he must satisfy himself completely. To do this, he must, at one stroke, satisfy his sense of justice and his love for men. There is only one way to accomplish all this, and that is to express his entire nature as it is gathered up in holy love. This perfect manifestation of holy love is in the death of Christ.

Before going further, let us summarize what we now have of Saint Paul's teaching:

1. Jesus Christ was constituted a sinner in our behalf by the simple fact that he died a bodily death, and so bore the exact historical penalty which belongs to man. He was a sinner by substitution.

2. By bearing this penalty of death Christ rendered God propitious; or he reconciled God to man, so that individual justification by faith became possible and ready.

3. The reason why the death of Christ was such a propitiation, or means of reconciliation, was that it satisfied, at one stroke, God's inherent sense of justice and his boundless feeling of love for men.

4. And, last, the reason the death of Christ could do such work in harmony, could satisfy God's sense of justice and his feeling of love, was that it manifested the divine moral love which is the holiness of God, the entire ethical nature of God, consummated in the perfection of the divine personal experience. In the death of Christ God ceases to express fragments toward men, and manifests *all he is*. And by manifesting all he is, he is supremely satisfied.

"*A people for his own possession.*" "Looking for the blessed hope and appearing of the glory of the great God and our Saviour Jesus Christ; who gave himself for us, that he might redeem us from all iniquity, and purify unto himself a people for his own possession" (Titus 2. 13, 14). In this passage Saint Paul passes clearly from the idea of redemption from iniquity to the idea of Christ's obtainment of a holy people for himself. The same thought appears in Rom. 8. 29—"that he might be the firstborn among many brethren." Besides this, under the conception of Christ as the second Adam, there is the thought that our Lord's redemptive work is to result in a holy company of men. Besides all this, and in deep association with it, is Saint Paul's conception of a glorious church, "holy and without blemish" (Eph. 5. 27), which Christ gave himself up for, and which he nourishes and cherishes, "because we are members of his body." All these teachings indicate plainly that redemption through the death of Christ, as Saint Paul understands it, is to have a great social outcome. Jesus Christ does not die to smite sin in the abstract, nor to save, here and there, an isolated moral person; he dies to obtain a people, a church, a holy community, so perfectly inherent in him that he and they constitute one body.

We have the same idea of a holy social organism in many places in the New Testament, and it is especially noticeable in our Saviour's last prayer, "that they may be one, even as we are one" (Saint John 17. 22); but here I desire only to bring out the social expansion of Saint Paul's central conception of the redemptional significance of the death of Christ. By his death our Lord not only reconciles God to man, and renders possible the justification of the separate sinner, but also obtains a people for his own possession.

"*That Jesus died and rose again.*" "For if we believe that Jesus died and rose again, even so them also that are fallen asleep in Jesus will God bring with him" (1 Thess. 4. 14). This association of our Lord's death with his resurrection is often found in Saint Paul's mind. It is found in Rom. 4. 25, where Jesus is spoken of as "delivered up for our trespasses and raised for our justification." It is found in that great fifteenth chapter of 1 Corinthians, where the apostle says: "For I delivered

unto you first of all that which also I received: that Christ
died for our sins according to the scriptures; and that he
hath been raised on the third day." And it is also found
in 2 Corinthians (5. 15), where Saint Paul says of our
Lord and his people "that they that live should no longer
live unto themselves, but unto him who for their sakes
died and rose again." By studying all of these passages
in their full connections it will be clearly seen that in
Saint Paul's thinking our Saviour's resurrection is not
merely an event which historically follows his death, it
is an event which teleologically follows his death in the
plan of redemption.

"Conformed to the body of his glory." "For our citizenship is in heaven; whence also we wait for a Saviour, the
Lord Jesus Christ: who shall fashion anew the body of
our humiliation, that it may be conformed to the body of
his glory, according to the working whereby he is able
even to subject all things unto himself" (Phil. 3. 20, 21).
This passage is of the most intense interest. Speaking
of this passage, in his treatise on Immortality, Cyprian
exclaims, Who would not crave "to arrive more quickly
to the dignity"! It is in this very epistle to the Philippians, in the chapter before, that we have Saint Paul's
most extended reference to the Incarnation. Evidently
he looks upon our Lord's body *there* as merely a part of
that humiliation which was completed in his being
"obedient even unto death, yea, the death of the cross."
The natural body of Jesus had no significance to Saint
Paul save as it was the instrument of a supreme ethical
self-sacrifice. But how exceedingly different is Saint
Paul's conception of the significance of our Lord's body
of glory! *That* is the type according to which shall be
fashioned all the final, glorious bodies of his own
people.

Now I will give, as I understand it, the closer interlacing of the most important features of Saint Paul's entire view of our Lord's redemptive work:

1. Jesus Christ *died*. In this bodily death our Saviour bore the exact, historic, divine penalty for man's sin, and therefore was a sinner in category, or a sinner by substitution. Bearing this penalty of death, our Saviour satisfied the holiness of God by fully expressing that holiness in its personal consummation of moral love. By thus satisfying the divine holiness Christ rendered God ethically open to the possibility of justification conditioned on faith.

2. Jesus Christ *rose from the dead*. By this event of his resurrection our Lord made justification more than possible—he made it redemptionally feasible. And through this process of justification actually carried out our Lord is gradually forming, person by person, believer by believer, a new spiritual community—a people organic in him—τοῖς ἐν χριστῷ Ἰησοῦ—one body in vitality of moral life, in identity of aim, and in the service and fellowship of love.

3. Jesus Christ rose from the dead *with a glorified body*. This spiritual community of saints who live in Christ is to be objectively completed in their organism when, in their resurrection, every one of them shall take on, not the body of the grave, but a spiritual body "conformed to the body of his glory." The saints are to be like Christ, not only in moral person, but also in their actual bodily life.

XXII. OUR LORD'S STRANGE HESITATION IN APPROACHING DEATH

His Primary Attitude. The strangeness of our Lord's hesitation will stand out more clearly, if we first notice his primary attitude, or the way that he as Redeemer looked upon his own death.

1. He did not regard his death as a natural incident terminating life; nor as an accident resulting from the disposition and deed of man. After the confession of Saint Peter ("Thou art the Christ, the Son of the living God") our Lord began definitely to speak of his coming death: "From that time began Jesus to show unto his disciples, that he must go unto Jerusalem, and suffer many things of the elders and chief priests and scribes, and be killed, and the third day be raised up" (Saint Matt. 16. 21; compare with Saint Mark 10. 33). The expression "that he must" (ὅτι δεῖ αὐτὸν) cannot mean that the circumstances, the hostile forces against him, render his death inevitable. We are certain of this point for several reasons: First, the rebuke to Peter implies that the *must* is moral. Second, such statements as that in the tenth chapter of Saint John ("I have power to lay it down, and I have power to take it again") show that Jesus regarded his death as a matter entirely within his own control. Third, the scene in Gethsemane further shows that Jesus regarded his death as finally a pure question of obedience to his Father (also compare with Saint John 10. 18). It is, then, beyond a doubt that our Saviour did not look upon his death as incident or accident, but did look upon it as a moral necessity, as an essential feature of his mission of redemption.

2. More precisely, our Lord regarded his death as a means of ransom for men. In Saint Mark's gospel (10. 45) we read: "For the Son of man also came not to be ministered unto, but to minister, and to give his life a ransom for many." This passage has been dealt with by Dr. Hollmann in a most radical fashion. The ἀντὶ πολλῶν he separates from λύτρον and connects with δοῦναι. The term λύτρον he renders *freeing* (Befreiung). With these radical changes, Hollmann makes the passage mean no more than this: "To free men from their stubborn pride and bring them to the spirit of repentance, Jesus gives up his life instead of many being obliged to give up their lives." If this arbitrary ingenuity is "advanced New Testament scholarship," then we must look toward the immediate future of the Christian church with deepening dread. But I have brought up this extremely radical interpretation by Hollmann to indicate how impossible it is to empty our Saviour's conception of his death of *all* redemptional meaning. Even in this comparative moral emptiness furnished by Hollmann, Jesus Christ considers his death as very important for the spiritual liberation of men.

3. Our Lord regarded his death as a covenant. At this point, again, there is such destructive work in criticism that in systematic theology, anyway, it is best to wait until some of the rationalistic caprice "is blown into the sea," before we try to do any thorough work. But we can easily get at a fragment of affirmation. Professor McGiffert says: "There can be no doubt that Jesus ate the Last Supper with his disciples, as recorded in all three of the synoptic gospels, and that he said of the bread which he broke and gave to his companions, 'This is my body,' and of the wine which he gave them to drink, 'This is my blood of the covenant which is shed for many,' and that he did it with a reference to his

approaching death." Let us for the present be content
and ask for no larger admission. What is the meaning
of that expression "blood of the covenant"? Probably
it refers back to the words in Jeremiah (31. 31–34): "Behold, the days come, saith Jehovah, that I will make a
new covenant: . . . for I will forgive their iniquity, and
their sin will I remember no more." This much, then,
we can affirm: Our Lord, at the Last Supper, looked upon
his death as the instrumental establishment of the prophe-
sied new covenant of grace under which sin could be
forgiven.

Our Lord's Hesitation. We are now prepared to note
the *strangeness* of our Saviour's hesitation when in the
garden he cried out: "My Father, if it be possible, let
this cup pass away from me." If, in his primary attitude, our Lord regarded his death as an essential feature
of the very plan of redemption for which he came into
the world; if he regarded his death as not merely important, but even the definite means of man's ransom; and if
he regarded this ransoming death as the actual inauguration of the new covenant and dispensation of grace; if,
in other words, every redemptional thing Christ was
aiming to do was, in his own estimate, to be achieved
only and precisely by his death, how could he, as Son of
God and Redeemer of men, *hesitate*, actually shrink back
from that death? Superficially, one would expect that
our Lord would approach death with solemn moral
eagerness, if not with such a spirit of joyous triumph as
that which made Saint Paul so ready to be offered.

Inadequate Explanations. Of this hesitation there have
been a number of purely humanitarian and rationalistic
explanations: By *Thiess*, that Jesus was suddenly "at-
tacked by some malady"; by *Heumann*, that "in addition
to his inward sorrow Jesus had contracted a cold in the
clayey ground traversed by the Kidron"; by *Strauss*,

that "Jesus on that evening in the garden experienced a violent access of fear"; and by *Renan*—one refuses to translate the sentimental indecency.

But a very different kind of an explanation, both in spirit and in fact, is that given suggestively by Principal Fairbairn in his Philosophy of the Christian Religion. He says:

"And Gethsemane represents the struggle of Jesus with the new problem which thus came before his imagination personified in Judas and the priests, and which he had to solve in the very face, if not in the very article, of death.

"And what was this new problem? Jesus was holy, and felt as only the sinless can the stain of sin burn like a living fire upon his soul. He had conceived himself as a Redeemer by the sacrifice of himself, as a Saviour by death. But now, when he comes face to face with this death, what does he find? That sin has taken occasion from his very grace to become more exceedingly sinful, to mix itself up with his sacrifice, penetrating and effacing it, transmuting it from a free and gracious act into a violent and necessitated death. His act of redemption becomes, so to say, the opportunity for sin to increase. The thing he most hates seems to become a partner with him in the work he most loves, contributing to its climax and consummation. Or, if not so conceived, it must be conceived under a still more dreadful form, as forcing itself into his way, taking possession of his work, turning it into 'a stone of stumbling and a rock of offense,' a means of creating sinners while it had been intended to save from sin. And there was an even more intolerable element in the situation: the men who were combining to effect this death were persons he was dying to save, and by their action they were making the saving a matter more infinitely hard, more vastly improbable, and changing the efficient cause of salvation into a sufficient reason for judgment. . . . From death as such he does not shrink, but from its mode and agencies, from death under the form and conditions which involve its authors in what appears inexpiable guilt, his whole nature recoils."

The spirit of this explanation is so large and sincere that one dislikes to make any criticism. But there are very serious objections, two of which I will indicate: First, there is, under the explanation, a confusing of sin with the expression of sin in crime. Sin is causal to crime, but crime is not causal to sin. From the standpoint of fundamental reality, the most dreadful thing, as far as those leaders who brought about the death of Christ were concerned, was not the crucifixion itself, but the fact that they were the kind of men they were. And a study of the life of Christ shows that he, long before, knew all about them. While he pitied the deluded and managed people, he branded the leaders with fiery invective. Second, the explanation is *redemptionally superficial*. It lies, like a sentimentality, on the surface of the awful deeps of redemption. That the Eternal Son of God could come into this world at infinite cost in self-sacrifice because of sin—"whole ages upon ages of bottomless sin"—and then, at the crucial point of his atonement for that sin, could have his redemptional consciousness exclusively occupied with one phase, one local item of the huge chaos of wrong, is to me entirely inconceivable. Principal Fairbairn is too profound a Christian thinker to be long satisfied with his own explanation.

The Clue to the Hesitation. When we read the account of our Lord's crucifixion, the clue to the hesitation becomes evident. It is in those words of agony: "My God, my God, why hast thou forsaken me?" Long before we have any heart to try to understand the meaning of these words of agony, we *feel sure* that they indicate the "cup" which Jesus Christ dreaded to empty. We feel sure of this because the two notes of agony, that of the prayer in the garden and that of the cry upon the cross, have the same intense spiritual accent, and the same indefinable suggestion of the depth of redemption.

XXIII. THE RACIAL THEORY OF OUR LORD'S REDEMPTIVE WORK

It may be helpful, as an introduction, to indicate the steps by which this racial theory was reached.

1. For twelve years I had a double attitude toward the three great historic theories of the atonement: On the one side, I was sure that they all were alike untrue to both the biblical data and the deepest Christian feeling. On the other side, I was just as sure that every one of the theories had a quality, if not a definite point, which should be preserved at any cost.

2. For six years I tried to preserve these three important qualities by the method of eclectic synthesis; but the result was so mechanical that I was at last obliged to throw it away.

3. I had become hopeless, when there suddenly came to me a vision of the full Christian meaning of the human race. This vision not only vitalized, but actually transformed, my entire theological situation. I saw not merely the atonement, but every doctrine, and the total combination of doctrine, in a new light. From that supreme hour (on one of the hills near Marburg) my one aim has been to get that racial vision into living expression.

4. My main work, after the vision, was to study the Bible more profoundly; and the consequence of this study was threefold: First, a realization of our Lord's bearing toward the one event of his bodily death. Second, a realization of the tremendous emphasis which the Bible places upon physical death as an abnormal human experience. Third, a realization that Saint Paul has in

his teaching the very backbone of a racial view of our Saviour's redemptive work.

5. Then I took the old theories in hand to see how much could be saved. And, to my astonishment, I found that the three qualities which had appealed to me could be preserved by a larger treatment from the racial standpoint. The satisfaction theory required that the attribute of justice should be exchanged for holiness, and that the idea of automatic necessity should be exchanged for the idea of a personal need of structural expression. The governmental theory required that there should be a profounder conception of the moral law, making it reach into the structure of the divine nature; and that the moral government should be granted a racial goal; and that penalty should be made a means of holy movement toward the racial goal. The moral influence theory required that its conception of love should be so united to moral concern as to furnish a new atmosphere of divine holiness. If I understand the *underlying intention* of such men as Anselm, Grotius, and Abelard, as Hodge, Miley, and Bushnell, the racial theory has caught the soul of all the theories. And, if I understand the New Testament, the racial theory has caught not only its formal teaching, but even its inner life.

The Purpose of God in Redemption. At the very beginning we need to clear the way by answering the simple question, What was God's primary purpose— what was he trying to do in redemption? There is, I am satisfied, only one final answer possible: *To obtain a race of holy persons.* He was not trying to get, here and yonder, a separate moral person ready to enjoy the divine glory. No, God wanted an entangled race—a personal organism of holy men—that was God's aim. In other words, God's purpose was the same in redemption that it had been in creation. The first plan, the ideal plan, failed because of sin; but this failure is now, in redemption, to be made over into a triumph. Out of the Adamic race, broken in organism, and doomed to destruction as a race, the work of Christ is to secure a new race completely personal, completely organic, and completely holy. Thus, the distinctive note in all we do must be *racial*. We do not drop the note of the moral person at all, but our outcome must be emphatically a racial redemption. This insistence is not a matter of mere words, it is the very core of the case. With this outcome in full view, a certain change of emphasis naturally takes place. The atonement itself, as a means to a large racial result, is to be treated as only one necessary feature of the entire redemptive work of our Lord. Such a connective treatment does not, in reality, minimize the doctrine of the atonement, but it does prevent the extreme and isolated emphasis which is found in theological works of a certain type.

The Dynamic Center of the New Race. It is not necessary to repeat what was said, in another discussion, concerning the racial peculiarity of the Son of man. Nor is it necessary again to affirm that the Incarnation was an abnormal event entirely due to man's sin, and in definite preparation for the atonement by the death of Christ. But what I said before was fragmentary. The Incarnation was more than a preparation for the atonement; it was also the provision of a dynamic center for the new race. Allow me to go back for a moment to the principle of individual supplement or complement ("The Racial Organism"). When all the saints have done their utmost to render every member of the race complete, the completion is not entirely effected. Men are made absolutely complete only through each other, *and in Christ*. The finishing dynamic help comes only from the racial center, and that center is our Lord. We cannot now dwell upon this wonderful point; but we need the mention of it that we may appreciate the significance of the suffering of Jesus. The experience of Jesus Christ cannot be fully understood from the standpoint of the single fact of the atonement; to that single fact must be added the further fact that he is, in all and through all, preparing himself by suffering to be the everlasting race center, the everlasting racial dynamic, the everlasting moral influence. By means of his humiliation, our Lord obtains that exhaustive human experience which perfects his racial efficiency. As the reservoir of supplement, so to speak, he has after the resurrection not only the power of God, but that sympathetic comprehension of the need of every man which could come to him only by suffering for men, with men, and as God become man.

The Absolute Necessity of Atonement. The ultimate purpose of Jesus Christ is to secure a new race of holy men; but before he can found this race he must make atonement for human sin. Is such an atonement an absolute necessity? or is it a relative expedient, either to protect moral government or to create a moral influence sufficient to move the sinner? The last two views I place together because philosophically they belong together. Practically they are not in the least alike. But philosophically they are alike; for in each theory the atonement is an expedient to produce influence, in one case an influence to act upon the saint, or upon the saint and the sinner; and in the other case an influence to act upon the sinner alone. Thus both views are essentially utilitarian. And because they are utilitarian I must regard them as superficial. The atonement for sin was an *absolute* necessity—*absolute* in the sense that the primary demand for it is in God's own nature: is not in God merely as he is *out there*, in relation to man; but is in God as he is *in there*, without any objective relations whatever.

More definitely, my view of the necessity of atonement is just as rigid as that held in the satisfaction theory. The pure satisfactionist holds that the satisfaction of justice, by the full expression of it, is absolutely necessary in the very constitution of the Divine Being. I hold that the satisfaction of *holiness*, by the full expression of it, is absolutely necessary in the very constitution of the Divine Being *personalized*. The further question whether the self-sacrifice of the Son of God was so absolutely necessary that nothing else could have taken its place is to be answered without hesitation in the affirmative. For it is inconceivable that a method so costly would have been chosen could God have entirely expressed his holiness in any other way.

Now we can come a little closer to our pivotal contention. With sin a fact, the situation is abnormal, rendering the complete expression of holiness, that is, the expression of moral love, for the time impossible. In such a situation God's holiness is expressed, but it is expressed by the most tremendous emphasis upon moral concern. The love of God cannot appear without an ethical basis firmly fixed. This emphasis upon moral concern is precisely what we find before the atonement is made. The destruction of the Adamic race by the abnormal method of death is the expression of God's moral concern, or of his eternal hatred of sin. In bodily death, *considered alone*, God does not say, "I love men"—he says only, "I hate sin."

The pivotal point can now be given. It is this: *In establishing a new race, in a situation still abnormal with sin, the holiness of God must be as fully expressed in moral concern as it was expressed by the destruction of the old race.* There must be complete ethical continuity between the two racial events. Not one step can be taken toward the final expression of moral love until there is as much hatred of sin manifested as was manifested before. This is only saying that in all situations God must be true to the law of holiness.

The Death of Christ. On the surface we have the physical fact of our Lord's death. In this bodily death he bore the precise racial penalty. Many contend that there could be nothing penal in the death of Jesus simply because he was not guilty. "Nor was Jesus *punished* for man's sin, he suffered for it. He could not be punished, for he was not guilty." Such a contention is properly made; but it lacks in discrimination, and it also lacks in any full understanding of the apostle Paul. Jesus Christ was not *personally* a sinner, and was not *personally* punished; that is certain. But, on the other hand, his suffering was not ordinary individual suffering—*it was official, representative suffering.* He suffered, as the Race-Man, for the whole race. *He carried the race in his consciousness.* Thus, Christ's death is a racial event from the double fact that he bears the racial penalty against the old race and that he is the racial center of the new race. And whether we consider the dying Saviour a sinner or not, depends entirely upon our point of view. From the Arminian standpoint of personal sin, he surely was not a sinner. Nor was he a sinner from the standpoint of depravity. But from the racial standpoint he was a sinner, because he stood for the race, and allowed himself to be shut into its category, and actually bore the racial penalty, actually died, and was broken off from the race like any son of Adam. It matters not so much about the words you use, though, if you only catch and firmly hold the idea that our Lord's death was a racial event through and through.

But this surface fact of physical death has also with our Lord a personal feature involved. By death he was not only separated from men, but also thrust into personal isolation. He, like any sinner, experienced the awful loneliness of death. He, too, entered the "chamber of silence" companionless. "But Christ was too strong, too regnant in personal resources, to feel such loneliness." My reply is not merely that our Lord had all natural capacity for human feelings, and not merely that the objection implies a misunderstanding of the nature of personality—my reply is that our Lord had, before his death, manifested an intense sensitiveness to personal loneliness: "What, could ye not watch with me one hour?"

With our Saviour, however, this personal isolation would not have been actual had he been able to find fellowship with his Father, *but his Father had forsaken him.* I dare not be ingenious and accommodating here—I must take these words to mean that God the Father was literally absent from the consciousness of his only Son. And, further, I think that the Christian consciousness will never allow the critical mangling of the text. The utterance, just as it stands, answers to the intuitive demand of the profoundest Christian experience. A sinner saved by grace shrinks back from the awful words, but in his heart he is certain that his redemption cost all that. The Eternal Father abandoned his own Son and allowed him to pass through death all alone.

There has been in theology a long discussion as to whether this divine abandonment was real, or only apparent—whether it shows the Father's personal attitude toward his Son, or shows a confusion of mind in the Saviour resulting from his terrible experience. But the entire discussion is on the surface. Under pressure, the two views amount practically to the same thing. The psychology of the terrible abandonment has no Christian, no redemptional import whatever. Suppose there was the mental confusion, and Jesus simply could not find his Father—then the Father *allowed* that confusion; the fact of the dreadful isolation was secured in the plan for it, and so the abandonment *does* express the Father's attitude toward his dying Son. In such a dire situation we are unwilling to spin our fine distinction between a bearing of sufferance and a bearing of exertion, for both bearings express, and equally express, *intention*. Do you all see it? Do you feel it? Suppose (to inflame the point) that a strong man and his child are standing on the brink of a precipice. The child is confused, cannot find the father's hand, and in an instant will fall over into the abyss. The father, standing there in his power, sees everything, and yet does not reach out and grasp the child's groping hand—the illustration is exceedingly inadequate, but it does suggest a situation where no one would be allowed to urge the difference between a bearing of sufferance and a bearing of actual exertion. The plain fact is that God the Father *intended* that his Son should pass through this awful experience of isolation, and had insisted upon it in the garden. With his Son he was ever well pleased; but now his Son does not stand in his own single selfhood. His Son is the Redeemer, the representative Race-Man, standing in death for a race of sinners, and the Father's attitude is an attitude of holiness toward the entangled entirety of the atoning situation. I am, after long, shrinking hesitation, unable to escape the conclusion that the Son of God, as the racial Mediator, met in the beginning of the isolation of his death the whole shock of the wrath of God against sin, that he was treated precisely as any sinner is treated. His death was more than the tearing apart of body and soul; his death had in its experience the extreme ethical content of personal isolation.

John Calvin taught that our Saviour in his soul experienced the anguish of the damned ("*quod diros in*

anima cruciatus damnati ac perditi hominis pertulerit").
This view is to us impossible if held, as it was held by
Calvin and others, under the terms of the satisfaction
theory. Nor can we hold the view as an explanation of
our Lord's "descent into hell." But Calvin's primary
feeling here, if not his theological insight, was profoundly
Christian. Indeed, the day is sure to come when all of
Calvin's deep Christian vitalities will be sharply separated
from his formal contentions. John Calvin himself was
much greater than his scheme of theology. I am convinced that Jesus Christ in his death actually suffered
infinite anguish. Toward this conviction I was started
by Calvin, but not alone by him. For a long time before
reading Calvin I had been growing dissatisfied with all
the little things which modern theologians are saying
about the death of Christ. It is the death of the Son of
God. It must be lifted totally out of the world of humanitarian mitigation. It must be made a boundless
agony in the experience of God himself. It must be
made such a finality in awful self-sacrifice that no Christian man, and no saint in all eternity, can ever think of it
without suffering.

But we are told that Christ, inasmuch as he had no
consciousness of guilt, could not suffer even as much as
one unrepentant sinner will suffer. At first this seemed
to me to be a point beyond question; but a larger contact
with the facts of life has led me to doubt the point.
Even among men, it is not the guilty man who suffers the
most, but rather the innocent friend who loves him and
wants to save him. Surely the friend cannot feel guilty
himself, but he can, in love and self-sacrifice and full
contact with the sinner, have something which the
sinner cannot have—purity's complete realization of the
condition and penalty and endless ruin of sin. This,
however, is but a suggestion to prepare us to look more

closely, and to appreciate more thoroughly our Lord's openness to anguish over human sin. Let us carefully note the combination of qualities and relations. As God, our Lord had a capacity constantly available for the intuitive seizure and mental comprehension of all reality and all possibility. As God become man, he was absolutely sinless and absolutely sensitive to even the faintest touch of evil. As the Race-Man, he gathered up into his consciousness the whole human race, so that mankind was almost a part of his very being. As Redeemer, he had come, with infinite love and at infinite cost, to save men from sin. And now, with this combination of qualities and relations—divine, human, racial, and redemptional—our Lord, without the fellowship of his Father, is by his death brought into *empiric contact* with the penalty and meaning of sin. Are we ourselves, with the intuitions of grace, not able, in some small degree of apprehension, to lay hold of the inner event? The Son of God, as Redeemer making atonement for sin, and as the Founder of a new race of redeemed men, will fully exhaust the possibilities of suffering, not merely the suffering possible to finite men, but even the suffering possible to the infinite God in human limitation. And so, there alone, our Lord opens his mind, his heart, his personal consciousness, to the whole inflow of the horror of sin— the endless history of it, from the first choice of selfishness on, on to the eternity of hell; the boundless ocean of its isolation and desolation he allows, wave upon wave, to overwhelm his soul.

The Complete Expression of the Holiness of God. When we remember who our Lord is, the only-begotten Son of God the Father; when we realize that the Father "spared not" his own Son, but delivered him up to this awful experience in death, surely we can begin to feel the *ethical intensity* of the entire redemptional deed. By this sacri-

fice of his Son God's relentless hatred of sin is expressed
as it could not be expressed by the total annihilation of a
universe of sinners.   The death of Christ does not, could
not, express justice of any kind, or in any degree whatsoever.   Never can you understand the death of Christ
if you cling to that vitiating idea of justice.   But the
death of our Lord does express moral concern, does show
that *God cares tremendously about sin*.   It is not a single
item, but the combination—the absolute deity of our
Saviour; his *personal* preëxistence in the eternal glory of
the Godhead; his *personal obedience* in giving up that
divine estate; his continued obedience even while shrinking back from the rending and isolation and divine abandonment and infinite anguish of death; the Father's
exhaustless love for his only Son; the Father's profound
need of his Son for full personal fellowship; and yet the
Father's unremitting insistence that redemption shall be
accomplished only by this measureless humiliation of his
Son and sacrifice of himself—it is this combination which
steeps the whole deed with intense ethical quality.   One
drop of humanitarianism; one drop of unitarianism, any
form of unitarianism; one drop of agnostic Ritschlianism;
one drop of even vagueness as to full self-consciousness
in the persons of the Trinity, and the ethical quality is
almost sure to vanish instantly.   In one sentence, we
may say that it is *the divine tenacity in holding fast to the
total penal event of death at such infinite cost in self-conscious self-sacrifice*—it is this tenacity of God so expensive
personally which reveals his moral concern.

This supreme revelation of bare moral concern is what
we find when we consider the death of Christ out of its
teleological connection, or when we consider it as merely
an atonement for human sin.   But the atonement itself
is not an end, but a means to an end.   The end is the expression of the moral love of God, or the expression of the

fullness of the divine holiness in a race of redeemed men.
Jesus Christ does not die to satisfy moral concern, he dies
to satisfy moral concern *in order that* he may be the
organizer of a new race. His death is an actual movement in penalty toward the racial goal. In treatment of
this penal movement toward the goal, one can immediately make use of important features of the governmental
theory and the moral influence theory; but these features
should be torn out of their utilitarian setting of expediency.
God's only aim and only method is to express all he
himself is in holiness. Utility is never planned, and yet
utility is necessarily involved. Every movement toward
perfect manifestation of holiness is as resultant of more
practical utility as every larger shining of the sun is
resultant of more heat. What we need is simply God,
God *out*, God entirely manifest in our sky. Such a
manifestation means necessarily all moral potency, all
moral support, all practical interests. God is not like
a finite Ruler ever balancing efficiencies, ever ponder-
ing expedients. His life is one harmonious intuitional
experience crowded with complex deposits of related
attributes; and his one perpetual purpose is to satisfy
himself by expressing all that he is. In a situation abnormal because of man's freedom and sin, such a complete divine expression may become temporarily unfeas-
ible or impossible; in such case God's immediate aim is to
move toward the complete goal by expressing his fundamental holiness in moral concern. The history of redemption, in its sweep of divine action, may be conceived
in this manner: First, there is an ethical start in racial
death. Second, there is an effective ethical movement
in the death of Christ. Third, there is a racial start in
the resurrection and ascension and session of our Lord.
Fourth, there is an effective racial movement in the
actual formation of the new race by the conversion of

moral persons.   Fifth, the holy racial goal is reached when the redeemed race, expressing the moral love of God, is completed in organism at the final resurrection of the body.

The Atonement.   The atonement is precisely in the death of Christ, because it is the death of Christ which ethically meets and covers the obstacle of human sin. Thus, we may truly say that the death of Christ propitiates God, or reconciles God to mankind, or is a moral satisfaction rendered unto God's holy nature.   Or, we can state the matter thus: Because God is holy he hates sin.   Because he hates sin, the expression of that hatred is fundamental to any expression of God whatsoever. The death of Christ is the fundamental and exhaustive expression of God's hatred of sin.   But, as I have intimated in several places, the death of Christ does not satisfy God, or reconcile God, or propitiate God, as an *isolated* expression of the divine hatred of sin.   To grant that point would, as you can readily see, imply that there was an atoning efficiency in the inauguration of racial death; for racial death also expresses God's intense hatred of sin.   The death of Christ satisfies God because it is an emphasis upon moral concern *unto the actual salvation of the human race as a race.*   The event of racial death could not satisfy God, and simply because it lacked the tremendous redemptional potencies and racial connections which belong to the death of our Lord.   Racial death is a *start* in moral emphasis, but it has no *speed*, no possibility of ever touching the goal.   The death of Christ is, on the contrary, a swift, urgent movement toward the actual expression of moral love in a race of redeemed men.   Thus, the divine satisfaction is not in the pure moral stress of the atonement, but rather in the total content and bearing of the atonement as a potent ethical emphasis rapidly provisional for the ultimate manifestation of all God is.

Definition.

>   Jesus Christ, as the representative Race-Man, endured in his
> death the precise racial penalty for human sin; and by the total
> event and experience under that penalty so expressed God's
> hatred of sin as to render possible the immediate foundation
> and gradual formation of a new race of men which shall at last
> perfectly manifest the moral love of God. The atonement is
> exactly in the death of Christ, if regarded in this comprehensive
> racial way.

Founding the New Race. The resurrection of our Lord
has a racial significance of much larger Christian consequence than its bearing upon the doctrine of personal
immortality. Indeed, the idea of personal immortality is
but a small item in the Christian conception of the future
life. The racial significance of Christ's resurrection lies
in two things: First, our Lord in his resurrection completed that human experience which prepared him to be
the dynamic center of the new race. Second, our Lord
in his resurrection obtained that "body of glory" which
is the type-model for the spiritual body of every member
of the new race. Thus, by our Saviour's resurrection the
racial center of organism becomes a finished fact.

Saint Paul is constantly inclined to relate the resurrection of Christ to our justification. For instance, in
Rom. 4. 25 we read: "Who was delivered up for our
trespasses, and was raised for our justification." This
fits into what I have said about the connectional import
of the death of Christ. His death reaches into the resurrection to obtain its redemptional feasibility. The racial
center must be finished by our Lord's resurrection before
it is feasible to justify men and thus constitute them
members of the redemptional organism.

The ascension of our Lord is sometimes considered as
the culmination of the resurrection; but it is better to
regard it as the formal historic induction into the racial
office of session. All such formal historic events (the

session, final judgment, etc.) are out of harmony with
the present drift in theology, but they must be recognized,
I believe, as real objective crises in the process of salvation. Even if the Scripture language is panoramic, it is
panoramic of actual formal history. The session of our
Lord is as truly outward history as is his birth or death.
In the New Testament, and especially in the Epistle to the
Hebrews, reference is often made to the session of our
Lord; but it is Saint Paul who brings out clearly the intercessory nature of the office. His words are (Rom. 8.
34): "Who is at the right hand of God, who also maketh
intercession for us." By this I understand that Christ is
become the perpetual Mediator between God and mankind.
As he has redeemed the race, and is now the center and
head of the redeemed race, it is through him—he is the
standpoint from which all human affairs are viewed.
Before this, all was tentative and provisional; but now
every human person and every human action and every
human experience—all are tested squarely and completely
by their relation to the person and work of Jesus Christ.
The whole world is now other to God because of what
Christ has done and because of what Christ is. Thus,
Christ is "seated at the right hand of God," that is, exalted to the throne of divine power; thus, we are forgiven
for Christ's sake; and thus, prayer is made in Christ's name.

We have, then, in the redemptive work of our Lord
a connected series of racial deeds:

1. *The Incarnation*, by which the Son of God becomes
the Race-Man.

2. *The Death of Christ*, by which he bears the racial
penalty and makes atonement for sin.

3. *The Resurrection*, by which our Lord founds the new
race of redemption.

4. *The Ascension*, by which our Lord is inducted into
the racial office of mediation.

5. *The Session*, by which our Lord is the mediatorial authority in the actual building of the new race and the final judge in determining the destiny of every human being.

Building the New Race. An atonement has been made for man's sin; the new race has been founded; and Jesus Christ is established in his mediatorial office. With all this done, there now begins the actual building of the new race, by saving men one by one through Jesus Christ. In a sense precise and full there was no Christian experience before the ascension of our Lord; also in a sense precise and full there is now and never can be any Christian experience where there is no faith in Christ as a personal Saviour from sin. Remember, though, I say no precise and full *Christian* experience; I do not say *religious* experience; and I am not here thinking of the question of ultimate salvation. I simply mean that the direct and positive building of the new race into Christ Jesus, with all the consequent personal experience, did not begin and could not begin until all his redemptive work, all his great racial deeds, were finished. In any fitting place, I am ready and eager to make essential connection between Christianity and the most worthy religious life; but I am not willing to becloud the splendor of peculiarity which belongs only to a man's experience in Jesus Christ.

In the next doctrinal division we are thoroughly to study the new man in Christ, but even now we need to glimpse a few notable points:

1. How God can forgive a sinner. Here you will miss much of the old terminology; but with a little patience you can, I think, adjust yourselves to the racial point of view. By faith in Jesus Christ, a man does, through the work of the Holy Spirit, make entrance into the new race. The man is spiritually joined to Christ, becomes a living part of that peculiar people organized in

Christ, and so is a part of that racial movement toward the glory of God. Fundamentally speaking, the atonement is the ground of forgiveness because the atonement purchased the very possibility of such racial union with Christ. But actually the sinner is forgiven *as making entrance into Christ*, which is precisely the same thing as making entrance into the new race. Now that the race is provided, God can forgive any man who does the full ethical task which is his side of the act of entrance. This task is *a moral faith* in Jesus Christ as a personal Saviour, or in Jesus Christ as the Son of God who has made in his death an atonement for all human sin. Because of the peculiarity of our time, I must insist upon the moral quality of the faith, by which I mean that it is a faith growing out of the profound moral experiences of conviction of sin and Christian repentance. Many a man's faith takes him *to* Christ, gives him a large appreciation *of* Christ, leads him to do countless deeds *for* Christ; but the man's faith has no moral quality, no driving urgency, and so it does not take him *into* Christ. *Personal salvation is realized only in Christ Jesus.* This is not rhetoric at all; we must make actual entrance into him, and must actually live in him forever. There is no other way for a sinner to be saved.

But does the faith save the sinner? Even if our answer were *Yes*, it would not mean that salvation comes by mere human "works," for this moral faith required, is itself a profound synergism, and would be impossible without divine contribution. But our answer to the question is *No*, positively, *No*. Faith has no redemptional quality; strictly speaking, faith is nothing but a *condition, the conditional act of personal entrance*. It is what one must do to enter Christ, but there is no redemption *in the bare act*, redemption *follows* the act. It is something like a man crossing the ocean. It is as a

condition exceedingly important that he have faith to
board the ship, but it is the ship itself which really lands
him safely on the other shore.

2. "Peace with God." Often the question is asked,
"How is a sinner's peace with God philosophically possible? How can he ever be satisfied with his sinful past?"
First, I will say that there is a large amount of false and
unwholesome teaching at this point. A sinner saved by
and in Jesus Christ is never satisfied with his sinful past
in the sense that he is complacent over it. To hear some
men talk, you would think that they had a sort of rich
rejoicing in the fact that they once were great sinners.
Whatever queer thing this may be, I have no interest in
discovering—I know that it has not in it even one pulse-
beat of real Christian experience. No Christian is satisfied with his sinful past; he wishes it were not there; he
hates it with untold might of hatred. But this hatred is
never a moral disturbance, never reaches into conscience.
Why not? First of all, because God has forgiven him.
But the redemptional psychology here is very profound.
It is not an arbitrary divine forgiveness which gives the
sinner peace, but a forgiveness *based upon the death of
the Son of God for his sins.* As I have said in another
connection: "A typical sinner is not a theologian; he has
no theory of the atonement; he does not pretend to know
what God requires, or what the moral law requires, or
even what he himself requires for abiding peace; but he
does believe that, whatever is required by anybody or
anything, the requirement is satisfied, because the person
upon that cross is God the Almighty trying to save him."
This, though, but leads to another question: How can this
peace be kept under a constantly expanding moral ideal?
The answer can be given in a word: The redeemed man
lives in Christ, and his expanding moral ideal is nothing
whatever but his growing conception of what Christ is

and what Christ wants him to do.   Thus, his life is full of
effort to be more and to do more, and yet the more he
struggles the deeper is his peace.

The Characteristics of the New Race.   The most economical way to conclude our long discussion of our Lord's
redemptive work is to gather up into definite points the
characteristics of the new race.   With these points before
us, we can, I think, understand why the holy God is
satisfied with such a race, or is satisfied with the death of
his Son as rendering such a race possible.

1. The new race is, by the death of Christ, so related to
the Adamic race, *penally*, as to express in perfect continuity God's condemnation of sin.

2. The center of the new race is the Son of God himself,
with a human racial experience completed by suffering.
And so the new race must forever express the awful ethical
cost at which it was obtained.

3. The new race is formed in such fashion that a man
can enter it only on the most rigid moral terms.   It is a
holy race by the very method of its formation.

4. This new race moves through history toward the goal
as the one thoroughly reliable servant of the moral concern
of God.

5. This new race grants to every moral person the
possibility of a holy completion of himself in his brethren
and in his Redeemer, and of coming to a perfect service, a
perfect rest, and a perfect joy.

6. This new race will, at last, be the victorious realization of God's original design in creation.

"And I heard a great voice out of heaven saying,
Behold, the tabernacle of God is with men, and he will
dwell with them, and they shall be his people, and
God himself shall be with them, and be their God."

THE FOURTH DOCTRINAL DIVISION
REDEMPTION REALIZED IN THE NEW MAN

Methought that the Lord showed me a heart into which he had put a *new* song. Where the heart was I do not know; but I heard it singing about the middle of its song. It *had* been singing, "What profit is there in my blood when I go down to the pit?" It had *been* singing the fifty-first psalm, and Jehovah had now put a *new song* into its mouth. He had done it; and the heart was *trying* to sing—I heard it in the middle of its song. It had been reading the fifth chapter of Revelation and *trying* to sing some of its numbers; and now it was at these words: "*For thou wast slain,*" and, O, how the heart was sobbing and breaking! how it was melting with a joyous grief and a grievous joy! O, how it faltered when it tried to sing, "*and hast redeemed us to God by thy blood*"! It was the song of one to whom much had been forgiven, and who, therefore, loved much, but it was the song of the chief of sinners, to whom most had been forgiven, and who, therefore, loved most. Yet it faltered and made wrong music; it jarred, and there was discord; and it grated on its own ear and pained it; and God was listening to the song—God who knoweth all things. But the song was presented to him through and by the Mediator: and if there was discord, it was removed by grace in atoning blood, by the sweet accents of intercession; for it came up as music in Jehovah's ear—melody to the Lord. It was not discord in heaven. I would know, O God, whose soul that is. O God, let that soul be mine.—*John Duncan*, New College, Edinburgh, 1843.

XXIV. THE PERSONAL DISPENSATION OF THE HOLY SPIRIT

The Question of Personality. When Professor Bey-schlag says that the notion of the Holy Spirit as a third divine person "is one of the most disastrous impor-tations into the Holy Scripture," he is writing as a ration-alist and not as a Christian scholar. We should admit at once, however, that there is for the personality of the Holy Spirit no such indisputable exegetical foundation as there is for the deity of our Lord. The fact is, that this is one of those peculiar places where Christian experience must approach the New Testament with a certain bias. With our Lord as a second person in the Godhead, the theolog-ical problem finds no further philosophical difficulty by making the plurality into a trinity. Indeed, for a certain type of speculative mind, the trinity actually helps us to understand the plurality. But the personality of the Holy Spirit is much more than an *easy addition* for the Christian man—it is almost a *necessary addition.* The Christian consciousness is ever more and more inclined to believe that the Holy Ghost is a person. In any time of rich quickening and deepening of the Christian life you will notice, in song and prayer and testimony, a con-tinual dwelling upon the personality of the Holy Spirit. And, as we would naturally expect, the bias of the Chris-tian consciousness enters into the interpretation of God's Word, as it certainly should.

All this frankly said, still the argument for the person-ality of the Holy Spirit is not weak, if it is not over-whelming. Separated from forced and dubious elements, the argument may be outlined as follows:

1. The most unartificial explanation of our Saviour's own conception is that the Holy Spirit is a person. If you study the sixteenth chapter of Saint John's gospel you will notice that the Spirit is always treated in careful separation from both the Father and the Son. Then, the term παράκλητος suggests much more than an impersonal influence. There is personal peculiarity implied. He is the intimate helper in danger, distress, sin, and all daily Christian need. To all this must be added that our Lord, after the resurrection, placed a separate stress upon the Spirit, "baptizing them into the name of the Father and of the Son and of the Holy Ghost" (Saint Matt. 28. 19). Some of the critics, I know, demand that this passage shall be given up; but I do not find their reasoning convincing. My conclusion is that there is indication that our Lord did not regard the Holy Spirit as a mere influence from himself, or from his Father, or from both the Father and the Son; but rather as a distinctly self-conscious Spirit.

2. In the early church the inspired Christian consciousness, as seen in the book of Acts, treated the Holy Spirit in distinction and emphasis just as he had been treated by our Lord. There are many such expressions as these: "The Holy Spirit said" (Acts 13. 2); "For it seemed good to the Holy Spirit" (Acts 15. 28). Surely these passages can be explained as figurative color, or more profoundly as psychological dramatization; but to take them as personal is less ingenious; and when connection is made with our Lord's teaching the case is yet stronger.

3. The teaching of Saint Paul can best be obtained by comparing Rom. 8. 26, 27 with the following: Rom. 8. 15, 16; 1 Cor. 12. 4–11; 2 Cor. 13. 14. To any student making this comparison in full, Saint Paul will certainly be regarded as holding and teaching the distinct personality of the Holy Spirit. And so the apostle Paul in

his epistles must be added to the book of Acts and to the teaching of our Lord.

4. In the antenicene period the Holy Spirit was in Christian consciousness clearly separated from the Father and from the Son, as could not have been the case had he been regarded as a mere impersonal influence from either or both of them. I have space for only one quotation. It is from Justin Martyr's First Apology (vi), and has been translated as follows: "And we confess that we are atheists, so far as gods of this sort are concerned; but not with respect to the most true God, the Father of righteousness and temperance and the other virtues, who is free from all impurity. But both him, and the Son . . . and the prophetic Spirit, we worship and adore."

What I would claim, then, is this: If we carefully examine the body of Christian utterance from the teaching of our Lord down to the most significant expression of the Christian consciousness before the organized church had any crucial doctrinal task on hand, we shall find that a belief in the personality of the Holy Spirit is naturally implied by that utterance. And I further claim that today the case is, for the Christian man, not one of exact exegesis and unbiased interpretation. For two reasons he has a practical and wholesome bias, which turns the above argument into personal conviction: First, the philosophical victory of Athanasius really makes for the personality of the Holy Spirit; and, second, the increasing deposit of Christian consciousness, for all the Christian centuries, more and more requires the personality of the Holy Spirit. It is not an instance of fundamental addition to the Word of God; but it is an instance where Christian history and Christian consciousness have rejected certain possible interpretations of biblical data and have resulted in an interpretation which is not satisfactory to any rationalistic scholar. But the rationalistic scholar himself has just as much bias as has the Christian scholar.

The Dispensation. When we speak of a "dispensation of the Spirit" we do not mean that Christ Jesus is now less in emphasis; nor do we mean that until now the Holy Spirit has been inactive; we mean simply that the peculiar work of building a new race into Christ is the work of the Spirit of God. This kind of work could not be done before because the new race was not founded. Thus, when it is said that the dispensation of the Holy Spirit was rendered possible only by the atonement in the death of Christ, the remark, however intended, is the exact truth. Details of conversion will be dealt with later; but, first of all, let us look at some of the general characteristics of this dispensation of the Holy Ghost:

1. The Superficial Quiet of the Dispensation. A very marked peculiarity of this dispensation of the Spirit is that, as a rule, the surface of life is so undisturbed. Now and then the Spirit's struggle with a soul shows itself in noise and external indications of battle, but usually the conflict is fought out entirely in the depths of the human soul. The man talks and laughs and plans a shrewd trade and takes his evening in pleasure and seems to be careless of all spiritual demand; but there is another chapter which you cannot read. Motives are being used, great self-decisions are now and again being made, silently there is deposit after deposit in moral character; and all this is watched and treated and lifted into full redemptional bearing by the swift and profound agency of the Holy Spirit. And there is a philosophy in this quiet, undramatic method, too; for were there constant noise and upheaval and terror there could be no genuine self-decision. It would be easy enough to make the whole race extremely religious by external coercive expedient. One crash of the planets would send every son of Adam

to his knees. But this religion of coercion would not
have even an atom of ethical meaning, and all the test of
probation would have to be made in some other way.
One word of exception is necessary here, however. There
are times when it is needful to arouse pure fear to break
up the habit of torpidity and render the operation of self-
decision possible. But even in these torpid situations
the fear must not be turned into overwhelming fright.
It is to contribute to self-consciousness and not to
smother it.

2. The Supreme Moral Quality of the Dispensation.
But this quiet, although it lends itself to moral test, does
not furnish the positive ethical quality of the Spirit's
dispensation. This ethical quality comes from two things:
First, from the actual stimulation which the Holy Spirit
gives to personality. There could be no realization of
moral demand unless the person were made strong enough
to remain in self-consciousness. Thus, the foundation of
all ethical movement lies in personality itself. And
whatever makes for strong personality always makes
for ethical possibility. In this statement is infolded the
main principle of all wise effort in reforming men. Second,
from the supremacy which the Holy Spirit grants to conscience. A full Christian experience involves the entire
man; but the Spirit's point of pressure is the conscience.
No Christian thing can ever be secured until the conscience is thoroughly utilized and thoroughly satisfied.
This does not conflict with anything that I have said in
our study of morality. No man can satisfy his moral
ideal when it is the cold, abstract, impersonal demand of
morality; but the moral ideal in the Christian process is,
by the Holy Spirit, quickly related to the personal God
and to Jesus Christ; and this Christian change profoundly
effects the entire moral situation. But what I wish now
to make emphatic is this: In building a Christian man the

Holy Spirit places the utmost stress upon conscience. To be a Christian man *you must take all your conscience along with you.* It is true that we are not come unto a "tempest and the sound of a trumpet," but the mountain unto which we are come has in it just as much moral quality as there ever was in Mount Sinai. And Mount Sinai had in it just as much moral quality as there ever can be in the loftiest pure morality.

3. The Infinite Gentleness of the Dispensation. There are times when the Holy Spirit seems to be furious, and he disturbs a wicked soul until there are no human words which can describe the awful torture. But when we look at the dispensation as a whole we find it full of gentleness. How patient he is with us! How he searches and searches for every faint beginning of better intention, to lift it more clearly into self-consciousness! How he waits for our final meaning, waits like an endless Friendship! And how extremely gentle his touch is! He handles a soul as a Great Mother handles a babe! He is so sensitive that even one vile thought grieves him, and yet he clings and clings to the worst sinner with the tenacity of holy love. "Thy patient love, at what a cost, at last it conquered me!"

4. The Inevitableness of the Test. From the very fact that the dispensation of the Holy Spirit is so quiet and so ethical and so gentle, the test of the moral person as to intention is inevitable. No man, whatever his outward life, whatever his individual inheritance, whatever his opinions, can escape the searching questions of the Holy Ghost. He is the one abiding Interrogator that cannot be evaded and cannot be silenced. He is the augmented Conscience bound to come to terms of clear understanding with the sinner. Every external test, and every mental test, can be avoided. A man may honestly believe a half truth, and himself manipulate a falsehood into per-

sonal conviction.   He may inherit prejudices which he
cannot now even wish to overcome.   He may live where
his environment is a lifelong disadvantage.   But under
all—environment, inheritance, chosen opinions—under
all the Holy Spirit squarely and repeatedly meets the
man and says: "What do you mean to do with your moral
ideal?"   Sooner or later the man must answer that
question.

5. The Finality of the Test.   If what I have said of
the Spirit's dispensation be true, then it follows that, in
the very nature of the case, there can be no further moral
test.   The test under the Holy Spirit is *final*.   Not because God is arbitrary and unwilling, but simply because
the dispensation of the Holy Spirit exhausts all moral
procedure.   *There is nothing more which can be done.*   Of
course, if sainthood were automatic, much more could
be done; but inasmuch as sainthood is and must be moral
(to be sainthood at all), the notion of a second probation is
inconceivable.

"*The sin against the Holy Ghost.*"   "Therefore I say
unto you, Every sin and blasphemy shall be forgiven unto
men; but the blasphemy against the Spirit shall not be
forgiven.   And whosoever shall speak a word against the
Son of man, it shall be forgiven him; but whosoever shall
speak against the Holy Spirit, it shall not be forgiven him,
neither in this world, nor in that which is to come" (Saint
Matt. 12. 31, 32; Saint Mark 3. 28–30; Saint Luke 12. 10).
The clue to these seemingly strange words of our Lord is
added by Saint Mark: "Because they said, He hath an
unclean spirit."   They could make an honest mistake
as to Jesus himself, they might not be able to look upon
him as their expected Messiah; but to say that all the
good Christ did was inspired by an unclean spirit revealed a heart fixed in hostility to the right—an irreme-
diable turpitude of the personal motive-life.   This sin could

never be forgiven because it was a finality in their intentional bearing. In brief, the sin against the Holy Ghost is the full personal rejection of all the moral demand which the Holy Ghost makes through conscience. In the sixteenth article of the Church of England, 1552, we read, "Blasphemy against the Holy Ghost is when a man of malice, and stubbornness of mind, doth rail upon the truth of God's Word manifestly perceived." Commenting upon this article, Dean Mansel says, "Thus interpreted, the sin is not a single act, but a spirit of hostility to Christ, manifesting itself in continued acts." The article and the comment have caught the spirit of the sin, but they are not profound enough to fit into the Saviour's statement. The sin is not directly against him, nor directly against the Scripture, but against moral concern itself. It is the culmination of personal sin into a fixed attitude of willful unrighteousness. And so it is the complete exhaustion of the pressure of the Holy Spirit. And so it is not forgivable—it is everlasting moral ruin.

ORDO SALUTIS

BUILDING THE NEW MAN IN CHRIST
THE TYPICAL PROCESS IN OUTLINE

I. THE PREPARATION FOR CONVERSION.
  A. *The Human Side of the Preparation.*
    1. The bearing of persons.
    2. The bearing of the Christian church.
      (1) The preacher.
      (2) The people.
    3. The bearing of the sinner himself.
  B. *The Divine Side of the Preparation.*
    1. The ordinary work of the Holy Spirit in conscience.
    2. The extraordinary work of the Holy Spirit in conscience.
      (1) Enlightenment.
      (2) Awakening.
      (3) Conviction of sin.
      (4) Invitation.
II. CONVERSION. The first point of Christian attainment—the loyal person.
  A. *The Human Side of Conversion.*
    1. Repentance.
    2. Faith.
  B. *The Divine Side of Conversion.*
    1. Justification.
    2. Regeneration.
    3. Adoption.
III. CHRISTIAN HOLINESS. The second point of Christian attainment—the holy person.
IV. THE INTERMEDIATE STATE. The third point of Christian attainment—the completed personal individual.
V. THE RESURRECTION OF THE BODY. The fourth point in Christian attainment—the completed new man in Christ.

XXV. THE PREPARATION FOR CONVERSION

FIRST of all, it may be well to remind you of the true philosophy of influence in any consistent Arminian theology; for many an Arminian is quite ready, after insisting that the influence of God cannot be coercive, to teach that the influence of men can actually and efficiently bring about the conversion of a sinner. Surely you readily perceive the underlying inconsistency. Let it be said, then, plainly and repeatedly, that no human influence is ever compulsory to the personal acceptance of Jesus Christ. But what, then, can we do by our influence? We can do very much. The Holy Spirit, in his dispensation, allows us to work together with him in doing two things: First, in clearing up the self-consciousness so there can be self-decision. Second, in furnishing a motive for *immediate* self-decision. Never can we coerce a moral person, but we can make it necessary for him *to do something instantly*. We also can do many very valuable things in relation to the surface of life; but with these we are not now concerned. For example, it is of worth to keep the life of a child outwardly moral by personal watchcare, but we are doing a superficial thing, after all, a thing which should not be in any manner confused with real conversion.

The Bearing of Persons. By the term *bearing* I mean much more than word or deed, although these may manifest the bearing. I also mean something different from the quiet influence of moral character, although such character is of the largest moment. "What you are speaks so loud I cannot hear what you say." I mean precisely this: You hold a certain noble ideal over against

a certain man—that he shall be a Christian of the largest
and profoundest kind—and steadily you bear toward this
man, without dropping the ideal, and without weakening
the demand. To yourself you say, day after day, and
perhaps year after year: "Ah, you cannot deceive me. I
will believe in you more deeply than your own estimate.
And I will not be satisfied with any makeshift. You
simply must be *this other man* which I have in mind."
The important thing is not how this bearing is expressed;
the important thing is that you *really have it*, that you
cultivate it, that you never give it up either before men or
before God. If we could only exchange our general
"passion for souls" for an unyielding heartache for
definite men, our influence would be greater. The mighti-
est thing we can ever do for a man is to insist upon
suffering for him until he is a new man in our Lord. But
it takes a great Christian to suffer, and to suffer wisely
and helpfully, for other men.

The Bearing of the Church. Here the problem is to
create for all the work of the church, and especially for
the church services, *a Christian atmosphere.* The first
thing to do is to unload the church of all its unchristian
features—music or ritual or anything which is planned
as a substitute for Christian pressure. It matters not
whether the church service is in form simple or complex,
beautiful or rugged, provided that every item makes its
positive spiritual offering to a Christian atmosphere. But
yet more important is the bearing of the Christian congregation. Every Christian person in the congregation
should *insist upon a Christian atmosphere*, praying for it,
preparing for it, expecting it, and so making personal
contribution to it. But yet more important is the bearing
of the preacher himself. He can, in combination with the
Holy Spirit, do more than the entire congregation. Again
and again I have known Dr. John Hall to come into his

pulpit and before he had spoken one word change the atmosphere from that of the world to that of the gospel. He brought Christian urgency with him; and personality began to rouse up, and conscience to make demand all over the room. The preacher's bearing was fully as important as his sermon.

The Bearing of the Sinner Himself. It is of the utmost importance how the sinner meets the different pressures against his life, and how he treats the moral ideal which he now has. Not infrequently we hear some man say: " But I have never had any *feeling* that I should become a Christian—I must wait for that." If the man's words are true to the fact, the probability is that his bearing has been unopen toward many small spiritual appeals. The work of the Holy Spirit is not arbitrary—it has root-connections. Just as the bursting blossom has a history which reaches down out of sight into the ground, so a spiritual crisis is the outcome of many unseen things in personal history. This I believe: any self-conscious person *can begin right where he is* and bear toward God. There is some right thing which he can choose—some moral beckoning which he can follow. This does not mean that conversion is immediately possible, but it does mean such a personal response to the Holy Spirit that more spiritual experiences can be given to a man. But from what I have said you are likely to infer that the work of the Holy Spirit is *always* in this measure-for-measure method? Such is not the case. The Holy Spirit will do, sooner or later, every possible gracious thing for a sinner; but it is in his wish to make use of people, and the sinner himself, as much as possible; and so again and again he waits for men, and precisely adapts his influence to their bearing. It is almost impossible to give a perfectly balanced statement of the entire case; but there are two points which you must tenaciously hold: First, that moral response is always possible to a self-conscious moral person.   Second, that such response *tends* toward conversion.

The Divine Side of the Preparation.   Every movement in conscience is the work, I believe, of the Holy Spirit; but it is impossible to obtain any exact and exhaustive psychology of this work.   We may, though, for the sake of redemptional emphasis, fairly divide the whole field, by making a distinction between the *ordinary* and the *extraordinary* operations of the Spirit.   What we find is precisely this: Beyond all those common moral experiences which I have covered with the phrase *sporadic morality*, there are certain additional experiences which are so momentously significant that they should be made to stand out, in all practical Christian discussion, as something more than the usual manifestations of conscience.   These additional experiences are in inherent correspondence with the higher experiences of the moral process, but they are deepened and augmented and corrected by GRACE.   By grace I understand neither more nor less than *that special intense action* of the Holy Spirit which is his response to the definite redemptional purpose of our Lord Jesus Christ as the Mediator in actual session between God and man.   What we have now under the *grace of Christ* is the filling out of the old moral indications.   Even those initial things are in the dispensation of the Spirit, and in consequence (logically) of the atonement, and in teleo-logical connection with the plan of salvation; but it is only in grace that we perceive the crowning peculiarity of the Spirit's dispensation.   What I want you all to do is this: First, ground the process of conversion in the moral process itself.   Then, lift the whole thing into positive Christian peculiarity.   *Keep the moral basis, but add grace.*

These extraordinary moral experiences, in as far as they belong to the preparation for conversion, are as follows:

1. *A Vision of Righteousness.* For the first time the sinner sees that all separate items of wrong are but splinters of *one vast wrong* which is in antagonism to *one vast righteousness.* It is not enough to do right, here and there, now and then. Thus, the man obtains a moral ideal, and a sense of personal obligation toward his ideal. Morally the man is in a new state, and the theological term which expresses this new condition is *enlightenment.* The sinner has been *enlightened* by the Holy Ghost. This term enlightenment is very convenient; but I would make no battle for the word. The main thing is to keep hold of the fact of this new conception of righteousness as a whole.

2. *A Vision of the Holy God.* In the bare moral process, this vision of the totality of the right secures no adequate outcome; but in the full Christian process it is but the beginning of a larger vision, namely, the vision of the Holy God. Righteousness is now made personal, but that is not all. There is a further note of *intense divine concern for righteousness.* The Holy God is not a mere person who is righteous; his whole being is on fire with it, and the flame of his awful purity is unapproachable by man. With this vision of the Holy God the sinner may be considered as having been *awakened* by the Holy Ghost.

3. *A Vision of Sin.* This is the completion of the vision of righteousness and God. Sin is seen to be not merely a violation of conscience, but an *unnatural rebellion against the Holy God, who is intensely concerned about it.* Now comes the real *conviction of sin.* "Against thee, thee only, have I sinned, and done that which is evil in thy sight." If we try to analyze the conviction of sin we shall find in it two features: First, the feeling that our sin is under God's absolute condemnation. In John Bunyan's case there was such a keen realization of impending judg-

ment that he was literally filled with terror. He says: "There was I struck into a very great trembling, insomuch that at some times I could, for days together, feel my very body, as well as my mind, to shake and totter under the sense of the dreadful judgment of God." This is an extreme case, and it would seem almost as if the terror were so great as to become coercive; but in all conviction of sin there is deep distress over the wrath of God. Second, there is a feeling of self-blame. When convicted of sin, a sinner does not begin to excuse himself. He does not blame his parents, the law of heredity, the people about him; he blames just himself. He actually joins in the divine condemnation; and, to keep Wesley's phrase, lets the law of God "glare upon him."

4. *Divine Invitation*. Were this conviction of sin the end, the sinner's situation in the Christian process would be more hopeless than it is in the moral process; but the end is not yet. Into this distress and severity and gathering despair there comes the *invitation* by the Holy Spirit. The form and outward circumstances of this invitation may be one thing or another—a friendly Christian look, a letter from home, a prayer, a sermon; but whatever the form, the content is the voice of God's Spirit, saying, "Come, come, my son; Jesus Christ wills to save you." The tenderness of this invitation is almost the most wonderful thing in all the action of the Holy Spirit. It is like a rainbow springing into the sky after a storm and lending a quiet hopefulness to every frightened creature and to every dripping thing.

With this invitation from the Holy Spirit, the entire preparation for conversion is completed.

XXVI. CONVERSION

THE HUMAN SIDE OF CONVERSION

WHEN we speak of a human side of conversion we are speaking practically and not profoundly. In repentance, as well as in faith, there is a synergism, where God's part is much more important than man's part; but for practical reasons it is man's part that we seek to emphasize.

Repentance. This is another place where we have to do not so much with the Greek words (μετανοέω—ἐπιστρέφω) as with the total teaching of the New Testament, and with the total Christian consciousness. We will start with a provisional "working definition." *Repentance is a personal sorrow for personal sin as against the Holy God.* In the first place, we should place the greatest emphasis upon the point that repentance is *personal.* I mean this in the most earnest sense. Repentance is not merely something done by a person, it is something done by a person *when he is self-conscious.* It is not a feeling of disturbance in consciousness, but a feeling of moral disturbance in *self*-consciousness. It involves a clear estimate of self under a moral ideal. No man can repent without real self-decision, and there can be no self-decision without full self-consciousness. In the next place, repentance is a personal *sorrow.* The sorrow itself is, I believe, the gift of God; but it comes to personal appropriation in self-decision, and expresses at last the personal bearing of the sinner himself. In the next place, this sorrow is *over the sinner's personal sin.* The sorrow is not over vice. One may be in distress over vice and not have the spirit of repentance at all. Our vices may imperil our ambitious plans, and ruin our friendships, and make us outcasts from

society, and injure our health, and even limit our pleasures
—and we may be greatly troubled over it all.   But such
trouble is not sorrow over personal sin.   Nor is repentance
a man's distressing disturbance *at being found out*.   Many
a criminal has been so extremely wretched, when caught
in his crime, as to be taken for a penitent; but his penitence
proved to be over his misfortune and not over his vileness
of heart.   In the last place, the sorrow is over the fact
that the sinner's personal sin is *against the Holy God*.
The final drop of bitterness in the cup of the repentant
sinner is that he is hostile to the Holy God.   He looks
upon himself as a miserable rebel; and, without one
clause of extenuation, his cry is only for mercy.

It is now possible and may be helpful to enter somewhat into the philosophy of repentance.   What we
really have in Christian repentance is *the conviction of sin
made hopeful*.   After the Holy Spirit's invitation the
sinner still keeps his vision of sin and the Holy God; but
the vision is not alone in self-consciousness, it is there
with the invitation.   And so the vision is refashioned by
being shot through and through with hope.   This gives the
sinner courage to make such a perfectly compliant response
that the Holy Spirit can do more, namely, *break the man's
hard heart*.   This is *contrition of heart*, and it is the very
marrow of Christian repentance.   But we are going a bit
too fast.   Contrition of heart is, closely speaking, the
broken heart, the work of the Spirit, accepted, personalized, made the sinner's very own act.   And the sinner
does all this by three personal attitudes: First, confession.   I do not mean words, although words are likely
to be used, but an attitude of complete acknowledgment
of guilt before God.   It is the hopeful enlargement of
the self-blame in conviction.   And, second, a hopeful determination to get right at any cost.   This is what Dr.
Whedon was wont to call the "purpose of righteousness."

The whole feeling is this: "God himself wants me to be right, then I can be right, then I will be right." And, third, personal hatred of his sin as ungodly. The repentant sinner begins to hate all his sin bitterly as a thing in antagonism with the holiness of God.

Final Definition of Repentance. To complete our provisional definition, we would say this: Repentance is a sinner's personal sorrow over his responsible sin, both in deed and in condition of heart; and involves a confession of the guilt of his sin, a purpose to get free from his sin, and an intense hatred of his sin as against the holy God. It is contrition of heart with three distinct notes—confession, determination, and moral hatred.

Faith. As a matter of fact, there is a certain element of faith necessary toward the Holy Spirit's invitation before there can be any repentance; but the full, culminating personal bearing of *saving faith* is properly placed here after repentance and in close relation to justification.

The Nature of Faith. The biblical writers do not aim to provide any exhaustive idea of the inherent nature of faith; but there is one suggestive passage, the familiar beginning of the eleventh chapter of the Epistle to the Hebrews: "Now faith is assurance of things hoped for, a conviction of things not seen." The meaning can be given thus: Faith makes the unseen things for which a person hopes certain to his soul. And I think we can go further and analyze the meaning to some advantage: First, the object of faith must be beyond the seizure of the senses, and beyond the entire field of coercive reality. You cannot have faith in anything which can be so exactly demonstrated as to overwhelm the personal equation. Second, this unseen object of faith must be *hoped for*. That is, the object of faith is a personal ideal which calls out the heart. Third, this unseen ideal faith turns into a personal conviction. The person is *convinced* that

the ideal is not a vagary, but an object as real as the
objects which are seen.   Indeed, sometimes to a great
saint the invisible world is much more real than is the
visible world.

But I want to examine more closely this term *hoped for*
(ἐλπιζομένων).   If I mistake not, the underlying idea is
the same that we find again and again in the New Testament, and especially in that verse of hot controversy in
the fifth chapter of Galatians: "For in Christ Jesus
neither circumcision availeth anything, nor uncircum-
cision; but faith working through love" (δι' ἀγάπης).
I will not join in the controversy over this last clause;
still I have no doubt whatever but that a sound interpretation requires the love to be regarded as a normal
feature of faith.   There can be no full faith without love,
and no faith at all without some heart-interest.   The
person's will cannot lay hold of the invisible ideal without
motive, and the motive is this heart-yearning which
idealizes the object and makes it attractive.   Every man
of faith is a spiritual idealizer—a poet, if you will.

But even with this contribution from the heart faith is
a *personal venture*.   I would state it in this way: Faith
is the personal venture by which we create that confidence in an ideal which is necessary to satisfy our entire
being.   My heart has turned the object into an ideal;
and now I need this ideal, not as a dream, but as a reality;
and by the power of my personality I actually make the
ideal real to myself.   Thus, in faith a man always *takes
a risk*.   But he takes this risk in the name of satisfied
manhood.

You must not, though, suppose that the mind has no
place in faith.   In all normal faith the mind is entirely
satisfied, only it is never allowed to make any demand
contrary to the needs of the whole man.   For illustration,
take the idea of personal immortality.   There is no

evidence adequate to satisfy the mind in isolation.   But if the mind takes its place in relation to all a man is in conscience—in heart; if the man, as a moral person, *hopes for* a world beyond the grave; if he, out of a spiritual life here, now, ventures on into perfect faith as to immortality, then his mind is satisfied completely.   Indeed, there is nothing more thoroughly rational in all thinking than a Christian man's faith in personal immortality. He is just as rational as is the rationalist.

I am not quite pleased with what I have written concerning the mind and faith.   It is true enough, but too vague.   The fact is that in normal faith the person makes his venture *with a satisfied mind*.   He does not, as some have taught, first believe in order that afterward he may satisfy his mind.   He never drops his mind; he never lets go of reality for an instant.   But the mind is not allowed to work alone, and the reality is lifted into an ideal for the whole man.   Come back to immortality. What we have there is not a *sheer fancy*, but an ideal conception which is rooted in a group of things of which the man is sure now in this life.   For this ideal conception there is no coercive evidence to reach the mind alone, but there is enough evidence so that when the man dares to make the personal venture, in the name of his ideal, and out of genuine spiritual need, his *mind goes with him, satisfied all the time*.

This is just the connection in which we may best grasp the difference between normal faith and that abnormal faith which is presumption.   In presumption the mind is never satisfied.   The venture is made in the most arbitrary way without any regard to reality.   A man of presumption is bound to have his own way even if he has to do violence to every fact in the universe.   Thus, the venture is likely at last to violate the moral nature.   A man of faith, on the contrary, wants nothing whatever

as a willful capture at the expense of reality. But he
does believe that reality is vast enough to satisfy thoroughly an entire man, heart as well as intellect. Here in
one incident is the difference in spirit between faith and
presumption. After trying to control the will of a
severely wounded man a certain "faith-healer" impa-
tiently exclaimed: "I cannot help you as long as you keep
believing that your head is cut open." The man answered:
"But it *is* cut open. I will not believe a lie even to get
well."

Different Kinds of Faith. There are two things which,
either separately or in combination, differentiate one kind
of faith from another kind. These two things are the
relation to conscience and the nature of the ideal object.
Perhaps our most useful plan will be to secure two main
divisions from the standpoint of moral quality, and then
the subdivisions from the standpoint of peculiarity in the
ideal.

I. *Non-Moral Faith.*

1. Secular Faith. Such faith we find wherever there
is an unrealized object which is not a matter of exact
knowledge, and yet is in some way an ideal toward which
a man goes out in full but unarbitrary aspiration. There
may be such aspiration toward such an ideal in national
life, or in science, or in invention, or in discovery, or even
in the ordinary world of business. In truth, the very
great things in secular affairs are usually done by faith;
sometimes admittedly by presumption, but more often
by such a combination of knowledge and hope and venture
as amounts to real faith.

2. Bare Religious Faith. This has already been noticed
in our Introduction, and no further word is required in
this connection.

II. *Moral Faith.*

3. The Lowest Phase of Moral Faith. A secular faith

may (as in the finest patriotism, or in the most noble philanthropy) involve the moral nature, and so become a moral faith, expressing not only mind and heart-interest and personal venture, but also a positive sense of duty.

4. The Lowest Phase of Moral Religious Faith. In the religion of the moral person it is possible to have a moral faith which is not definitely theistic, and so we protect this fact in our classification.

5. Theistic Faith. Here the ideal is either the personal God or the moral law considered as the manifest will of the personal God.

6. Messianic Faith. The Old Testament faith, at its highest, is much more than a theistic faith; for the ideal is saturated with a peculiar redemptional expectancy. The Old Testament prophet, deal with him as critically as the Christian consciousness will permit, is looking on— on to a coming Redeemer from sin; and this Messianic element gives to the object of faith a moral intensity which is not possible to any form of naked theism.

7. Christian Faith. To the Christian man the Redeemer is no longer an expectation—*He is come!* And this one fact lifts every phase of Christian faith into a completeness which is merely suggested by other kinds of faith.

The Faith that Saves a Sinner. In New Testament usage, the word πίστις has a number of very different meanings. Sometimes it means fidelity; again it means a trust in a divine promise; again it means a man's entire attitude of confidence toward God; and again it means the essential body of Christian teaching. But beyond all this there is, especially in Saint Paul's epistles, a conception of a definite faith which saves a sinner; and this *saving faith* is the root of every phase of Christian faith. This saving faith is "faith in Jesus Christ" (see the third chapter of Romans). But the Christian meaning does not all appear in the phrase.   It is not Jesus as a person, nor Jesus as a teacher, nor Jesus as a Master; but Jesus as the Son of God become our actual Saviour from sin. Bishop Lightfoot, in his commentary on Galatians, says that to understand the force, and to appreciate the leading conception, of Saint Paul's teaching as to faith, "it would be necessary to take into account the atoning death and resurrection of Christ as the central object on which that faith is fixed."   In any normal situation the full object of saving faith is this: Jesus Christ as God in self-sacrifice become man; and having by his death made full atonement for sin.   This double emphasis makes the essential ideal, but often it has been enlarged to cover the resurrection and even the present mediation of our Lord. I would not say, however, that in every individual case to-day the sinner's faith in Christ involves the entirety of this double emphasis, and that without it there is no real conversion.   I dare not say so much.   But I do say that a sinner who has been convicted of sin, and who has responded in thorough repentance, *needs*, in his object of faith, both the deity and the death of our Lord; and when either is lacking his Christian experience is likely to be extremely superficial.

DEFINITIONS

Concise.

Saving faith is the perfect trust of a repentant sinner in Jesus Christ as his divine Saviour from sin.

Enlarged.

Saving faith is the perfect trust of a repentant sinner in Jesus Christ as his divine Saviour from sin; and involves the entire man—mind and sensibility and will.

Comprehensive.

Saving faith is a personal bearing of the entire man; presupposing that sense of moral need which is completed by repentance; and involving, normally, a conviction that Christ is God, and that his death was an atonement for sin; and further involving a feeling of both duty and love toward Christ; this whole bearing being gathered up in a positive venture out upon Christ as a personal Saviour.

The Divine Side of Conversion

Those exact distinctions which are made in systematic theology between justification, regeneration, and adoption are not supported by modern biblical investigation. In presenting the Christian life, not only has every New Testament writer a way of his own, but, what is still more confusing, no writer aims to secure any philosophical consistency in his different statements. Saint Paul comes the nearest to fundamental consistency; but when we apply the modern method to his epistles, the most of his assertions are seen to be practical and literary rather than philosophical. Justification and adoption, for example, are not separate and exclusive things in Saint Paul's mind, as if God first justified a sinner before the law and then adopted him into his family. The apostle is all the time writing about the same thing, only with two literary forms in mind, and so from two different practical points of emphasis.

Still there is great advantage, for some minds at least, in so lifting out of all vagueness the different practical points of emphasis as to separate them into distinct *momenta* of the divine side of conversion. Such separation gives us a clearer view of the magnificent total of Christian experience, and need not mislead anyone, if he only keep in mind that we are dealing not with several basal things, but with one basal thing in its several practical relations.

Justification. The Greek word here is δικαιόω. Whether we hold, with some commentators, that the word means *to make righteous*, or hold, with other commentators, that the word means *to pronounce righteous*, is really of no great concern. In either case, the meaning is merely *forensic*. The sinner's new condition is a legal condition. The use of this term does not indicate in the least the present subjective state of the sinner, but only that the law has no further claim against him.

In a most characteristic passage Cardinal Newman admits that δικαιοῦν means only to declare righteous, but adds that the divine declaration is *creative*. "It is not like some idle sound, or a vague rumor coming at random and tending no whither; but it is 'the *word* which goeth forth out of his mouth'; it has a sacramental power, being the instrument as well as the sign of his will. It never can 'return unto him void, but it accomplishes that which he pleases, and prospers in the thing whereto he sends it.' Imputed righteousness is the coming in of actual righteousness. They whom God's sovereign voice pronounces just, forthwith become in their measure just." How like Newman all this sounds! So original, so uplifting, and yet so empty of reality and so distant from Saint Paul! Through Newman's discussion one can seldom catch even the faintest and most flashing glimpse of the apostle.

What, then, does Saint Paul mean by the justification of a sinner? He does not mean that God *actually wills the condition of subjective righteousness into the soul of a sinner*. Nor do I think that Saint Paul means that God forgives a sinner, or pardons a sinner. Those words, forgiveness and pardon, answer well enough in ordinary speech; but neither one of them is quite large enough to express *all* the apostle means by justification. Perhaps I can best bring out the Pauline view by a paraphrase: "I am thinking of those who are *in* Christ Jesus, in him by faith and the work of the Holy Spirit. How are they now related to God? They are to him *as righteous men*. The past is blotted out, and they are in a class now fully under his favor, to be treated as men saved by the death of Christ. In one word, they are justified, for no longer are they under the condemnation of the law."

Dr. Latimer's Definition.

"We therefore define justification to be that gracious act of God, as Moral Governor, whereby, on the ground of the atonement, and on condition of faith in Christ, he pardons the penitent, and treats him as though he had not sinned, and receives him into positive favor."

Popular Definition.

Justification is God's acceptance of a sinner who joins himself by moral faith to Jesus Christ.

Descriptive Definition.

When a repentant sinner has faith in Jesus Christ as his divine Saviour, God forgives the man's sin, and receives the man himself into full favor, because Christ died for him. Thus, the sinner is *justified.*

Final Definition.

Justification is that change in personal bearing, whereby God, because of the death of Christ, and on condition of a repentant sinner's faith in Christ as his divine Saviour, receives him into full favor.

Regeneration. I cannot agree with Professor Sanday when he says that "the Christian life is made to have its beginning in a fiction." Such an idea of fiction in justification comes from failing to remember that justification is but a phase, one relative aspect, of a fundamental experience. That fundamental experience is union with Christ. And, while one phase of this union is a new relation to God's favor, another phase is a new spiritual life in the sinner himself, a new life which is obtained by a new relation to the Holy Ghost. To use John Wesley's words, "There is a *real* as well as a *relative* change." "No man is justified without being regenerated."

The Scripture Data. In coming to the New Testament we are to seek only data, and not any philosophy of regeneration; and such data we find in great abundance. First, we have Saint Peter's phrase, "having been begotten again" (1 Pet. 1. 23). Then, we have Saint John's words: "Whosoever believeth that Jesus is the Christ, is begotten of God" (1 John 5. 1; also see 1 John 2. 29; 3. 9;

4. 7; and compare with Saint John's gospel 1. 12, 13). Then, although Saint Paul is peculiarly the teacher of justification, still he now and again seems to have in mind the change which takes place in the sinner himself. In Galatians (4. 19) he writes, "until Christ be formed in you." In 2 Corinthians (5. 17) he writes, "Wherefore if any man is in Christ, he is a new creature" (καινὴ κτίσις); and in Ephesians (4. 23, 24), "And that ye be renewed in the spirit of your mind, and put on the new man, that after God hath been created in righteousness and holiness of truth."

Many students have difficulty in understanding our Lord's words to Nicodemus: "Except one be born of water and the Spirit, he cannot enter into the kingdom of God." Our Saviour's meaning becomes quickly evident when we note that the word *water* makes connection with the peculiar mission of John the Baptist, which Christ was eager to recognize. John's baptism was one of water with the most tremendous emphasis upon repentance. Our Lord said to Nicodemus in substance this: "To enter the kingdom of God you must have a new birth, a birth which begins with repentance on your part, and is accomplished by the power of the Holy Spirit. You must start with John's teaching, but go away beyond that, and rely upon the Spirit of God, who can make you all over again."

A Psychology of Regeneration. Can we, though, get this fact of regeneration into any terms of psychological clarity? I think so. When a repentant sinner, through moral faith, comes into union with Jesus Christ, Christ as his Saviour, in the very nature of the case, has some place in the affection and in the conscience of the sinner. There is some heart-interest in Christ and some sense of obligation toward Christ. Were this not so, there could be no moral faith in Christ. Now think your way back to our discussion of motives, and you will see that this introduction of Christ into the motive-life is an event of large psychological possibility. My conception of regeneration is simply this: The Holy Spirit takes this new motive and vitalizes it, and organizes the sinner's entire motivity, his entire range of interest, about it to this extent, namely, that in every full mood of self-consciousness the regenerate man cares more for his Lord than for all other things. Not yet can we say that the man is *altogether* organized, but the whole new plan of manhood is established, and the center of this plan is *loyalty to Jesus Christ*.

Nor is this all of regeneration. There is something much more glorious. *This new plan of organization in motivity is kept vital by the actual indwelling of the Holy Ghost.* Recall Saint Paul's words (Rom. 8. 9): "if so be that the Spirit of God dwelleth in you" (οἰκεῖ ἐν ὑμῖν). The apostle does not mean here any ordinary residence of the Holy Spirit in a man; but a residence of peculiar Christian efficiency. When a sinner is really united to Jesus Christ by moral faith, the Spirit of God makes his own home in that man, and it is the Holy Spirit who completes the union with Christ, and vitalizes the new motive, and grounds the new plan of spiritual manhood, and remains in the man, sending pulses of power through his whole being. Regeneration is not merely a new motive of loyalty to Christ, and not merely this motive vitalized and placed by the Holy Spirit; regeneration is loyalty to Jesus Christ vitalized as a motive, made supreme as a motive, and kept vital and kept supreme by the actual indwelling of the Spirit of God.

Definition.

Regeneration is the primary reorganization of a person's entire motive-life by the vital action and abiding presence of the Holy Spirit so that the ultimate motive is loyalty to Jesus Christ.

Adoption. In the fourth chapter of Galatians (verse 5) Saint Paul says, "that he might redeem them that were under the law, that we might receive the adoption of sons" (ἵνα τὴν υἱοθεσίαν ἀπολάβωμεν). This term υἱοθεσία is peculiarly Pauline, and is used in at least three of his epistles. By this term the apostle never means *sonship*, but always and exactly *sonship by adoption*. Unrelated to the work of Christ, men are sons of God potentially, are sons by plan; but actually they are slaves and can realize sonship only by divine adoption.

More deeply, though, what is meant by adoption? Saint Paul did not get the idea from the Old Testament; but, as Dr. Ball has convincingly shown, from the Roman law, under which a stranger by blood could become a member of a family as really as though he had been born into it. "He became identified with the family in a higher sense than some who had the family blood in their veins, than emancipated sons, or descendants through females. He assumed the family name, partook in its mystical sacrificial rites, and became, not on sufferance, or at will, but to all intents and purposes, a member of the house of his adoption." The question now arises, Have we in this adoption nothing but Saint Paul's doctrine of justification, given in a second forensic setting? I think not. As stated before, the underlying Christian fact of union with Christ is the same in all these relative phases of experience; but adoption is a phase, and is just as distinct from justification as justification is distinct from regeneration. In the doctrine of justification the practical meaning is this: "When a sinner is in Christ Jesus the attitude of the Holy God toward him is a new attitude of positive favor." In the doctrine of regeneration the practical meaning is this: "When a sinner is in Christ Jesus he has a new motive of loyalty to Christ, about which his personal life is reorganized by the indwelling

Holy Spirit." In the doctrine of adoption the practical meaning is this: "When a sinner is in Christ Jesus he has *a new family*, God is actually his Father, Christ is his Elder Brother, all the redeemed are his own brethren; and there is provided for him a great inheritance and an everlasting home."

Definition.

Adoption is a legal term which Saint Paul borrowed from the Roman law to express the social phase of conversion, namely, that a saved sinner is not only justified and regenerated, but actually incorporated into the family of God to enjoy its fellowship and to share its destiny.

The Witness of the Holy Spirit to Our Adoption as Sons. In the Epistle to the Romans (8. 15, 16) we find another passage in relation to adoption: "For ye received not the spirit of bondage again unto fear; but ye received the spirit of adoption, whereby we cry, Abba, Father. The Spirit himself beareth witness with our spirit, that we are children of God" (compare with Gal. 4. 6, 7). I am fully convinced that this passage has been misunderstood by a number of our greatest interpreters of Christian experience; but, in such matters, their judgments, and even their intuitions, are usually so reliable that it is only with very great hesitation that I undertake to give my own view of what Saint Paul means by the witness of the Spirit that we are the children of God. Perhaps, though, the most economical way to reach a clear result will be to outline my entire view of the Christian assurance of conversion:

1. We may be assured *by inference*. When Saint John says that "we know that we have passed out of death into life, because we love the brethren," he indicates an assurance which is by pure inference. Almost endless are the combinations of this sort of assurance, but the inner movement is ever the same: "I *was* that kind of a man;

I *am* this kind of a man—*therefore.*" Naturally this assurance by inference increases as the Christian life matures by taking on the "fruits of the Spirit."

2. We may be assured *by conscience.* When we have what Saint Paul calls "peace with God through our Lord Jesus Christ" it is the end of a struggle in conscience, and for the first time the sinner can face his moral ideal without any sense of condemnation. Thus, there is an intuitive element of assurance in the fundamental operation of conscience itself in moral settlement. But with my conception of conscience, even this peace with God is not a mechanical thing, but truly the work of the Holy Spirit.

3. The assurance by conscience may be *augmented and transformed.* As we read the lives of typical Christians, we soon perceive that sometimes, at conversion or later, this peace in conscience becomes so intense and penetrating that it really amounts to a new intuition that God has forgiven the sinner and taken him into his rich favor. This is what many mean by "the immediate witness of the Holy Spirit." And while the language about the fact is usually popular and inexact, nearly always the language is essentially true to the fact. Indeed, it is impossible to exaggerate the wonder and potency of this experience.

4. *We may have yet another assurance.* But no one of these three is what Saint Paul means when he says: "The Spirit himself beareth witness with our spirit, that we are children of God." The standpoint from which Saint Paul is now speaking is neither that of justification, nor that of regeneration, but definitely that of adoption. The assurance, therefore, is not that the saved sinner has the forgiveness and favor of God, but that he is in the family of God. If it be said that to be sure of God's favor is also to be sure that he is our Father, I answer that such is not *inevitably* the case. You must remember that

we are dealing with spontaneous personal seizure. A man may come to full self-consciousness, may lay hold of every item in the vision, may have the profoundest peace under his moral ideal, and yet may have *no filial sense* whatever. It is one thing to *think* "God is my Father!" and quite another thing to *feel* it within. Many a man has for years preached about the Fatherhood of God, and never once intuited it in personal experience, never once burst like the breaking day into the quick and inevitable intuition, "Abba, Father!"

The exegetes make much of Saint Paul's use of the verb συμμαρτυρέω, but to me the synergistic nature of the witness is more convincingly evident from a large study of all the operations of grace, in connection with a close study of human personality itself. What takes place is essentially this: The moment the Holy Spirit begins the reorganization of a man he begins to help the person to recover the filial sense which man had lost in depravity. The person, now loyal to Christ, struggles toward the realization, but cannot fully achieve it, no, not even in his loftiest mood. Then, there comes a crisis (not necessarily an external crisis) when with a deeper sense of need, or with a more thorough consecration, or with a greater purpose to serve men, the man opens himself entirely to the wish of the Holy Spirit. Into this new opportunity the Spirit rushes eagerly and completes the broken intuition; and now the self-conscious person has the glorious filial sense, and his home-life in the family of God is as real to him as his peace in conscience.

I myself deem this intuitive grasping of the fact of adoption as the crowning experience in this world. I deem it so because it lifts the saved sinner out of that extreme emphasis upon his single self, upon *his* salvation, upon *his* life with God, and makes him actually live in the fellowship of the whole family of God. You cannot misunder-

stand me if I say that sainthood has often shown an inclination to isolate its life of rapture, and to forget that
we are one organic brotherhood in Christ Jesus, with one
Father, one social relation, and one final home. Surely
there should be the most tremendous emphasis upon the
one moral person, upon what he is, upon what he ought
to do, and upon what he may become; but that exaltation
of the person is not *all* of the Christian life, is not the
Christian *finality*. The finality is where the Christian
man finds himself all over again in the large experience
of the mighty family of God. And one important step
toward this Christian finality is that experience where
the whole vision of self-consciousness is luminous with
the spontaneous assurance that we have been adopted
as sons, and now belong in title and privilege and service
to the household of God the Father Almighty.

PERSONAL HOLINESS

I have made a little exposition of Methodism, but I see it will be too long to present in full. I sum it all up in one or two sentences. As to its theology, it takes the old theology of the Christian church, but it takes one element which no other Christian church has dared to put forward as a prominent feature of theology. In ours it is the very point from which we view all theology. Now listen; I want that to be understood. Knowing exactly what I say, and taking the full responsibility of it, I repeat, we are the only church in history, from the apostles' time until now, that has put forward as its very elemental thought—the great central pervading idea of the whole Book of God from the beginning to the end—the holiness of the human soul, heart, mind, and will. Go through all the confessions of all the churches, and you will find this in no other. You will find even some of them that blame us in their books and writings. It may be called fanaticism, but, dear friends, that is our mission. If we keep to that, the next century is ours; if we keep to that, the triumphs of the next century shall throw those that are past far into the shade. Our work is a moral work—that is to say, the work of making men holy. Our preaching is for that, our church agencies are for that, our schools, colleges, universities, and theological seminaries are for that. There is our mission—there is our glory—there is our power, and there shall be the ground of our triumph. God keep us true.—*John McClintock, the first president of the Drew Theological Seminary;* from an address delivered at the Methodist Centenary Celebration in New York, January 25, 1866; reported in the Methodist, issue of February 3, 1866.

XXVII. PERSONAL HOLINESS

PSYCHOLOGICALLY this doctrine belongs to the general subject of conversion, for holiness is really the completion of regeneration; but there are practical reasons for a separate discussion and formal emphasis.

Our wisest course is to avoid the many controversies, and go back to John Wesley himself. We could not fairly deal with the controversies without making use of certain books which, while very penetrating and suggestive, manifest a spirit so narrow and ungenerous as to create an atmosphere unworthy of the theme. Of all the places in Christian discussion, this is the one place where it is more wholesome to have a weak argument than to have a vitiating atmosphere. And, further, there are three positive reasons why it is of the larger importance to go back to Wesley: First, Wesley was the central point of Christian consciousness in a special doctrinal epoch. Historically, Wesley had almost the same epochal relation to the doctrinal emphasis upon holiness that Luther had to the doctrinal emphasis upon justification by faith, or that Athanasius had to the doctrinal emphasis upon the Deity of our Lord. Second, because Wesley was the leader in such an epochal movement, he had at hand *quantity in data*. The flaw in some of the modern discussions of Christian perfection is not so much in the reasoning as in the want of sufficient data to reason upon. The author is like a botanist giving out a *dictum* about a rare plant which he has cultivated in a hothouse. Every word he says is the truth, but it is not the *typical truth*. There is sometimes a genuine Christian experience which is so individualistic as to be almost worthless for theology. Third, quantity of data, however, is of small worth unless there be surety in Christian discrimination. There are several recent scientific studies of Christian experience which would be almost priceless in value had the authors only known the difference between reality and imitation. It is possible to obtain a thousand answers to a list of set questions and have only a hundred of them with any real Christian meaning. It is just at this point that John Wesley was a master in Israel. He did almost no fundamental thinking, not merely because he was ceaselessly occupied with practical affairs, but mainly because his mind, like that of Gladstone, was receptive and not creative. But Wesley had such extraordinary spiritual insight, and such sanity in judgment, that often his most casual statement, especially in his Journal, is more illuminating than many a profound monograph in theology.

The Wesleyan Doctrine of Christian Perfection

Wesley's Own Experience. John Wesley was always loath to reveal the deepest things of his Christian life. He freely gives you his opinions and delights to talk about his work; but it is only now and then that you can catch any glimpse of "the inner chamber of introspection." And yet, by careful search, we can discover a few very significant points of self-revelation.

1. It is significant that Wesley was greatly impressed by Jeremy Taylor's discussion of *purity of intention.* Forty years afterward, in his Journal, May 14, 1765, Wesley writes: "I was struck particularly with the chapter upon *intention*, and felt a fixed intention 'to give myself up to God.'" For a young man twenty-two years of age, and having Wesley's ecclesiastical surroundings, to lift this one idea of intention into potent emphasis is

not only remarkable, but also momentous.   It is, indeed, Wesley's prophetic start.

2. About five years later we find another significant point.   He has now become "a man of one Book," and he perceives that love is the key to the full Christian life. In his Journal, same date as already quoted, he says: "I then saw, in a stronger light than ever before, that only one thing is needful, even faith that worketh by the love of God and man, all inward and outward holiness; and I groaned to love God with all my heart, and to serve him with all my strength."   Let us now note precisely what Wesley has: He has a clear idea that the person's central purpose is an important feature of the Christian life; but he perceives that it is not enough to hold passively this purpose, it must be positively expressed in a faith which works by love.   Further, he has a craving both for a supreme love toward God and for a life giving out that love in the largest service.

3. But did Wesley actually reach the experience for which he yearned?   In his Journal, December 23–25, 1744, we read this: "I was unusually lifeless and heavy, till the love feast in the evening; when, just as I was constraining myself to speak, I was stopped, whether I would or no; for the blood gushed out of both my nostrils, so that I could not add another word: but in a few minutes it stayed, and all our hearts and mouths were opened to praise God.   Yet the next day I was again as a dead man; but in the evening, while I was reading prayers at Snows-fields, I found such light and strength as I never remember to have had before.   I saw every thought as well as every action or word, just as it was rising in my heart; and whether it was right before God, or tainted with pride or selfishness.   I never knew before (I mean not as at this time) what it was 'to be still before God.'   *Tuesday, 25.*   I waked, by the grace of God, in the same spirit;

and about eight, being with two or three that believed in
Jesus, I felt such an awe and tender sense of the presence
of God as greatly confirmed me therein, so that God was
before me all the day long.   I sought and found him in
every place, and could truly say, when I lay down at night,
'Now I have lived a day.'"   To anyone familiar with
John Wesley's careful, realistic manner of speech, it is
evident that we have here the same sort of testimony to
the experience of holiness that we have in his Journal,
May 24, 1738, to the experience of conversion.   If the one
is not quite so near a full definition as the other, it surely
is just as expressive of the fact.   I find it almost impossible to read Wesley's words in the light of all his later
utterance about the doctrine of Christian perfection, and
not consider this date, December 24, 1744, as the probable
time when he began to love God supremely.

4. In a letter (CCCLIII) from London, June 19, 1771,
there is another important reference to Wesley's own
experience: "Many years since I saw that 'without holiness no man shall see the Lord.'   I began following after
it, and inciting all with whom I had any intercourse to do
the same.   Ten years after, God gave me a clearer view
than I had before of the way to attain this, namely, by
faith in the Son of God.   And immediately I declared to
all, 'We are saved from sin, we are made holy, by faith.'
This I testified in private, in public, in print; and God
confirmed it by a thousand witnesses.   I have continued to declare this for above thirty years; and God
hath continued to confirm the word of his grace."   By
using this passage as a supplement to all we had before,
I think it would be possible to make out quite a probable
history of Wesley's movement in grace from the point
where he was impressed so deeply by Jeremy Taylor on
to his own actual experience of holiness; but such a history is not what I am really after.   I want these refer-

ences by John Wesley to his own experience simply to prepare the way for our better understanding of his teaching, and for our better appreciation of the quiet intensity and certainty manifest in his demand that Christian people should be holy.

Wesley's Teaching Analyzed.

1. The Name. It is to be noted, first of all, that Wesley called the experience of holiness "*Christian* perfection, or *scriptural* perfection." (See especially Letter CCCLI.)

2. As to Conduct. Such perfection does not mean perfection in conduct. "But these souls dwell in a shattered, corruptible body, and are so pressed down thereby that they cannot exert their love as they would, by always thinking, speaking, and acting precisely right. For want of better bodily organs, they sometimes inevitably think, speak, or act wrong" (Letter CLXXXVI; also see Letter CCXXIX).

3. As to Individual Character. The imperfection is deeper than conduct and belongs even to the individual character itself. "These very persons feel more than ever their own ignorance, littleness of grace, coming short of the full mind that was in Christ, and walking less accurately than they might have done after their Divine Pattern; and are more convinced of the insufficiency of all they are, or do, to bear the eye of God without a Mediator; are more penetrated with the sense of the want of him than ever they were before" (Letter CCCLI).

4. As to Temptation. Nor does Christian perfection secure freedom from actual temptation. In a letter to the Bishop of London (vol. viii, p. 484) Wesley says: "There is no such perfection in this life as implies an entire deliverance from manifold temptations." And in commenting on the Journal of Elizabeth Harper (vol. xiv, p. 278) Wesley says: "She was exceedingly

tempted, after she believed God had cleansed her from inbred sin." (Also see Plain Account, sec. 25, question 14.)

5. As to Sinless Perfection. Wesley himself avoided the phrase *sinless perfection*, because, in a generic sense, sin is any want of individual conformity to the law of God. But Wesley's own final definition of sin was strictly personal. In a letter (CCCCII) he writes: "Nothing is sin, strictly speaking, but a voluntary transgression of a known law of God." But I have found no way of harmonizing all of Wesley's statements at this point; and I am inclined to think that he never entirely cleared up his own thinking concerning the nature and scope of sin. At first I believed that a path out of his seeming inconsistency might be found by means of an exact chronology, but a severer examination of all his writings forced me to give up even that hope.

6. As to Love. While again and again Wesley makes much of personal intention, this intention of the person is not enough; the intention must be gathered up into a positive fullness of love. To be a perfect Christian is nothing other than being perfect in love toward God and man. In his Journal, August 27, 1768, Wesley writes: "I mean, 'loving God with all our heart, and our neighbor as ourselves.' I pin all its opposers to this definition of it. No evasion! No shifting of the question!" And the same statement, in slightly varying words, can be found all through Wesley's writings.

7. As to Time. In Brief Thoughts (January 27, 1767) Wesley says: "As to time, I believe this instant is generally the instant of death, the moment before the soul leaves the body. But I believe it may be ten, twenty, or forty years before. I believe it is usually many years after justification; but that it may be within five years or five months after it, I know no conclusive argument to

the contrary." In another place (not taken from the London edition) Wesley says that "some of the most unquestionable witnesses of sanctifying grace were sanctified within a few days after they were justified." And in his Journal, September 7, 1765, there is an account of what Wesley deems a most remarkable case—"a person convinced of sin, converted to God, and renewed in love, within twelve hours." And Wesley adds: "Yet it is by no means incredible, seeing one day is with God as a thousand years." I have found no testimony in Wesley's writings that justification and entire sanctification ever take place at the same time; but it is plain enough that in his last years he was unwilling to set any limit. As his experience with men widened, and his pastoral intuitions deepened, he became less conservative on all questions of divine grace—was more open to new and astonishing results in the work of the Holy Spirit.

8. As to Growth. On the surface there seems to be a contradiction in Wesley's teaching at this point. At times, apparently, he teaches that a regenerated man can actually grow into Christian perfection. In Sermon CVII, on God's Vineyard, we read: "And as, in natural birth, a man is born at once, and then grows larger and stronger by degrees; so, in spiritual birth, a man is born at once and then gradually increases in spiritual stature and strength. The new birth, therefore, is the first point of sanctification, which may increase more and more unto the perfect day." There are a number of passages to the same effect. To harmonize this view of growth with Wesley's other statements, some have said that he believed Christian perfection is obtained either by growth or by instant and crucial faith; but the truth, I think, is that Wesley regarded the *decisive stroke* in attainment as always instantaneous, growth being but a preparation for the stroke, or an after work in utilization and enlarge-

ment. In the Minutes of Several Conversations, Wesley says: "The substance, then, is settled, but, as to the circumstance, is the change gradual or instantaneous? It is both the one and the other. From the moment we are justified, there may be a gradual sanctification, a growing in grace, a daily advance in the knowledge and love of God. And if sin cease before death there must, in the nature of the thing, be an instantaneous change; there must be a last moment wherein it does exist, and a first moment wherein it does not" (viii, 328). Again to the same purpose in the Plain Account (sec. 19): "Is this death to sin, and renewal in love, gradual or instantaneous?" His answer is in these very striking words: "A man may be dying for some time; yet he does not, properly speaking, die till the instant the soul is separated from the body; and in that instant he lives the life of eternity. In like manner, he may be dying to sin for some time; yet he is not dead to sin till sin is separated from his soul; and in that instant he lives the full life of love. And as the change undergone, when the body dies, is of a different kind, and infinitely greater than any we had known before, yea, such as till then it is impossible to conceive; so the change wrought when the soul dies to sin is of a different kind, and infinitely greater than any before, and than any can conceive till he experiences it. Yet he still grows in grace, in the knowledge of Christ, in the love and image of God; and will do so, not only till death, but to all eternity." Again in Brief Thoughts, Wesley touches upon the method of attainment: "I believe this perfection is always wrought in the soul by a simple act of faith; consequently, in an instant. But I believe a gradual work, both preceding and following that instant" (xi, 446).

9. As to Assurance. In the Plain Account, sec. 25, question 16: "How do you know that you are sanctified, saved from your inbred corruption?" Answer: "I can

know it no otherwise than I know that I am justified. . . . We know it by the witness and by the fruit of the Spirit. And, first, by the witness. As, when we were justified, the Spirit bore witness with our spirit that our sins were forgiven; so, when we were sanctified, he bore witness that they were taken away. Indeed, the witness of sanctification is not always clear at first (as neither is that of justification); neither is it afterward always the same, but, like that of justification, sometimes stronger, and sometimes fainter. Yea, and sometimes it is withdrawn. Yet, in general, the latter testimony of the Spirit is both as clear and as steady as the former."

10. As to Losing the Experience. At first Wesley believed that the experience of Christian perfection could not be lost, but finally he was convinced that it could be. In a letter to his brother (LXVII, London, February 12, 1767) Wesley writes: "Can one who has attained it fall? Formerly I thought not; but you (with Thomas Walsh and John Jones) convinced me of my mistake." In the month before (January 27) Wesley had said: "By perfection I mean the humble, gentle, patient love of God and our neighbor, ruling our tempers, words, and actions. I do not include an impossibility of falling from it, either in part or in whole. Therefore, I retract several expressions in our hymns which partly express, partly imply, such an impossibility." In his Journal (July 25, 1774) Wesley writes: "I went on to Sheffield and on Tuesday met the Select Society. But it was reduced from sixty to twenty; and but half of these retained all that they once received. What a grievous error, to think those that are saved from sin cannot lose what they have gained! It is a miracle, if they do not; seeing all earth and hell are so enraged against them; while, meantime, so very few, even of the children of God, skillfully endeavor to strengthen their hands."

11. As to the Primary Compromise. "From long experience and observation, I am inclined to think that whoever finds redemption in the blood of Jesus, whoever is justified, has then the choice of walking in the higher or the lower path. I believe the Holy Spirit at that time sets before him the 'more excellent way,' and incites him to walk therein, to choose the narrowest path in the narrow way, to aspire after the heights and depths of holiness—after the entire image of God. But if he does not accept this offer he insensibly declines into the lower order of Christians. He still goes on in what may be called a good way, serving God in his degree, and finds mercy in the close of life through the blood of the covenant" (Sermon LXXXIX, on The More Excellent Way).

12. Personal Conclusion. By constant association with an author we may come to have a conception of his real meaning in spite of all his inconsistencies. For our conception has been gradually formed by a number of features in a complex combination—by his peculiar silences; by his spontaneous repetitions; by the way a certain paragraph closes, or a certain discussion culminates; by the instant and eager answer to an unexpected question; and even by his choice of phrase in a crucial situation. My view of John Wesley's meaning is of this indefensible sort. I am sure of his doctrine of Christian perfection, as sure of its essential import as I am that I walk the earth; but I am unable to relate my view, in an exact way, to all of his statements, or even to all of his very important statements. I will give my own personal conception without quotation and without defense. According to John Wesley, a sinner has three things the matter with him: First, he is *guilty;* second, he is morally *powerless;* and, third, his inherent and inherited *disposition is wrong.* Or, as I would say, the individuality is out of harmony with the ideal of the moral person. When a sinner is

justified the guilt is canceled.   When he is regenerated
he receives a nucleus of power, not enough to exterminate
his wrong disposition, but enough "to fight it to a stand-
still."   In Christian perfection, there is no such fight
with the disposition, "no civil war at all," for the wrong
impulse never enters the consciousness as motive.   Now,
when you ask, "What becomes of the wrong disposition?"
Wesley can give no fundamental answer, for the simple
reason that he was all mixed up in his psychology.   I
am not one of those courageous men who dare to say that
John Wesley had at the bottom of his thinking a consistent psychology.   My opinion rather is that he was
a very crude realist, but usually restless under that
unspeakable curse, and trying to break away, without
ever being fully able to accomplish his purpose.   This
"slavery of the man to the lump" is not surprising, if we
only remember that many of the recent Christian books,
and many more of the modern scientific books, have been
written with an underlying realism so gross that any
serious thinker should have been unwilling to grant it
toleration at any time since the death of Immanuel Kant;
and I almost said at any time since the death of Plato.
But Wesley does this much for us: he holds that the civil
war in the perfect Christian is rendered impossible by
love, supreme love toward God and man.   Whether the
natural disposition is extirpated or only overwhelmed, it
does not appear in a consciousness full to the brim of pure
love.

It will help us all, probably, if I can give a concrete
illustration of Wesley's view.   Here is a man, a Christian
preacher now, who has from infancy been naturally
jealous.   He is not only converted, but is a noble Christian man, ready to sacrifice for his Lord, and equally
ready to serve his brethren.   But he is still jealous in
disposition.   Yesterday he heard another preacher's ser-

mon receive large commendation, and, like an uprush of mercury in the heat, that old feeling of jealousy rose into consciousness. His volition, his personality, had no more to do with it than his will had to do with the coming on of night. But the moment our preacher realizes that he is jealous he makes Christian battle, and forces the disposition back, back into its cave. Now, we have here an exceedingly strange psychological situation, for the man's struggle is plainly Christian in its revelation of the moral ideal, and yet the struggle reveals a motive-life which no Christian ought to have at all. Or, we can say this: The victory is truly that of a Christian man—but as a Christian man he should have been without the possibility of that kind of a battle. Now comes a pivotal inquiry. As our preacher grows what does his growth in grace accomplish? According to Wesley, the growth does not affect the inherent disposition of jealousy at all; but it does bring the regenerate man himself to a more potent attitude, both of intolerance toward the disposition and of trust toward Jesus Christ. With this more potent personal attitude the man dares to believe that his Lord can and will take that jealousy, and every wrong disposition, out of his life. In full, simple faith he asks Christ to do it; and, precisely as when he was converted, *it is all done at one stroke*. Now what is the man's condition? On the one hand, he never is conscious of jealousy. Rather does he spontaneously rejoice in another man's success. On the other hand, he never comes to self-consciousness without being filled, like the prodigality of a freshet, with the love of God. This, as I understand him, is what John Wesley means by the conquest of inbred sin through supreme love. And if there is one man here to whom Wesley's view of inbred sin suggests no reality, no point in kindred experience, he most surely is to be regarded as extremely fortunate.

Christian Perfection and Biblical Theology

Is there, though, for this Wesleyan doctrine of Christian perfection any support in biblical theology? In Wesley's day there was such an arbitrary and fragmentary and superficial use of Scripture, even by the finest scholars, that many students have gained the impression, if not the belief, that the scriptural argument for Christian perfection cannot endure the test of our modern method of studying the Bible. I am certain that the test can be endured; but, before taking up that matter, I wish to enter a protest against the prevailing notion that before we can accept a Christian doctrine every feature of it must have exact Scripture proof. The Bible is not to be used in that hard and fast manner. The Bible is the *normative* authority on Christian doctrine; but we must also provide for the larger and larger interpretations by the developing Christian consciousness. For example, it would be enough to show that Christian perfection is not in contradiction of any Scripture, but harmonizes with the *trend of emphasis* in the New Testament upon moral love; and is the loftiest ideal belonging to the most normal and most thoroughly developed Christian consciousness. If we can make it indubitable that the Bible itself never allows the great saints to rest until they hold and experience this doctrine of supreme love, we will have secured quite as good a basis for the doctrine as could be secured by any amount of precise scriptural proof.

Saint John's Doctrine of Love. The essence of the message of Saint John to the Christian man is in this glowing passage (1 John 4. 16 to 5. 5): "God is love; and he that abideth in love abideth in God, and God abideth in him. Herein is love made perfect with us, that we may have boldness in the day of judgment; because as he is, even so are we in this world. There is no fear in love:

but perfect love casteth out fear, because fear hath punishment; and he that feareth is not made perfect in love. We love, because he first loved us. If a man say, I love God, and hateth his brother, he is a liar: for he that loveth not his brother whom he hath seen, cannot love God whom he hath not seen. And this commandment have we from him, that he who loveth God love his brother also.

"Whosoever believeth that Jesus is the Christ is begotten of God: and whosoever loveth him that begat loveth him also that is begotten of him. Hereby we know that we love the children of God, when we love God and do his commandments. For this is the love of God, that we keep his commandments: and his commandments are not grievous. For whatsoever is begotten of God overcometh the world: and this is the victory that hath overcome the world, even our faith. And who is he that overcometh the world, but he that believeth that Jesus is the Son of God?"

When we separate the real message of this passage from its rhetorical mannerism, we find the connected points to be these: First, in Saint John's conception of God the finality is love. Second, we make entrance into this love of God by being "begotten of God," and this takes place when we believe "that Jesus is the Christ." Third, we are prepared for the day of judgment by having this love of God made perfect in us; and this perfection of love can be achieved in this life—"because as he is, even so are we in this world." Fourth, the marks of this perfect love are that it "casteth out fear," that it makes a man "love his brother also," and that it enables him to "do his commandments," and to have that perfect faith which "overcometh the world."

Saint Paul's Teaching. In coming to Saint Paul's teaching, I wish to be sure of avoiding not only all personal bias, but also all Methodist bias, so I will make use of Professor Bartlet, Mansfield College, Oxford. In his article on Sanctification in the Hastings Dictionary of the Bible, Professor Bartlet writes of Saint Paul's teaching as follows: "There is a state possible to Christians, corresponding to the ideal of their calling, in which they can be described as 'unblamable in holiness' (ἀμέμπτους ἐν ἁγιωσύνῃ), and into which they may be brought by the grace of God in this life. Therein they stand hallowed through and through (ὁλοτελεῖς), every part of their being (ὁλόκληρον ὑμῶν τὸ πνεῦμα καὶ ἡ ψυχὴ καὶ τὸ σῶμα) abiding by grace in a condition fit to bear the scrutiny of their Lord's presence without rebuke (ἀμέμπτως ἐν τῇ παρουσίᾳ τοῦ κυρίου ἡμῶν Ἰησοῦ Χριστοῦ τηρηθείη). Such is the teaching of 1 Thess. 3. 13 and 5. 23. The fidelity of God to his purpose in calling men to be Christians is pledged to this achievement (1 Thess. 5. 24), though there is no definite time, as measured from the initial hallowing of the Spirit in conversion, at which it must needs be accomplished. God, who begins the good work in the soul, also continues to work at its perfecting (ἐπιτελεῖν) right up to the day of Jesus Christ (Phil. 1. 6); and yet, ere that day dawns, Christians may become already 'pure in purpose' (εἰλικρινεῖς = Christ's καθαροὶ τῇ καρδίᾳ, Matt. 5. 8) and 'void of offense,' and so remain 'until the day of Christ' (Phil. 1. 10). It is this state of realized sanctification of conduct, or 'walk,' so as to 'please God,' that Saint Paul has constantly in view in exhorting his converts to holy living (for example, 1 Thess. 4. 1). This is what he means, at times, by his use of ἁγιασμός. But the conception needs to be carefully guarded and explained by other aspects of his thought. Thus (1) it represents a growth *in* holiness rather than *into* holiness out of something else; (2) it is conceived as realizable by a definite act of faith—claiming and appropriating its rightful experience by an act of will informed by the living energy of the Holy Spirit— rather than as the cumulative result of a slow, instinctive process after conversion; (3) it is not the same as absolute moral perfection or consummation ($\tau\epsilon\lambda\epsilon\iota o\tilde{v}\sigma\theta\alpha\iota$), but is rather the prerequisite to its more rapid and steady realization."

Our Lord's Injunction.   "And he said unto him, Thou shalt love the Lord thy God with all thy heart, and with all thy soul, and with all thy mind.   This is the great and first commandment.   And a second like unto it is this, Thou shalt love thy neighbor as thyself.   On these two commandments hangeth the whole law, and the prophets" (Saint Matt. 22. 37–40).   This one passage should forever settle the entire controversy as to both the ideal and the possible achievement in the Christian life.   From the Old Testament (Deut. 6. 5 and Lev. 19. 18) our Lord takes the two items of supreme moment, and lifts them into a Christian primacy of injunction.   It has been said that our Saviour did not intend to give an actual injunction, but only to suggest a Christian ideal.   But I do not understand how anyone can hold such a view; for a study of the Saviour's life will show that love toward God and love toward man were the two tests which he used in determining all religious values.   And the fact is that to-day the Christian consciousness anywhere grasps the Master's words as injunction, and responds to them as such, making them the final test of life.   Every Christian deed *is* Christian, every Christian thought *is* Christian, every Christian feeling *is* Christian, precisely to the extent that it expresses this supreme love.   Ignatius clearly apprehended the whole thing when he said: "The beginning of life is faith, and the end is love.   And these two being inseparably connected together, do perfect the man of God; while all other things which are requisite to a holy

life follow after them. No man making a profession of
faith ought to sin, nor one possessed of love to hate his
brother. For He that said, Thou shalt love the Lord thy
God, said also, And thy neighbor as thyself."

A Psychology of Personal Holiness

With my conception of a perfect Christian very much
more is required than perfection in motive, and so I prefer
the expression *personal holiness*. The holiness is *personal*
because it is holiness exactly from the standpoint of self-
consciousness and self-determination. What you have is
holiness in personality.

The Transformed Motive. As we have seen, the motive-
life of a regenerate man is organized about the motive of
loyalty to Christ. This motive of loyalty is not a simple
motive, but is made up of two elements, one of love and
the other of duty. At rare moments these two elements
are in self-consciousness with equal force, but usually the
sense of duty is paramount. The regenerate man, in any
typical situation, is seeking to do his duty. His common
remark is: "I will be true; I will not deny my Lord."
This loyalty is very different from the loyalty of the
moralist; and for two reasons, namely, it is loyalty to a
person, and it is rooted in the enthusiasm of a positive
personal affection. And yet the Christian loyalty has
some of the same psychological weakness which renders
morality so ineffective. Duty always implies a conflict,
a civil war. The sense of the ought is, like a bugle, intended to call the person into battle. And while this
moral battle is great, it is less than the highest mood.
You will see what I mean if you think of a home where
husband, wife, parents, children are ever trying to do
their duty by each other. What a dreadful home that
would be! Not one day with the simple, rejoicing impulse of dominant love.

Now we can quickly uncover the fundamental flaw in the condition of the regenerate man. In his life of struggle to do his duty he cannot organize his inner personal life. He has the beginning, the ground plan, so to speak, of an organism, but he cannot carry out the plan. And the reason of his failure is that when duty is paramount in consciousness, even though it be the most noble sense of duty, the personal task is done under fear; and fear is never an organizing motive.

In personal holiness this motive of loyalty is transformed into the simple motive of pure love. There remains all the ethical quality of duty, for the new supreme love is a moral love; but "the whip of the ought" is gone. The holy person does not do things because it is his duty to do them, but *because he loves to do them.* But note this closely, the important thing here, psychologically, is not the *vastness* of the love (that is a matter of endless growth), but simply that the love *entirely occupies the self-conscious mood.* Whenever the person comes to self-consciousness it is crammed with love to the very edges. Thus, there is a perfect personal organism, because all the man's motivity is nothing but love in a variety of shapes. In the man's personal life there is no antagonism, no civil war whatever. He may be tempted, as we shall see, but he cannot be tempted by his own inorganic condition, by his own depravity.

The Exhaustion of Wrong Motive. The old question, "Suppression or eradication?" I cannot fairly consider; for my psychological point of view is different from that of the combatants about that question. But if you will recall my early discussion of motivity you can see what I think takes place when the motive of loyalty is transformed. The new motive of pure love is not used in a negative conflict, but is used positively; and by this positive use the wrong motives are exhausted. There is no longer any heart-interest in them. They are mere ideas empty of all urgency toward the will. It is not that they are *for the time being* shut out from consciousness; no, the work is profounder than all that, they cease to have any existence as motives. The full use of pure love has exhausted them.

The Question of Growth. Is this experience of personal holiness obtained by growth? First of all, the practical concern in the matter leads me to say that the very word *growth* is a word which should be used, in this discussion, only with extreme care. For to many people growth means a natural, an unurged development from an implanted germ. Now, there is no such unurged development in the Christian life. The whole thing is personally strenuous from conversion until death. But is personal holiness obtained gradually by earnest endeavor? Looking at it in the most comprehensive way, our answer should be in the affirmative; for the crisis itself is profoundly involved in all that has led up to it. Some of the evangelists to the contrary notwithstanding, no man can arbitrarily leap into that faith which is the condition of the divine gift of supreme love. It may, now and then, look like such a leap, but psychologically it is not so. You can leap into self-assertive presumption, but never into real faith.

And yet John Wesley's emphasis upon the ultimate stroke is exceedingly important. For there is a great difference between the last phase of the regenerate life and the first phase of the life of supreme love. As it is only in the latter case that the motive of loyalty *entirely* loses the note of duty; only in the latter case that love absolutely fills self-consciousness to its rim; so only in the latter case that all the wrong motives of disposition are exhausted.

But the question has been asked, "Why, on the principle of your discussion of motivity, may a regenerate man, with his motive of loyalty, not simply fight his way into personal holiness?" My answer is this: To exhaust all wrong motive by a sheer negative fight would require more time than belongs to our earthly life; and even if there were time enough the victory would exalt the element of duty and not the element of love in the motive of loyalty. What we are after is so to escape sin as to escape the bondage of conscience itself, and, like God himself, live the life of moral love.

But I have yet one suggestion to offer. I can conceive of another way of obtaining Christian perfection in love. It is, anyway, a theoretical possibility that a man might at the beginning of his Christian life lay hold of the under element of love in his loyalty, and *emphasize that*. He might by self-sacrifice express his love for Christ in the most complete manner. He might in prayer cultivate the mood of love for Christ. And so on and on until his love for the Saviour absolutely filled his consciousness, and his entire service was one of rejoicing love, and not one of moral obligation. There are a few of the saints whose experience is at least a hint of this kind of earnest growth into the fullness of love.

Falling Away from Personal Holiness. If it be true that the wrong motives of our depraved, inorganic individuality are thoroughly exhausted of their urgency, then the question arises, How is it possible to fall away from personal holiness? I answer: No Christian who is perfect in love can fall in the same way that a regenerate man may fall, by yielding to a motive which springs out of individuality into consciousness in antagonism to the moral ideal. But this higher life itself, as strange as it may seem at first, is a life of the most extreme self-assertion. It is *spiritual* self-assertion, but it is fundamental self-assertion, all the same. And out of this spiritual self-assertion there may come three motives, any one of which may bring on struggle, and with the struggle the possibility of personal defeat. These three motives are: First, spiritual discouragement. A saint in this world, in situations where Christ is not triumphant, can have a sort of discouragement which actually grows out of his supreme love for his Lord; and there is very great peril in such a mood. Second, spiritual pride. There is no experience so lofty in this life to a moral person as entirely to protect him from spiritual pride. In studying the temptations of our Saviour you see the whole method of its approach. A regenerate man is not half so likely to have this temptation as is the saint who is filled with love. Third, spiritual ambition. A holy man may have an ambition to be a great leader in the church, or a great preacher, or a great evangelist; and his ambition may have been created by his love for Jesus Christ; and yet there may come such a turn in his affairs that he must choose between his ambition and his Master. That is, his ambition is so interesting to the man now that it stands over against the very love which created it.

I am inclined also to think that sometimes this supreme love has created a subordinate love in some human person, which has grown and grown, until at last, in an abnormal crisis, the saint was obliged to make a choice between his human friend and his Saviour. But beyond all our psychological theorizing we positively know that there are peculiar temptations which are characteristic of the life of personal holiness; and, such temptations once in force, there is ever the possibility of falling away from the experience. The Christian battle is not over until through death we pass into the intermediate state.

THE INTERMEDIATE STATE

Possunt etiam spiritus mortuorum aliqua quæ hic agunter quæ necessarium est eos nosse, et quos necessarium est ea nosse, non solum præterita vel præsentia, verum etiam futura Spiritu Dei revelante cognoscere.—*Saint Augustine*, De Cura pro Mortuis gerenda, xv.

Sometimes I think that those we've lost,
   Safe lying on th' Eternal Breast,
Can hear no sounds from earth that mar
   The perfect sweetness of their rest;
But when one thought of holy love
   Is stirred in hearts they love below,
Through some fine waves of ambient air,
   They feel, they see it, and they know.

As rays unseen—abysmal light—
   Are caught by films of silver salt
When these are set to watch by night
   The wheelings of the starry vault,—
So may the souls that live and dwell
   In one great Soul, the Fount of all,
Feel faintest tremblings in the sphere
   On which such footsteps gently fall.
No evil seen, no murmurs heard,
   No fear of sin, or coming loss,
They wait in light, imperfect yet,
   The final triumphs of the Cross.
           —*The Duke of Argyll*, Our Dead.

Their kingdom is not one of works and deeds, for they no longer possess the conditions upon which works and deeds are possible. Nevertheless, they live a deep spiritual life; for the kingdom of the dead is a kingdom of subjectivity, a kingdom of calm thought and self-fathoming, a kingdom of *remembrance* in the full sense of the word, in such a sense, I mean, that the soul now enters into its own inmost recesses, resorts to that which is the very foundation of life, the true substratum and source of all existence.—*Hans Lassen Martensen*, Christian Dogmatics, p. 458.

XXVIII. THE CHRISTIAN DOCTRINE OF THE INTERMEDIATE STATE

WHATEVER one may think of the doctrine of the intermediate state from a merely religious standpoint, it has large Christian importance. For no one can see total Christianity, no one can grasp the philosophy of the Christian faith, until he has caught the peculiar significance of that personal experience between death and the resurrection. The systematic theologian is wont to consider the intermediate state as a doctrinal fragment of eschatology; but to me the profounder connection is soteriological; and I will, therefore, consider the intermediate state as a further stage in the progress of the realization of redemption in the new man.

Guiding Principles. Before we try to construct the doctrine, I wish to indicate the principles which should guide us in our very difficult task.

1. Not merely the surface teaching, but also the *ethical spirit* of the New Testament must be protected. Take, for example, the utterance of our Lord. Suppose we come to some word of his message, and there are two fair exegetical explanations possible; then, I contend, that we are bound to accept the explanation which has in it the greater moral outcry, the more serious warning for sinful men. If we do not do this we cannot be true to the severity of the moral insistence of the New Testament.

2. We should give to this earthly life a full philosophical significance. After reading certain books which teach that the intermediate state is a continued probation I have felt like saying: "Then, my dear man, *this* life is a waste.

It would have been economical, to say the least, to have *begun* with the next life." Just as I would not expect a chrysalis inside its silken cell to do all over again the work of a silkworm, so I would not expect the probation of the years to be repeated. No, we must keep a separate Christian meaning for this period of temporal struggle.

3. In the same spirit of Christian economy we should give also to the intermediate state a full philosophical significance. We cannot allow any theologian to make out that the intermediate state is a *useless pause* on the way to glory. Something, in that state, must take place of everlasting value. To borrow John Wesley's beautiful phrase, the saints there "will be continually ripening for heaven."

4. The view of personality and individuality and bodily life, already gained, must be maintained watchfully. For example, we must resist, on the one side, the temptation "to put the person to sleep"; and, on the other side, the temptation to grant a social life to a bodiless person.

5. The doctrine must be so constructed as to protect the awful Christian emphasis upon death, and also the Christian note of triumph. In Christian thought the intermediate state is not like Homer's dreary world of the dead, where they flit about like shadows, and gibber like bats, and "follow vaguely and emptily the old pursuits." If we are thinking of the redeemed we are to think of their bodiless life as one of triumph and rich experience in Jesus Christ. But we are never so to regard the doctrine of the intermediate state that it even suggests *heaven*. The terrible stress upon death is yet lingering there, for no man is complete, no man can be complete until the resurrection.

The Construction of the Doctrine.

1. The intermediate state is *not an unconscious state*. To a certain type of man there seems to be a fascination

in the idea of "soul-sleep" between the grave and the final resurrection. The idea took hold of Isaac Taylor, and even Archbishop Whately had an evident fondness for it. The idea is supposed by some to have scriptural support in such passages as 1 Thess. 4. 14: "For if we believe that Jesus died and rose again, even so them also that are fallen asleep in Jesus will God bring with him." But even if such expressions as "fallen asleep" be taken for more than a poetic turn of speech, to suggest the quiet rest which the saint has after death, they could be fully protected by saying that the intermediate state is a condition in which all objective relations are broken. As a matter of fact, it has never been proved that our natural sleep is an unconscious state. I myself think that the argument to the contrary is much the stronger. What we know about natural sleep is that the person has retreated into isolation, has lost his social connections, has given up all objective relations. To *get at him* again you must wake him up. In his System of Biblical Psychology, in speaking of the "false doctrine of the soul's sleep," Professor Franz Delitzsch says: "Scripture calls death a sleep, so far as the disappearance of the soul of a dying person out of the body resembles the retreat of the soul of a person falling asleep out of corporeally evidenced external life; but it nowhere says that souls vanishing out of their bodies sleep."

But my deeper objections to this idea of "soul-sleep" are two: First, it passes beyond the real Christian emphasis upon the value of the body, and takes on the first tinge of materialism. Second, for the important personal task of the intermediate state self-consciousness is very essential.

2. The intermediate state is *not a second probation*. When we fairly study such a view of second probation as was given by the Andover teachers in their Progressive

Orthodoxy, we see that the inner impulse of the discussion is peculiar. It does not originate in the old spirit of universalism, nor in the new spirit of critical biblical investigation; but rather in a spirit of equity, in the moral sense of fair play. Rejecting the idea of coercion, they demand a fair, full probation for every responsible person, but they can discover no way to provide such a probation for every person in this life. Hence there must be a probation beyond the grave for those who do not have their opportunity of test here. Indeed, it is not too much to say that the spirit of Christianity itself created the inner impulse of the Andover discussion. And if we regard the discussion as a strong echo from Dr. Dorner, the case is much the same, for his own discussion is thoroughly Christian in motive.

While I am eager to grant so much, the work of the Andover teachers seems to me to result from a serious misunderstanding of Christianity. They condition personal salvation upon actual acceptance of the historical Christ. This sounds intensely Christian; but it is essentially false to Christianity, for it turns salvation from a moral thing into a mental thing. Finally the contention amounts to this: Whatever a man means morally, he will be lost forever if he holds an untrue opinion about Jesus Christ. As I understand the teaching of our Lord, and the teaching of his greatest apostle, precisely the opposite is the Christian principle: a man is not saved by opinion, nor lost by opinion; the ultimate test is in the person's moral meaning. Surely the historical Christ may, as a rule, be the immediate test, but this is so for a moral reason, namely, because the man has in conscience come to feel a moral obligation toward Jesus Christ.

Were the contention as to the historical Christ a sound one, the Andover teachers would need to widen greatly their practical application. For not only the heathen and idiots and insane people have no adequate mental probation in this life—thousands upon thousands of people, typical in both mind and situation, have never for one hour mentally apprehended Christ, never for one hour seen him as he is. This precise division of men into two classes, those who have heard of Christ and those who have not heard of him, is so untrue to the facts. If any man of you imagines that every person who has read a Christian book or a Christian newspaper, or who has listened to an average Christian sermon, has *heard of Christ*, with any intellectual reality, such a man needs to make a larger study both of the obstinacy of human bias and of the impotence of human appeal. Why, there were a number of the finest souls and greatest minds New England ever produced, who lived for years almost within hailing distance of Andover Seminary itself, and yet they never accepted the historical Christ—*did they ever "hear of Jesus Christ"?* If so, they are all lost, in spite of their nobility in moral purpose. No, no, the Andover distinction is artificial. Hearing of Christ is not a matter of catching in thought the phrases and idioms of Christianity. As Dr. Dorner himself says: "Even within the church there are periods and cycles when the gospel does not approach men as that which it is."

The true Christian view, as I apprehend it, is essentially this: First, the entire possibility of personal salvation is based upon the atonement of Jesus Christ. Second, the actual Christian experience, in its definiteness and fullness, does involve the necessity of belief, a mental attitude toward both the work of our Lord and his person. Third, but *final salvation* is a matter of personal moral bearing, a bearing which is manifest in repentance and faith under a supreme moral ideal. Fourth, thus every person with a conscience has in this life a fair, full probation; for he has a fair, full test of moral intention. As I once wrote: "It is this test of personal moral intention which gives real significance to this life. In all the differences of climate, nationality, ancestry, environment, under all business, in all pleasure, with the stroke of sorrow or in the tumult of joy, there is just one thing being said: 'What do you *mean?* What do *you* mean?' For this, the sun shines and the winds blow; for this, all formal history is made; for this, dreadful accidents are allowed and more dreadful crimes are for now left unpunished. God is giving every moral person a chance to settle it forever whether he will love righteousness or not."

3. A Work in Adjustment. If the intermediate state is not a second or continued probation, if it makes no change whatever in moral intention or bearing, what, then, is it for? First of all, and under all, its work is to adjust a person's mental life to his moral meaning. This world is planned merely or mainly for ethical test, and we all reach death holding all sorts of false or fragmentary opinions. These opinions do not determine our central intention, do not even influence our personal attitude toward our moral ideal; but they do confuse *the expression* of intention, they do prevent entire consistency at the point of judgment. Therefore, in the intermediate state, our relation to truth and reality is to be fully cleared up. No longer will a perfect purpose be held back by an imperfect judgment. No longer can any man's moral meaning be hidden under a false opinion.

This clearing up of the mental life may result in a new formal adjustment to Jesus Christ. If a man in his earthly probation has really come to a spirit of repentance and faith; if he passes out of his probation longing for all Christ Jesus is, although he has never known him, then, in the intermediate state, the formal adjustment to his Saviour will be instant and complete. As Dr. Shedd once wrote: "For although the Redeemer has not been presented historically and personally to him, yet he has the cordial and longing disposition to believe in him." Said in one positive sentence: In the intermediate state every man must see Jesus Christ as he really is; and seeing him as he is, every man who is in harmony with Christ's nature will accept him; while every man who is not in harmony with Christ's nature will reject him. Thus the intermediate state merely turns the essential experience into the formal experience.

We have, though, another and a most difficult point in adjustment, namely, to adjust to Jesus Christ those children who die before they have any personal and moral bearing. I now remember only one Arminian theologian who seriously tries to say a consistent word concerning this difficult matter. Indeed, the usual Arminian procedure is to make the stoutest contention against Calvinism up to this point, then suddenly to borrow the very pith of the Calvinistic philosophy, disguising it under some such phrase as "unconditional regeneration," and so to *coerce the children into salvation.* Whatever failure we may have in our thinking, let us never do *that!* Never should we admit that any human being can be saved by omnipotence. Never, never, should we admit that any human being will be saved by pure divine favoritism worked out in a providential plan. I say it carefully, but I say it with every atom of manhood I have, that if one moral person can, anywhere, by any process whatsoever, be coerced into righteousness, then all our sense of God-given equity demands that all men shall be saved. Could I be a necessitarian for one swift instant, I would have to be a Universalist forever.

My own conclusions as to infant salvation are as follows: First, it is a fact of Christian consciousness that we all now believe that those children are saved who die before they reach personal responsibility. Our discussion, therefore, is not for the purpose of getting a belief; but merely for consistency, merely to harmonize with the fundamental principles of our theology a belief which we already have. Second, these children are *persons*. We cannot for one moment tolerate the teaching, however poetically couched, that these children, snatched from our homes, are nondescripts, more than *thing*, but less than *person*. There can be no such nondescript. In the intermediate state all these children come to full personal experience just as surely as our children do in this life. Third, these children are *moral* persons. Not only do they come to self-consciousness with all the motives originally intrinsic to created personality, but also they feel the urgency of these motives as persons under moral demand. Fourth, under moral demand and with this contrariety of motive, these children apprehend and freely accept their Saviour; and, in companionship with him, they achieve, in the intermediate state, the full equivalent of a perfect Christian experience. Thus, they are saved under a personal and moral test, but not in a formal probation. Fifth, the reason these children are treated in this special manner, the reason for their being taken out of this life and granted an essential test in place of a formal test, is, I conjecture, this: They are exceptional persons who have no need of a prolonged probation to fix their moral destiny; and their death is so entangled with the probation, or with the development, of other persons as to be of more providential worth than is their continued life in this world. That is, they die not to get advantage but to give service. And yet they are peculiarly honored. To be so selected by our Lord, to be taken at once into his profound life, to get their entire Christian education, so to speak, directly from him, should be regarded as a glory beyond our largest estimate in speech.

If to any one of you this view of infant salvation seems to be, either practically or philosophically, the same thing as to open up the intermediate state, as a formal contingent process in probation, to persons who in this life come to a clear realization of the difference between right and wrong, I can only say: "I am totally unable to look at the matter in your way, and totally unable to sanction any sort of coercion."

4. *Getting Ready for the New Race.* But the quiet, rich wonder of the intermediate state does not become manifest until we relate it to the final social organism of the Redeemed. When at the resurrection all the saints take up their full membership in that new race of which Christ Jesus is both the dynamic and the formal center, they are to serve each other, and to fit into each other, in the most absolute fashion. This does not mean that personality will be weakened, or that individuality will be given up; but it does mean that every member of the new race will be made free from all that is untrue or unreal. I am not now thinking of the wasteful clashing in polemics. Certainly there could be no Christian organism were polemics to last over into eternity. But polemics will not last over, for the development of the Christian consciousness itself will do away with every phase of polemics long before the ultimate church begins her splendid history in this world. No, I am thinking of completeness in supplemental fellowship and service. Perfectly to enter the life of his fellow men, perfectly to serve them, perfectly to augment their being with his own, the saint needs to be at his best. And he cannot be at his normal best if he thinks that which is untrue or believes that which is unreal. It is not now a matter entirely of personal motive and moral character; it is also a matter of sound judgment, and integrity in the make-up of the total manhood. I claim that service is injured anywhere

by every particle of error held by a man; and not even two men can have absolute companionship, if either one of them has an iota of untruth clinging to his mind. Moral love *and reality* are both required for the organism of the new race. Moral love is gained in this life. Reality is gained in the intermediate state.

5. *The Question of Method.* In the method of the intermediate state there are three features: First, *revelation*. It is not necessary to hold that all truth and all reality will be given in the intermediate state. We cannot be sure that all truth and all reality can ever be communicated to finite creatures. But they can have *enough* so that they will live altogether in the vitalities of truth and reality. And, then, perhaps, there will be a larger and yet larger revelation forever. Second, *perfect introspection.* Many times I have made reference to a man's substructure of individuality, that vast mystery of being which is the basis of personal manhood. From an ethical standpoint this individuality is mastered when it no longer antagonizes the moral ideal in a self-consciousness filled with love for God and man. And yet this moral mastery is in a sense superficial, for by it no man comes thoroughly to fathom himself, to know what he is. Indeed, he cannot in this earthly life know what he is, for his self-consciousness is too feeble, too flashing, too fleeting. But in the unbroken quiet of the intermediate state, with no body, no objective demand, no social distraction, the man can enter the recesses of his individuality and can find out precisely what he is, and so can finish his great task of self-personalization. Thus, we have in the intermediate state, the last triumph of personality in *the completed personal individual.* Third, *companionship with Christ.* I will startle you with a thought which you have never had before: *In all his Christian history, from his conversion on through the long*

reaches of eternity, the intermediate state is the only period when the redeemed man is altogether alone with his Saviour. Saint Paul calls it being "at home with the Lord." Do you remember his inspiring words? "We are of good courage, I say, and are willing rather to be absent from the body, and to be at home with the Lord." And this thought of companionship with Christ is to lend its inspiration to our consideration of the entire purpose and method of the intermediate state. The revelation is from Christ. The introspection is with the presence and help of Christ. The minute preparation for the coming social life in the new race is under the constant teaching of Christ. His own people, whom he hath redeemed, he prepares, now alone and personally, for their glorious destiny.

XXIX. THE RESURRECTION OF THE BODY

This doctrine, like that of the intermediate state, is usually discussed as an important division in eschatology. And there are reasons why it should be discussed in such a connection. Were we thinking of *all* men in their relation to the *last things*, surely we would need to treat the general resurrection as one of those last things. But according to my view, we can best understand the totality of redemption by keeping at the front its positive intention and actual accomplishments. Therefore, it is in my plan to make emphatic the redeemed, and to give merely an incidental reference to those who reject Jesus Christ. Besides all this, it is, I am confident, fairer, and more illuminating, to consider the everlasting ruin of those who will not be saved, as a problem in philosophical theodicy. As, then, my purpose is to emphasize the positive process of redemption, I wish to bring out the important fact that the redeemed man, the new man in Christ, is made complete only by the resurrection of the body. Here I will quote a striking passage from Chancellor Bernard's article on "The Resurrection": "Saint Paul's expression of Christian hope is not deliverance from the body, but redemption of the body. The redemption of the body is the last stage in the great process of adoption (υἱοθεσία) by which we are made 'sons of God'" (Rom. 8. 23).

Points in Personal Belief. The full discussion of the resurrection runs necessarily into such complications of detail as to be out of perspective with the plan of this book. I will, therefore, barely state my personal conclusions:

1. The body of the resurrection is not produced by the development of an indestructible *germ* which is within the body of this life.

2. It is not produced by a *natural force* which in some way belongs to the body of this life.

3. It is not an *ethereal body* which, before or at the time of death, was within the physical body as the shell is within the husk of a nut.

4. It is not the literal body of the grave *reconstructed*, whether by using all, or many, or a few, or even one, of the old material atoms. All this chasing through the universe to get the identical particles of matter, or enough of them to constitute "a proper identity," is not only an absurdity in philosophy, but a serious misinterpretation of Saint Paul.

5. The body of the resurrection is not the result of any natural law, any habitual divine volition, such as brings on the buds and blossoms of spring.

6. The body of the resurrection *is* a purely spiritual body (not bound by the laws of this world); made by the direct and new intention of God; *but so made as to be conditioned by the body of the grave.* Every glorified body is in occasional connection with a single physical body just as really as my body to-day is in occasional connection with the body of my childhood. The child's body conditions the man's body—is the start, the initial indicative, the determining fundament, in God's own process of identity. The body I have now is *what it is* because the body of my childhood was *what it was.* I have lost every old particle of matter, times and times, but I have remained in *my own category of identity.* Not for an instant has my body leaped into another man's category. Precisely so a man's body of glory *is his own body under the law of identity*, and can be traced back to its conditioning clue, namely, the body which that one man had at the

time of death.   Every abiding element, the entire intrinsic plan and meaning of the material body, is by the resurrection brought again into fact and made glorious.   Indeed, were it feasible to enter into a thorough philosophical discussion to show what *matter* actually is, such a discussion would, I believe, make it evident that the body of the resurrection is nothing other than *God's volitional repetition of the body of the grave—with splendid additions.*

Saint Paul's Analogy.   "But some one will say, How are the dead raised? and with what manner of body do they come?   Thou foolish one, that which thou thyself sowest is not quickened except it die: and that which thou sowest, thou sowest not the body that shall be, but a bare grain, it may chance of wheat, or of some other kind; but God giveth it a body even as it pleased him, and to each seed a body of its own" (1 Cor. 15. 35–38).

Against bald literalism Saint Paul distinctly pronounces when he says, "Thou sowest not the body that shall be;" and his entire teaching may be gathered up in the phrase, "resurrection by seed-process."   Here is a fair paraphrase of what the apostle says: "You place a seed in the ground; and by means of that seed you get a precisely corresponding plant, you know not how; even so you place in the ground a natural body, and by means of that, in God's own mysterious process, you get another, a spiritual body, which is to be identified with the buried body as a plant is exactly identified with its own seed."

A Catholic Union in Him.   It is not necessary again specially to note the social significance of the body; or to show that the Christian doctrine of the resurrection gives the most important emphasis to that social significance. But we do need to look more closely at the structural meaning of the saint's glorified body.   It is, on the one hand, a spiritual repetition of the body of his temporal probation.   Thus comes the accentuation of the distinct person himself. Never is he to lose connection with his own past. Not only by memory, but by his very objective life itself, he is to be reminded that he is the same man who lived that life on earth. Most seriously I urge you to work out the wholesomeness of this thought that the line of identity is everlastingly sacred, that *no man, in all the solemn eternities, can begin all over again.*

Not only so, but this repetition of the earthly body is a perpetual objective insistence upon the fact that every redeemed man once belonged to that old Adamic race which was broken up by death and because of sin. Thus, the entire social life of the new race will ever suggest the sad history of the old race. No saint can ever make a gesture, or look into the face of another saint, without projecting large hints of the story of a costly redemption. Indeed, the whole objective life of the saints in glory is so planned that it has memorial force, like a great sacrament.

The inspiring point, though, is now to come. The glorified body is, on the other hand, made according to the type of our Lord's own glorious body. And, as you quickly see, thus comes the emphasis upon the new race in Christ. The one distinct personal individual is kept emphatic; but he is, even in his bodily life, brought into union with his Redeemer. Thus the new race is formally, as it was before spiritually, given actual solidarity with Jesus Christ. There is a mighty social republic, kingdom, church, where every item of association is a tribute to "Him who hath redeemed us." In the Gospel of the Resurrection, there is one great passage which I am eager to give you now: "In this way the doctrine of the resurrection turned into a reality the exquisite myth of Plato. . . . And, at the same time the notion of civic union, in which lay so much of the strength and virtue of classical life, is freed from the dangers of party and class, and

extended to the utmost limits of human brotherhood.
. . . Christianity satisfies the instinct and harmonizes
the idea of a special relationship to a divine Lord with
that of a catholic union in him."

THE THREE COSMICAL SPHERES

I had written a paragraph on "the three cosmical
spheres," when, to my surprise, I found it almost word
for word in Bishop Martensen's Dogmatics. Evidently
my own work was nothing but Martensen as held in memory through a number of years. And yet my own movement in thought naturally would have reached the same
conception. Here is the passage from the Christian Dogmatics: "According to the fundamental representations
of revelation, the life of man is to be lived in three cosmical spheres: First, the sphere in which we dwell in the
flesh, ἐν σαρκί, our present life, whose prevailing bias is
sensible and outward—for not only is all spiritual activity
conditioned by sense, but the spirit groans under the
tyranny of the flesh; next, a sphere in which we live, ἐν
πνεύματι, wherein spirituality and inwardness is the
fundamental feature, and this is the intermediate state;
and, lastly, a sphere in which we shall again live in the
body, but in a glorified body, and in a glorified nature,
which is perfection, the renewal and perfecting of this
world to its final goal" (comment on 2 Cor. 5. 2, 8).

THE FIFTH DOCTRINAL DIVISION
REDEMPTION REALIZED IN THE NEW RACE

Das Reich Gottes ist das von Gott gewährleistete höchste Gut der durch seine Offenbarung in Christus gestifteten Gemeinde; allein es ist als das höchste Gut nur gemeint, indem es zugleich als das sittliche Ideal gilt, zu dessen Verwirklichung die Glieder der Gemeinde durch eine bestimmte gegenseitige Handlungsweise sich unter einander verbinden.—*Albrecht Ritschl*, Unterricht in der christlichen Religion, § 5.

Our Lord nowhere simply identifies his kingdom, or the kingdom of God, with the church which he came to found. As we have seen, his kingdom is visibly represented in his church; but there are insuperable obstacles to treating the two things as convertible. Our Lord founded a society which was to be visible like a city seated on a hill that cannot be hid (Matt. 5. 14), but the kingdom of God is visible only to faith—the kingdom of God is within you—the church is present and actual, the kingdom of God is present and yet future, actual and yet ideal. The kingdom of God is the supreme end, the visible church a means and instrument to that end. The kingdom of God is in its essential idea the reign of God; those over whom he reigns, and who answer to that reign by loyal allegiance constitute a kingdom in the sense of a body of subjects, and this is the ideal toward which the church must ever be advancing.—*Archibald Robertson*, Regnum Dei, the Bampton Lectures, 1901, pp. 75, 76.

The kingdom of Christ, not being a kingdom of this world, is not limited by the restrictions which fetter other societies, political or religious. It is in the fullest sense free, comprehensive, universal. . . .
It is most important that we should keep this ideal definitely in view, and I have therefore stated it as broadly as possible. Yet the broad statement, if allowed to stand alone, would suggest a false impression, or at least would convey only a half truth. . . . The conception, in short, is strictly an *ideal*, which we must ever hold before our eyes, which should inspire and interpret ecclesiastical polity, but which nevertheless cannot supersede the necessary wants of human society, and, if crudely and hastily applied, will lead only to signal failure. As appointed days and set places are indispensable to her efficiency, so also the church could not fulfill the purposes for which she exists, without rulers and teachers, without a ministry of reconciliation—in short, without an order of men who may in some sense be designated a priesthood. . . . But the priestly functions and privileges of the Christian people are never regarded as transferred or even delegated to these officers. They are called stewards or messengers of God, servants or ministers of the church, and the like; but the sacerdotal title is never once conferred upon them. The only priests under the gospel, designated as such in the New Testament, are the saints, the members of the Christian brotherhood.—*Joseph Barber Lightfoot*, The Christian Ministry, Dissertation I in Com. on Philippians.

XXX. THE CHURCH OF OUR LORD

The Kingdom of God. Before stating my own view of the significance of the "kingdom of God" I wish to call your attention to a scholar's protest which has been made by Professor Briggs against the modern Protestant practice of sharply distinguishing between the meaning of βασιλεία and the meaning of ἐκκλησία, as these terms are used in the Word of God. He says: "Let me say that I have carefully examined all the uses of these and cognate terms in both Testaments, and as a result of my investigations I declare that nothing can be more false than the distinction between 'kingdom' and 'church' asserted by many moderns. These are chiefly men who are displeased with the historic church and seek refuge in the kingdom as taught by Jesus Christ in the conceit that this is something larger and better. In fact, 'church' and 'kingdom' differ only as synonymous terms. There is nothing of importance which can be asserted of the kingdom of God which may not be also asserted of the church of God, if we faithfully use biblical material without speculation and theorizing. Jesus is King of the kingdom, and he reigns over it, subduing all external enemies under his feet, or transforming them by his grace into citizens of his kingdom. He is also the head over all things to his church. The church and the kingdom are coextensive; both are Old Testament institutions and New Testament institutions; both are institutions of this world, and both are eternal institutions of the world to come; both are organizations in the midst of the world and of the universe; both will eventually subdue and absorb the world and also the universe; the one is as spiritual as the other; the one is as external as the other."

The conclusions of Professor Briggs as a biblical scholar have, and should have, great weight with us; still I can but feel that in this instance his entire study of the scripture teaching has been superficial. When, for one example, our Lord says, "Thy kingdom come," can we believe that by *kingdom* he means exactly the *church* which he came to establish and to which he committed the sacrament of baptism? I cannot believe so. It is contrary to the whole tone and drift of his teaching. I am quite ready to admit that now and again the two Greek words, as we see them in the New Testament, slip into each other's province, and that a line of absolute consistency in usage it is impossible to trace through all the various writings; but I hold that there are plain indications of facts which are not the same; and that these facts should not be confused in our thinking, if we are ever fully to understand the Word of God and all Christian history.

My own view I can give economically as follows:

1. Let us start with God's unrealized plan to have an ultimate kingdom. Most comprehensively considered, the kingdom of God is the final, universal, absolute, everlasting dominion of God. All persons, all events, all creation will express the one fact—*God rules*. This is the sublime ideal toward which the universe struggles. But there is another sense in which the kingdom of God is a present reality. It has already *begun* in the hearts of angels and saints. And all its great spiritual laws are in operation—"the world of invisible laws by which God is ruling and blessing his creatures." The entire movement in the moral government is in an important sense expressive of the kingdom of God.

2. In this ultimate kingdom of God there is to be a *cosmic sweep*. The final universe—everything as formed

and placed and used—every person in either his character or his condition—will manifest the sovereign holiness of God. I mean that in God's ultimate kingdom the entire cosmos will not merely conform to his will, but will show forth his nature. The obedience will reveal something more than power, it will reveal the perfect divine holiness.

3. Within this cosmic kingdom, there is to be "the kingdom of heaven." This inner kingdom will be made up of all holy persons, all those having "the vision of God," and experiencing the ineffable felicity of the divine fellowship. The *beginning* of this kingdom of heaven is in the present life of the angels of God; but the kingdom will be fully realized only after the general resurrection.

4. Within this kingdom of heaven there is to be "the kingdom of Christ." This is a very definite matter, even that new race of men redeemed by the death of our Lord, and organized in him, and glorified in bodily conformity to him. This kingdom of Christ is also now in existence in an incomplete way, and comprehends all those persons who are by saving faith actually joined to Jesus Christ. The test is this actual union with Christ and not whether the persons are members of the Christian church or not.

5. These three, the cosmic kingdom, the kingdom of heaven, and the kingdom of Christ, are to be conceived under the figure of three concentric circles (recall our discussion of the moral government); so that the kingdom of heaven is the inner dominion of the cosmic kingdom, and the kingdom of Christ is the inner dominion of the kingdom of heaven, and also the innermost dominion of the cosmic kingdom, and all three constitute the kingdom of God.

6. This kingdom of God, taken in its entirety, is the kingdom of God the Father, which is the kingdom referred to in the Lord's Prayer. The full consummation of this kingly dominion of God the Father is to take place

when our Saviour "shall deliver up the kingdom to God, even the Father, . . . that God may be all in all" (1 Cor. 15. 24–28). This does not mean that Christ is to become anything less to his own people whom he hath redeemed, but merely that Christ and his kingdom are to become an integrant feature of the larger kingdom of God over which only the Father is to be the absolute and everlasting Ruler. It is the last extreme emphasis of that idea of the inherent subordination of the Son of God which is a fundamental idea in the whole system of Christian doctrine.

7. What, then, is the church of our Lord? It is the concrete exponent of the kingdom of Christ. It is a formal organization of men which stands for the kingdom of Christ while that kingdom is in the process of formation. Not exactly, as Kahnis said, "an æon of the kingdom"; but rather, as Dräseke said, "the workshop of the kingdom"; or, as Neander most beautifully said, "the seminary for the heavenly community." I am willing to allow just this much: The church of our Lord *belongs* to his tentative kingdom; but it is not coextensive with that kingdom (even as that kingdom exists to-day), and cannot be coextensive with it until, anyway, there is what Saint Paul terms "a glorious church, not having spot or wrinkle or any such thing" (Eph. 5. 27). But even this admission is somewhat misleading, for to many it will suggest that the difference between the kingdom and the church is merely that one is perfect and the other is imperfect. That, though, is not the fundamental difference. The fundamental difference is one of essential structure. The kingdom is a simple personal and spiritual organism. The church is a formal and complex organism. The kingdom is a life of fellowship mediated only through Jesus Christ. The church is a machine; at its best a machine full of life and expressing life, and yet a machine.

In its worship and in all its service the church has, and must have, some sort of outward instrument—forms, symbols, creeds, what not; but the kingdom needs only the complete man. If, as some believe, the Christian church itself is to be purified, completed, glorified, and then taken into eternity for everlasting worship and service, even then it will not be, strictly speaking, the kingdom of our Lord, but merely the formal instrument of that kingdom. It will be, perhaps, to the kingdom as a whole what the glorified body will be to the one moral person—the instrumental means of perfect objective manifestation. The kingdom of Christ may, so to speak, show its life to the entire universe through a glorified church—Saint Paul's ἔνδοξος ἐκκλησία.

The Holy Catholic Church. As Protestants we cannot afford to surrender this great historic phrase. Nor should we transform its original meaning into that of "the invisible church of Christ." The holy catholic church is precisely the visible church of our Lord, that is, the entire body of persons who are in actual organization about the two points, the gospel and the sacraments. Whenever a company of men unite, in any way whatsoever, to maintain the preaching of the gospel of redemption, and to secure the administration of the sacrament of baptism, and to have Christian communion in the sacrament of the Lord's Supper, that company of men constitutes a Christian church; and the sum total of such churches is the holy catholic church. Forms of ecclesiastical government, and preferences in ceremony, and peculiarities of denominational belief, have no large significance; the essential points of organization are simply the two sacraments and the preaching of the gospel. This church of our Lord is *holy*, not in the sense that every member is now entirely holy in personal life, but in the sense that the church is our Lord's own instrument in building up a holy kingdom. The whole plan and movement of the church are unto holiness. This holy church is *catholic* in the sense that it is *for all men*. In it there is no ethnic limitation. Its ambition is for world-wide conquest. Catholicity is to the church just what the racial plan is to the kingdom of Christ. It is the humanity-note. In this holy catholic church there are three kinds of membership: First, there is *formal* membership. In many situations there are men who submit to all the tests used, and become members of an organized church, and yet do not have any redemptional relation to Jesus Christ. Of course the question soon arises, "Are these formal members really members of the church of our Lord at all?" I myself find it best to regard them as in the holy catholic church, but not members of the kingdom of Christ. This view renders possible large emphasis upon the absolute need of having a Christian experience; and yet, with this emphasis, a certain practical wisdom in pastoral work. And, further, the view is helpful when we try fairly to estimate the situation in any of the great national churches, or when we try to understand the condition of the whole Christian world. Second, there is *dynamic* membership. I mean by this more than any one term can denote. The power of the holy catholic church is due to the Holy Spirit. But his action is (not wholly conditioned) largely related to those members of the church who are also members of the kingdom of redemption. They may be called the dynamic personal points of his action. For example, the force of a sermon, or the influence of a sacrament, depends, in quite a measure, upon the reality and vitality of the Christian experience of the congregation. And so every member of the church who actually lives in Christ Jesus adds a veritable dynamic to the church. Third, there is membership by *Christian claim*. The church of our Lord has the right and the duty to claim the helpless. She should take into her atmosphere and association and (if possible) service all people who are unable to make a choice for themselves—not only all irresponsible children, but all the feeble-minded, and all those unfortunate souls who have been mentally wrecked by woes too terrible for human fortitude. Of course, there are involved here serious questions in church economy, but they all can be met and mastered, if we are determined to make the church of Christ a worthy instrument of the kingdom of Christ.

But surely you will not misunderstand me here—you will not think that I intend to teach the possibility of a mechanical salvation. No human being is saved, or can be saved, by membership in the holy catholic church—salvation is only by *personal* union with Jesus Christ.

The Organism of the Church. To appreciate the philosophy of the organism of the holy catholic church, we need to remember that, as the concrete exponent of the kingdom of Christ or the new race, the church is also designed to be a brotherhood of moral persons dominated by Jesus Christ. Thus there are three features to be protected and emphasized in the church-organism: 1. The personal. 2. The societary. 3. The spiritual, in fellowship with Christ. I can get at these three features most lucidly, I think, by comparing the organism of the church to the structure of an ellipse, with its two *foci* and a major axis.

First, in the church, there is *the personal focus.* This is the preaching of the gospel. Not merely the Christian sermon, but all personal testimony, everything which is done in the church to show what the gospel means to separate persons. The purpose is to bring about the conquest of the world by the church through this personal feature of preaching. And how wonderful it all is, this giving to the world the entire message of redemption through the experience of men! The most effective Christian sermon is really nothing other than a chapter of the inner life of a person who lives in our Lord Jesus Christ. The moment the sermon loses that personal quality, that moment the sermon ceases to be effective. Do you not begin to apprehend the philosophy—one might almost say the strategy—of this personal focus? Why, we reach the great Christian verities through each other, our very apprehension of the finalities of the gospel is only by entering the living personal experience of Christian men. And so every time you grasp a Christian truth it prepares you to understand better the life of Christian men; and to live—helpfully, joyously, to live with them forever. Thus, the whole Christian brotherhood comes to its mighty certainties of faith in one great entanglement of personal experience, the very emphasis upon personality making a contribution to ultimate fellowship.

Second, *the societary focus*. But it is not enough to preach the gospel through persons; the Christian society, as an organized body, must have a chance to express itself. Hence the second focus, which is the focus of the Christian sacraments. Not now are we to consider the significance of each sacrament; I merely wish you to note the fact and worth of the sacramental idea in the organism of the church. This focus is a perfect balance to the other. As the aim of preaching is to stir up personality, to make men think, to keep the personal life from stagnation, so the sacramental aim is to fill consciousness with the sense of Christian companionship, to make the person realize that he is only a part of the large Christian community. In both sacraments it is the holy catholic church which dominates the scene. The person is there surely, but he is there for submission and fellowship. His very meditation and confession and consecration are *in the midst*.

Third, there is (to keep our ellipse in mind) *a major axis*. This major feature in the organism of the church is, some would insist, the Holy Spirit. Such insistence is a mistake. Indeed, there is, I fear, in our day, an emphasis placed upon the Holy Spirit which is not quite true to the New Testament. To protect with words every side of the matter is extremely difficult; but I will say this: *No emphasis is ever to be given to the Holy Spirit which, in any moment or in any degree, shuts our Lord out from the Christian consciousness.* The real work of the Spirit always exalts Christ; *that* is his mission. As to the church, the Holy Spirit is the very life of it all. The preaching, the sacraments, the service, are literally nothing without his presence and power. But the major axis is only Jesus Christ our Redeemer. And just what do I mean by this? I mean that the spiritual organism of the church requires actual fellowship with Christ. You have a complete organism to just the extent that in the sacraments and in the preaching and in all the work the people are in conscious union with Jesus Christ. This implies, you easily perceive, that it is only dynamic membership which contributes to the spiritual organism of the church. O, if we all could only feel this; if every Christian preacher could only realize that *size* is not what the organism requires for its completeness and efficiency, but fellowship, actual fellowship with Jesus Christ. If you say that conversions are the test of church efficiency, I will say that conversions will follow if the church is in living union with our Lord.

A further word of caution is necessary in this connection, owing to certain widespread tendencies: Fellowship with Christ cannot normally be secured in the church by exalting his person at the expense of his atonement. It verily seems as if the whole realm of Christian scholarship was trying to minimize the death of the Son of God.

The tendency is not only wrong, but even pernicious. Fully to enter into the life of Christ, one needs to be overwhelmed by his death as Saint Paul was overwhelmed by it until he could hardly think a thought which was not colored by its sacrificial meaning.

Christian Unity. At this point I cannot speak an effective word; for I am out of sympathy with every effort to crush out the denominational churches in the name of Christian unity. I believe in uniting all those churches where the fundamental interpretation of the Christian faith is the same; but I do not believe in asking any church to yield any real conviction. In the present state of things there is more Christian vitality in these denominational convictions than in all the superficial combinations of forced external conformity. Solidarity is the ultimate, is the Christian ideal; but real Christian solidarity cannot come by sacrificing personality to machinery. I fully appreciate the dreadful fact of waste; but a waste of life is better than any artificial economy.

XXXI. THE CHRISTIAN SACRAMENTS

COMING now closer to the Christian sacraments, we find that they have, without losing at all their societary significance in the organism of the church, very important functions in relation to the Christian person himself.

1. Each sacrament is *a token of personal Christian intention.* In baptism the candidate expresses his personal intention of entering the church of Christ. Here his self-decision is something more than to submit to Jesus Christ as his Redeemer, it is to acknowledge Christ's command, and "to be a Christian man before the world." Thus baptism becomes a public profession of the faith. In the Lord's Supper there is no less an expression of personal intention, for the communicant, by his answer to the invitation, declares that he intends "to lead a new life." Thus the member of the church is made often to recommit himself to the Christian purpose, and so there is repeatedly a renewal of that intense personal bearing in self-decision which he had as a candidate in baptism.

2. Each sacrament *is a symbol of an event in grace.* Baptism is to us the symbol of regeneration. To be comprehensively true to all the different ways in which the writers of the New Testament associate baptism with salvation, we should, I think, use a larger fact than regeneration, and say that Christian baptism is the symbol of redemptional union with Christ. Allowing such usage, baptism would be, first, a token of personal intention to enter the church of Christ; and, second, a symbol of actual entrance into the kingdom of Christ. But, as a matter of history, the Christian consciousness has never

treated all passages of Scripture as of equal importance; and, in this instance, the Christian tendency has been to make baptism precisely a symbol of regeneration. The Lord's Supper is the symbol of the death of Christ, or, more exactly, a sign of the personal appropriation of the person of Christ in his death. By grace the person takes the crucified Saviour as a spiritual nourishment of soul; and the use of the bread and wine symbolize that deep event of grace. The phrase "by grace" means that the communicant receives the extraordinary aid of the Holy Ghost.

3. Each sacrament is *a means of grace*. We are to understand this point, first of all, in the sense that the full use of either of the sacraments enables a person to open up his inner life more largely to the personal operation of the Spirit of God, and this more searching work of the Holy Spirit always results in Christian growth. But, in this connection, there also comes to mind the old question of "baptismal regeneration," a question concerning which a sane word is now very much needed. Several Protestant New Testament scholars, in their exposition of "the washing of regeneration" (see Titus 3. 4–7), hold that Christian baptism is, in this phrase, most closely connected with regeneration, not merely because it symbolizes it, "but also, and chiefly, because it effects it." At once we want to know what exactly is meant by the expression "effects it." If the intention is to teach that baptism is automatically effective of regeneration, or even that baptism is a fixed and only condition of regeneration, the view should be rejected; for it is contrary to the trend of teaching in the New Testament, and also is not the best interpretation of the Pauline passage involved. If, however, it be held that baptism may be such an energizing personal expression of the faith of a repentant man as naturally to prepare the way, or to

render feasible actual regeneration by the Holy Ghost, I can see no forcible objection to the view. In other words, Christian baptism not only is a symbol of regeneration, but also may be a means of grace unto the event of regeneration. It does not practically follow, however, that a pastor should always be willing to baptize any repentant person. Indeed, as a rule, it is wiser, I think, to baptize men only after complete conversion.

The Number of the Sacraments. The discussion of the term *sacramentum*, as to its history and meaning, is of some interest, but of no great worth in reaching a decision concerning the number of the Christian sacraments. The question is, mainly, one of pure obedience in carrying out our Lord's intention as to what features are essential in the structure of his own church. He really organized his society about the preaching of the gospel and exactly two sacraments; and therefore exactly these two sacraments the church should have. It matters not how sacred and useful other rites may be, the Saviour him-self did not place them in the organism of his church, and we have no right to enlarge upon his will. The name *sacrament* is not worth long contention, but baptism and the Lord's Supper should together have a name which is not given to any other feature of the church service, or to any other rite in sacred ceremony.

How far the new discussion of the significance of our Lord's last supper with his disciples and the origin of the eucharist (by Harnack, Jülicher, and others) may influence Christian scholarship, it is now impossible to surmise; but I do not expect to see any essential modification of the consensus of evangelical opinion by this extremely erratic discussion. For Christian men, it certainly would seem that Saint Paul's statement to the Corinthians should settle the entire matter forever. In an article on the Lord's Supper in the Hastings Dictionary of the Bible,

Alfred Plummer wisely writes as follows: "In what sense is the tradition represented by Mark and Matthew 'the earliest'? That given by Saint Paul was written earlier, and is the earliest written record of any words of Christ. It had been previously communicated to the Corinthians. And Saint Paul had derived it direct from the Lord himself (1 Cor. 11. 23). His words can mean no less. Had he merely been told by apostles he would have had no stronger claim to be heard than hundreds of other Christians. The silence of Matthew and Mark does not warrant us in contradicting such explicit testimony, which would be sufficient, even if it were unsupported, for the unvarying belief of the church from the earliest ages, that it was on the night in which he was betrayed that Christ instituted the eucharist, and gave the command, 'Continue to do this [pres. imp.] in remembrance of me.' The proposal to place the institution of the eucharist as a permanent rite later than the last Supper is as unnecessary as the proposal to place it earlier."

The Formula of Christian Baptism. In 1 Cor. 6. 11 we read: "And such were some of you: but ye were washed, but ye were sanctified, but ye were justified in the name of the Lord Jesus Christ, and in the spirit of our God." Such references to Christ in connection with baptism, together with the fact that in the New Testament there is no mention of any person as being baptized in the name of the Trinity, has led many to believe that at first the trinitarian formula was not used in the Christian sacrament of baptism. This belief I cannot regard as well founded. These references to Christ are to be taken, I am inclined to think, as mere statements of the fact of Christian baptism, with the emphasis, in rhetorical manner, upon Jesus Christ—an emphasis which under the militant circumstances of the early church is just what one would naturally expect—and not as exact indications of the formula used in the administration of the sacrament. There stand our Lord's words, "baptizing them into the name of the Father and of the Son and of the Holy Ghost"; and unless there is thoroughly convincing evidence to the contrary, we surely must suppose the apostolic church, so eager to do the will of their crucified and risen Lord, would carry out his last command.

Nor is the recognition of the Trinity in baptism an unimportant matter; for it is of the greatest concern that the Christian church fundamentally and perpetually recognize the fact that, while Jesus Christ is our Redeemer, redemption is the plan and work of the entire Godhead. The baptismal command of our Lord, in taking leave of his disciples, is as if he had said to them, "I have now finished my work on earth, and provided for every man the possibility of salvation, but you are ever to remember that this free salvation is not a gift from me alone; but is from the whole of God, even the Father, the Son, and the Holy Ghost."

The Mode of Baptism. Exhaustively to consider the question of mode in Christian baptism is a physical impossibility under the limited plan of this book. But, fortunately, the old-style discussion, which spent pages upon βαπτίζω and the classical history of the Greek pronouns, is no longer necessary. Christian archæology has changed all that. We now know what the early church *actually did.* All reliable scholarship is, I think, in agreement that the typical baptism in the apostolic church was in the mode of trine immersion. But from the very beginning, with the type ever at the front, there was in use a principle of liberty, a deep distinction being made between the essential act of baptism and the mere mode. The whole spirit of the situation is expressed in this passage from The Teaching of the Twelve Apostles:

"Having first said all these things, baptize into the name of the Father, and of the Son, and of the Holy Spirit, in living water [that is, fresh-running water]. But if thou have not living water, baptize in other water; and if thou canst not in cold, in warm. But if thou have not either, pour out water thrice upon the head into the name of Father and Son and Holy Spirit." This principle of liberty has been used by different branches of the holy catholic church until the typical mode of baptism has been thrust into a practical banishment, and the exceptional mode (and the most exceptional mode, too) has become the type. As Dean Stanley said, "It is a striking example of the triumph of common sense and convenience over the bondage of form and custom."

From the standpoint of the Baptists, Dr. George Dana Boardman says, "The church has no more right to change a divine symbol than to change a divine command." To this I would answer: If the church decides that she can better carry out a divine command by changing the form of a symbol which she believes is not a divine command, then she has not merely the right, but even the obligation, to make such a change. Indeed, this same principle of liberty has been used by our Baptist friends themselves, for they do not practice *trine* immersion.

Dr. Boardman also suggests, as his *irenicon*, that the Baptists shall give up their insistence on immersion as a qualification for communion, and that the non-Baptists shall return to the primitive mode of immersion. This suggestion is made in such a large Christian spirit that one can only wish it could be accepted and acted upon; but it is out of range with the urgency of the situation which the Christian church is now facing. We are now fighting for nothing less than the whole supernatural peculiarity of Christianity, and such a question as the mode of baptism is, for the time, of no great Christian concern.

The denominations would much better stay just as they are until this serious battle is won—then there will be a new Christian perspective, and we all shall be able to look at our polemics in a new way, I believe.

"*A Communion of the Body of Christ.*" For the sake of emphasis, I have kept for this place the deeper consideration of the Lord's Supper. This sacrament is, as was indicated, a general means of grace; but it is also a most peculiar means of grace, for it furnishes to the communicant the possibility of an experience which is properly called *mystical*. The modern Christian man seems to be afraid of this term mystical, but it is the only term which can indicate some of the highest Christian experiences, those experiences which are so transcendent that, like the peace of God itself, they pass all understanding. Allow me, in this connection, to say that the teaching of Zwingli concerning the Lord's Supper has been very strangely misunderstood. He taught something much more profound than "the memorial view," for he taught that the body of Christ was *mystically present*. And, in the Methodist church, the mystical presence has also been taught. Dr. Latimer's "dynamical presence," by which the communicants are "penetrated" so that Christ "assimilates them to himself," was Zwingli's view stated in a most inspiring manner. I say it was Zwingli's view; but I am not sure but Dr. Latimer intended to go further and to be almost as mystical as was John Calvin, who had an exceedingly profound and spiritual conception of the Lord's Supper. Had Calvin's influence only prevailed, the superficial Socinian conception of our Saviour's table would never have made such headway as it has made, although it fits into the rationalistic tendency to cheapen into clarity every feature of Christian experience.

In 1 Corinthians, the tenth chapter, Saint Paul says: "The cup of blessing which we bless, is it not a commun-

ion of the blood of Christ?　The bread which we break, is
it not a communion of the body of Christ? seeing that we,
who are many, are one bread, one body: for we all partake of the one bread." In all of Saint Paul's epistles
there is nothing more mystical than is this passage, and it
is extremely difficult to get at his exact meaning. But
let us earnestly try. The key to the passage is, I am
sure, the one word κοινωνία, translated "communion"
in the English text quoted above. What does this word
mean? That it does not mean a mere "partaking of" is
at once indicated by the fact that Saint Paul, in the last
clause of the passage, expresses that meaning by another
word ("for we all partake of"—μετέχομεν). Then,
again, when we study κοινωνία, in its derivation, and as
it is used in various connections, we discover that the
pith of its meaning is in the idea of *active fellowship*. That
is, a fellowship where both parties give as well as take.
Now, is it possible to interpret the Lord's Supper in terms
of an active transcendent fellowship? I think it can be
done in the following way:

1. The bread and wine of the Lord's Supper, when
used in a thoroughly Christian manner, become, under the
operation of the Holy Spirit, the means of a transcendent
realization of the death of Christ. That death not only
occupies the communicant's thought, it also dominates
his feeling. It becomes absolutely real to him. It is
reproduced in his consciousness. Spiritually, mystically,
in overwhelming effect, it is to him as if the crucified
Saviour, broken and bleeding, were *actually there*, in complete grasp by the senses. This is the mystical presence
of our Lord's body and blood. And it has been the
actual experience of thousands of Christians who have
fully prepared themselves for this sacrament. This mystical presence is the first stage of Saint Paul's κοινωνία.

2. This realization of the death of our Lord is a means

(again under the operation of the Holy Spirit) of an active fellowship with Christ. The believer absolutely yields his person to that transcendent vision of his crucified Redeemer, and thus enters into communion with Christ himself. Christ takes him, penetrates him, and "assimilates him to himself." Even the mystic's phrase, "He becomes a part of the body of Christ," I do not deem beyond the fullness of the experience. This is the second stage of Saint Paul's κοινωνία; and it is really only an intense emphasis in personal consciousness of that actual union with Christ which every truly Christian man obtains in his conversion.

3. This active fellowship with Christ is the means (still under the operation of the Holy Spirit) of a further fellowship—a transcendent fellowship by the communicant with the Christian people who are about him at the Lord's table; and to just the extent that they are in active fellowship with Christ. Thus, one man can gather up into his consciousness all sorts and conditions of men, and enter into their sorrows and their joys, and live large moments of supreme unselfishness. And thus it is possible for a Christian society, all partaking "of the one bread," to become "one body." This is the completion of Saint Paul's κοινωνία, the communion of the body of Christ. And with a thought of the matter you will see that this communion is for the church but a predictive foretaste of the completed new race in Christ, as the members of that race will live in glory. Forever will the death of Christ be absolutely real to them; forever will they have active fellowship with Christ; and forever will they have active fellowship with each other.

XXXII. THE CHURCH MILITANT

HAVING considered the church in its sacraments, in its organism, and in its essential relation to the kingdom of God, we are now prepared to look at the church militant, that is, the church actually at work in the great struggle to conquer the world.

The Christian Preacher. It is with serious purpose that I place the Christian preacher in just this connection, for he has no significance save from the standpoint of the militant aim of the church. The Christian preacher is not an apostle. He has neither the authority nor the inspiration to make any fundamental addition to the word of God. Nor is the Christian preacher a priest, excepting in the sense in which every Christian man is a priest, "to offer up spiritual sacrifices, acceptable to God through Jesus Christ." The Christian preacher does not belong (as do the sacraments) to the organic structure of the church. There could be a real Christian church without any minister at all. He is not even necessary to preach the gospel. But he is necessary for economical and efficient service. He is an important feature in the economy of Christian conquest. A careful study of the Christian church in the New Testament will convince you that the difference between the clergy and the laity, of which high-church writers have made so much account, was merely a difference in practical service. To accomplish anything, without perpetual waste, the early church had to have machinery, had to have some sort of government, and had to have regular officers for this machinery and for this government. But these officers did not have any redemptional dignity in the church. Especially note the words of Bishop Lightfoot, who wrote as a master of the early history of the Christian church: "But the priestly functions and privileges of the Christian people are never regarded as transferred or even delegated to these officers. They are called stewards or messengers of God, servants or ministers of the church, and the like; but the sacerdotal title is never once conferred upon them. The only priests under the gospel, designated as such in the New Testament, are the saints, the members of the Christian brotherhood."

This false, unchristian sacerdotal importance once entirely rejected, we are quickly and eagerly to place the largest emphasis upon the worth of the Christian preacher to the church. I would go so far as to say that without him a living, efficient church is practically impossible. He is essential not only to the surface economy of the church, in using its machinery to advantage—he is essential also, and even more, to the deeper spiritual economy, in advising and developing and uniting and using in service the persons who make up the Christian community. In any church there are almost sure to be many kinds of people, perhaps no two of them in the same spiritual condition, perhaps no two of them with the same conception of the details of duty in Christian activity; and there is pressing need of "a master in Israel," who has the time and calling to study the entire situation from the standpoint of the ideal of a Christian church, and then has the definite purpose to lead the people, by preaching and by pastoral method, on toward that churchly ideal. To make out of many elements a living, efficient church; a church in which the sermon and the sacraments are ever quick with the Holy Ghost; a church with the atmospheric expectation of conversions; a church where the tempted are environed with victory; a church where the imperfect are made to see their larger need of Christ; a church where the peculiar consolations of God are given to the afflicted; a church where Christian men begin even on earth to be a Christian brotherhood; a church which constantly bears toward the whole world with sacrifice in its heart and conquest in its purpose—to make such a church, a church of the long major axis, that is the work of the Christian preacher. For such work in the church the Christian preacher needs at least four things in qualification, namely: First, a Christian experience so deep that it fills the consciousness with urgent reality; second, a comprehensive knowledge of the Holy Scriptures; third, an unfailing grasp of all the peculiarity of the Christian faith as a system of redemptional doctrine; and, fourth, the capacity and the courage for spiritual leadership among men. Other qualifications the Christian preacher may have to advantage, especially for the oratorical phase of his service; but these four things mentioned he *must* have to build up a living and potent church of Christ.

The Christian Church and the Home. From the beginning it has been a point in what may be called Christian strategy to gain vantage in the home. When Saint Paul teaches (see 1 Cor. 7. 14) that "the unbelieving husband is sanctified in the wife, and the unbelieving wife is sanctified in the brother," he is not thinking of personal holiness at all. No unbeliever can be holy by proxy. But a home itself is under the divine plan a little organism, and to get into it even one point of Christian faith lifts the entire home into a new category for the church. The church can treat that home as its own spiritual property, so to speak, and plan for it and even pray for it with a sense of Christian ownership. The question as to the worth of such Christian treatment of people who are not actually Christians in their personal life, should be answered from the standpoint of the philosophy of human influence. While every man's decision must be at last

his own self-decision in his own freedom, yet we do influence each other; for we can be instrumental in bringing
motive to immediate urgency. Thus there is a true sense
in which one can be a means in another's conversion.

On the whole, this is the connection which I deem the
most fitting for a statement of view concerning the baptism of infants. My view as to the baptism of infants has
very naturally a close relation to my view of the salvation
of infants in the intermediate state, for in both views there
is involved their personal and moral condition. Already
I have given the one view, and the other may be succinctly stated thus:

1. Inasmuch as infants have not yet come to the possibility of personal volition, their baptism has not the
meaning which Christian baptism has in the case of adult
believers. That is, the baptism of an infant is not a token
of personal intention, is not a symbol of an event of grace,
and is not a means of grace. Of course, we can say that
the parent or sponsor has personal intention and all that;
and we can also say that the child is in a spiritual condition which is the equivalent of the regenerate state;
and we can also say that later in life baptism will become
to the child a means of grace. These things, or some of
them, I have myself often said in the past; but they now
seem to me to be mere verbal ingenuities made for the
defense of a practice; and I deem it much fairer and
much more wholesome to place the baptism of infants on
a basis of its own.

2. Inasmuch as infants are not personal sinners, they
are innocent. It is, I believe, only of this simplicity in
innocence that our Saviour was thinking when he said,
"of such is the kingdom of heaven;" and his words are
not to be taken in a hard and fast doctrinal way.

3. These helpless and undeveloped and innocent children the Christian church has a right to claim as her own

wards, to bring them up on the inside of the rich life of
the holy catholic church.

4. But the best way (and often the only feasible way)
to do this is to do it through the home, which belongs to
the church entirely or essentially. And so the church
turns to the home and says: "If you will consecrate unto
your Lord this child, and act for us until we can get at
his personal life, we will baptize him into membership of
the Redeemer's church on earth."

5. And so the baptism of an infant is the most forcible
recognition and utilization of the home on the part of the
Christian church.

6. If now you ask what infant baptism precisely stands
for as a rite, the answer should, I believe, be this: It stands
for the sacramental acceptance by the church of the consecration unto Christ of a babe by a home. The church
officially joins in with the home in dedicating the child
unto the Redeemer, and does this by making the child
a member of the holy catholic church under the principle
of Christian claim. The two rites, infant baptism and
adult baptism, are alike only in that both are forms of
entrance into the church of Jesus Christ.

The Church and the Nation. "The nation is to work
in the realization on the earth of his kingdom who is the
only and the eternal King. It becomes, then, no more
the kingdom of this world, but the kingdom of Him
whose reign is of eternal truth—the reign in which, in
the realization of personality, there is the freedom of man.
Its advance is only in his advent; its destination is toward
him. Its new ages are the days of the coming of the Son
of man. Its freedom is only in his redemptive strength.
It is no more the life of the first man, of the earth earthy."

It is certainly fitting that I begin with these seerlike
words quoted from the greatest tribute ever paid to the
significance of national life; for it was this tribute, in

Elisha Mulford's The Nation, which, many years ago, started a line of thinking to culminate in my present conception of the profound relation between the church and the nation as two coördinate features in the vast work of God for mankind. But to bring out the full conception, as it lies in my mind, I will refer again to the family. For these three, the family, the nation, and the church, belong to one divine plan, which through the centuries moves steadily toward the distant goal. This goal is that perfect brotherhood which is to be the everlasting kingdom of Christ, the inner circle of the kingdom of heaven, and the innermost circle of the whole kingdom of God. For this final brotherhood there are these three different ventures in social solidarity. They might properly be called the three educational movements toward human brotherhood. First, there is the family, where, as in a primary school, we learn our first lesson in solidarity. It is the first check on pure individualism. In a home, even in a very imperfect home, the total family must at times become the point of view. Not yet, perhaps, is there any real unselfishness, but there is an escape from the merely individual outlook, and a first exercise in social entanglement. Then, in a finer home, what chances there are to live in each other and for each other, and to form an almost perfect social organism. Next comes the nation; and how all the utilitarians fail to understand the grandeur of its meaning! They seem to think that a nation is a union of men to secure material prosperity. But a nation is a divine institution, like the family; and its purpose is to give another and larger check to pure individualism. Here again one may be selfish; but he must combine with many men and in a measure understand them and think of their interests and yield to their judgment. Thus there is increasing social interlacing all the time. And, in the most noble relation to the nation, in patriotism, there is a complete surrender of the individual to the good of the whole, for a patriot is a man who lives absolutely for his country in feeling and thought and deed. Now, do you not see what a preparation the family and the nation have made for the Christian church? They have introduced and emphasized the very principle of solidarity which the church seizes and applies to all mankind. The church cries out: "Yes, live for each other in the family; live in the entire length and breadth of national concern; but all mankind redeemed in Jesus Christ is the final family and the final nation; let us join together to express that largest social solidarity even in this world."

Holding such a view of the significance of the nation, we cannot tolerate the Romish idea that the nation is subordinate to the church. Nor can we receive the Erastian idea that the church is subordinate to the state. Nor are we satisfied with the idea that each is supreme in its own province, but the two provinces have no relation to each other save as they cross lines in material things. The church and the nation are to be regarded as two allies, each working by its own method, to prepare the way for the kingdom of our Lord. Just as the moral process is a preparation for the full redemptional process, so the nation should be a real preparation for the work of the church. Perhaps we would better say an *indirect* preparation, as what we mean is that the nation should aim to become a moral brotherhood, where every law and every institution is for the benefit of all and under a moral ideal. This view I myself carry out into many details, some of these details involving action as a citizen; but all I wish to urge upon you is the general conception that the church is to look upon the nation, not as an accident brought about by men, but as a sacred agency of God in working out the plan of his final kingdom.

The Church and Socialism. Some years ago, in one of our great cities, I heard a socialist try to answer the question, "What must I do to be saved?" Substantially stated, his answer was this: "The Christian idea that to be saved a man must be convicted of sin, have faith in Christ, and be converted, and lead a holy life, is altogether wrong. A man is not saved by what he himself does or allows God to do. A man is saved by society. Let society make a man's environment right, and the man can't help being right. Let society make a man's environment wrong, and the man can't help being lost, that is, being bad. Our task, men, is to put about every brother man that which is true and beautiful and good."

Not every socialist would make or entirely sanction this statement as it stands; and yet the statement brings out sharply the main difference between socialism and Christianity, namely, one emphasizes environment while the other emphasizes personality. According to Christianity, the individual person *must do something* to be saved; and all that is done for him (and Christianity believes that much must be done for him) is done in some under relation to his personal action. According to socialism, the man is a product very completely of the situation in which he is placed. Indeed, I think it is not unfair to say that all unmodified socialism is materialistic either in fact or in tendency.

But when we go back to those pregnant times which followed the French Revolution, when the workingman woke up to the astonishing fact that *he* had not been benefited by that revolution, and then follow the course of socialism through all its intensely interesting history, especially in Europe, we can discover, it seems to me, that socialism has a personal root in spite of all its anti-personal theory. The root of socialism is *the personal hunger for brotherhood*. The disappointment over the

French Revolution was deeper than any question of material advantage. The man with money had shown in the outcome that he did not care any more about the workingman than royalty had cared for him. And from that day until now the workingman has felt that no one has any concern in his real welfare. Surely the Christian church can never go over to the socialistic point of view to any such extent as would tend to weaken our insistence upon personality and personal salvation; but it does seem to me that the Christian church should make a much more serious study of socialism and the whole industrial situation; and should make a Christian contribution to the settlement of such questions as involve a principle of equity; and should find some way to convince the workingman that the church of Jesus Christ is the very brotherhood which he needs. But it is not of much use to try to convince him, until we ourselves more nearly realize the Christian ideal, and actually *are* such a brotherhood.

The Church and the City Problem. There is no place where, as a Christian man, I come quite so near to dreadful discouragement as I do in one of the great cities of our Christian civilization. I say to myself, "We have preached the gospel here so long, and yet we have not conquered this place!" I have no heart thoroughly to enter into the matter, endeavoring to make you see all that I see. But there is one hopeful sign—a very hopeful sign, I think—and that is the new Christian attack upon "the slums." I know very well how superficial, from a Christian standpoint, some of this work is. It is mere philanthropy. But not all of it is so; some of it is as profoundly Christian as any work done by the church anywhere. And the movement, as a movement, has taken the right method, namely, the method of a convincing brotherhood. Even superficial things are no waste, if in the end they make for brotherhood. The greatest thing you can do for a man is actually to lead him to Jesus Christ, but next to that greatest thing is it to love the man and make him believe that you are his brother. And often these two kinds of service are not far apart.

What is now needed is to lift this slum work out of what may be called its sociological stage, and to make it truly Christian by placing it upon the conscience and heart of the entire church. The church should have much the same attitude toward the slum work that she has toward the foreign missionary work—an attitude of self-sacrifice, determination, conquest. The time shall come when the Christian church will consider the great cities points of such strategic importance that she will master them at any cost.

The Church and Foreign Missions. In the very nature of the case, the supreme work to a thoroughly militant church is, and should be, in the field of foreign missions; for it is this field which most promptly utilizes the aggressive Christian spirit of world-wide conquest. The gospel is not for ourselves alone, but for the whole race. But there need be no antagonism between the work abroad and the work at home. Neither one should be exalted and cultivated at the expense of the other. The truth is that all work really done for Jesus Christ is one and the same thing, and must be done with that aggressive spirit which cries out, *Every human being has been purchased by the death of our Lord, and we must reach them all with his gospel.*

I will state the true missionary motives, as I see them; but first I wish to quote a passage from Dr. D. D. Whedon. I have selected this passage from a number, because it expresses in a forcible way that view of the salvation of the heathen which has been current in the teaching of the Methodist church from John Wesley to John Miley:

"Bold assertions in missionary speeches and sermons that all the world without the pale of Christendom is damned in mass never quicken the pulse of missionary zeal. On the contrary, they ever roll a cold reaction upon every feeling heart and every rational mind. Our better natures revolt, and, alas! a gush of skepticism is but too apt in consequence to rise in the public mind, especially where precise ideas in regard to the question have not been formed and fixed. We had far better argue the missionary cause from the danger to our own salvation from that low standard of Christianity which does not subdue the world to the righteousness of faith; from the vast *increase* of the number saved through a universal gospel; and from the rich reward and unspeakable glory of winning every isle and continent to Christ, securing him the crown of our entire planet."

Our true motives for foreign missionary work are, as I see them, these:

1. A desire to obey our Saviour's command to go into all the world and preach the gospel to every creature.

2. A desire to furnish to all men the present blessings of the gospel.

3. A purpose to keep the church at home so filled with the militant temper of foreign missions as to render all her members unselfish and aggressive.

4. A purpose to keep before the mind of the entire church *the size of the plan of redemption*.

5. A purpose to begin to realize the idea of a universal human brotherhood in Jesus Christ.

6. A purpose *to hasten under all possible Christian pressure the salvation of men*, and thus to prepare them for the largest service and the largest destiny in the final kingdom of our Lord.

XXXIII. THE CHURCH TRIUMPHANT

The Second Coming of Christ. This is the one subject in systematic theology which I would gladly avoid, were such a course possible in fairness, for the data are so dubious as to meaning in important places that I have been unable to reach such conclusions as amount to positive convictions. There are several discussions which I value very highly (notably Bishop Merrill's for its sanity and Dr. Terry's for its scholarship); but I have not found a discussion which fathoms and harmonizes the whole of the teaching of the New Testament. The best I can do for you is to outline the case as it now stands in my mind:

1. There are a number of Scripture passages often marshaled in this connection which have no bearing whatever upon the question in dispute. For they refer to the ordinary Christian event of the coming of Christ into the human heart by means of the Holy Ghost.

2. There are other Scripture passages where the reference is (*probably*) to the appearance of Jesus to his disciples immediately after his resurrection. Such a passage is that where our Saviour says, "A little while, and ye behold me no more; and again a little while, and ye shall see me" (Saint John 16. 16).

3. There is one passage which may be quite reasonably explained as a special coming of Christ to meet his disciples, each one at his death. I mean the passage in the gospel of John (14. 3) where Jesus says, "And if I go and prepare a place for you, I come again, and will receive you unto myself; that where I am, there ye may be also."

4. The effort to explain such passages as that of Saint

Matt. 26. 64 as the coming of our Lord in an event of judgment having no association with his personal advent, seems to me to be entirely unconvincing.

5. I find it impossible to get all the teaching of the synoptic gospels into one consistent view; but, on the whole, this seems to be the teaching: At the end of the gospel dispensation ("*post-millennium*") Jesus Christ will return to this world in person, visible and glorious, to raise the dead; to judge all men; to punish sinners and reward saints; and to complete the formation and placement of his everlasting kingdom. And, further, this synoptic teaching is entitled to the theological right of way, for it is not only exceedingly emphatic but also bound up with important Christian doctrines.

6. This brings us to what has been called "the passage of torment," in the twentieth chapter of the Revelation. All I can say personally about this passage is that all the attempts to fit it into the synoptic conception of our Lord's second coming seem to me to be forced and therefore inconclusive. But the fairest thing for me to do is to place two great specialists in biblical theology over against each other. Professor Salmond says: "However the circumstance is to be accounted for, and however it is to be related to the general teaching of the New Testament, it must be admitted that this remarkable paragraph in John's Apocalypse speaks of a real millennial reign of Christ on earth together with certain of his saints, which comes in between a first resurrection and the final judgment." Professor Terry, in commenting upon verses 7–10, says: "It is a great symbolic picture, and its one great teaching is clear beyond the possibility of doubt or misunderstanding, namely, that Satan and his forces must all ultimately perish. This is written for the comfort and confidence of the saints. But that final victory is in the far future, at the close of the Messianic age, and it is

here simply outlined in apocalyptic symbols. Any presumption, therefore, of determining specific events of
the future from this grand symbolism must be regarded
as in the nature of the case a species of worthless and
misleading speculation."

The New Race in Full Fact. This triumph of the
church at the second coming of Christ is not the Christian
culmination, but simply a final instrumental stroke unto
that culmination. Christian history culminates only in
the full fact of the new race in Jesus Christ. In different
places and at different angles of vision, I have tried
gradually to prepare your minds and hearts for this sublime racial culmination; but now that we are actually facing the culmination there are several things which should
be brought out with the greatest possible stress. The
first of these points for extreme emphasis is that in this
new race there is guaranteed *the immortality of the person.*
This new race is, indeed, conceivable only in terms of
personality. The very organism is personal. The members are bound together *as persons.* The very glory of
their wonderful social life is that all the interchange of
blessing, all the interlacing in self-sacrifice, is self-conscious. Not only do they live for each other and in each
other, *but they want to.* There is a sense in which the
individual at last is an expressive feature of the divine
life, but this does not come about by the pantheistic
method, it comes about by a personal union with God.
In all his earthly probation no saint was ever so intensely
personal, so intensely self-conscious, so intensely self-
decisive, as he is now in the new race. His whole being
is filled with the realization of where he is and what he is
and what he is doing for other men and what they are
doing for him. He loses his life ethically only to find it
personally.

If this conception of personal immortality in the new

race is thoroughly before you, I will ask you to throw it
into sharp contrast with Herbert Spencer's benumbing
view of the outcome of human life.   In his last book Mr.
Spencer wrote: "And then the consciousness itself—what
is it during the time that it continues?   And what becomes of it when it ends?   We can only infer that it is a
specialized and individualized form of that Infinite and
Eternal Energy which transcends both our knowledge
and our imagination; and that at death its elements lapse
into the Infinite and Eternal Energy whence they were
derived."

Another point which should receive extreme emphasis is
that the social intercourse *is ethically achieved*.   It is precisely at this point that our modern imagination has most
widely gone astray.   We cannot imagine what the life
of the redeemed is like without sentimentalizing the scene
out of its pure ethical quality.   To illustrate what I mean
take John Milton's famous lines:

> "There entertain him all the saints above
> In solemn troops and sweet societies,
> That sing, and singing in their glory move,
> And wipe the tears forever from his eyes."

Here we have a most beautiful social scene surely, but
it is too soft, too empty of moral quality, to represent the
final life of our Lord's people.   If you do not feel the force
of my criticism, read the last part of the seventh chapter of
the book of the Revelation, the very passage which probably suggested to Milton his lines.   Saint John's picture
is strongly ethical, as every truly Christian thing always
is.   In the new race, the whole motive of action is moral
love.   The saint serves another saint not because he loves
him, but because he *morally loves him*.   That is, the love
itself is a flaming passion for righteousness.   And the
peculiarity of the social enlargement of the one man is that
it is his moral ideal itself which more and more deeply

drives him into the lives of the saints about him, until he is in living intercourse with every person of the new race. And so the size of the social experience of any one saint is the size of his moral experience as well as the size of the entire race. Nor does this mean a dead level in experience, for every person is rigidly himself with his own native and acquired individuality, which was completely personalized in the intermediate state; and the vast social life is caught up in thousands of points of individual peculiarity in self-consciousness.

As to the question of special individual friendships within the new race, we need to speak carefully. But our Saviour's relation to Saint John furnishes a hint; and our principle of human complement or supplement furnishes another hint; and our philosophy of probation furnishes yet another hint. Putting together all there is of such suggestion, I have reached this speculation: The social life of the new race is to be a large network of special friendships. Some of these friendships begin in this life. Perhaps a mother gradually transfigures her natural relation to her child into a moral fellowship which can go on forever because it is worthy of the eternal life. Perhaps a pastor becomes so much to a young man that their spiritual intercourse can never wear out. Indeed, I dare to think that every right natural relation is an invitation, an opportunity, for an eternal transaction; that, inside of a man's supreme probation, are many subordinate probations, where the voice of the situation is: "Will you let this thing fly away with time? or will you pack it full of everlasting riches?" Other special friendships may be rapturous discoveries of the eternal life. I like to dream of two men doing their work here faithfully, but with lonely person and starving heart, suddenly meeting on some highway of heaven, and finding out their mutual adaptation for intimate friendship, and exclaiming in one celestial explosion, "I have found you at last!" But these special friendships do not weaken the service and the joy of the larger social life of the whole race; rather do they strengthen it. Just as now and then we see a Christian home where every secret gladness in the home circle inspires every member of it into a more generous concern for all the town, all the nation, all the world—so all the little points of special heavenly joy shall only help the whole race to live and rejoice in one another.

The main point, however, for extreme emphasis is that *the dominating center of all this morally achieved social life is Jesus Christ our Redeemer.* Already I have urged upon you in several ways this supreme position of Christ in the everlasting racial and social organism of the redeemed; but now let us dwell upon it with lingering love. When I try to put into a sufficient symbol our Saviour's final relation to his own people, I find nothing quite so grandly suggestive as Dante's figure of the many lamps all enkindled by the one blazing sun:

> " In bright preëminence so saw I there
> O'er million lamps a sun, from whom all drew
> Their radiance."

Yes, that is it, all the countless little lamps of friendship throughout the society of the new race catch their flame from the Lord Jesus Christ! But just what do we mean by this figure here? We mean that the very motive for all this friendship, the motive which urges the saint out into social interlacing is his love for Jesus Christ. It is because the saint loves Christ supremely that he *can* love this or that man specially, and then give himself to all the redeemed. The saint's capacity for holy friendship is actually made by his love for his Lord. But—you are thinking it—did I not say that in the new race the whole motive of action is moral love? I certainly did say that; but the redeemed man's love is moral, not because he has gone back to Mount Sinai, or because he is seeking to be conscientious; but simply because he loves Jesus Christ with all his soul. It is Christ who creates the ethical passion and makes righteousness to the glorified an element of their spontaneous life. Let me say, then, that for the new race Jesus Christ amounts to the whole significance of eternity. Take him away, and everything would lose its attraction, and immortality itself would not be worth the having. It is only your Christian longing to be with Him "whom not having seen ye love"—it is only that boundless gratitude which Christ gives you in the supernatural experience of salvation—it is only that foretaste of glory which you now have in communion with your Lord—brethren, brethren, it is not the endless years but our blessed Redeemer that draws us on toward the eternal scene!

But are there not purely natural desires for the life beyond the grave? Yes, there are. Several such natural desires belong to the very nature of personality itself. One of these is a normal person's quick interest in self-assertion. In the clear vision of self-consciousness no normal person can tolerate the thought of ceasing to exist. He wants to assert himself and then to keep at it. He is bound to live forever. He wills at immortality as immediately as ten thousand creatures in the air will themselves into continued and swifter flight. Now they are flying they like to keep on flying.

Then, there is the motive of personal curiosity. There are times when, however much we may wish to remain here, we become impatient to find out what the eternal life is. In this case the further world is attractive to us not so much because it is a continuation of existence as because it is an unexplored realm.

"What a strange moment will that be
My soul, how full of curiosity,
When winged and ready for thy eternal flight
On the utmost edges of thy tottering clay,
Hovering and wishing longer stay,
Thou shalt advance and have eternity in sight!
When just about to try that unknown sea,
What a strange moment will that be!"

In this way we could go on, and out of our personal life, and out of our personal relations, especially those relations which yield our finest earthly friendships, we could bring into position quite a convincing series of natural desires to live beyond bodily death. And often this series is brought into striking position, in book or sermon, and is allowed to stand in place alone, as if there were no other side to the matter. But there is another side, the individual side. The man as an individual is not yet altogether personal. Many times he is in a state of consciousness far below self-consciousness. Many times he is but an individual dimly remembering his higher personal experiences. And many times he is an individual altogether exhausted by the intense personal and moral conflict out of which he has dropped. Now, this individual man, this man only partly personalized but realizing in long, dreary reaction all the weariness and sense of failure following the personal battle—this tired individual, I say, *does not want to live forever*. Grant him no supernatural reënforcement, no memory of association with God, no word from God, no habit of prayer, no church ministry, no Christian fellowship; and, in his weariness, he would be quite inclined to vote for annihilation. Well does he understand the fascination which certain forms of pantheism have for men; for he himself craves rest in the absolute extinction of all consciousness, he himself longs to fall back into the silent, meaningless abyss, even as a restless, storm-driven, foam-crested wave becomes quiet at last as it falls back into the deeps of the sea.

We are told that the men of our day are losing their interest in the question of immortality, "that the tide of human interest is steadily ebbing away from the shores of another life." This waning concern is just what we should expect as a consequence of the perpetual exploitation of the individual at the expense of the person, which has taken place since the publication of Charles Darwin's epoch-making book. In natural science, in psychology, in ethics, and even in theology there have not been (taking the four together) more than ten writers of influence who have given encouragement for the serious cultivation of a personal life and a keen sense of moral responsibility. And over against this, our dire poverty, Mr. Spencer has had hundreds of able helpers in making men believe that personal experience itself is an automatic deception. Has there been anything quite so pathetic and quite so enervating in the entire history of human opinion? I think not. We must—*we must* find some way to turn this tide, and to bring into general appreciation the majestic meaning of man's personality, and with that the tremendous responsibility of man's moral life. Such appreciation will tend to banish the present lethargy of the individual and so to recreate an interest in immortality.

But I should say much more. The natural personal desires for eternal life, even when they are at their best, are not capable of long resistance under strong attack. And in an experience of profound sorrow they are almost certain to fail. We need the Christian hope, and we need this hope in its apostolic purity. An urgent thing to do is to lead the church of our Lord out of all feeble sentimentalities concerning the life beyond. Let us stamp out every trace of spiritism. Our blessed dead should be so related to Jesus Christ that our thoughts of them are but tender repetitions of our thoughts of him. Our Lord must be in all and over all. Let us not have any longing for anything which can exist outside of him. Let us not only in our thinking and in our imagination build the entire company of the redeemed into a solid race of which Christ is center and source, but also find our interest in eternity itself, as Saint Paul did, through our desire to be forever with our Lord and those who love him supremely. Such an interest in eternity will resist any attack; will penetrate every affliction with consolation; will inspirit the individual even in his lowest mood; and will make the Christian fearless in life or death. While so many are seeking a "scientific demonstration of immortality," I would urge the whole church to seek that kind of certainty which comes only through an apostolic passion for Jesus Christ.

The Entire Sweep of the Plan of Redemption

Now that in our thinking the church of our Lord is made glorious by becoming the new race in full fact, we are ready to place together all the points of Christian attainment, and thus to have before us the entire sweep of the plan of redemption.

1. Starting with free personality and the moral nature of man, the plan first secures, under the supernatural work of the Holy Spirit, *the loyal person.* This loyalty to Christ makes a positive connection between the old moral ideal and all the new possibilities in Christ. That is, by becoming a Christian no truly moral thing is thrown away.

2. The compound motive of loyalty is turned into the simple motive of moral love, and thus is secured *the holy person.* By this method a perfect *moral organization* is obtained, by which I mean that in self-consciousness there

is harmony under the new moral ideal. A holy Christian does not violate the standard given by his moral judgment.

3. In the intermediate state the total individuality is personalized. And as the person is already holy the result is *the holy personal individual*.

4. By means of the resurrection this perfect personal individual obtains a glorified body, which is a perfect instrument of expression; and the result now is *the perfect man*, body and personal soul, capable of an objective life equal to his subjective life. This is the completed *new man in Christ*.

5. Here we make an important turn to obtain the final Christian point of view. The perfect man is not to exist alone. The glorified body is not furnished merely to finish out manhood, it is furnished for actual social life. Nor is social life the idea to stop at. The glorified body is a *racial body*. It is made and given precisely to connect this complete man, having all this social possibility, with the whole race of redeemed men. Thus the plan of salvation sweeps on and on until it provides a great racial outcome for every man saved by means of our Lord's death.

Having now this more comprehensive racial point of view, let us for an inspiring moment look back and quickly trace the preparatory stages for the racial consummation. These preparatory stages are five, and may be outlined as follows:

First, the free moral person becomes the person loyal to Jesus Christ.

Second, the loyal person becomes the holy person, loving his Lord supremely.

Third, in all the Christian life, from its beginning on to death, there is provision for a *probational training in brotherhood*. This training is by means of the holy catholic church, which, if not the new race in full fact, is the new race in tentative expression.

Fourth, in the intermediate state the holy person, alone with his Saviour, is *utterly* made ready for all the fellowship and service of the ultimate brotherhood in Christ. The intermediate state is the university, where the education for eternal brotherhood is completed. *And our Master is the whole Faculty!*

Fifth, by means of the glorified body of the resurrection this completed saint actually enters into the vast community of the redeemed, not only a perfect man, but also a *perfect brother*, capable of perfect fellowship and service. This vast community of perfect brothers, all saved by Jesus Christ, all completed by Jesus Christ, all organized by Jesus Christ, all living in union with Jesus Christ, is *his race in full fact*.

Is there possible in all human thinking a more sublime conception of destiny than this plan of redemption when taken in its entire sweep? And if we add the stupendous price paid for its possibility, what shall we say?

MEN OUTSIDE THE NEW RACE

The idea of the endless conscious suffering of the wicked is the most unwelcome thought ever suggested to my mind. My whole soul revolts against it. There is no sacrifice I would not willingly make to get rid of it. It is the horror of all horrors. Such is the attitude of my mind to the question. But against my wish, and all the feelings of my soul, I am constrained to believe that God sees it differently, and with infinitely greater capacity to know what is best and proper, and with infinitely greater love and tenderness than any of his holiest children can claim, has incorporated the dreadful fact of permanent conscious suffering as a possibility in his plan.—*Randolph S. Foster*, Beyond the Grave, pp. 130, 131.

XXXIV. MEN OUTSIDE THE NEW RACE

Rejected Views. The theory of second probation I have already rejected in our study of the intermediate state; and I am obliged also to reject three additional views concerning those who die in a personal attitude of moral antagonism to righteousness. The first of these views is *the restoration of the wicked by a coercive process.* The essence of this view was popularly expressed by this remark: "If God desire to save men and cannot, he is not God." After all I have said in regard to the moral person and God's dealing with him, it surely is unnecessary to uncover the crude, false thinking which underlies this remark, or to show why we should instantly reject the idea of any sort of coerced sainthood. The second view may be fairly called *the agnostic view.* For it amounts to saying that we cannot come to any positive conclusion, and the whole matter would better be left in the vague. When handled with apparent piety and unapparent ingenuity this view seems to be the high-water mark of Christian reserve; but it is practically a most dangerous hesitation, for it serves to encourage those germinal feelings which soon grow into some phase of universalism. Indeed, I have usually found that in theology an agnostic position is a wayside inn where men rest a bit on their way to extreme liberalism. The third view is *the anni-hilation of the wicked.* This view is taught in several different ways and in several different relations to the basal philosophy; but its most powerful setting forth is in the theory of "conditional immortality" as held by that growing group of men represented by Edward White. That White's book, Life in Christ, is one of the *real* books of modern times, actually throbbing with an earnest message to men, I am even eager to admit. But I cannot accept the message. There is much temptation to take up the exegesis, but I will leave that work to the biblical scholars. My own main objections to the theory of annihilation, however it may be grounded and elaborated, are just two: First, it is entirely lacking in that *ethical quality* which belongs to every truly Christian doctrine. Wherever we land in our theories, we simply should not, will not, land in a bog of moral mitigation. And to me this view is worse than mitigation. Preach annihilation to a sinner, and you preach *with his own inclination.* In his highest personal state the sinner would dread annihilation, but in his more usual individual state he would crave it. The statement will be contradicted by many, but I am very sure that this theory of annihilation is even less ethical than is the theory of second probation. Proclaimed generally in the church, it would rot the moral fiber of the message of the gospel. Second, the theory of annihilation is *impossible in theodicy.* That God in his omniscience would create men only to throw them away at last, a useless waste, "as rubbish in the void," is to me inconceivable from any standpoint possible in theodicy. The harsh theory of an eternity of torture in physical flame was surely hard enough to deal with in theodicy. But one could discover at least the possibility of a moral value in the torture. For it was barely conceivable that the structure of the final universe required an endless objective record of the sinner's dreadful rejection of God's mercy. Annihilation, though, I cannot relate to theodicy in any way whatever. Once I tried to see if it might not be morally utilized through the memory of the saints in their eternal life, but soon in earnest thinking the point became finical and impossible.

A Purely Personal Problem. It may be that constantly

I should have reminded you of the limited claim behind all my theological discussion. For pedagogical reasons the method of presentation changes here and there; and now and then the tone becomes almost one of authority; but all the time there is taking place only one thing, namely, a personal testimony as to what is essential in theology to enable a man to see the Christian faith *as a redemptional total*. I claim merely that to apprehend the Christian system consistently I myself need thus and thus to interpret and relate Christian doctrines. Now, in our consideration of the future condition of the wicked, there are very peculiar and important reasons why I should ask you to keep my moderate claim clearly in mind.

My own personal problem, then, I will give you frankly and exactly. I have no problem whatever as to the general content of the Christian doctrine. Not one word have I to say in depreciation of the sincerity and ability of such men as John Frederick Denison Maurice. I simply say that for me the New Testament teaches persistently the endless punishment of all men who die in personal hostility to righteousness. The case does not rest with the meaning of the one word αἰώνιος—whether it is a quantitative or a qualitative word. I think that it is (precisely like our own word *eternal*) sometimes quantitative and sometimes qualitative, and sometimes both at one stroke; and so its meaning in any given place is to be determined by the context, or by using larger exegetical principles. But I have no great interest in the discussion of this word. No Christian doctrine depends upon the significance of a word; or even upon the significance of an isolated text. Every Christian doctrine *eventuates!* It is a whole trend of Scripture come to necessary issue. When we further ask whether this endless punishment is a *conscious* punishment or not, my answer is this: To protect the tremendous moral urgency of the New Testament, that awful voice of warning, I require the feature of consciousness just as much as I require the feature of endlessness. The content of the doctrine, as I must hold it, is this: For all the wicked who die obdurate there will be a divine punishment which will be realized by them consciously and everlastingly.

My problem, the problem which for many years has been not only in my mind, but also on my heart, is to harmonize this awful doctrine of eternal punishment with our complete Christian conception of God. In other words, my problem is to place the doctrine in a Christian theodicy.

The Problem Met. With diffidence, because I well know that many Christian ideas and feelings I have not utilized, I will briefly indicate in what way it has been necessary for me to meet the problem. And when I say "necessary for me to meet the problem" I mean both that I had to meet the problem, and that I had to meet it in this precise manner. Some of the safest thinkers we have in the Christian church do not believe that it is wise to try to push an inch further than the content of the New Testament doctrine. I fully appreciate their discretion; but I must see a doctrine touch some possibility in theodicy or I cannot rest. I cannot carry about in my Christian life a bundle of mysteries which seem to hide an antagonism in doctrine. And I speak out only to help men who are constituted as I am myself. No, there is yet another motive for utterance; for I am hoping sooner or later to get some important indications at this difficult point from the range of Christian consciousness about me.

In speculation I have met my problem in the following way:

1. Our stopping place, the point beyond which theodicy does not require us to go, is the idea that, under the law

of expression, there is to be a vast final universe, which shall absolutely manifest the holiness of God as culminating in moral love. That is, the final arrangement of all persons and all things must plainly evince the facts that the structural finality in God is holiness, that his personal relation to this holiness is one of intense and unyielding concern, and that his infinite love itself is but the supreme phase of this moral concern.

2. In this final universe there are to be, just as really as there are in this world, two kinds of service—a voluntary service given by the creature in freedom, and an involuntary service yielded by the creature under compulsion.

3. Like the angels themselves, all men are *created for this final universe.* In the plan of their destiny the divinely fixed fact is that they must live forever, that they must, whether or no, become a part of the final universe, and make an endless contribution in service. Are you holding this crucial thought? Within God's ideal, and having no item contingent upon personal freedom, he has an inner plan, a primary teleology, which will be accomplished entire; and all men are as fast in this inner plan as the Stanser Horn is fast in the Alps. In our usual thinking about a man we ignore this primary design; we quietly assume that when God created the man his *only* aim was to obtain a saint. And then when the man in his personal freedom refuses to become a saint the result appears to us to be a complete defeat of the Creator. Now, I insist that in creation the idea of service is more fundamental than the idea of a certain kind of service. The saint *may* be; the servant *must* be. God will have service—there can be no failure here; the final universe shall be a universe of service; and every man is made primarily to take a task in the eternities and endlessly to serve the great ends of holiness.

4. Although a man is created primarily for the final universe, and must render an endless service in the evincement of holiness, yet he is created a free moral person, and in his freedom he can and must decide the *manner* of his destiny. He can and must decide whether he will render his eternal service under compulsion, as a slave is driven to a burden; or in liberty and love, as a saint does the will of his Lord. The significance of this earthly probation lies not in that it determines whether a man is to have an eternal existence or not, but only in that it determines in which of the two possible categories of eternal service he is to exist.

5. Before I closely consider this conception of involuntary service I wish to prepare our hearts for the point by making a serious protest against the sweeping affirmation that a final universe, with lost men in it, is not only an idea obnoxious to Christian sentiment, but also an idea inconceivable in a Christian theodicy. For my own sake, to get my own point of departure, let me begin with the creation of men. What does their creation mean to God under the law of expression? In the creation of men God expresses more than his purpose to have service, he expresses his *desire* to have voluntary service. Whenever a man is born there is the manifestation of a thing deep in God, his ideal, his personal longing, so to speak. In the very make-up of a man (or any moral person, for that matter) there is trace of what we may dare to call the divine finality in ambition. Every time a new man comes into being fresh from God's will the event cries out, "God will have this particular man added to his final universe—*and*—God's desire, God's ideal, God's ambition is to have this man there as a free, loving, rejoicing saint." Thus, I hold that, whatever the outcome, whatever the man may do or become, the bare creation of him as a free moral person manifests the divine ideal and so

must have for God the beginning of worth under the law of expression. I do not say or intimate that such initial worth *taken alone* could become the motive for creation; but I urge the reality of the worth, nevertheless. I wish ever to begin with this emphasis upon the law of expression because it helps me to strike out a course of thinking free from that humanitarian utilitarianism which has poisoned so much of our theology. We all are inclined to believe (and sure to feel) that the ultimate test of any view is in its answer to this question: How much pleasure and profit will man get? We never think of God.

Dropping those intermediate connections which are not essential to our discussion, let us now try to look at the final universe from God's point of view. His final universe certainly will not be what he most profoundly wanted, it will not be his ideal realized. God wanted a final universe comprehending every moral person created; and all these created persons in a voluntary service of holy purport; and all this eternal service resplendent and enraptured with the holy vision of God. In such an ideal universe the involuntary service, all the tasks of compulsion as far as such tasks might be needful, would not be done by vitiated persons, but rather by automatic creatures, even as coercive service is furnished in this world by beast and bird. But God saw his ideal plan in wreck through the very freedom absolutely necessary to its actualization. *There is no "felix culpa"!* Sin has destroyed the possibility of our finest eternity. The final universe will be nothing but a second best, a drop down from the wish, an ideal mangled. Sin will not be triumphant, but sin has infringed the dream, has placed the glory of the outcome in everlasting check. You are not quite ready to say so; but there is a minor voice which can be heard in spite of our rejoicing; a voice which sounds louder as the soul deepens in moral love for God and

men; a voice which silences at last all our easy, unethical optimisms; a voice which will speak with a tender
but moral emphasis through all the ages upon ages of
human destiny: "*This is not the universe God wanted!*"

But, although the final universe will not *be* all God
wanted, it will *tell* all he wanted. As an everlasting
cosmic utterance it will be altogether sufficient. The
mitigating minds in theodicy seem to think that God in
his transcendent regard for his creatures has no inherent
rights, that all he is and all he needs should be sacrificed
regardless. Any speech which I am able to command is
too clumsy for the task, the very word *rights* is entirely
inadequate; but the false notion ought to be contradicted
at once in some way, and so I will assert that God himself
has rights. He has the right to come fairly out into cosmic
fact. He has the right to manifest the whole range of his
holy life. He has the right to fasten into the eternities
his changeless hatred of sin. He has the right to have a
final universe which shall forever declare the *entirety of
meaning* in his moral love for men; that it was *moral* love;
that it was *moral love*. God loved these lost men precisely as he loved those who are now his saints. He
made them moral persons. He gave them freedom.
He provided moral pressure in conscience. He gave
them motive after motive toward righteousness. He
sent his only Son to render possible their redemption.
Their sin entered into Christ's infinite agony. God
watched their wandering steps with his sleepless providence. Their faintest moral effort he met with instant
help. Again and again, and yet again, he poured the
power of the Holy Spirit upon their withering moral
desire—yes, until there was no moral desire. To save
these lost men God the Omnipotent spent all the resources
of the Triune Godhead; and the final universe should say
so—*and it will say so!*

6. More closely now, what do we mean by this involuntary service? By using the word *involuntary* I do not intend to teach or suggest that lost men are crushed into mere "thinghood." They are, I believe, below the possibility of any moral action, or moral concern. Their conception of right and wrong is an intellection empty of all feeling. And they are, I think, also below the possibility of any real self-decision. They are creatures of fear. They are like persons in this life when personality is entirely overwhelmed by the bare sense of what we call "physical fear." The lost are in consciousness totally occupied, as far as they feel the urgency of motive, with a fear which has in it not one throb of moral meaning. Their personal rebellion is all gone, and they obey God swiftly; but they obey him not because they eagerly recognize a moral obligation in his command, they obey merely because they are afraid. As a frightened creature cowers at the rush and thunder of an avalanche, so the lost are afraid of God. Incapable of the vision of God, incapable of the love of God, incapable of any moral regard for God—and yet doing God's behest under the slavery of torturing fear—that is the eternal punishment; that is the worm which "dieth not "; that is the fire which is "not quenched." And do you not see that this awful condition is not an arbitrary infliction, but a punishment intrinsic to the nature of sin? God does not build an environment on purpose to torture the wicked. Hell (like heaven) is in the Bible made real to us by an objective scene, and those who need it may keep the scene; but the moral message is much more terrible than the superficial scene. The punishment of hell is the suffering of a man become entirely and eternally inorganic. The man was made to fear God; but the original fear had in it great moral possibility, possibility sweeping on, under the plan of redemption, even into the lofty rapture of moral love.

The obdurate sinner, though, in his freedom, has emptied all moral quality out of his fear; and now the naked terror, beating alone in consciousness, drives him on forever.

My thought is that in the final universe there is a service of fear over against the service of love. Even this obedience of fear *is obedience*, and can be so placed and so used that God's holiness *entire* is expressed as it could not be expressed by the annihilation of the wicked; yes, and is expressed as it could not be expressed, if no one of these lost men had ever been created. It is *the sum total* of the final universe which will project into the eternities all that God is, all that he has done, and declare all that he longed to secure.

7. If you have fully caught the significance of my discussion you surely see that I have been indirectly trying to do several things: First, to meet the point of the restorationist, that, to evince the love of God, the final universe must be made up *entirely* of righteous persons; second, to meet the point of the annihilationist, that the obdurate sinners must be blotted out of existence as having no longer any teleological worth; and, third, to modify Calvinism into a system of true moral freedom, and yet to keep the basal notion of divine decree. Instead of saying that God has decreed *the whole destiny* of a man, I say that the coercion covers only the one fact of everlasting service, and the man himself freely determines the kind of service he will render. It may be urged that under the attribute of omniscience my modification amounts only to a matter of words; but it amounts to a moral reality, for it fairly introduces the element of moral responsibility. According to my view, God is not causal to any ultimate condition of personal character. And, further, and in harmony with this view, the moral joy of everlasting sainthood is not an automatic outcome, but is a truly personal rejoicing won, with God's aid, by thor-

ough ethical procedure.   My thought can be crowded into a sentence: *The rim of destiny is by God's decree, but the personal center of destiny is by man's choice.*

8. I cannot close this discussion without lifting into notice another point, a point which I am anxious to lodge in your hearts and to leave there.   These lost men are *outside the new race.*   Their service of fear belongs to the final universe; but it belongs to the cosmic sweep of the kingdom, and has no possible place in the kingdom of Christ.   They have lost their race.   In the most wholesomely rigid thinking, they are no longer men.   Every real *man*—every moral person realizing the essential scope of manhood—*every real man* will yield to Christ and enter the new race and love his Lord, and love *all men* forever. The final brotherhood will have lost only those who refused to be men complete.

THE SIXTH DOCTRINAL DIVISION
THE TRIUNE GOD REVEALED IN REDEMPTION

The doctrines of the Incarnation and the Trinity seemed to me most absurd in my agnostic days. But now, as a *pure* agnostic, I see in them no rational difficulty at all. As to the Trinity, the plurality of persons is necessarily implied in the companion doctrine of the Incarnation. So that at best there is here but one difficulty, since, duality being postulated in the doctrine of the Incarnation, there is no further difficulty for pure agnosticism in the doctrine of plurality.—*George John Romanes*, Thoughts on Religion, pp. 174, 175.

Athanasius, then, held to a trinity of three personal Beings. . . . But if Athanasius held to three persons in the strict sense, how did he save himself from tritheism? I answer: In the same way as his predecessors had done before him, by the doctrine of one supreme cause. . . . The Latin fathers before Augustine universally held to a trinity of three personal beings united in a generic nature by community of essence. They held to the real subordination of the Son to the Father.—*Levi Leonard Paine*, A Critical History of the Evolution of Trinitarianism, pp. 45, 47, 62.

Perhaps, however, one may be allowed to doubt whether, *in all respects*, the term *person* may not be taken to signify "the same thing" in us as in God. It is true, as before observed, that three *persons* among men or angels would convey the idea of three different and separate beings; but it may be questioned whether this arises from anything *necessarily* conveyed in the idea of *personality*. We have been accustomed to observe personality only in connection with separate beings; but this separation seems to be but a circumstance connected with personality, and not anything which arises out of personality itself. . . . In God, the distinct persons are represented as having a common foundation in *one being;* but this union also forms no part of the idea of personality, nor can be proved inconsistent with it.—*Richard Watson*, Theological Institutes, i, 449, 450.

But how this community in unity is possible is one of the deepest mysteries of speculation. The only suggestion of solution seems to lie in the notion of necessary creation. Such creation would be unbegun and endless, and would depend on the divine nature and not on the divine will. If now we suppose the divine nature to be such that the essential God must always and eternally produce other beings than himself, those other beings, though numerically distinct from himself, would be essential implications of himself. There would be at once a numerical plurality and an organic unity.—*Borden P. Bowne*, Theism, The Deems Lectures for 1902, p. 288.

Each is necessarily and eternally one in Being with the Others; there are not three Gods. Each is not the Others; there are three Persons.—*H. C. G. Moule*, Outlines of Christian Doctrine, p. 23.

THEOLOGY, or the doctrine of God, is usually discussed at the beginning of systematic theology, and doubtless there is much formal advantage in the usual method; but there are several reasons why I have kept this great doctrine for our last work together. In the first place, this system of doctrine has been largely a study of the divine movement in redemption, and now at the end of our study it is fitting to ask the question, What is the conception of God which has been gradually revealed in this redemptional movement? In the second place, the atmosphere of our study has been intensely and intentionally anthropological, and I wish, if possible, to change the atmosphere, and leave you thinking of our God who hath redeemed us, the Father, the Son, and the Holy Ghost. I want you, as the last thing in systematic theology, to lay hold of that true Trinitarian conception of God which is both the fundament and the culmination of all real Christian thinking. And, in the third place, I have a pedagogical reason. As a teacher I deem it a mistake to discuss the Trinity with only the preparation which comes from theism. The student needs that new world of ideas and feelings which is created by following the stages of salvation. The Trinity is not a doctrine which can be made clear and vital in any situation and by mere rational equipment. It is a doctrine among the finer culminations of Christian requirement. And a teacher may wisely adjust himself to this fact.

Perhaps also I should add a personal reason. I myself reached not only my interest in the doctrine of the Trinity, but also my full conception of its meaning, by means of my years of study of the ways of God with men in their redemption. I had almost no interest in the doctrine of the Trinity—it was a vague burden in my mind—until I felt the significance of the work of Christ; then I *saw* the Christian doctrine of God for the first time.

XXXV. THE ATTRIBUTES OF GOD

BEFORE taking up the doctrine of the Trinity, it is important for us to make a study of the divine attributes. But our study will be a brief one, inasmuch as I consider the subject entirely subordinate to our work on the doctrine of the Trinity.

What is a Divine Attribute? It is any characteristic which we must ascribe to God to express what he really is. The question comes up here: Does an attribute express a divine reality or merely a way in which we need to conceive of God's nature? My answer, as implied in my definition, is: *Both.* Surely an attribute expresses our human conception, and so it is a relative truth probably; but there is a point of reality in the human conception. I hold that the revelation of God in redemption is *reliable.* By this I do not mean that we get the *total reality;* but we do get *some reality*, and all the reality possible to us in this life. Deeper down, this must be connected with our discussions of knowledge, Christian certainty, and the intermediate state.

Kinds of Divine Attributes. There are two kinds of divine characteristics: 1. *Definitive attributes*, or those which are essential to an adequate definition of God; 2. *Descriptive attributes*, or those which are essential when we aim to describe more closely the Being that we have already defined.

There is always a temptation to say that what I call a definitive attribute is more fundamental than a descriptive attribute; but I am not quite ready to say so. For example, I am not sure that personality is any more fundamental, any more necessary to the very existence of God, than is moral love, although surely personality is more primary in our own thinking about God.

Definition of God. The characteristics which we need to define God are the following: 1. Spirituality; 2. Unity or individuality; 3. Personality; 4. Moral bearing; 5. Absoluteness; 6. Triunity.

With these six characteristics we can so define God as to have in terse speech the basis—not the practical basis but the philosophical basis—of the Christian conception of God, namely: *The God of the Christian faith is one Spirit, personal, moral, absolute, and triune.* A better definition for homiletical use is this: The God of redemption is a personal Trinity, one God of absolute moral love. In many connections it is enough to say: God is moral love. Or, where the moral background is entirely protected, we may say, with Saint John, simply, God is love.

PLAN OF THE DESCRIPTIVE ATTRIBUTES

I. BELONGING TO THE PERSONAL NATURE.
   Omnipotence, the characteristic of God's will.
II. BELONGING TO THE PERSONAL AND MORAL NATURE.
   Righteousness, the first characteristic of God's personal relation to holiness.
   Moral Love, the second and culminating characteristic of God's personal relation to holiness.
III. BELONGING TO THE ABSOLUTE NATURE.
   Aseity, the characteristic of God's absolute relation to causation.
   Eternity, the characteristic of God's absolute relation to time.
   Immutability, the characteristic of God's absolute relation to the process of history.
   Omnipresence, the characteristic of God's absolute relation to space.
   Omniscience, the characteristic of God's absolute relation to reality.
IV. The structural characteristic of the one Triune Spirit is *holiness*.

COMMENT ON SOME OF THE ATTRIBUTES

In other connections enough has been said concerning righteousness (moral concern), moral love, and holiness;

but there are some of the attributes remaining which require explanation, and others which require more or less notice.

Omnipotence. By the divine omnipotence we are not to understand that God can will anything whatsoever. To will anything, even God must have a motive, and so he never can make any volition contrary to his own nature. Not only so, but all the features of his nature come together in a perfect organism, under the law of holiness, and so no volition can spring out of a fragment of God.

Aseity. This means merely that God *causes himself.* "God's essence is his own act." "God eternally makes himself what he is." Two things are really covered by the attribute: 1. That God is *uncaused.* He is (as in theism) the First Cause; and so he is, in causation *a se*, from himself. 2. There is a profounder idea, namely, God is *absolute life.* All the infinite potencies of being he has just in himself. He is life, life, eternal, absolute life.

Eternity. As aseity emphasizes God's vitality from the standpoint of the idea of causation, so the attribute of eternity emphasizes that vitality from the standpoint of the idea of time. In his own life God is *timeless.* The surface thought is that God has neither beginning nor end. The deeper thought is that his being is so absolute that he is independent of the time process and has only a living present. Dr. Latimer used to say that the succession in God's thinking was logical but not chronological. And Saint Augustine, in commenting on the ninetieth psalm, says: "In the life of God nothing will be as if it were not yet; or hath been as if it were no longer; but there is only that which is; and this is Eternity." But the attribute of eternity does not mean that God is incapable of taking our point of view, and perfectly treating us under the terms of the time process.

Immutability. When we say that God never changes, that "He is the same yesterday, to-day, and forever," we do not mean that his personal bearing is ever the same. For the record in the Bible indicates change after change in God's dealings with men. And, in the very nature of the case, man being free, the divine volitional attitude must vary somewhat to meet the changing conditions in man's life. The very joy of God over the conversion of a sinner, for example, would mean some change in the divine bearing toward the sinner. No, what we mean is that in being, nature, character, motives of action, God is unchangeable. *You can always rely upon him.* In our employment of the term *immutable* we are not seeking, we are not predicating a rigidity of personal life, with no fresh pulsation in self-consciousness and no new movement in self-decision; we are seeking simply a personal and ethical reliability. Such absolute reliability, of course, implies perfection ever, and shuts out the pantheistic notion of a developing God.

Omnipresence. This might well be called the spot of ingenuity in systematic theology; for right here the theologian (even if he have not an atom of basal metaphysics) tries to see what new thing can be said. Bishop Martensen says: "As the bird in the air, as the fish in the sea, so all creatures live and move and have their being in God." A striking amplification of Saint Paul, but *not extremely elucidating!* Dr. Samuel Clarke taught that God is omnipresent "by an infinite extension of his essence." What that means I do not know. I always feel some gratitude, though, toward Richard Watson for his *hesitation* at Dr. Clarke's view! Dr. Shedd says: "The divine omnipresence means rather the presence of all things to God than God's presence to all things." This is an unintentional evasion growing out of an unconscious deism. Dr. Miley says: "In the plenitude and perfection of these personal attributes God is omnipresent in the truest, deepest sense." This is entirely true, and on the right trace; but it needs as much explanation as the term it aims to explain.

In considering the divine omnipresence we would better quickly make distinction between the practical message of the doctrine and the philosophy of the doctrine. The practical message of the doctrine is very plain. It means simply that space is no hindrance to God. Wherever a thing may be hidden, God can get at it. Wherever in the universe you may be, the whole of God is *there available* for judgment, or help, or companionship. The underlying philosophy should *begin* with the swift banishment of deism. How that unspeakable curse hides and lingers in the Christian church! Already I have several times suggested what I myself need as a substitute for deism, namely, a universe entirely and constantly dynamic of God, a universe which is nothing other than God in cosmic action. If you are unable to accept such a philosophy, then it is wiser to be content with the practical message of the doctrine of omnipresence, for the rhetorical ingenuities in explanation will never land you in any reality. Merely quote Saint Paul without the bird in the air and the fish in the sea!

THE ATTRIBUTE OF OMNISCIENCE

By the divine omniscience we mean that attribute whereby God perfectly and eternally knows himself and all reality and all possibility. The moment we say that God's knowledge is perfect and eternal we are really affirming that it is *not acquired*. There is no process, no progress from what is known on and on to further knowledge. In other words, the knowledge of God is *intuitive*.

The Point of Difficulty. How can God know a contingent event before the event has any beginning? About this point of difficulty there has been hot dispute both in theology and in philosophy, some of the strongest thinkers claiming that divine foreknowledge of a truly contingent event is impossible. For an elaborate discussion I cannot afford the space; but I will notice the most important points.

Main Objections Noted and Answered. The main objections to the doctrine of divine foreknowledge of contingent events are these:

1. An event contingent upon a future free volition is not an object of knowledge, for there is nothing to know until something begins to take place.

Answer: When it is said that *there is nothing to know* the objector is really quietly assuming that God's knowledge is *acquired*, and our claim is that God *intuits* the contingent event.

2. Were there foreknowledge of what a person will decide to do, the foreknowledge would *necessitate* his decision, and so his personal freedom would be destroyed.

Answer: The idea that foreknowledge would be coercive arises from the confusing of certainty with necessity. A future event may be *certain* to take place, and yet it may not be *necessary*. The foreknowledge is not *causal*. "A thing will not take place because God foreknows it, but he foreknows it because it will take place." Knowledge of any sort is purely subjective and can bring nothing to pass unless it can employ an efficient will. Can you not see how entirely inoperative knowledge alone is? If as a teacher I *could* in any way come absolutely to foreknow that Brother Z. will master one lesson next week, would my secret knowledge, by just being there in my mind, *compel him* to master the lesson? If I had such knowledge, the event, his mastery of the lesson, would be a *certainty*, but it would not be a *necessity*.

3. In actual history God treats men *as if* he were uncertain as to their ultimate decisions, for he treats all men with redemptional urgency.

Answer: The supposition here is that God would not *try* to save any sinner who will ultimately reject salvation, if he foreknew the fact of the ultimate rejection. The supposition is entirely wrong. Take this case: The Holy Spirit urges a sinner to repent—what does that urgency mean? It means just three things, neither more nor less: first, that the sinner *can* repent; second, that the sinner *needs* to repent; and, third, that God *wants* the sinner to repent. Whatever God might know or not know as to the final outcome, the moral love of God would never give up striving with a sinner as long as there was any conscience remaining.

4. Here the objector relates the doctrine of foreknowledge to the doom of the lost, and says: To create a man foreknowing his everlasting doom is out of harmony with the conception of God necessary in a Christian theodicy.

Answer: Not to repeat my own discussion in theodicy, I will meet this objection narrowly. The idea that an adequate theodicy can more easily be constructed under the terms of divine nescience than under the terms of divine foreknowledge is precipitant and superficial. Even a nescient Deity would *now know* that some men have irretrievably rejected righteousness, and yet he continues to create free moral persons. And, deeper than all that, conceive of the Creator starting a race of men, every one of them having the *possibility* of eternal damnation, and yet not having any certainty as to the outcome! The doctrine of nescience has in it no superior possibilities in theodicy.

The Unanswerable Argument. Along the line of prophecy a Scripture argument of great force can be formulated;

but the argument which to me is unanswerably convincing is this: If God has no foreknowledge of contingent events, then he not only arranged a vast and complex plan of redemption without knowing that *even one* moral person would ever be saved; but in carrying out this plan of redemption he actually sent his only Son as Redeemer into the reality of human temptation without knowing that this Son, Jesus Christ, would resist the temptation. To accept this strange, strange doctrine of divine nescience I would need to become a necessitarian, and once a necessitarian I would not have any need for the doctrine at all.

Fact and Method. Of course, the divine foreknowledge cannot be comprehended by us; but in this respect it is not different from many features in God's life; indeed, it is not different from some features in our own life. How extremely easy it is for shallow minds to think, because they are familiar with certain phases of human activity, that they comprehend the deeps of manhood! About all we can do in any chapter of search is to lift a bit of reality up into apprehension. And that is all we aim to do with the doctrine of God's foreknowledge—to apprehend it, to make it seizable mentally.

In trying to apprehend the doctrine of foreknowledge, there are several helpful things which we can do:

1. We can carefully distinguish between *fact* and *method*. That is, we can *narrow our difficulty*. We can, if convinced by the evidence that God does foreknow contingent events, say, "I grant the fact, but I do not see *how* there can be such knowledge, I do not apprehend the *method* of it." If you say that you cannot make this distinction between fact and method, I will insist that you can; for you have already apprehended many facts without even trying to lay hold of the method. What I urge is this: It is not wise—neither is it fair—to let

your difficulty vaguely spread all over the doctrine, and to hesitate before the evident fact merely because you are unable to get a clue to the method.

2. The fact once seized, we can do *something* in apprehending the method. For one thing, we can *get rid of time*. Even if you are not willing to touch the point in metaphysics, you already, with the attribute of eternity, have the idea that *God himself is absolutely independent of time*. If God, then, in grasp of reality is unhindered by time, why do you say that mere futurity, one phase of the time process, can shut him away from an event? Why do you require the Eternal God to plod through your tenses? But you say, "I cannot think away time." You mean that you cannot *picture* it away; you can *think* it away.

3. One further thing we can do in lifting the method of foreknowledge into apprehension. We can emphasize the point that God's knowledge is all *intuitive* knowledge. We ourselves have a certain degree of intuitive experience, not very much, surely, and yet enough so that we have a clear point of departure in our thinking about God. With this point of departure, I find it possible to apprehend God as having an absolute and eternal self-consciousness, and this consciousness as being filled with the certainty of all reality and all possibility.

XXXVI. THE CHRISTIAN DOCTRINE OF THE TRINITY

The Doctrine in Essential Statement

The Aim. The aim here is to express the doctrine of the Trinity in *bare essentiality.* How much is essential to any real Trinitarianism?

Rejected Views. First, let us approach the case negatively. All Trinitarians reject the following views:

1. The Humanitarian view that the Trinity is God the Father, the man Jesus Christ, and a divine influence called the Spirit of God. There are a number of phases of this view, but in every phase Christ is nothing other than a man.

2. The Arian view that the Trinity is God the Father, Christ a highly exalted creature, and the Holy Spirit a less exalted creature. There are variations also of this view, but they have no significance in this connection.

3. The Modalistic view (Sabellian) that there is one God and three successive and peculiar manifestations of him in history. Or, one person with three aspects, modes, relations toward the world.

4. The Swedenborgian view that the Trinity is one God with soul (the Father), body (the Son), and operation (the Holy Spirit).

5. The Tritheistic view that the Trinity consists of three divine individuals.

All these five views are regarded as heresy by every man who has the right to call himself a Trinitarian at all.

Essential Points of Belief.

1. There is only one God.

2. Of this one God there are three historical manifestations, namely, the Father, the Son, and the Holy Ghost.

But these manifestations are not "mere masks." As Dr. Dorner says, "A trinity of Revelation is a misrepresentation if there is not behind it a trinity of Reality." *Therefore,*

3. These three historical manifestations express three inner distinctions in the Godhead. "The faces are turned not merely outward toward the world, but inward toward himself, so that they behold themselves in mutual reflection."

4. These distinctions are not only internal, they are so fundamental as to be necessary to the ongoing of the divine life.

5. As these distinctions are thus fundamental, they are eternal. God did not develop into them. They always have been and always must be essential to his existence.

6. These three historical manifestations—the Father, the Son, and the Holy Ghost—expressing three inner, fundamental, and eternal distinctions in the Godhead, are in the Scriptures *treated as personal;* and so we name them Persons.

Ways of Meeting the Trinitarian Problem

The Problem. The problem of the Trinity does not come merely from an effort to interpret the command of baptism and other passages of Scripture, but mainly from a larger effort to harmonize with the unity of God the Christian conception of redemption as involving the Father who gave his only-begotten Son, the absolute deity of Jesus Christ, and the personality of the Holy Spirit. On the one side we must hold fast to monotheism, to the rigid conception of one God, and yet, on the other side, we must protect the three personal manifestations, "the three persons out in history." To bring up the old test, the Trinitarian problem is, "Not to divide the substance and not to confuse the persons."

Ways of Meeting the Problem.

1. The most popular way of meeting this problem is not to meet it at all, but to declare the reality beyond human apprehension. Of the many agnostic statements, I will give only one. Dr. W. L. Alexander says: "What I gather from it [the Bible] is, that there are three manifestations of God in relation to the created universe and the work of human redemption, described severally as Father, Son, and Holy Spirit, and that these three manifestations of God correspond to distinctions in the Godhead for which we have no names, and of the nature of which nothing has been revealed to us; of which, in fact, beyond the simple fact of their existence, we know nothing. What is very plainly made known to us is the *economical* distinction between Father, Son, and Holy Spirit—a distinction that may be stated in the most intelligible form, and made clear by a reference to the works ascribed in Scripture to these three respectively; and to this we are led to believe that a distinction of some sort in the divine nature corresponds, but of *what* sort we do not know and therefore do not pretend to say. This way of stating the doctrine has the advantage of avoiding modalism on the one hand by asserting a real distinction in the divine nature, while on the other it keeps clear of the unintelligible and self-contradictory statements of the Catholic doctrine by simply asserting the fact of a distinction in the divine nature without pronouncing upon the *kind* of distinction as personal or capable of being described by any term, direct or analogical, in use among men; and by confining the distinction expressed by the words Father, Son, and Holy Spirit to the

economical distinctions in the divine manifestations in relation to creation and redemption."

2. Another way of trying to meet the problem is to consider these inner distinctions as less than personal. Whatever the manifestations out in history may be, the distinctions are not actual persons as they exist in the life of the Godhead. For example, to Nitzsch they are *ineffable fundamental powers;* and to Dorner they are something *between an attribute and egoity* ("zwischen Eigenschaften und Ichheit oder Persönlichkeit," ch. Glaubenslehre, i, 368).

3. The most speculative view is a theological dripping out of the German philosophy, a view which is quite often found in American theology. It is stated in several slightly different ways, but essentially amounts to this: In the full self-consciousness of God there are three movements, each movement yielding an eternal reality in being. God the Infinite Person makes himself (*Thesis*) the object of his own thought (*Antithesis*), and then identifies subject and object (*Synthesis*). The *Thesis* is the Father; the *Antithesis* is the Son; and the *Synthesis* is the Holy Spirit.

4. In this, the last view to be mentioned, the divine *persons* are considered real eternal persons, each one capable of self-consciousness and self-decision, and yet all so bound together as not to be separate individual Gods. In Jonathan Edwards's Observations Concerning the Scripture Œconomy of the Trinity and Covenant of Redemption we find such a remark as this: "And that there was a consultation among the three Persons about it, as much, doubtless, as about the creation of man (for the work of redemption is a work wherein the distinct concern of each Person is infinitely greater than in the work of creation), and so, that there was a joint agreement of all; but not properly a covenant between them." How strange this

sounds over against all the recent timidities of theological utterance on the Trinity! It almost seems as if Athanasius had spoken again!

A Study of Our Lord's Obedience

1. Our Saviour's bearing is ever that of obedience to his Father.

This bearing appears even in Christ's boyhood. "How is it that ye sought me? knew ye not that I must be in my Father's house?" (Saint Luke 2. 49.) Again: "My meat is to do the will of him that sent me" (Saint John 4. 34). And yet again, in the Garden: "And he said, Abba, Father, all things are possible unto thee; remove this cup from me: howbeit not what I will, but what thou wilt" (Saint Mark 14. 36).

This bearing of our Lord involves a discrimination in his consciousness between himself as a person and his Father *as a cotemporaneous person;* and then a distinct self-decision of obedience toward his Father. Of course, there can be obedience in the sense of doing one's duty under the moral ideal in conscience. But you cannot study the life of Jesus Christ, and conclude that by his Father he meant merely a moral ideal in conscience; for with him the Father had many associations, not precisely moral, but intensely personal.

The significance of our Lord's obedience, then, should in the very nature of the case exclude every form of modalism. Whatever we may come to in our view of the Trinity, that unbiblical idea, found here and there even now in disguised forms, that the Trinity is one God with three successive and exclusive *historic attitudes* must be cast out of the church, not only in the name of Christian doctrine, but also in the name of sane biblical scholarship. There could be no obedience of our Lord toward his Father, if that Father were a special historic attitude of

488 THE CHRISTIAN FAITH

God no longer in existence. To fairly interpret the Scripture, the Father and Son can only be regarded as *real persons, now over against each other, one claiming obedience and the other yielding obedience.*

2. The background of our Lord's obedience, as the entire matter is held in his own self-consciousness, is a preëxistent personal state which he had with his Father.

In Saint John's gospel (17. 4, 5) we read: "I glorified thee on the earth, having accomplished the work which thou hast given me to do. And now, Father, glorify thou me with thine own self with the glory which I had with thee before the world was" (compare Saint John 6. 62 and 8. 58).

Here our Lord is thinking of his finished work of obedience, and he prays that he may again experience the glorious estate which he had given up in carrying out his Father's command. The earthly obedience is to him but a feature of the whole scheme of obedience that first required the giving up of the life in eternal glory. We have in this passage no mere longing for rest, no mere desire such as the saint has "to go home to God"; the scene is too sharply cut to be explained in such a manner; there is every indication of actual personal remembrance.

I am loath to grant the time and space, but there is sure to be a legitimate expectation at this point that some serious reference will be made to Beyschlag's view of our Lord's preëxistence. According to Beyschlag, our Saviour's preëxistence was not *personal*, but merely *ideal*. Jesus, in his own self-consciousness, was but the ideal Son of man come down from heaven. "Jesus thinks of himself as preëxistent, not because he knew himself to be a second God, and remembered a former life in heaven, but because he recognized himself in Daniel's image (Dan. 7. 13) as the bearer of the kingdom of heaven, and because this Son of man as well as the kingdom which he brings to earth must spring from heaven." This is the ordinary way in which our Saviour regarded his preëxistence, but now we come to the extraordinary way. The ideal taken from the Old Testament is, in moments of spiritual exaltation, transformed into seeming personal remembrance! "Especially in the tense final period of his life, in excited moments and conflicts, . . . and, above all, in the frame of mind of the intercessory prayer, where he is raised above the world and time, it appears quite credible that such a consciousness of eternal existence should at times flash up in him like a mental vision."

In plain terms, this view of Beyschlag means that Jesus Christ could and did delude himself into seeming to remember that he had lived before the world was created and verily shared the glory of the Eternal God! And *a man—of that kind*—actually founded the Christian faith, and gained the following of men like Saint Paul! And now undoubted Christian scholarship finds it easier, finds it more rational, to believe *that* than to believe that our Lord *was* God, and that he *did* share the glory of his Father before the ages began! Surely there are wonders in psychology as well as wonders in grace!

But my main objection to Beyschlag's view is not that it is rationalism, and rationalism almost as irrational as that of Paulus, but that it destroys the peculiar ethical character of our Lord's self-sacrifice in his work of redemption. This brings us to the great utterance of Saint Paul, which we must now look at from a second point of view.

3. "Have this mind in you, which was also in Christ Jesus: who, being in the form of God, counted it not a prize to be on an equality with God, but emptied himself, taking the form of a servant, being made in the likeness of men; and being found in fashion as a man, he humbled

himself, becoming obedient even unto death, yea, the death of the cross. Wherefore also God highly exalted him, and gave unto him the name which is above every name; that in the name of Jesus every knee should bow, of things in heaven and things on earth and things under the earth, and that every tongue should confess that Jesus Christ is Lord, to the glory of God the Father" (Phil. 2. 5–11).

We do not need to recall my former exegesis of this passage. I only ask you to read the passage over and over again until its meaning and its majesty fill your soul. Saint Paul traces back the life of Jesus Christ to its pre-existent point in the Godhead. Back there in the eternities there was *somewhat* in God that afterward became the being "found in fashion as a man" and called Jesus Christ. Now I ask every man who is a Trinitarian at all, What was this *somewhat?* A mere ideal conception? A phase of the one complete self-consciousness of God? Something between attribute and egoity? An ineffable, fundamental power? An agnostic entity which cannot even be named? If you make any one of these answers, then I must insist that when the Son of God became man, in the event of becoming man, *there was no obedience*. Nothing short of a person can obey. Obedience means self-decision, and self-decision is impossible without self-consciousness. And if there was no obedience there was no *self-sacrifice* on the part of the Son of God in becoming man. No ideal, no phase of self-consciousness, no something between attribute and egoity, no ineffable, fundamental power, no agnostic entity which cannot be named, *could* sacrifice itself, *could* empty itself, *could* voluntarily give up the glory of God and take on the form of a servant. No impersonal thing, describable or indescribable, could with awful self-cost become man to redeem us from sin. In the presence of all these hesitations and timidities and ingenuities and evasions, I insist in the name of ordinary consistency that every Trinitarian should clearly make choice—either to give up the whole moral content of the Pauline doctrine of the infinite self-sacrifice of the preëxistent Son of God in our behalf, or to grant to the preëxistent Son of God self-decision, self-consciousness, personality.

4. One more step we need to take. Our Lord's obedience was *the obedience of a subordinate Son*. He was not obedient to God as an angel might be obedient to God. He was the Son of God, and obedience was the expression of the most fundamental relation of his being. His divine Sonship involved two things in relation to God the Father: first, an equality in nature; second, a subordination in person. And both this equality and this subordination are ever manifest in the spirit and manner of his obedience.

In Saint John's gospel these two things, equality and subordination, are expressed again and again; but there is one remarkable passage (5. 25–27) which I wish you especially to note: "Verily, verily, I say unto you, The hour cometh, and now is, when the dead shall hear the voice of the Son of God; and they that hear shall live. For as the Father hath life in himself, even so gave he to the Son also to have life in himself: and he gave him authority to execute judgment, because he is the Son of man."

This passage not only teaches subordination and equality as clearly as do those passages which show our Lord's obedience more definitely; but it goes further, it does a profounder thing, for it reveals the fact that our Lord's equality with his Father has been *given to him*. The Son hath life in himself (that is, he is an absolute *source* of life) even as God the Father hath life in himself; but the Son's life is not *original* (no reference here to sequence, merely to causation) with him, it is derived from his Father.

As a result of this brief study of our Lord's obedience we have two conclusions which should have large consideration in our final construction of the doctrine of the Trinity: First, as the preëxistent Son of God, our Lord was a *real person*, having self-consciousness and making self-decision. Second, our Lord's subordination is so fundamental that his very absolute fullness of life is itself a *derived life*, a life which is an effect, a life which is *caused by his Father*. In the profoundest sense, our Lord's obedience is the obedience of a Son who is both personally and essentially subordinate to his Father.

Consistency in Systematic Theology

One very glaring inconsistency is often found in the conventional works in systematic theology. Their teaching in Christology is that Jesus Christ is one person with two natures, a divine nature and a human nature; but the human nature is *impersonal*, merely a bare nature added to the divine nature of the one Eternal Person. Our Lord is (to quote a typical statement) "a conscious, intelligent Agent, who preserves from eternity into time and onward to eternity his own unbroken identity. And this we not inaptly or unreasonably term his undivided personality." Some of these theologians, indeed, are so anxious to protect the full personality of the Son of God in the event of the Incarnation that they find it necessary to reject every form of the doctrine of *the kenosis*. Not only so, but in their discussions of our Lord's preëxistence these theologians are wont to maintain, and to maintain with commendable energy, that his preëxistence was *not* ideal, but *was* personal. And yet to these very men, in their cautious, theistic treatment of the doctrine of the Trinity, the eternal Son of God, the second person in the

Godhead, is "not what we mean by a person"—*no, he is an agnostic nondescript to remain in mystery until a veritable person is needed in Christology!*

Another inconsistency almost equally pronounced is to be found in the work of many defensive theologians, namely, an inconsistency in their teaching concerning the Holy Spirit. In their theology, in the doctrine of God, the Holy Ghost is viewed as something less than a real person; but in every other place, where any reference is made to the nature or to the dispensation or to the activity of the Spirit, he is regarded as having not only functions of his own, but also a will of his own. Indeed, some of the men I have in mind devote precious pages to prove "the proper personality" of the Holy Spirit and look upon the point as essential to genuine orthodoxy. Now, how the Holy Spirit can be a person making actual self-decisions out in the application of redemption to men, and yet nothing but a principle, or potency, or impersonal entity, in the deep life of the Eternal and Immutable God, is "a mystery so boundless that no man can understand it, and I will therefore not pretend to understand it"!

CONSTRUCTION OF THE DOCTRINE

Special Points to Be Protected. In constructing the doctrine of the Trinity, under the demands of the Trinitarian problem as already stated, there are certain special points which we must constantly seek to protect. These points are:

1. The Feature of Structural Unity. It is not enough to provide for a "moral unity," or the unity of three persons who are united in moral and personal purpose. Christian theism requires us entirely to avoid tritheism; and we need, in some way, to conceive of God as *one individual structure* with only one attitude of personal will.

2. The Feature of Subordination. We should protect that profound bearing of subordination which the Son of God ever shows in his obedience to his Father. And we should also protect, at the same time, the subordination of the Holy Spirit to both the Father and the Son, for this is revealed in the Scripture almost as clearly, and the point is fully confirmed in the history of the Christian consciousness.

3. The Feature of Self-sacrifice. Not only are we to protect the moral costliness of Redemption to God the Father, but we must also protect the whole tremendous fact of self-cost to the Son of God in becoming man to carry out the plan of salvation.

4. The Feature of Equality. We must protect the absolute equality of the Father, the Son, and the Holy Spirit in *every* attribute of Deity. It is not enough to construct the doctrine so that the three persons are equal in such attributes as righteousness and love, and leave the matter there: the divine persons are so to be conceived as to be equal in the attribute of omnipotence, in the attribute of eternity, and in every attribute belonging to the absolute nature of God. In yet plainer speech, I mean that the relation of subordination is not to be allowed to impair, in our doctrine, the absolute deity of the Son and of the Holy Spirit.

5. The Feature of Moral Love. Just as I have emphasized moral love in my entire treatment of the philosophy of the Christian faith, so now we must aim so to construct the doctrine of the Trinity as to exalt the divine attribute of love.

Relation to Athanasius. That no one of you may be misled in even the slightest degree, I will, before going on to more positive work, clearly indicate my relation to Athanasius. For a number of years I was influenced— yes, I would better say dominated—by the patristic interpretation of a class of scholars converging in Dr. Dorner; and during those years I supposed that Athanasius, in his mighty struggle with the Arians, had no clear conception of the nature and significance of personality. And I actually came to think that Augustine's doctrine of the Trinity (from which our present perilous Trinitarian situation has largely come) was a normal development out of what Athanasius *probably meant at the bottom!* But after a long period of doctrinal unrest and search it began to dawn upon me that it was *they*, my patristic authorities, who had no clear conception of the nature and significance of personality; and that, precisely because of their own lack of fundamental thinking in philosophy, they were, in spite of all their fine, technical scholarship, incapable of a complete mastery of the meaning of Athanasius. Now there is not the touch of a doubt in my own mind but that the view Athanasius held of the Trinity was essentially this: The Father, the Son, and the Holy Ghost are three persons, each having personal consciousness and personal will; but the Father is the Supreme Cause, and because of this the other two persons are subordinate to him.

In getting at the bearing of the Christian consciousness upon the interpretation of the doctrine of the Trinity, the important man to me is not Augustine, but Athanasius. For this choice I have two reasons: First, Augustine seems to me never to have caught the Christian view of God. In fact, much that he says about God and the ways of God is *Christianity so tampered with* as to lose the spirit of the New Testament altogether. Second, Athanasius was providentially placed. He stood, in his defense of the Christian faith, in a crisis *where he had to grasp* the basal import of the Trinity. For, such a grasp was necessary before he could see how to protect in statement the absolute deity of Jesus Christ. In other words, Athanasius was at one of those crucial turning points in the development of doctrine, or, more exactly, in the development of the Christian seizure of doctrine, where the Holy Spirit finds a wise opportunity to deepen one phase of the Christian consciousness. My idea, in truth, of the progress in doctrine is that this progress is seldom or never *gradual*, but rather *zigzag*, from crisis to crisis; and that between crises the church may not only make no headway, but even miss the route entirely. Thus, the mere fact that one thinker or leader is later than another in the years does not necessarily mean that the later man has more doctrinal insight. It is quite possible that he can see nothing beyond the indorsements of the *Zeitgeist*.

While Athanasius is of the greatest importance to me, and is really my point of philosophical departure, I shall not be found clinging to him in a slavish literalism. I will construct the doctrine of the Trinity to satisfy, in Christian freedom, my own heart in its relation to our Lord; and my own judgment in its relation to the entire utterance of Christian men, in so far as that utterance is known to me; and my own mind in its relation to the teaching of the Word of God.

The Use of Terms. My use of terms in this connection is the same that it has been in every other connection; but it may be useful to recall precisely some of the most important of the definitions:

1. *A person* is any being capable of self-conscious decision. Or, a person is a self-conscious, self-decisive agent.

2. *An individual* is a distinct item of being (or a punctual entity) that cannot be divided without losing identity.

3. *The nature* of anything is the structural law by which the thing is precisely what it is.

4. *An organism* is a complex of essential parts; all the

parts in dependent reciprocity; and every part making contribution to a common end.

In a spiritual organism of persons there is a further feature, namely, every person is in the organism both means and end. He is a means by which the organism works toward its end, and also a part of the end for which the organism exists. He lives for the entire organism, and the entire organism makes perpetual contribution to his life.

Then there is *an absolute organism*, by which I mean one that is absolutely self-sufficient *as an organism*. No feature of the organism is self-sufficient, no feature could exist at all alone; but the organism *as a whole* is self-sufficient.

The Full and Final Statement.

1. God is *one individual*. Taken as a total, God is an indivisible finality. And so God is an individual in the precise sense that a man or an angel is an individual—that is, an itemnic being, a punctual entity, an actual existence that cannot be divided without loss of identity.

2. This one divine individual has *one nature*. There is only one μορφή, only one complex of attributes, only one structural law of action.

3. In this one individual, with this one nature, or under this one structural law, there are three Persons—three Agents with self-consciousness and capacity for self-decision. That is, the whole divine individuality is grasped, and estimated, and consciously appropriated, and used as the background of decision, at three personal points and not merely at one.

4. But, while the basal nature is ever one and the same, it is *personalized* in three very different ways. The First Person is conscious of himself *as the Father*, and to him every feature of the Godhead is mediated by that peculiarity of self-consciousness. He thinks as the Father,

he wills as the Father, he loves as the Father. In like manner, the Second Person is conscious of himself *as the Son;* and the Third Person is conscious of himself *as the Holy Spirit.* This is the philosophy of the ἰδιότης in general; but this point of personal peculiarity I will consider more definitely and more deeply somewhat later in the statement.

5. Inasmuch, though, as the three Persons have the one individual nature, are under one structural law; inasmuch as they have the same attributes in quality and quantity; and inasmuch as they are ever in the profoundest personal fellowship, there is a constant intercommunion, a currency of personal joys, an exchange of personal experiences. And so each Person is vastly more than his isolated self could be. He lives by augment. He lives in and through the other two Persons. His ineffable experience is the combination of three peculiar divine experiences, of three different ways of personalizing the Godhead. This is that sublime feature of God's life which has been called the περιχώρησις.

6. Interlaced in this infinite interchange of experience, and living under one structural law, the three divine Persons constitute an *absolute personal organism.* Not only are all three Persons organically essential; not only do they contribute to a common end; not only do they depend upon each other in reciprocity; and not only is each Person both means and end; but there is an eternal self-sufficiency which is due to the organism and to that alone. Not one of the three Persons, not even the Father, could exist at all out of the organism. He partakes of the attribute of *aseity* itself only as he is a part of the organism. Thus we make the *unity of God* fundamental to our entire conception of God.

7. And yet the Father is original in supremacy as to just one thing, namely, *causation.* All the process in

organism *originates* with the Father. Again and again we are told that to be thus the causal origin the Father must have existed first, and then begun the line of causation. It is not so. The Father *lives only as cause.* To cause is his method of existence—his eternal breathing, so to speak. Creation proper, the making of stars and men and all creatures, is a personal matter—an option under motive and the motive urgent under the law of personal expression; but infinitely beyond all this personal urgency to create is the Father's intrinsic and eternal necessity to be the causal source in the organism of the Godhead. *Begetting* the Son and *causing* the Holy Spirit are not at all a matter of optional personal expression; but are *the method and means of self-existence.* This is but saying in another way that the whole triune organism must exist or none of it can exist.

8. This prepares the way for our bringing out and making emphatic the fact that the fundament of all being is *social.* In our modern thinking there are two views which are in perpetual clash. In one view the fundament of all being is an impersonal somewhat; in the other view the fundament is a solitary person. Either view, if thoroughly developed, should be a bottomless horror to any man with a warm Christian experience. The fundament of all being is not an impersonal somewhat —a blind Infinite evolving into heartless and meaningless destiny. Nor is this fundament a solitary person—an isolated iceberg of self-consciousness—an omnipotent loneliness. No, no, no, the causal fundament of all being is *an actual Father who must be a Father to exist at all.*

Nearly every vagary has in it the hint of a great truth toward which the vagary is wandering; and this is the case with that German vagary concerning the divine Antithesis in consciousness. God the Father *needs* his Son for the fullness of his own self-consciousness. He needs the Son (and they both need the Holy Spirit) precisely as much as the Son needs him. Thus their essential equality reaches into the very structure of the divine organism.

9. We are able now, I think, to deepen our former philosophy of creation, and perhaps to change our sentiment concerning that philosophy. In their effort to protect such Scripture teaching as that found in the third verse of the first chapter of Saint John's gospel ("All things were made by him"), some theologians have seemed to show a tendency to minimize the Father's effectual relation to creation. If there really is such a tendency it is all wrong. The clue to the entire truth lies in the fact that all creation is *a social act*. The Father is primarily the Creator; but he creates, under the law of personal expression, *through his Son*. And the Son *confirms* the creative will of the Father in *the fellowship of moral love*. And then this *double will* is carried out into the event by the Holy Spirit.

Not only so, but the race of man (and all creation that pertains to man) the Father has created *for his Son*. Whatever men might do to stay it, the Father made a plan that his only Son should have an everlasting kingdom within the vast kingdom of God—*and the Son will have it as an expression of his Father's love!*

10. Can we not now see our Lord's obedience in a somewhat larger bearing? The Son of God must obey his Father. The very organism of the Godhead involves the absolute necessity of such obedience. Did I not tell you that the idea of service under the supreme will of God is a finality in the universe? Every created thing is made to obey. Not even free personality can escape that finality. But where does that final principle of doing the supreme will come from? It comes from the Godhead. The Son of God must obey the supreme will of his Father.

The Son, though, does not obey his Father under the motive of necessity. Nor does he obey his Father under the motive of moral obligation even, he obeys him under the motive of moral love. The obedience is thus ethical and yet more than ethical. All the Son's moral concern for the law of holiness is but the central fire of his personal love for his Father, and this love for his Father becomes the total motive of his obedience. What we find here, then, in the case of our Lord, is exactly what will be found in the eternal life of every saint, namely, a necessary service lifted into a service of personal love and moral love.

Probably this is the most fitting place to correct a certain notion which you are likely to meet in crude Christian thinking. God the Father and his Son, our Saviour, are regarded as having two very different attitudes toward the salvation of men. The attitude of the Father is one of *holy obstacle*, while the attitude of the Son is one of *eager mediation* between sinners and the angry Father. The same feeling, if not the same notion, is repeated in the Roman Catholic conception of the mediation of the Virgin Mary. As it is in Chaucer's verse, "Gracious maid and mother, *help* that my Father be not wroth with me." It is exceedingly important that this notion, and especially this feeling, about God the Father should be crushed out of Christian life. For it is false through and through. The moral obstacle to superficial pardon is equally in every Person of the Trinity. Not only so, but the plan of redemption *is primarily with the Father*. He it was who gave his only-begotten Son. *The Father's plan* was confirmed by the Son in obedience and self-sacrifice, and again confirmed by the swift and silent redemptional response of the Holy Spirit. Even Jonathan Edwards has not, at this point, quite gained the New Testament accent. It is true, however, that every

Christian heart in full health has, must have, a peculiar love for Jesus Christ; but this peculiar love has no necessary relation to the origin of the plan of redemption; rather does the love grow out of the four facts that the Son of God in his self-sacrifice became man to redeem us, that he actually did redeem us by his death, that in conversion we are united to him, and that he remains man, "our Elder Brother," forever.

11. An additional word can now be given concerning the ἰδιότης, or personal peculiarity, of each Person in the Trinity. The peculiarity of the Father is *that of origination*. Not only is he the causal source of the divine organism, but also his will is original and supreme. It is his will that we refer to in the discussions of Christian theism. It is his will that springs the worlds into existence and binds them into harmony in their majestic courses. When we speak of "God" without qualification we always mean the Sovereign Father. His will is confirmed, doubly confirmed, *but it is his will that is confirmed*. Philosophically a Trinitarian is as rigidly monotheistic as any Unitarian can be, or even as any deist ever was, and as well prepared for any problem in theism.

The peculiarity of the Son of God is *that of personal obedience*. Here we need to be intensely attentive, or we will not get the idea truly. This obedience is active, personal, *self-assertive obedience*. It is full of humility, but the humility never flings the Person into effacement. Notice the ring of authority and dominion: "I will draw all men unto me." "Verily, verily, I say unto you." "The Son of man shall come in his glory." The fact is that nothing can be more tremendously aggressive than the will of Jesus Christ, the Eternal Son of God.

Even more difficult is it to understand perfectly the personal combination of quality in the Holy Spirit. His peculiarity is *that of personal self-effacement*. His obedience is not obedience merely, not loving obedience merely, but personal effacement in obedience. I despair of making this divine principle of voluntary, eager self-effacement real and sublime to an age which refuses even to try to understand Saint Paul's inspired conception of a Christian home; and I will make no endeavor to do so. An intimation, though, is necessary for the completeness of my Trinitarian message. What we may term the organic peculiarity of the Holy Spirit is that he is as subordinate to the Son of God as he is to the Father; but his personal peculiarity is the wonderful way in which, in moral love, he treats this organic limitation. He takes hold of it with enthusiastic assent, he transfigures it, he turns it into his everlasting rejoicing. Not only so, but also instead of obeying by an aggressive self-assertion, he actually obeys by self-effacement. Of men, for instance, the Holy Spirit wants nothing for himself. He wants us only to belong to Christ, only to serve Christ, only to love Christ supremely. If your consciousness is totally occupied with love for your Saviour, the whole longing of the Holy Spirit is satisfied. He for himself wants nothing, excepting the infinite love of the Father and of the Son. He rejoices not in obedience, but in that particular kind of obedience which never blossoms into personal emolument. He, too, is ever urged on by the law of personal expression, but he expresses all he is, and all he desires, in bare service —not service *and something*—not service and a universe— not service and a final kingdom—the Spirit of God expresses himself simply and totally in service. And what a service, what a service it is! Whether God will send a river flowing to the sea, or will set a sunset blazing in the western cloud, or will quiet the fears of a terrified child, or will break the proud heart of a sinner, or will unite a willing man to Jesus Christ, or will add a further grace to the triumphs of a saint, or will pour the surprising consolations of heaven into a hopeless grief, or will take an old man who is timid before the gathering mystery of death and fill his soul with the peace of God and the certainties of faith—the work, the finishing volition, the efficient eventualization of it all is given over to the Holy Spirit—*he alone is sent!*

THE MORAL LOVE OF THE TRIUNE GOD

This, the moral love of the Triune God, is our last theme, our last work together in this system of doctrine!

First of all, I want you to get the entire force, and the inner spirit, of that conception of the love of God as the love of a solitary Infinite Benevolence, a conception which is now apparent almost everywhere in the Christian church, and which is almost certain to become dominant. I have, therefore, selected two typical passages for quotation, choosing one passage for its spirit and the other passage for its meaning. Professor Ritschl, in his finest *ad hominem* manner, says: "In a certain quarter of theological speculation we are met by the principle that perfect love requires the similar mutual relation of two personal wills. In so far as love is the principle of perfect fellowship between two personal beings, this may be true. But the perfect love, as motive power and guiding principle of the individual will, is independent of responsive love (Matt. 5. 46); on the contrary, just there, where it meets with no answering love, perfect love proves in every possible case its peculiar sublimity."

The other passage comes from W. L. Walker's remarkable book, The Spirit and the Incarnation, and reads as follows: "It is often argued that the love that God is must eternally produce an object to which it can impart itself, and from which it must be eternally reflected back again. It is thus that some theologians have argued for the existence of a Divine Son of God, and for what has been termed a 'social Trinity'. But this, if the love is not to be a mere self-love, would imply such a distinct and separate person in the Son as would be wholly inconsistent with the unity of the Divine Being, and as would even savor of the mythological. This is not the inference which we seek to draw from the existence of God as love. The scriptural doctrine is that God *is* love, and 'the Son' must be that same love in one mode of its existence. The love that God *is* is not merely 'the affection of one person for another,' as of individuals, but that holy, universal, infinite love which forever seeks to impart itself, and which causes *all* persons to arise. The Son is that love as it goes forth to impart itself to others conceived in the divine image. The Son in God is thus at once the ideal and the potency of the creation. The perfect love that God is, just because it is perfect love, can never keep itself to itself, but must be eternally giving itself and going forth creating."

Professor Ritschl (to take up the less important quotation first), it seems to me, twists the Saviour's meaning out of shape. Our Lord does not mean that the sublimest love has no *desire* for response, but rather that such love can and should be a motive when there is no response, and even in the face of hatred. There is something lofty in loving an enemy, but there is nothing lofty in being *content* with the enmity. And, yet deeper, to love an enemy requires a moral love, and, in the very nature of moral love, it craves an answer of moral love. Then, coming to God himself, it is not true that he "maketh his sun to rise on the evil" because he is indifferent to response. He treats *his* enemies as he does because he wants them to drop their enmity and love him in return. I will deny the whole contention that the highest kind of love is independent of response. On the contrary, I believe that the more nearly perfect, the more nearly divine the love is, the more one suffers, out of sight, if there be no response. How, then, is a love asking for response to be protected from mere selfishness? The answer is ready: *By moral quality.*

To the teaching (as I grasp it) of the second quotation, I have three objections which are strong and unyielding:

1. Inasmuch as this view of the love of God grants the preëxistent Son of God neither self-decision nor self-consciousness, it would in our thinking entirely destroy that ethical quality of self-sacrifice on the part of the Son in his Incarnation, a self-sacrifice which is clearly taught by Saint Paul, and which is vital to any really Christian conception of redemption. Urge and reurge this point I will upon the church, for it concerns the total practical efficiency of Christian preaching.

2. Carried out in consistency, this view of the love of God certainly means either one or the other of two things: Either, first, that an impersonal "seed" or potency of Deity so develops under temporal conditions as to *become* personal—in which case there is *now* personal duality in the Godhead (the Father and the Son Jesus Christ), and the old problem of divine unity must be faced and answered by the very men who object to the Athanasian solution—or, second, that our Saviour is but a man, or at the most a personal creature, having in his nature a *deposit of Deity;* in which case the outcome is nothing other than Unitarianism, essentially akin to that kind of Unitarianism (James Freeman Clarke) which regards Christ as "divine by peculiar endowment." That the second theological option is the one likely to be taken I have been convinced by much observation, and especially by a study of the effects of the Ritschlian movement upon American and British theology.

3. A divine love which "can never keep itself to itself, but must be eternally giving itself and going forth creat-

ing," amounts, precisely, I think, to that "infinite and eternal craving to create" which so often comes to the fore in the pantheistic philosophy. Under the terms of such a view there could be in creation neither beginning nor end, for the entire motive of creation is love as an *unsatisfied* attribute. Indeed, the view seems to me to be not only impossible in a rigidly Christian theism, but also out of harmony with all the fundamental Christian doctrines, and even inconsistent in its own structure.

Dropping all this negative work of criticism, I will now give you simply and yet positively that conception of the love of God which I look upon as belonging to the philosophical fiber of the Christian faith. In doing this I have an extremely delicate preparatory task, namely, to make you all see and feel the deep difference between the motive of *unsatisfied* love and the motive of *satisfied* love. I am far from being sure that my modicum of literary skill is enough for the task; but the matter is so fundamentally important that I must do what I can. There is many a human home where a child has been adopted to meet the inherent craving of a hungry heart. Sometimes such homes are very noble, sometimes they become very happy; but, profoundly regarded, always they are abnormal and very pathetic. Right over against one of these abnormal homes I ask you to imagine another kind of a home, a home of the Bunsen type, where the father and the mother and all the children are tenderly and usefully and unselfishly entangled in a love well-nigh boundless. Now, this home—*all of them*—adopts a waif, let us say. Are any of you able to discover any deep difference between the two cases of adoption? There *is* a deep difference. In the one case, the motive is an *unsatisfied* love—*the home needs the child*. In the other case, the motive is a *satisfied* love—*the child needs the home*.

Now I will try to gather up into more definite point

my entire view of God's relation to creation. Searching
for creation-motive, I find that there are in the divine
life three main features which are to be considered: First,
there is the feature of personality. As I have said in
various ways, personality likes to create, is eager to express the inner secret. Because of this intrinsic personal
eagerness, there is divine motive to outplace objects of
actual expression. But this motive is purely personal,
and very unlike the "unfolding instinct" of pantheism;
for the will of God is *not driven into creation.* God creates
because he *would* and not because he *must.* Again let me
borrow Martensen's fine thought, the creation is a "*superfluity*" for God. God has joy in the cosmos, but God
does not *need* the cosmos. Neither personality nor any
divine attribute gets, in creation, any new fullness. You
cannot do any thoroughly Christian thinking until you
lay fast hold of the idea that our God is eternally perfect
and so self-sufficient. He is not an infinite craving endlessly striving to satisfy his own nature and fill out the
underlying plan of his own being. Second, there is the
feature of moral concern. This second feature must be
quickly added to the first. It is inherent for personality
to want to get out into expression, but this inherent desire
is much more urgent in moral personality. Moral concern
mightily longs to spring into cosmic fact. The philosophy
of this is partly in the nature of righteousness itself and
partly in the way moral concern vitalizes personality.
Now, therefore, we have in mind another range of divine
motive. Personality alone is enough to explain a vanishing universe of things, continents, and daffodils tossing
in the breeze, and all that; but to explain, to show motive
for a final, everlasting universe with men and angels and
archangels, we need to *begin* with personality and come
on swiftly to God's moral concern. Third, there is the
feature of moral love. But we cannot *stop* with moral

concern. To obtain a *Christian* conception of the final universe, we must think of personality and moral concern as culminating in the one divine motive of moral love. In other connections and at differing angles in meaning and emphasis, I have spoken of the final universe, and probably I have left the impression that our extreme point of emphasis should be that the final universe must express the holiness of God as culminating through moral concern in moral love. To correct this impression, I have been waiting for this very place. My full view is that the final universe is to manifest, in finite measure, the entirety of God's life. To do so much, the final universe must express, not merely the fact of God's moral love, but additionally the fact that this divine love is a *satisfied* moral love. What do I mean by this? I mean that the final universe will come to climax in perfect sainthood —in personal moral creatures who have, in their freedom, been made perfect in storm and pain and test. Freedom was granted them simply because there is no other process under which a finite being can become morally like God. Because of this climax of sainthood, every other feature of the final universe takes on its last touch of significance. What, then, is God's relation to this sainthood? That of Creator with the motive of a satisfied love. Forever will it be evident that these saints were created, not because God *needed them* to moderate his own craving for love; but because, out of the eternal fullness of a satisfied love, God wanted them to bring their little cups of finite possibility and fill them with everlasting joy out of his shoreless ocean. Thus the very law of expression itself becomes at last more than merely personal, even more than merely personal and moral—it becomes absolutely altruistic.

One last look at the new race, and our work is done. Not yet, in this immediate discussion, have we provided for the finite expression in the final universe of the *entirety* of the life of God. For we made no provision for the expression of the absolute personal organism of the Godhead. Do you not see what we need as our ultimate feature? We again need the new race in Jesus Christ. The cosmic sweep of the kingdom of God will manifest the divine holiness as personalized in moral concern. The kingdom of heaven will manifest the satisfied love of God as benevolent motive. But the kingdom of our Lord will express *more*—it will express the love of God—moral and satisfied—in a personal organism which will be a finite copy of the unity of the Persons of the Trinity, and will have a racial imitation of the glory of their inter-communion.

"Neither for these only do I pray, but for them also that believe on me through their word; that they may all be one; even as thou, Father, art in me, and I in thee, that they also may be in us: that the world may believe that thou didst send me. And the glory which thou hast given me I have given unto them; that they may be one, even as we are one; I in them, and thou in me, that they may be perfected into one; that the world may know that thou didst send me, and lovedst them, even as thou lovedst me. Father, that which thou hast given me, I will that, where I am, they also may be with me; that they may behold my glory, which thou hast given me: for thou lovedst me before the foundation of the world."

And now unto the God of our redemption, unto the Father, and unto the Son, and unto the Holy Ghost, do we ascribe all power and all dominion and all glory, world without end, Amen and Amen.

NOTES ON THE TEXT

I. The Man and the Animal

PAGE

7   Charles Morris, Man and His Ancestor, chap. viii. The Macmillan Co., 1900.

9   Haeckel, Die Welträthsel, kap. xiii, the McCabe translation. Harper, 1901. One hundred and fifty thousand copies sold in Germany alone. See Hibbert Journal for July, 1905, p. 741.

10   The quotation from Darwin. See Man and His Ancestor, p. 14. Also Descent of Man, p. 154, revised edition. Appleton, 1902. Mr. Darwin says: "If the above explanation is correct, as seems probable, the direction of the hair on our own arms offers a curious record of our former state; for no one supposes that it is now of any use in throwing off the rain; nor, in our present erect condition, is it properly directed for this purpose."

11–13 As to God's relation to the world, compare with statement on pp. 147, 148.

II. Personality

17   Spencer's Facts and Comments. Appleton. Preface written in March, 1902. See p. 12.

19   Hegel's statement in his Philosophie der Religion (i, 64) is this: "Ich bin nicht einer der im Kampf begriffenen, sondern ich bin beide Kämpfende und der Kampf selbst."

20   "The crushed worm." See the Clark edition of the Microcosmus, i, 250.

20   Fife ponies. See article by Kellogg Durland in Blackwood's Magazine, January, 1902.

23   Julius Müller, Lehre von der Sünde, ii, 32.

III. The Moral Person

27   The best discussion of the characteristics of the dog may be found in chap. xvi of Romanes's work on Animal Intelligence. Appleton, 1897.

PAGE
29-31 "The institution of taboo." Frazer's article in the Encyclopædia Britannica, xxiii, 15. Jevons's Introduction to
the History of Religion, chaps. vi, vii, and viii. Methuen,
1902. Andrew Lang's Magic and Religion, chap. xiv.
Longmans, 1901.

IV. FREEDOM, PERSONAL AND MORAL

39 Jonathan Edwards's conception of the "strength of a
motive" is to be found on p. 8 of his Inquiry, London edition,
1831.

James M'Cosh, The Method of the Divine Government, p.
271. New York, 1856.

48 Robert Browning, Saul, xviii.

51 The Methods of Ethics. Macmillan, 1901. The entire
fifth chapter is of importance. Especially note the following passage (pp. 74, 75): "It is sometimes vaguely thought
that a belief in Free Will requires us to maintain that at any
moment we can alter our habits to any extent by a sufficiently strong exertion. And no doubt most commonly
when we make such efforts, we believe at the moment that
they will be completely effectual. We will to do something
hours or days hence with the same confidence with which we
will to do something immediately. But on reflection, no
one, I think, will maintain that in such cases the future act
appears to be in his power in the same sense as a choice of
alternatives that takes effect immediately. Not only does
continual experience show us that such resolutions as to
the future have a limited and too frequently an inadequate
effect, but the common belief is really inconsistent with the
very doctrine of Free Will that is thought to justify it; for
if by a present volition I can fully determine an action that is
to take place some hours hence, when the time comes to do
that act I shall find myself no longer free. We must therefore accept the conclusion that each such resolve has only a
limited effect, and that we cannot know when making it how
far this effect will exhibit itself in the performance of the
act resolved upon. At the same time it can hardly be denied that such resolves sometimes succeed in breaking old
habits; and even when they fail to do this, they often substitute a painful struggle for smooth and easy indulgence."

51 "A recent book." Professor Frank Thilly's Introduction
to Ethics, p. 334. Scribner, 1900.

52   "The sternum in poultry." The Life and Letters of
George John Romanes. Longmans, 1896. Letter to Mr.
Darwin dated November 7, 1875, p. 45.

53   Professor Wundt, The Principles of Morality, p. 39. Swan
Sonnenschein & Co., 1901.

54   Professor Huxley, Life and Letters of Thomas Henry
Huxley, vol. i, pp. 352, 353. Appleton, 1901. Compare
with passage in Collected Essays, i, 163.

56   Professor Bowne, Theory of Thought and Knowledge,
p. 243. Harper, 1897. See also Professor Bowne's discussion of "Freedom and Necessity" in part iii of his Metaphysics, revised edition; and the chapter on "Will and
Action" in part i of his Introduction to Psychological
Theory.

V. Personal Morality

65   For a sufficient discussion of "the categorical imperative"
see chap. xiv of Kant, by William Wallace, Blackwood's
Philosophical Classics.

69   John Caird. The quotation is from the Croall Lecture for
1878-79, chap. ix, 291.

71   The translation of the line from Homer is by Max Müller.

VI. Religion

79   John Stuart Mill. Read his entire essay on Nature.

82   The quotation from Edward Caird's The Evolution of
Religion is more largely given on p. 78.

84   Samuel Johnson. Boswell says: "He had another particu-
larity, of which none of his friends even ventured to ask an
explanation.   It appeared to me some superstitious habit,
which he had contracted early, and from which he had never
called upon his reason to disentangle him.   This was his
anxious care to go out or in at a door or passage by a certain
number of steps from a certain point, or at least so as that
either his right or his left foot (I am not certain which)
should constantly make the first actual movement when he
came close to the door or passage. Thus I conjecture; for I
have, upon innumerable occasions, observed him suddenly
stop, and then seem to count his steps with a deep earnest-
ness; and when he had neglected or gone wrong in this sort of

magical movement, I have seen him go back again, put himself in a proper posture to begin the ceremony, and, having gone through it, break from his abstraction, walk briskly on, and join his companion." The edition in Macmillan's Library of English Classics, i, 357.

84   "The folklore of Brittany." See Dealings with the Dead. London, Redway, 1898. It comprises selections from La Légende de la Mort en Basse Bretagne.

85   Fichte, Ethik, i, 23, quoted by Mulford.

86   Professor James, The Varieties of Religious Experience, p. 34. Longmans, 1902.

88   Professor Seth. There is nowhere a more penetrating discussion of Hegel's philosophy in its relation to personality than is to be found in the last two lectures of Andrew Seth's Hegelianism and Personality.

VII. The Theistic Argument

98   Democritus. See Ferrier's Lectures on Greek Philosophy, the lecture on the "Atomic School."

98   For a criticism of Mill's explanation of the origin of the cosmos see Dr. Miley's Systematic Theology, i, 82–85.

99   For the bearing of modern scientific study upon theism read the little book by John Fiske called The Idea of God as affected by Modern Knowledge.

100   Professor Everett's book (Macmillan, 1902) is one of the most suggestive discussions of the last ten years. See p. 164.

VIII. Revelation

107   Herbert Spencer's last fragment published, in Facts and Comments, is on "Ultimate Questions." The intense gloom of the fragment is manifest in this passage: "But it seems a strange and repugnant conclusion that with the cessation of consciousness at death there ceases to be any knowledge of having existed. With his last breath it becomes to each the same thing as though he had never lived."

108   In his essay on "Nature" Mill says: "In sober truth, nearly all the things which men are hanged or imprisoned for doing to one another are nature's everyday performances. . . . Nature impales men, breaks them as if on the wheel, casts them to be devoured by wild beasts,

burns them to death, crushes them with stones like the first Christian martyr, starves them with hunger, freezes them with cold, poisons them by the quick or slow venom of her exhalations, and has hundreds of other hideous deaths in reserve, such as the ingenious cruelty of a Nabis or a Domitian never surpassed. All this Nature does with the most supercilious disregard both of mercy and of justice, emptying her shafts upon the best and noblest indifferently with the meanest and worst; upon those who are engaged in the highest and worthiest enterprises, and often as the direct consequence of the noblest acts; and it might almost be imagined as a punishment for them. She mows down those on whose existence hangs the well-being of a whole people, perhaps the prospects of the human race for generations to come, with as little compunction as those whose death is a relief to themselves or a blessing to those under their noxious influence."

108   "A certain journalist." Editorial on "Increase of Joy" in Harper's Weekly, November 14, 1903.

IX. THE CHRISTIAN RELIGION AND THE MORAL PERSON

120   Professor J. R. Seeley, the author of Ecce Homo. His book Natural Religion is almost as important as the work which made him famous.

121   Adolf Harnack. "Die Predigt Jesu wird uns auf wenigen, aber grossen Stufen sofort in eine Höhe führen, auf welcher ihr Zusammenhang mit dem Judentum nur noch als ein lockerer erscheint, und auf der überhaupt die meisten Fäden, die in die 'Zeitgeschichte' zurückführen, unbedeutend werden."—*Das Wesen*, i, 10.

126   Das Wesen des Christentums. Leipzig, 1900. Translation by Thomas Bailey Saunders, What is Christianity? second edition. Putnam, 1902. There are two strong replies to Harnack's book: a conservative reply by Professor Hermann Cremer, and a rationalistic reply by Abbé Loisy. The latter has been translated into English, and may be found in the introduction to The Gospel and the Church. Scribner, 1904.

X. THE CHRISTIAN RELIGION AND THE HUMAN RACE

131   Emerson. An article on "The Personality of Emerson," by Thomas Wentworth Higginson, in the Outlook, May 23, 1903. The passage almost entire is as follows: "It is not the sea and poverty and pursuit that separate us. Here is Alcott

by my door—yet is the union more profound? No! the sea, vocation, poverty, are seeming fences, but man is insular and cannot be touched. Every man is an infinitely repellent orb, and holds his individual being on that condition. . . . Most of the persons whom I see in my own house I see across a gulf; I cannot go to them, nor they come to me." Compare with Emerson's essay on "Self-reliance."

132   Thomas Arnold (the younger). From an article in the Century Magazine, May, 1903.

XI. Christian Certainty

This discussion has been worked out from starting points which I gained, strangely enough, from the two antipodal men, Dr. Fr. H. R. Frank and Professor Albrecht Ritschl.

148   "One system." Compare with what is said on pp. 11–13.

155   "Christianity taken by hazard." The quotation is taken from the book The Rational Basis of Orthodoxy, by Dr. Albert Weston Moore. Houghton, Mifflin & Co., 1901. See the first chapter, on "The Rationality of Faith."

XII. The Christian Book

160   Professor Sanday's university sermon is given as an appendix to his Bampton Lectures on Inspiration.

161   Professor Huxley's Hume, English Men of Letters Series, part ii, chap. vii.

161   Professor Wellhausen's Sketch, originally published in the Encyclopædia Britannica, vol. xiii, and then published as a monograph by Adam and Charles Black.

163   "The Recession of Miracle." The editorial is to be found in the Independent, December 4, 1902.

163   Cardinal Newman, Oxford University Sermons, sermon x, on "Faith and Reason, Contrasted as Habits of Mind."

The present tendency to "reduce the miracle" is referred to by Matthew Arnold in this way: "To reduce the miraculous in them [the Bible miracles] to what are thought reasonable dimensions is now a favorite attempt. But if anything miraculous is left, the whole miracle might as well have been left; if nothing, how has the incident any longer the proving force of a miracle? Let us treat so absurd an attempt as it deserves. Neander supposes that the water at the marriage feast at Cana was not changed by Jesus into wine, but was only endued by Jesus with wine's brisk taste and exhilarating effects. This has all the difficulties of the miracle, and only gets rid of the poetry. It is as if we were startled by the extravagance of supposing Cinderella's fairy godmother to have actually changed the pumpkin into a coach and six, but suggested that she did really change it into a one-horse brougham."—*God and the Bible*, chap. i, sec. 4.

175   Professor Paul W. Schmiedel, Professor of New Testament Exegesis, Zürich. See his article on "Gospels" in the Encyclopædia Biblica, vol. ii.

XIII. SYSTEMATIC THEOLOGY

183   In this connection I wish to quote a most significant passage from Dr. Abraham Kuyper's discussion of the "Liberty of Scientific Theology": "Hence there is no question of desiring to free the theologian as such at the bar of his own conscience from his obligation to his subject, his principium, or the historic authority of the church; what we should object to is that the study should be prevented from pursuing its own way. That a church should forbid a minister of the Word the further use of her pulpit when he antagonizes her confession, or that a board of trustees should dismiss a professor, who, according to their view, does not serve the end for which he was appointed, has nothing whatever to do with this *liberty of studies*. A shipowner, who dismisses a captain because he sails the ship to a different point of destination from what the shipowner designated, in no wise violates thereby the personal rights of the captain. When a church appoints a minister of the Word, she and she alone is to determine what she desires of him, and when he is no longer able to perform this, she can no longer retain him in her service. And in the same way, when the curators of a university appoint some one to teach Lutheran dogmatics, and this theologian meanwhile becomes Romish, it is not merely their right but their duty to displace him. Yea, stronger still, a theologian who, in such a case, does not withdraw is dishonest, and as such cannot be upheld. But these cases have nothing to do with the liberty of studies, and at no time does the churchly liberty of the theologian consist of anything but his right to appeal to the Word of God, on the ground of which he may enter into a spiritual conflict with his church, and if he fails in this, to withdraw.

Thus when the liberty of theology is spoken of, we do not mean theology as attached to any office, but theology as an independent phenomenon.   The question simply is, whether, after it has separated itself from this office, and thus makes its appearance as theology only, it is or is not free.   And the answer is that every effort to circumscribe theology by any obstacle whatever is antagonistic to her nature, and disables her for her calling.   The law of thought will not allow you to call the thing black which you see to be white."—*Encyclopedia of Sacred Theology*, pp. 594, 595, the De Vries translation from the Dutch.   Scribner, 1898.

In a time when "mental reservation" is making meaningless so much public subscription to doctrine, these unequivocal words from Dr. Kuyper are exceedingly wholesome. And yet he does not seem to be aware of the extreme complication of the present theological situation.   Oftentimes the church to which a theologian belongs is itself far from being a consistent unit in theological trend and interpretation; and the man stays in place, not because he is dishonest, but because there is no clear indication of duty.   Dr. Kuyper's distinction, however, between theology and theology as attached to an elective office is of the greatest importance.

XIV. The Creation and Fall of Man

192   "The primitive style of narration."   Taken from a lecture delivered by President W. R. Harper, of the Chicago University, reported in the Standard, and this report then summarized in the Independent.   His view is of so much worth to me that I will quote more largely and from the summary: "What Genesis really teaches is that man exists as a creation of God, that he received a nature superior to that of all other animals, that he is in the image of God in his spiritual nature.   What portion of the narrative is to be taken literally it is difficult to say.   The account is not an allegory nor a myth nor a mere legend or tradition; it is an historical fact revealed by God to the first men and preserved in the primitive style of narration characteristic of the age in which it was written.   He says the Eden story was intended to make known the fact that evil in the world had its origin in disobedience to the divine command.   The account is historical, but, as in other cases, is given in the narrative form.   While it is so referred to in the New Testament that we must accept it as describing a real event, still it is not to be read or understood in the method of bald literalism.   Man fell into sin by yielding to temptation and thus forfeited that which had

been originally provided for him, and brought not only upon himself but upon his posterity the curse of evil in its various forms. He failed under the trial to which his Creator subjected him. The description of the garden is to be held as ideal, grounded in tradition, but not to be taken as geographically correct. The narrative has in this connection an historical basis, but makes a free use of symbols in setting forth the historical facts of the first sin and its consequences."

195   Bishop Martensen, Christian Dogmatics, sec. 59, p. 114.

XV. The Doctrine of Sin

200   Bishop Foster, Sin, vol. vi of his Studies in Theology. Especially note pp. 33, 117, 119, 229, and 230.

200   In the history of Arminian theology there is no position so entirely inconsistent and indefensible as that of Dr. William Burt Pope on "hereditary guilt." See his Compendium of Christian Theology, American edition, vol. ii, p. 48.

XVI. The Deity of Our Lord

211   "Five methods." 1. The historical argument, as used by Dr. Dorner. 2. The combination argument, as used by Canon Liddon. 3. The scriptural argument, as used by Dr. Miley. 4. The argument in biblical theology. 5. The argument based entirely upon the claims of Christ.

211   "Saint John's gospel." The literature is too extensive for indication here; but the best recent discussion of the subject is by Professor George Park Fisher in chap. xi of his Grounds of Theistic and Christian Belief, revised edition. Scribner, 1902.

212   "The kingdom of God." My view of this kingdom will be precisely given in my consideration of the doctrine of the church.

224   William Bright, D.D., Canon of Christ Church, Oxford, Regius Professor of Ecclesiastical History. See Waymarks in Church History, p. 65. Longmans, 1894.

229   "Passage from an editorial." "Who is He?" in the Outlook, February 15, 1902. This editorial is signed "L. A." Compare with an editorial in the same paper, "The Divinity of Jesus Christ," June 29, 1901. This editorial, however, is not signed.

230 Professor Ritschl. See chap. vi of the second edition of The Christian Doctrine of Justification and Reconciliation. T. & T. Clark, 1902. The German of the quotation runs as follows: "Als Träger der vollendeten Offenbarung ist Christus gegeben, damit man an ihn glaube. Indem man an ihn glaubt, versteht man ihn als den Offenbarer Gottes."

XVII. The Incarnation of the Son of God

233 Rothe, Dogmatik, ii, 22.

233 "Only a minor matter." Professor Briggs's The Incarnation of the Lord, p. 217. Scribner, 1902.

235 Bishop Martensen, Christian Dogmatics, p. 260.

236 Professor James Orr, The Christian View of God and the World, second edition, pp. 322, 323.

239 Canon Gifford, The Incarnation. Dodd, Mead & Co., 1897. Expositor, September and October, 1896. Critical Review, October, 1897.

242 Professor Bowne. Read the entire chapter on "The Nature of Things," in his Metaphysics.

249 "In another connection." The quotation is from an article, "The Authority of Our Lord, and of the Bible to the Christian Man," published in the Independent, November 11, 1897.

250 Canon Gore, The Incarnation of the Son of God, p. 212. Scribner, 1896.

251 "Two wills." Canon Liddon says: "Christ has a Human Will as being Perfect Man, no less than he has a Divine Will as being Perfect God."—Bampton Lectures, eighteenth edition, p. 264.

252 "The double life." See Martensen's Christian Dogmatics, p. 264.

252 Proclus of Cyzicus.
ὁ αὐτὸς ἐν ἀγκάλαις μητρὸς
καὶ 'ἐπὶ πτερύγων ἀνέμων—Orat. i, 9.

252 Professor Briggs, The Incarnation of the Lord, sermon v.

XVIII. The Holiness of God

257 "The most striking characteristic of the Old Testament."

Read the remarkable article by Professor A. B. Davidson on "God (in Old Testament)" in vol. ii of the Hastings Dictionary of the Bible.

259   Professor Sanday. In his article on "God (in New Testament)," written to complete Professor Davidson's article.

259   Mr. Lidgett. He says: "The Fatherhood of God therefore means the Father regnant. The emphasis must be laid in turn both upon the subject and upon the adjective. It is *the Father* who reigns. Therefore his law is a law of grace and love from beginning to end. Even that which is sternest in its nature and administration is ordained in the interests of love and life. And the Father is *regnant;* for he calls into existence, constitutes, and maintains a world which is absolutely and irrevocably controlled by his own perfection, and controlled in the interests of that spiritual life which love creates and would perfect. Love reigns, therefore, by law in the interests of life."—*The Fatherhood of God*, chap. vi. T. & T. Clark, 1902.

262   Professor Stevens, The Hastings Dictionary of the Bible, vol. ii, p. 399.

266   Bishop Martensen on the wrath of God: "Though God eternally loves the world, his actual relation to it is not a relation of love, but of holiness and justice, a relation of opposition, because the unity of his attributes is hindered and restrained. There exists also a contradiction between the actual and essential relations of God to mankind; a contradiction which can only be removed by the destruction of the interposing principle of sin. The expression, the *wrath of God*, simply embodies this truth, that the relations of God's love to the world are unsatisfied, unfulfilled. The expression is not merely anthropopathic, it is an appropriate description of the divine pathos necessarily involved in the conception of a revelation of love restrained, hindered, and stayed through unrighteousness."—*Christian Dogmatics*, sec. 157, p. 303.

XIX. THE MORAL GOVERNMENT

269   Hugo Grotius, Defensio Fidei Catholicae de Satisfactione Christi. Basileae, 1732. There is an excellent translation by Dr. Frank Hugh Foster, but unfortunately it is out of print.

270   Saint Paul's conception of the law. See Professor Denney's discussion in the Hastings Dictionary of the Bible, vol. iii, p. 77.

271   Dr. Dale. His view is given in lecture ix of his work on The Atonement.

280   For a trenchant criticism of the governmental theory of the atonement, see Professor George Nye Boardman's "Estimate of the New England Theory" in A History of New England Theology. A. D. F. Randolph, 1899.

XX. The Christian Meaning of Death

281   Walt Whitman. As I remember it, the poem was first published in the Century Magazine. But it has been added to Leaves of Grass in the Boston edition of 1897.

281   Here is one more selection out of a number of modern poems which I have collected:

"Do you think that I fear you, Goodman Death?
    Then, sir, you do not know;
For your grim white face and your frosty breath,
    And your dark eyes browed with snow,
Bring naught to me but a signal of love.
My Father sent you; he dwelleth above,
    And I am ready to go."

282   Newman Smyth. The book was published in 1898 by Charles Scribner's Sons. See p. 28.

283   Professor Davidson, article on "Eschatology" in the Hastings Dictionary of the Bible, i, 739.

284   Professor Charles. Published by Adam & Charles Black in 1899. See p. 353.

288   Herbert Spencer. The sixth edition, Appleton, 1902. See p. 70.

288   Bishop Dahle, Life after Death. See p. 26 of the Beveridge translation.

290   Professor Charles. See p. 415 of his Eschatology.

292   Professor Delitzsch: "Wie der Baum des Lebens die Kraft der Unsterblichkeit in so zu sagen sacramentlicher Weise in sich schloss."—Neuer Commentar, Gen. 2. 16, 17.

PAGE
292 Dr. Latimer. The quotation is taken from my own class-room notes.

292 Professor Denney, The Death of Christ. Armstrong, 1902. See pp. 127, 128. Compare with lecture iv in his Studies in Theology.

292 Professor Bruce. Chap. ii, especially p. 64.

293 Alfred Russel Wallace, Fortnightly Review, March, 1903. Also the book Man's Place in the Universe. McClure, Phillips & Co., 1904.

XXI. THE TEACHING OF SAINT PAUL

302 Professor Sanday, commentary on Rom. 3. 25. Note his discussion of "The Death of Christ Considered as a Sacrifice," pp. 91–94.

305 Professor Stevens, The Theology of the New Testament. part iv, chap. v, p. 378.

XXII. OUR LORD'S STRANGE HESITATION IN APPROACHING DEATH

311 Dr. Hollmann. For a noteworthy criticism of Dr. Hollmann's view ("Die Bedeutung des Todes Jesu nach seinen eigenen Aussagen auf Grund der synoptischen Evangelien"), see the Critical Review for November, 1901.

311 Professor McGiffert, A History of Christianity in the Apostolic Age. Scribner, 1898. See note, pp. 68–70.

312 "Inadequate explanations." See in The Life of Jesus by David Friedrich Strauss, George Eliot's translation, part iii, chap. iii, sec. 125.

313 Renan. "Se rappela-t-il les claires fontaines de la Galilée, où il aurait pu se rafraîchir; la vigne et le figuier sous lesquels il aurait pu s'asseoir; les jeunes filles qui auraient peut-être consenti à l'aimer?"—*Vie de Jésus*, xxiii, 391.

313 Principal Fairbairn, The Philosophy of the Christian Religion, book ii, part i, chap. v, sec. iv. The Macmillan Company, 1902. Read pp. 430–432.

XXIII. THE RACIAL THEORY OF OUR LORD'S REDEMPTIVE WORK

321 "Nor was Jesus *punished*." "Nor was Jesus *punished* for man's sin, he *suffered* for it. He could not be punished, for he was not guilty. He endured no equivalent for the appro-

priate penalty of our wrongdoing; he did something far more valuable. God the Father did nothing so immoral as punish some one in the stead of some one else. It was sinful man, not God, who crucified Christ. Sin did its very utmost when it took the life of the Son of God, but it could no further go. It might have taken that life in any one of a hundred ways. It might have hanged, or drowned, or burnt him; but it chose the cross, and by so doing made the cross the symbol of our salvation. But observe—it could not make him sin. Here is just the point where the death of Christ saves us." —*R. J. Campbell*, in British Weekly, March 31, 1904.

323 John Calvin, Institutio Christianae Religionis, liber ii, caput xvi, 10. Edinburgh, 1874.

333 "A typical sinner." "The Authority of Our Lord, and of the Bible to the Christian Man," the Independent, November 11, 1897.

XXIV. THE PERSONAL DISPENSATION OF THE HOLY SPIRIT

336 In a letter to Dr. Albert H. Plumb, written in 1888, Professor Edwards A. Park says, concerning this passage from the works of the "wonderful John Duncan": "I suppose I have read it forty times. I shall probably read it many times more. It has a great effect upon my mind." See The Memorial Collection of Professor Park's Sermons, p. 9. The Pilgrim Press.

337 See John Fletcher's "Portrait of Saint Paul," p. 170, part ii, vol. iii, New York edition of his works.

337 Professor Beyschlag, New Testament Theology, vol. i, p. 279. T. & T. Clark, 1895.

339 Justin Martyr, The Antenicene Fathers, American reprint of the Edinburgh edition, vol. i, p. 164.

344 Dean Mansel. See his comment on Saint Matt. 12. 31, 32, in The Bible Commentary (Speaker's).

343, 344 Also read the article on "Blasphemy" in the Hastings Dictionary of the Bible, vol. i, p. 305.

XXV. THE PREPARATION FOR CONVERSION

352 "Wesley's phrase." "The inward, spiritual meaning of the law of God now begins to glare upon him."—*Sermon IX*, on "The Spirit of Bondage and of Adoption."

XXVI. CONVERSION

355   "Now faith is assurance." See Professor A. B. Davidson's Handbook on Hebrews.

356   "Great saint." In his Apologia pro Vita Sua Cardinal Newman writes (p. 4): "In isolating me from the objects which surrounded me, in confirming me in my mistrust of the reality of material phenomena, and making me rest in the thought of two and two only absolute and luminously self-evident beings, myself and my Creator . . . "

359   The best discussion of Saint James's conception of faith as over against Saint Paul's conception of faith is to be found in the introduction to Professor Joseph B. Mayor's commentary on The Epistle of Saint James. Macmillan, 1897.

362   Cardinal Newman, Lectures on Justification, iii, 8.

363   "Dr. Latimer's definition." Taken from my notebook of 1879.

363   Professor Sanday. Read his entire discussion beginning on p. 34 of the commentary on Romans.

366   Dr. Ball. Saint Paul and the Roman Law, by W. E. Ball, LL.D. T. & T. Clark, 1901.

367   The witness of the Spirit. Read chaps. viii, ix, and x in Professor Beet's The New Life in Christ.

XXVII. PERSONAL HOLINESS

372   Concerning Dr. McClintock's statement Professor Faulkner, of the Drew Theological Seminary, says: "I find this to be true: (1) The Methodists were the first Christians who *officially, and as a united body, without deviation, and with the power of a church behind them to make it effective,* taught the New Testament doctrine of Christian perfection. (2) Absolutely they were not the first to teach it. Not speaking of individuals in the ancient and mediæval church, the Arminians taught the doctrine. But they were not a united and responsible church in the same sense that the Methodists were, nor did they continue to maintain the doctrine in a living way. The Friends also taught it. Elsewhere I say: George Fox's ' opinion on Christian perfection is exactly similar to Wesley's, excepting that he did not emphasize any *special* work of sanctification, but said that faith in Christ would save from all sin.' But the Friends are not a church at all in the New

Testament sense, much less in the ordinary Protestant sense; and besides, they are broken up into schools, one of which is almost, if not quite, rationalistic."

374 The quotations from John Wesley are, as a rule, taken from the London edition, 1829–31, in fourteen volumes.

376 The expression "above thirty years" should, I think, be "about thirty years."

387 Professor Bartlet, vol. iv, pp. 391–395.

Of the many books on Christian perfection the following I regard as the most important: Love Enthroned, by Dr. Daniel Steele; Growth in Holiness toward Perfection, by Dr. James Mudge; Sin and Holiness, by Dr. D. W. C. Huntington; The Story of Gottlieb, by Dr. William F. Warren; Thoughts on Christian Sanctity, by Bishop Moule; Christian Perfection, by Dr. P. T. Forsyth; The Higher Christian Life, by Dr. Alvah Hovey; Sanctification—Right Views and Other Views, by Bishop Merrill. And among the old books on the subject two are especially worthy of notice: John Fletcher's "Last Check"; The Philosophy of Christian Perfection. A psychological study. Anonymous. Philadelphia, 1848.

XXVIII. THE CHRISTIAN DOCTRINE OF THE INTERMEDIATE STATE

399 "Progressive Orthodoxy," chap. iv in the book; or see the Andover Review, August, 1885.

400 Dr. Dorner. It is only justice to say that Dr. Dorner's Eschatology should never be separated from his full System of Doctrine.

401 "True Christian view." Dr. Whedon says (Will, p. 349): "Of the SPIRIT OF FAITH it may be said that though it is not a perfect faith in Christ, yet it is a faith more or less distinct, recognized by the searcher of hearts and trier of the reins, in that of which Christ is the concrete and the embodiment. It may be safely assumed that if the true Redeemer were presented in proper correlation to that faith at the moment of its full existence he would be cordially accepted." Read the entire chapter, "Equation of Probational Advantages."

XXIX. THE RESURRECTION OF THE BODY

408 Of the more recent articles on the resurrection of the body, I will name three as especially worthy of attention: 1. "Our

Humiliation," in the British Weekly, January 29, 1903. 2. "The Resurrection of the Body," in the Expositor, February, 1901.   3. "Resurrection," Hastings Dictionary of the Bible, vol. iv, p. 231.

410   " Saint Paul's analogy."   The best study of 1 Cor. 15 is to be found in The Resurrection of the Dead, by Professor William Milligan.

411   The Gospel of the Resurrection. Macmillan, 1898. The author is Bishop Westcott. See p. 155; but read the entire chapter "The Resurrection and Man." The book is a most important contribution to the philosophy of the Christian faith.

412   Martensen's Christian Dogmatics, p. 461.

XXX. The Church of Our Lord

415   Professor Briggs. "The New Testament Doctrine of the Church," an article in the American Journal of Theology, January, 1900.

418   On 1 Cor. 15. 24–28, see the commentary by Principal Edwards, and also the commentary by Professor Beet, and also the commentary by Bishop Ellicott, to bring out a somewhat different view.

XXXI. The Christian Sacraments

427   " The new discussion." See commentary on Saint Mark (14. 24) by Professor H. B. Swete; also Professor McGiffert's Apostolic Age, p. 68, footnote. In this note the important German discussions by Harnack, Spitta, and Jülicher are indicated; so it is unnecessary to refer to them here in a separate note.

428   Alfred Plummer, Master of University College, Durham. See vol. iii, p. 147.

429   The Teaching of the Twelve Apostles, chap. vii. The translation is from the American edition of The Antenicene Fathers.

430   Dr. Boardman, The Church, pp. 74, 75, and 91.

429, 430   In Professor C. W. Bennett's Christian Archæology, as revised by Dr. A. W. Patten, we find the following (p. 454): "The conclusion to which the evidence leads us is that a large liberty has prevailed from the beginning as to the mode of administering the rite of Christian baptism. The root idea is found in the cleansing prescribed by the Jewish ceremonial purification, the application of water as a symbol of moral renewal. No stereotyped forms are given in the New Testament. Fundamental ideas are given, but the details are left to be adjusted to varying conditions. In this conclusion the latest Christian scholarship concurs." This statement seems to me to be almost but not quite fair to the situation. A little more emphasis should be placed upon trine immersion as the *typical* form.

432 κοινωνία. See the discussion by Professor J. Armitage Robinson in the Hastings Dictionary, vol. i, p. 461.

XXXII. The Church Militant

435 Bishop Lightfoot. See dissertation i (181–269) in commentary on The Epistle to the Philippians.

439 Elisha Mulford's The Nation. Houghton, Mifflin & Co., 1890. A book which every preacher should master.

441 "French Revolution." See in the American Journal of Theology, October, 1901, an article by Martin von Nathusius, on "The Duty of the Church in Relation to the Labor Movement."

443 " The church and foreign missions." For Methodist opinion on the salvation of the heathen I make reference as follows: John Wesley, sermon cvi, on " Faith," London edition, vol. vii. John Fletcher, vol. i, p. 40, "First Check." Richard Watson, Institutes, ii, 445. Dr. Pope, Compendium, iii, 428. Dr. Summers, Systematic Theology, i, 342. Dr. Whedon, Will, chap. xi, 343. Professor Terry, Methodist Review, May–June, 1889. Dr. Miley, Systematic Theology, ii, 436. Dr. Raymond, Systematic Theology, ii, 316.

XXXIII. The Church Triumphant

445 " The second coming of Christ." Most valuable articles and books as follows:

1. *Articles*

By Professor Harnack on "Millennium," in the Encyclopædia Britannica, vol. xvi, 314. By Professor Fisher on "Millennium," in McClintock and Strong's Cyclopædia, vol. vi, 264. By Professor W. Adams Brown on "Parousia," in the Hastings Dictionary, vol. iii, 674. By Professor R. H.

PAGE
478 " The attribute of omniscience." The strongest complete statement of the argument for divine nescience of contingent events has been given by Professor L. D. McCabe. There are two books by him: The Foreknowledge of God (Cincinnati, 1878); and Divine Nescience (New York, 1882). See a review of Professor McCabe in Methodist Review, January, 1883.

482 "Get rid of time." See Professor Bowne's Deems Lectures on Theism, pp. 186–190, and compare with the discussion of "Time" in his Metaphysics, pp. 164–194.

XXXVI. The Christian Doctrine of the Trinity

483 "Bare essentiality." The question here is not, What is essential to Trinitarian consistency? but merely, What is essential to any view properly termed Trinitarian?

483 "Essential points of belief." Professor Edwards A. Park gives us a definition from this essential standpoint: "The Father is God; the Son is God; the Holy Spirit is God; the three are distinct from each other by a necessity of their very substance; neither is God without the others; and there is only one God."—*The Bibliotheca Sacra*, vol. xxxviii, p. 335.

485 Dr. W. L. Alexander, A System of Biblical Theology, vol. i, p. 109.

486 " German philosophy." See Dr. Shedd's Dogmatic Theology, vol. i, pp. 186, 188, for a discussion of the process of self-consciousness in God. My statement is not quite just, for there are kindred speculations further back than any German philosopher.

486 Jonathan Edwards. This essay was published in 1880, with an introduction by Professor Egbert C. Smyth (see p. 55). In 1881 (Bibliotheca Sacra, vol. xxxviii, articles v and ix) Professor Edwards A. Park published his "Remarks of Jonathan Edwards on the Trinity." Then, in 1903, the Scribners published An Unpublished Essay of Edwards on the Trinity, with remarks on Edwards and his theology by Professor George P. Fisher. The claim that all the statements in the writings of Edwards on the Trinity cannot be harmonized does not seem to me to be well founded. What he did was to try to put a profounder philosophy under the view of Athanasius without impairing that view.

PAGE

488   Beyschlag.   See New Testament Theology, Clark translation, vol. i, pp. 249–255.

492   "A typical statement."   The quotation is from Dr. W. B. Pope's Fernley Lecture (1871) on The Person of Christ, p. 5.

494   Athanasius.   See the first chapter of Professor Levi Leonard Paine's A Critical History of the Evolution of Trinitarianism. Houghton, Mifflin & Co., 1900.

498   περιχώρησις. Compare with my conception of the process of supplement in the Racial Brotherhood.

504   Professor Ritschl.   See Justification and Reconciliation, Clark translation, p. 453.

504   W. L. Walker.   The passage is to be found on p. 239.

INDEX

Westminster definition, 195. Also see Individual sin.
Sin against the Holy Ghost ("the unpardonable sin"), 343.
"Sinless perfection," 378.
Sinner, awakened, 351; convicted, 351; enlightened, 351; his own bearing, 349; how forgiven, 331; how satisfied, 333; invited, 352.
Smyth, Newman, 282.
Social act of creation, 500.
Social fundament of all being, 499.
Social life in heaven, 447.
Social nature of the Christian religion, 137.
Socialism, 441; and the Christian church, 442; and the French Revolution, 442.
Solidarity of mankind, 135.
Son of God, the, 498; and creation, 500; and obedience, 500; his kingdom, 500; his mediation, 501; his peculiarity, 502; his self-assertion, 502; his subordination, 502.
Son of man, 213.
Sonship by adoption, 366.
"Soul-sleep," 399.
Speculation, 187.
Spencer, Herbert, 17, 107, 288, 448.
Spirit, the, and the Incarnation, 506.
Spiritual organism, 497.
Stanley, A. P., 210, 430.
Stevens, G. B., 213, 262, 305.
Strauss, D. F., 313.
Subordination, in the Trinity, 494; of our Lord, 491.
"Sum total of final universe," 468.
Supernatural, the, 70, 79; analyzed, 80; and religion, 92; and the Christian religion, 164; origin of man's sense of the supernatural, 82.
Superstition, 84.
Supper, last. See Lord's Supper.
Swedenborgianism, 483.
"Sweep of the plan of redemption," 454.
Systematic theology, 183; defined, 188; its personal element, 186; its purpose, 183; related to biblical theology, 185; related to Christian consciousness, 185; related to speculation, 187; related to the Bible, 185; value, 184.

Table of our Lord, the. See Lord's Supper.
Taboo, institution of, 29, 31.
Taproot, the, of moral concern, 69, 72.
Taylor, Isaac, 399.
Taylor, Jeremy, 374.
Teaching of the Twelve Apostles, 429.
Temptation, and Christian perfection, 377, 378; of our Lord, 248.
Ten Commandments, 278.
Tennyson, Alfred, 21.
Terry, M. S., 445, 446.
Tertullian, 224, 256.
Theism, 95, 102.
Theodicy, and eternal punishment, 462, 460; and foreknowledge of God, 480; and nescience, 480.
Theology, 473.
Thiess, on Gethsemane, 312.
"Thing in itself," 146.
Thoreau, H. D., 58.
"Three cosmical spheres," 412.
Tiele, C. P., 78.

Time, and Christian perfection, 378; and foreknowledge of God, 482.
Tolstoy, 150.
"Total depravity," 200.
"Transformed motive," 389.
"Tree of life," 291, 294.
Trine immersion, 429.
Trinity, the, 265, 483; and baptism, 429; and causation, 498; and equality, 494; and German speculation, 486; and Latin fathers, 472; and moral love, 494; and new race, 510; and self-sacrifice, 494; and subordination, 494; consistency required, 491, 492; doctrinal construction, 493; essential points of belief, 484; final statement, 497; ἰδιότης, 498; μορφή, 497; περιχώρησις, 498; rejected views (agnostic, 485; Arian, 483; humanitarian, 483; modalistic, or Sabellian, 483, 487; Swedenborgian, 483; tritheistic, 483); the Father, 497; the Holy Spirit, 498; the Son, 498; three real persons in one absolute organism, 497, 498; use of terms in constructing the doctrine, 496.
Tritheism, 483.
Triumphant church, 445.
Truth, 145.
Turretin, 278.
"Two Infinites," 271.
Two wills in Christ, question of, 251.

Ultimate condition of the wicked. See Lost men.
Unitarianism, 499, 506.
Unity, Christian, 424; in the cosmos, 100; of God, 493, 498; of the church, 424.
Universe, final, and lost men, 464.
Unpardonable sin, the. See Sin against the Holy Ghost.

Vaughan, on Romans 5. 12, 286.
Verbal theory of inspiration, 177.
Vice, 353.
Virgin birth, the, 233.
Virgin Mary, the, 501.
Vision, of righteousness, 351; of sin, 351; of the Holy God, 351.

Walden, 58.
Walker, W. L., 504.
Wallace, A. R., 7.
Ward, James, 38.
Warren, W. F., 78, 183.
Watson, Richard, 472, 477.
Wellhausen, Julius, 161.
Wesen, das, des Christentums, 126.
Wesley, John, 363, 373, 391, 398; his definition of sin, 199; his own religious experience, 374; his teaching on Christian perfection analyzed, 377; his view of a sinner's condition, 382; personal conclusion as to Wesley's real meaning in his teaching on Christian perfection, 382.
Westminster definition of sin, 195.
Whately, Richard, 399.
Whedon, D. D., 38, 46, 47, 291, 294, 443.
White, Edward, 459.
Whitman, Walt, 281.
Wicked, the, ultimate condition. See Lost men.

SCRIPTURE REFERENCES